TEXAS POLITICS

TEXAS

SIXTH EDITION

POLITICS

AN INTRODUCTION

JAMES E. ANDERSON
Texas A&M University

RICHARD W. MURRAY
University of Houston

EDWARD L. FARLEY

HarperCollins*Publishers*

Sponsoring Editor: Lauren Silverman
Project Coordinator: Arlene Grodkiewicz
Design Supervisor: Lucy Krikorian
Cover Design: Jan Kessner
Cover Photo: © The Stock Market/Kunio Owaki, 1989
Photo Researcher: Mira Schachne
Production Manager/Assistant: Willie Lane/Sunaina Sehwani
Compositor: ComCom Division of Haddon Craftsmen, Inc.
Printer and Binder: R. R. Donnelley & Sons Company
Cover Printer: The Lehigh Press, Inc.

For permission to use copyrighted material, grateful acknowledgment is made to the copyright holders on page 326, which is hereby made part of this copyright page.

Texas Politics: An Introduction Sixth Edition

Copyright © 1992 by HarperCollins Publishers Inc.

Library of Congress Cataloging-in-Publication Data

Anderson, James E.
   Texas politics: an introduction / James E. Anderson, Richard W. Murray, Edward L. Farley. —6th ed.
     p. cm.
   Includes bibliographical references and index.
   ISBN 0-06-500511-2
   1. Texas—Politics and government—1951- I. Murray, Richard W., 1940- . II. Farley, Edward L., 1937- . III. Title.
JK4816.A53 1992
320.9764—dc20   91-34948
                                         CIP

91 92 93 94 9 8 7 6 5 4 3 2 1

Contents

Preface

In this introduction to the fascinating and sometimes frustrating Texas political arena, our main focus is on the description and analysis of political institutions, processes, and behavior at the state level. However, in addition to including a chapter on local governments, we also say much that is pertinent to local politics in other chapters. Basically, we view politics as being the very essence of democracy, as involving conflict and struggle among individuals and groups over issues of public policy and governance. Bargaining, negotiation, and compromise are some of its features. There is, of course, also a seamy side to politics—various forms of selfish and nefarious activity occur, and occur more frequently than we would prefer. In preparing this text, however, we have chosen to present neither an expose of Texas politics nor a defense of the status quo. In the pages that follow we do believe that we have fashioned a realistic framework for understanding Texas politics, whatever the reader's particular ideology or interests. We have chosen not to grind our own axes here but have hewed closely to the facts as we see them.

This sixth edition generally updates the material in the book. New or expanded material is included on the 1988 elections, gubernatorial politics, legislature redistricting, public school finance, the Texas population, budgeting and taxation, and group politics. We have included some more Ben Sargent cartoons and, for the first time, some photographs relating to Texas politics.

We have always sought to keep this volume reasonably short, although it has grown somewhat through its various editions. To this end, we have not defined or explained all of the basic political science terms and concepts that appear in the text. We assume that the students who constitute the book's main body of readers either will have had a general course in American government or will be enrolled in one. Such a course should provide the needed background for our book.

A limited amount of material on political or governmental reform is included, although this was once a major part of the content of textbooks on Texas government and politics. This is done, not because the Texas political system is fine as it is or because we are opponents of all change. Rather it is our belief that a solid understanding of existing political institutions and practices should precede the considerations of reform if it is to be meaningful and realistic. Moreover, what some think is a necessary change, such as term limitations, is regarded as an abomination by others. Not having space to discuss everything, it continues to be our practice to devote our full attention to the discussion of existing institutions, practices, and behavior. This in itself is a large and useful task.

We have included only one chapter—that on taxing and spending—devoted primarily to public policy matters. Again, a disclaimer and an explanation are in order. We are not uninterested in public policies, but holding down the size of the book was again a consideration. We have, however, sought to use policy materials throughout the book as illustrations and examples in order to provide some understanding of the substance of Texas politics. The chapter on the administrative system particularly includes discussions of various public policies.

We wish to acknowledge the assistance of various friends and colleagues who provided information, advice, and helpful criticism. Ronald Stidham, Lamar University; Melissa P. Collie, University of Texas/Austin; and Sean Kelleher, University of Texas/Permian Basin, who were the reviewers for HarperCollins, deserve special credit for their useful comments, suggestions, and encouragements. Ben Sargent of the *Austin American Statesman* kindly gave us permission to reprint several of his political cartoons. The editorial staff at Harper patiently did their best to get the revision process started, to keep it moving, and to bring it to a successful conclusion. The book is better because of their efforts. We especially want to acknowledge the help of political science editor Lauren Silverman and project editor Arlene Grodkiewicz. Try as we might to prevent it, some errors likely have found their way into the book. For these we reluctantly accept responsibility.

James E. Anderson
Richard W. Murray
Edward L. Farley

TEXAS POLITICS

chapter *1*

The Constitutional Context

The Texas Constitution begins with a bill of rights.

In the United States, written constitutions provide an overarching legal context for the "great game of politics." A constitution is essentially a set of basic rules, regarded as superior to ordinary law, that are intended to regulate the political process in a particular community, such as the United States or the state of Texas. To this end, a constitution typically indicates the manner in which the government shall be organized, assigns powers and responsibilities to the various units or branches of government, and places some specific limitations on governmental action, as, for example, by a bill of rights. Constitutions may differ substantially in their style, length, and detail in treating these matters, as a comparison of the U.S. and Texas Constitutions will readily indicate. The use of written constitutions to limit governmental power is an American contribution to the practice of government, and, as a people, Americans tend to be much enamored with things constitutional.

A study of its constitution may provide important insights about, but not an adequate understanding of, how a government operates. For instance, there may be a sharp divergence between formal constitutional rules and actual political behavior. Although the Fourteenth Amendment to the U.S. Constitution provides that the states shall not deny equal protection of the laws to anyone within their jurisdiction, in the past they have discriminated, and occasionally still do discriminate, against racial and religious minorities. Constitutional authorizations for governments to legislate on various matters usually tell us little about the actual policies that result. While it is necessary for a government to have constitutional power to levy taxes, a variety of political and economic factors help determine the types and levels of taxes actually levied, exemptions from particular taxes, how they are collected, and the like.

Nonetheless, governmental action in the United States appears to be in substantial conformity with the relevant constitutional rules, which are often quite general. Americans are still much concerned with questions of constitutional power and practice, especially when personal rights and liberties are involved. But the regulation of economic activity, while not lacking in controversy, does not stir the intense constitutional debates it did a few decades ago.

It is useful, and traditional, to begin an examination of the Texas political system with a brief description of its constitutional context. To this we now turn.

THE AMERICAN FEDERAL SYSTEM

As a member of the federal union, the government of the state of Texas is affected in what it can do by the U.S. Constitution and federalism, as well as by the Texas Constitution.[1] The U.S. Constitution divides governmental power between the national government and the several state governments, places some limitations on them, and sets forth some obligations of each to the other.

Certain powers are delegated to the national government, such as those to regulate interstate and foreign commerce, establish post offices and post roads, raise and support armies and navies, and tax and spend for the general welfare. The national government is also given all power necessary and proper (implied power) to carry out its delegated powers. Powers not delegated to the national government (reserved powers) are left to the states or the people. The basic arrangement is succinctly stated in the Tenth Amendment: "The powers not delegated to the United States by the Constitution, nor prohibited by it to the States, are reserved to the States respectively, or to the people." Essentially, the U.S. Constitution is a source of power for the national government and a series of limitations on the state governments. The latter are free to do anything not prohibited to them by the U.S. Constitution (unless they limit themselves through their own constitutions) and are thereby in a semiautonomous position.

Some limitations on the states are contained in the main body of the U.S. Constitution. In Article I, Section 10, a variety of state actions are prohibited, such as entering into treaties or alliances, coining money, passing bills of attainder and ex post facto laws, and taxing exports or imports. Other limitations are found in amendments to the Constitution. The Fourteenth Amendment broadly prohibits the states from depriving persons of their lives, liberty, or property without due process of law; from abridging the privileges and immunities of citizens of the United States; and from denying persons within the states' jurisdictions the equal protection of the laws. By judicial interpretation, the liberty protected by the due process clause has been held to protect most of the rights listed in the Bill of Rights against state action, including all of the rights enumerated in the First Amendment. The Fifteenth and Nineteenth amendments provide that the right to vote cannot be denied on the grounds of race or color and sex, respectively.

Some limitations on the states are implicit in the U.S. Constitution. By judicial construction, the states are forbidden to burden interstate commerce or interfere unduly with the exercise of national power. As a general rule, the delegations of power to the national government act as limitations on the states, the inference being that power granted to the national government is denied the states. The two levels of government do have concurrent power to tax, including the power to tax the same objects, such as personal income and tobacco products. Neither, however, can use its taxation power to interfere with the basic governmental functions of the other, as in the operation of their court systems.

Article VI provides for national supremacy. According to the "supreme law of the land clause," the Constitution, laws made in pursuance thereof, and treaties made under the authority of the United States take precedence over conflicting provisions in state constitutions and laws. In short, when national and state actions come into conflict and the national government is acting within its area of constitutional power, the conflicting state action must give way. Thus, a provision of the Texas Constitution authorizing separate schools for "the white and colored children" became null and void because it conflicted with the equal protection clause of the Fourteenth Amendment, as interpreted by the Supreme Court in *Brown* v. *Board of Education* (1954). Congress, however, may choose to yield to state action in some matters. A notable example is Section 14(B) of the Taft-Hartley Act, which permits the states to enact laws outlawing the union-shop arrangement, although it is permitted by national law. In the absence of this provision, the Texas "right-to-work" law, which bans the union shop in the state, would be unconstitutional, as it would then conflict with national policy.

Some limitations may also arise out of the obligations the states owe one another. For example, Article IV of the U.S. Constitution ordains that the states shall give "full faith and credit . . . to the public acts, records, and judicial proceedings of every other State" and that fugitives from justice shall be returned, upon request, to the state from whence they fled. The return of fugitives has been held to be a moral rather than a mandatory obligation, there being no effective way to compel a state to meet this obligation against its wishes. Customarily, though, requests for the return of fugitives do receive compliance.

Within the framework of these various limitations, the states can legally take whatever actions they see fit on economic, social, and political matters, subject to whatever limitations they may impose upon themselves. Indeed, the states are probably more restricted in many matters, such as taxation and economic regulation, by their own constitutions than they are by the U.S. Constitution. Although much comment relating to the decline in power of the states is made about the "march of power to Washington" and the like, the states have greatly expanded the range of their activities in the twentieth century. They have frequently been encouraged to do this by national grant-in-aid programs, which in 1990 funneled nearly $134 billion to state and local governments.

At this point it should be helpful to indicate the general scope of governmental powers available to the states. They are grouped conventionally into four categories.

Police Power   This can be defined broadly as the power of the states to protect and promote the public health, safety, welfare, and morals. This can entail such actions as the enactment and enforcement of criminal laws, licensing of occupations, regulation of local businesses and utilities, regulation of wages and working conditions, control of fire hazards, operation of welfare programs, promotion of economic activity, and control of diseases and pests (e.g., fire ants). Exact definition of the police power is not possible.[2]

Taxing Power   The states possess full power to tax, subject to self-imposed limitations and the requirement of noninterference with national governmental activities. Although the basic purpose of taxation is to raise revenue to finance the government, it can be used for other purposes. Various states have shown substantial ingenuity in the types of taxes they levy. High tax rates may be used to discourage the consumption of some products, and favorable tax provisions may be used to encourage or promote desired activities.

Proprietary Power   This designates the power of the states, or their subdivisions, to own and operate economic enterprises. As far as the U.S. Constitution is concerned, the states are free to engage in as much government ownership of enterprises (a practice that some might call "socialism") as their inhabitants desire. Although there is no single standard definition of *public enterprise* (as is the case with most political phenomena), the term can usefully be held to designate activities of a commercial or businesslike nature that could be handled by private enterprise. Collectively a variety of government enterprises can be found in the several states—power production facilities, public forests and parks, recreational facilities, liquor stores, airports, subways, bus companies, cement plants, and insurance companies, to name a few. Texas is among the less innovative and active states in the enterprise field.

Eminent Domain   The states possess power to take private property for public use, upon payment of just compensation for the property so taken. This power can be used, for example, to acquire rights-of-way for highways, sites for public buildings, and land for public parks. It can also be granted to public utility companies to secure easements and the like for utility lines. In cases of the sort mentioned, the theory runs that private rights should give way to the general welfare. Public officials, of course, make these determinations; and such acts may stir considerable controversy, as when a utility company seeks land for a nuclear power plant.

These four categories comprise the "pool of power" available to Texas and the other states under the U.S. Constitution. The extent to which and purposes for which a state exercises the power available depend first of all on two general factors: (1) limitations imposed by the state constitution and (2) internal political processes. To illustrate the first factor, the Texas Constitution prohibits the state government from spending more than one percent of the state budget in a biennium on public assistance programs for the needy. (Texas is the only state to have such a limitation.) Although the state is constitutionally free to levy personal or corporate income taxes, it has not done so—despite revenue needs—because of the strong political opposition to such taxes, especially from conservative citizens and businesspersons; here, then, the limitation is political rather than constitutional.

The Position of the States

Two comments need to be made here concerning the division of power between the national and state governments in the American federal system. First, the division of power is not a clear-cut, never-changing allocation. The actual division of power has fluctuated as changing social, economic, and political conditions have given rise to new or different interpretations of the broad general language of the U.S. Constitution or to action to shift the balance of power. Second, the two levels of government do not operate in separate and distinct spheres but, rather, act jointly in many areas (e.g., highway construction, welfare, and pollution control), with both cooperation and conflict characterizing their relationship. To use a metaphor, the American federal system is best thought of as a marble cake, rather than a layer cake, because of the extensive intermingling of national, state, and local activities, as in the several hundred federal grant-in-aid programs.

The twentieth century has seen a vast expansion of national governmental power and activity, whether measured by such indexes as civilian personnel employed (208,000 in 1900, 3.1 million in 1990), size of the national budget ($521 million in 1900, $1.2 trillion in 1990), or number and range of programs undertaken. Among the causes often mentioned for the expansion of national action are the following: (1) Many problems, such as inflation, unemployment, monopoly, energy shortages, and poverty, are national in scope and can be dealt with only by a government having nationwide jurisdiction. (2) National defense, of course, is solely the prerogative of the national government. (3) The states have been unable or unwilling to act, or act effectively, on many matters because of constitutional limitations, deficient legislatures, poor administrative systems, and internal political factors. (4) The national government has better financial resources and greater ability to act than have the states. But whatever the causes, and whether or not one considers the expansion of national power desirable, the national government is clearly a much more powerful and active entity today than it was a few decades ago.

Various attempts have been made in recent years to "return" more power to the states. One notable effort was the State and Local Fiscal Assistance Act of 1972, better known simply as "revenue sharing," which was initiated by the

Nixon administration. Through this program, state and general local governments (cities, counties, and townships) were provided as much as $6.5 billion annually to use largely for whatever activities they chose. General revenue sharing proved to be very popular with state and local officials, one of whom called it "the best thing since the milking machine." This program was terminated in 1986 (the state governments were dropped from it in 1983) at the request of the Reagan administration and because of the financial pressures created by large federal budget deficits.

A second notable effort was the Reagan administration's "New Federalism," which was intended to separate more distinctly the roles of the national and state and local governments. In 1981, 57 categorical federal grant-in-aid programs, which provided funding for fairly narrowly defined purposes (such as rural library services), were combined into 9 block grant programs. Block grants cover broader areas, such as urban development, and give state and local governments more discretion in the use of funds. The administration subsequently proposed that the national government take over the Medicaid program for the needy, which is administered by the state and local governments. In return, the states would assume complete responsibility for Aid to Families with Dependent Children (AFDC) and the food stamp program. Strong opposition to this proposal quickly emerged, and no action was taken. State officials, for instance, were concerned that it would require increased state spending.

Although the growth of national power and programs has produced much handwringing and many dismal proclamations about both the present and future positions of the states in the American federal system, the states and their local governments remain important governmental units. They have a large and immediate impact on the day-to-day lives and happiness of most citizens. To neglect state and local governments in the study of American government and politics is to neglect much of the subject.

The state governments have also greatly expanded the range and scope of their activities in recent decades and appear considerably stronger than in the past, at least in a relative sense. Total expenditures by state and local governments in the United States increased from $10.9 billion in 1942 to $775 billion in 1987. In Texas, the state government's spending rose from $165 million in 1940 to $22.8 billion in 1987. If we focus attention only on domestic expenditures, we find that spending by all governments in the United States on domestic programs totaled $1511 billion in 1990. Of this amount, the state and local governments accounted for $773 billion, or 51 percent. Again, in 1987, of the 17 million civilian government employees in the United States, 13.9 million (82 percent) were employed by the state and local governments, whose employment level has been growing much faster than that of the national government.[3] Such policy areas as public and higher education; highway and street construction and maintenance; law enforcement; land use controls (e.g., zoning); local business regulations; occupational licensing; and the management of parks, recreation facilities, and wildlife are still significantly financed and administered by the states and their subdivisions. Although these are rough measures of state and local government activity and its importance, collectively they convey an impression of growth and vitality rather than of decline.

THE TEXAS CONSTITUTION

The present constitution of the state of Texas, adopted in 1876, is the seventh constitution under which the state has been governed. Previous constitutions were adopted in 1827, for Texas and Coahuila (under the Republic of Mexico); in 1836, for the Republic of Texas after it became independent from Mexico; in 1845, when Texas entered the Union; in 1861, when Texas left the Union to join the Confederacy; in 1866, when Texas reentered the Union; and in 1869, to meet the requirements for Reconstruction laid down by the Radical Republicans in Congress. The Constitution of 1876 has thus lasted substantially longer than all of its predecessors combined, notwithstanding long-continued criticism and a variety of efforts toward revision.

Framing the Constitution

After the Constitution of 1869 was adopted, a Radical Republican regime led by Governor E. J. Davis (1870–1874) came to power. Both the constitution and the Republicans apparently caused a great amount of dissatisfaction within the state, especially on the part of the Democrats. A standard interpretation of the era asserts, "The Radical Republican regime in Texas was one of oppression, corruption, graft, and blackmail. It sought to centralize the government and brought about a large growth in government expenditures, an increase in taxation, and a rapid accumulation of a comparatively heavy debt."[4] Whether fully accurate or not—and some recent historical research indicates it is not—this was apparently the view of things that influenced the majority of the framers of the Constitution of 1876. It is, after all, what people *believe* to be real or true that influences their behavior.

In 1872 the Democratic party had regained control of the legislature and in the following year elected the governor and other state officials. Two years later, after the Democrats had taken complete control of the state government, they turned their attention to the state constitution, which to them was a symbol of Republicanism and carpetbagger domination. After an abortive attempt to use a joint legislative commission to write a new constitution, in 1875 the legislature adopted a resolution calling for a constitutional convention, subject to the approval of the voters. The voters agreed, and three delegates from each of the state's 30 senatorial districts were elected to a constitutional convention that met in Austin in the fall of 1875.

The constitutional convention was composed of 76 Democrats and 14 Republicans (of whom 5 were blacks).[5] Forty-one of the delegates were farmers, 29 were lawyers, and the others had occupations such as merchant, editor, and physician. Many were either members of the legislature or had other governmental experience. Thirty-eight were members of the Grange, a major nineteenth-century farm organization, which had a strong following in the state. More than 20 had served as officers in the Confederate Army. Generally, the delegates were "old-line Texans" and were of a conservative mood. Accounts of the constitutional convention agree that the Grange, with its program of "Retrenchment and Reform" in government, was the most important single influence on the convention. The economy-mindedness of the delegates was manifested in such actions as their refusal to employ a stenographer or have the proceedings of the convention published because of the financial costs involved.

The constitution written by the delegates provided for a governmental system intended to be characterized by more popular control, greater economy in operation, and less power to act than that under the Constitution of 1869. Most state officials, including judges, were to be elected; they were generally bestowed with low salaries, short terms of office, and limited power. Many limitations were imposed on the legislature, and the state debt was limited to $200,000. Adequate provision was made for regulation of railroads and corporations, matters of special concern to the Grangers. Concerning the handiwork of the convention, Professor Rupert N. Richardson comments:

> All in all, the constitution complied with public opinion quite faithfully. Biennial sessions of the legislature, low salaries, no registration for voters, precinct voting [the previous constitution had required voting at the county seat], abolition of the road tax and a return to the road-working system, a homestead exemption clause, guarantees of a low tax rate, a more economical [and segregated] school system under local control, a less expensive court system, popular election of officials—all these were popular measures with Texans in 1876. The constitution was the logical product of its era. It was to be expected that men who were disgusted with the vagaries of a radical regime would design a government that was extremely conservative. Furthermore, the low prices and low wages of hard times had created a demand for the severest economy in government.[6]

Although there was considerable criticism of the new constitution (especially in more urban counties), because of its restrictive nature, it received popular ratification in February 1876 by a vote of 136,606 to 56,652. Generally, rural areas voted strongly in favor of it, while most larger cities, including Dallas, Galveston, Houston, and San Antonio, were opposed.

Constitutional Development

The meaning of a constitution can be altered and expanded or restricted in a number of ways to meet new needs and conditions. Methods of change include custom and usage, judicial interpretation, statutory elaboration, formal amendment, and general revision. All of these methods except the last have been important in the development of the U.S. Constitution, while formal amendment has been the primary means of constitutional change in Texas since 1876. The state courts have generally taken a restrictive view in their interpretations of the

Texas Constitution; this attitude has had the effect of further stimulating and necessitating formal amendment. Between 1881 and 1990 some 481 amendments to the Texas Constitution were proposed, of which 326 were adopted. Partly a consequence of the length, detail, and rigidity of the constitution, this plethora of amendments has further added to the length, detail, and rigidity of the document. In a very real sense, detail begets detail.

The procedure for amending the constitution was itself changed by a constitutional amendment adopted in 1972. Amendments are proposed by resolutions approved by two-thirds of the members elected to each house of the legislature. This can be done either during a regular biennial session or (since 1972) a special session opened to such action by the governor. Although the governor can recommend amendments or approve proposed amendments, the governor has no constitutional power to veto proposed amendments.

The ratification of amendments is a task for the voters, at either regular general elections or other elections called specifically for the purpose, as determined by the legislature. A brief explanatory statement of the amendment, including the way the proposition will be worded on the election ballot, is prepared by the secretary of state with the approval of the attorney general. The approval procedure was provided because it was thought too dangerous to permit one person alone to prepare explanations of proposed amendments; personal viewpoint might bias the explanation. An absence of trust is noticeable here, as is often the case in Texas politics.

The secretary of state's statement is published twice in most newspapers in the state several weeks prior to the election, and a complete copy of each proposed amendment is posted in each county courthouse at least 30 days before the election. (Under the old procedure the actual amendments, without any explanation, were printed four times prior to the election in a newspaper in each county in which one or more newspapers were published.) The thought behind the new publicity procedure is that it will better inform voters of the meaning of proposed amendments. Given their legalese, constitutional amendments are probably only slightly more comprehensible than insurance policies. Under the old procedure, most of those voting on amendments probably had little knowledge of what they were voting on. Whether the new procedure has improved the situation is conjectural.

Approval of an amendment requires favorable action by a majority of those actually voting on it. As evidenced by voter turnout, there is considerable public indifference to the amending process. When amendments are voted on at special elections, only a very small proportion of the voters participate. In November 1973, nine amendments submitted to the voters drew a turnout of approximately 600,000, about 15 percent of the eligible voters. When amendments are voted on at regular elections, a phenomenon called "voter fatigue" occurs, and only about half of those who vote for major elective offices vote on amendments. Voters tend not to vote on matters on which they have little or no information, and constitutional amendments clearly fall into this category for many.

The range of constitutional amendments has been quite broad in recent years. Consequently, voters may have had great difficulty in separating the vital from the trivial, the necessary from the merely desirable for some group—assuming they had the information and inclination to attempt the task. Table 1.1 lists the 13 constitutional amendments that appeared on the ballot in November 1985, all of which were approved because no significant opposition to most of them developed. An exception was the amendment authorizing water development bonds. Most of the amendments did not involve matters of a really fundamental nature. Certainly the typical voter would be hard-pressed to exercise an informed judgment on such a diverse range of matters. Nor is there reason to expect that voters in most areas of the state would be much interested in precincts in Chambers County or county offices in El Paso County.

In 1987 the legislature submitted a record 25 constitutional amendments to the voters, who approved 18 of them. Several of the amendments approved authorized the issuance of bonds (which will increase the state's debt). These were part of the "Build Texas" program promoted by the governor and legislature as a remedy for the state's economic recession. Also on the ballot were referenda on parimutuel betting on horse and greyhound races (which won) and retention

Table 1.1 CONSTITUTIONAL AMENDMENTS, 1985

HJR 6*	Authorizing issuance of additional Texas water development bonds to create special water funds for conservation and development.
HJR 19	Authorizing issuance of general obligation bonds to provide financing assistance for purchase of farm and ranch land.
HJR 27	Relating to number of precincts in Chambers County.
HJR 54	Authorizing legislature to enact laws permitting a city or town to spend public funds and levy assessments for relocation or replacement of water laterals on private property.
HJR 72	Authorizing legislature to require prior approval of expenditure or emergency transfer of other appropriated funds.
HJR 89	Relating to authority of legislature to regulate provision of health care by hospital districts.
SJR 6**	Relating to placement of state inmates in penal or correctional facilities of other states.
SJR 9	Providing additional bonding authority for veterans' housing assistance program and changing definition of those veterans eligible to participate.
SJR 10	Granting Supreme Court and Court of Criminal Appeals jurisdiction to answer questions of state law certified from federal appellate courts.
SJR 14	Creating Judicial Districts Board and providing for reapportionment of judicial districts by that board or by the Legislative Redistricting Board.
SJR 16	Relating to manner in which a person is charged with criminal offense and to jurisdiction of courts in criminal cases.
SJR 21	Authorizing use of proceeds from sale of permanent school fund land to acquire other land as part of permanent school fund.
SJR 27	Abolishing office of county treasurer in Andrews and El Paso Counties and abolishing office of county surveyor in Collin, Dallas, Denton, El Paso, Henderson, and Randall Counties.

*HJR = House Joint Resolution
**SJR = Senate Joint Resolution

of an appointed State Board of Education (which lost). A record turnout of approximately 20 percent of the state's voters participated in the election. The controversial referenda were likely of major importance in creating voter interest and turnout.

The frequency with which the constitution has been amended has increased over the long term, as Table 1.2 indicates. (The table does not include the first amendment, which was adopted in 1879.) As the constitution has become more detailed through amendment, and as government has become more active—especially since the New Deal era—amendments have proliferated. The need for frequent amendment of the constitution can be taken as one indication of its inadequacy. On the other hand, given the rigidity of the constitution, frequent amendment has helped keep it somewhat viable and responsive to pressing needs.

In a study of the amending process for the 1951–1972 period, Professor Janice C. May indicates some of the reasons for amending the constitution.[7] These include (1) avoidance of financial restrictions, such as those on government debt and taxation; (2) elimination of limitations on the activities of local governments; (3) responses to national policies and court decisions, as in welfare and suffrage; and (4) accommodation to decisions of the Texas courts and opinions of the state attorney general, as in workmen's compensation and dissolution of hospital districts. Many amendments are proposed to amend previous amendments because the initial amendments were either narrowly drawn or poorly drafted. Also, amendments defeated by the voters are frequently resubmitted by the legislature. Legislative pay proposals are the leaders here, nine having been submitted and only one having been adopted.

The Constitution Today

As it exists today, the Texas Constitution is a long, detailed, cumbersome document. As a consequence of its original length, plus over 300 amendments, it is approximately 65,000 words in length. Only three state constitutions are longer, with the range extending from fewer than 8,000 words for Vermont to approxi-

Table 1.2   CONSTITUTIONAL AMENDING ACTIVITY, 1881–1987

Decade	Number of Amendments Submitted to Voters	Number of Amendments Approved
1881–1890	15	7
1891–1900	15	9
1901–1910	20	11
1911–1920	34	10
1921–1930	25	15
1931–1940	45	32
1941–1950	35	22
1951–1960	43	37
1961–1970	84	56
1971–1980	67	42
1981–1990	98	85

Source: Texas Legislative Council, Information Report No. 9–3, August 1990.

mately 172,000 for Alabama. The Texas Constitution is not very readable because of its length and complex, legalistic language.[8] A brief description of its content follows. (Table 1.3 lists the articles in the constitution.)

Bill of Rights   The Texas Bill of Rights is contained in the first article of the constitution and includes 29 sections. All of the provisions of the U.S. Bill of Rights, plus many of the personal guarantees in its main body (e.g., the prohibitions of ex post facto laws and bills of attainder), are repeated in the Texas document. Also included are a variety of guarantees and declarations not found in the U.S. Constitution, such as the provisions that there be no imprisonment for debt and no religious tests for public office—with the stipulation that one "acknowledge the existence of a Supreme Being"; some profess to see an inconsistency in the latter guarantee.

The provisions of the Texas Bill of Rights fall generally into three categories.[9] First, there are statements of general political values and philosophy, as in the declaration that "the maintenance of our free institutions and the perpetuity of the Union depend upon the right of local self-government unimpaired to all the states." Second, there are declarations of substantive rights to liberty and property. Illustrative are the guarantees of liberty of speech and press, prohibition of the "outlawry" of citizens (an action that would make them legally "fair game" for all shooters), and protection of the right to keep and bear arms. Third, several provisions deal with procedural rights, especially in criminal proceedings, such as the guarantees of trial by jury, due course of law, and no double jeopardy.

Governmental Organization   The three branches of government—legislative, executive, and judicial—are established by Articles III, IV, and V, respectively.

Table 1.3   THE TEXAS CONSTITUTION: ARTICLES

Preamble	
Article I	Bill of Rights
Article II	The Powers of Government
Article III	Legislature Department
Article IV	Executive Department
Article V	Judicial Department
Article VI	Suffrage
Article VII	Education
Article VIII	Taxation and Revenue
Article IX	Counties
Article X	Railroads
Article XI	Municipal Corporations
Article XII	Private Corporations
Article XIII	(This article, which dealt with the Spanish and Mexican Land Titles, was repealed in 1969.)
Article XIV	Public Lands and Land Office
Article XV	Impeachment
Article XVI	General Provisions
Article XVII	Mode of Amending the Constitution of This State

Provision is made for the qualifications, selection, and tenure of members of each branch; their powers and duties are set forth; and limitations on them (particularly on legislators) are imposed, all in substantial detail. Not only does the constitution deal with the substantive power of the legislature, but it also includes many provisions pertaining to the internal organization, behavior, and procedure of that body. In contrast, the U.S. Constitution leaves most of those matters to Congress itself to determine. Many of the state's important executive offices and the structure of the court system are also provided for by the constitution.

Article II explicitly ordains that the state government shall be organized according to the principle of separation of powers:

> The powers of the government of the State of Texas shall be divided into three distinct departments, each of which shall be confided to a separate body of magistracy, to wit: Those which are legislative to one, those which are executive to another, and those which are judicial to another; and no person, or collection of persons, being of one of these departments, shall exercise any power properly attached to either of the others, except in the instances herein [elsewhere in the constitution] expressly provided.

Other sections of the constitution create a system of checks and balances whereby each branch is given some power to interfere with, or check, the exercise of power by the other branches. Thus, the governor is given legislative veto power, the Texas Senate is authorized to approve most gubernatorial appointments, the courts can hold legislative acts unconstitutional, and so on. The courts, however, have tended to construe the separation of powers quite strictly, with a slight encroachment by one branch on the powers of another being held unconstitutional.

The Texas Court of Criminal Appeals in 1987 held that a statute requiring that juries in criminal cases be instructed on the effects of parole was unconstitutional because it infringed on the executive power of clemency possessed by the governor and the Board of Pardons and Paroles.[10] No evidence or explanation was provided as to how a jury's knowledge of parole conditions might interfere with the executive's exercise of clemency powers. Rather, the focus was on the abstract character of governmental functions. The court's decision was overcome by a constitutional amendment in 1989. Decisions of this sort variously add to the rigidity of the constitution or stimulate the addition of detail to it.

Local Government   Various articles and sections cover the establishment, organization, legal authority, and selection of officials of local governmental bodies, including counties, municipalities, school districts, and various forms of special districts. In legal theory, local governments are dependent on the state government for their formal powers and, under the Texas Constitution, the state legislature is empowered to enact a variety of legislation involving local governments. Such legislation is supposed to take the form of general laws pertaining to all local governments, a point emphasized by the detailed constitutional prohibition against most local or special legislation; however, this prohibition has often been breached in practice.[11] The constitution also contains provisions permitting cities to adopt home-rule charters (see Chapter 9).

Citizen Political Participation   The constitution prescribes the qualifications for voting in state and local elections; provides for the disfranchisement of particular persons, such as "idiots and lunatics" and convicted felons; and authorizes the annual registration of voters. By requiring the election of many state and local officials, referenda on many tax levies and bond issues, and popular approval of amendments, the constitution ensures a long ballot at elections.

Substantive Material   Many sections of the constitution are concerned, often in minute detail, with matters of substantive public policy. Among the topics dealt with at some length are public education, taxation, welfare programs, the veterans' land program, retirement programs for teachers and public officials, conservation and resource development, public lands, and liquor control. For example, there are provisions in Article VII for the creation of a permanent university fund for support of the University of Texas and Texas A&M University, regulation of the way this fund can be invested, and control of the use of the income derived therefrom. As a consequence of the large volume of material of this sort, the Texas Constitution takes on the appearance of a legal code. Few would argue that it contains items only of a "fundamental" nature.

An Evaluation of the Constitution

Scholars, public officials, and interested citizens have expressed several major criticisms of the Texas Constitution. First, it is too long and detailed, poorly written, badly organized, and often unclear in meaning. Stylistically, the constitution leaves a lot to be desired. Second, it is not confined to fundamental matters and contains a lot of essentially statutory material. Third, the constitution's excessive detail and *restrictive* orientation hamper the operation of the government and help prevent it from adequately meeting the needs of a modern urban society. Fourth, it contains a lot of deadwood, that is, provisions that are no longer necessary or applicable. The "deadwood argument" was substantially countered by a 1969 amendment that deleted 52 outdated of superfluous sections. Some of the provisions eliminated were those that denied the right to vote or hold office to persons who engaged in dueling, authorized pensions for those who fought in the Texas War for Independence (1835–1837), permitted the appropriation of funds for a state centennial celebration in 1936, and dealt with Spanish and Mexican land titles. Some deadwood remains, as in the case of an authorization for the governor to use the militia to "protect the frontier from hostile incursions by Indians and other predatory bands" (Article IV, Section 7).

   Although the length and detail of the Texas Constitution, as such, are not especially important, the *consequences* of the length, detail, and complexity and their impact on the operation of government and its ability to respond to public problems *are* significant. Much of the detail is statutory in nature (e.g., the sections on hospital districts, the veterans' land fund, and taxation of agricultural land), in that it seeks to solve problems rather than simply authorize someone to solve them. But, whether the detail is conceived as statutory or fundamental, much of it has the effect of helping some groups and hindering others in getting what they want from government. As one authority remarked: "Many constitutional provisions protect a variety of interests. People like to be remembered in the Texas Constitution; but, unfortunately, not all people are remembered equally, and the sum of those special interests protected does not necessarily add up to the general or public interest."[12]

Much of the detail is designed to prevent the enactment of legislation or otherwise restrict governmental power. Thus, more than half of the 64 sections in the article dealing with the legislature involve restrictions on it.[13] In all, the state government is undoubtedly more limited by its own constitution than by the U.S. Constitution when it comes to the enactment of social and economic legislation. Much of the criticism of the Texas Constitution has come, unsurprisingly enough, from those who want a more active and positive government.

Because the states possess reserved powers under the U.S. Constitution, it is not necessary for state constitutions to authorize the enactment of particular laws in the fashion of the Texas Constitution. However, once started, the process of adding detail and specific authorizations leads to further detail as needs and circumstances change. Professor Duane Lockard comments:

> If the wealth of details grows sufficiently complex, it may become necessary to authorize a particular kind of legislation for the simple reason that so many kinds of legislation are authorized that doubt may be cast on the constitutionality of a law unless it is possible to point to some authorizing constitutional provision.[14]

This appears to be the case in Texas, as indicated by the flood of proposed amendments since 1960 (see Table 1.2), many of which were designed to authorize particular changes in state programs or specific actions by designated local governments. The amending process, because of constitutional restrictions and details, tends to displace the regular legislative process on many policy matters. An illustration of this involves Sections 59, 60, and 61 of Article III: Section 59, adopted in 1936, authorized workmen's compensation for state employees; Section 60, adopted in 1948, extended coverage to county employees; Section 61, adopted in 1952, covered municipal employees. Section 60 was itself amended in 1962 to permit coverage of employees of special districts. It would seem that one general amendment when the problem first arose would have been a sound constitutional approach.[15]

A constitution containing much detail and many restrictions on the actions of public officials will not guarantee good government or responsible officials. Although apparently such was a consideration motivating the framers of the Texas Constitution, a variety of provisions directed to requiring honesty in government have not prevented Texas from having its share of dishonest officials and political scandals. Neither, however, will a constitution confined to fundamental matters and general statements and phrased in clear language automatically yield

GETTING AROUND THE CONSTITUTION

A much noted characteristic of the Texas Constitution is the many restrictions that it imposes on state government. However, constitutional restrictions can be circumvented in various ways. One is simply to ignore them, as a number of counties do when they fail to elect the four justices of the peace required for each county. Another is to rely on interpretations and practices that permit the avoidance of limitations. Two examples are noted here.

State debt is limited to $200,000 (Article III, Section 49). However, a substantial amount of debt has been authorized by constitutional amendments, as in the instances of bonds for the veterans' land program, water development, and the superconducting super collider. Their value in 1989 was $2.3 billion. There also exist revenue bonds, as for student housing at state colleges, toll roads, and prisons, which are not guaranteed by the full faith and credit of the state's general revenues but are backed by fees or loan repayments. Technically, these do not fall under the prohibition on state debt. Their value in 1989 was over $4.3 billion. Total state bond debt thus was over $6.6 billion; the constitutional prohibition clearly does not depict actuality.

In an attempt to prevent legislative meddling in local government affairs, the Constitution prohibits the enactment of local legislation applying to named local governments on a wide array of topics. The legislature circumvents this limitation by the use of "bracket" legislation, that is, legislation that looks general but which contains such precise population or other limits as to apply to only one or a very few local governments. Many laws of this sort have been enacted, frequently at the request of local officials needing legal authority to handle particular local problems.

Should such actions as these simply be accepted as necessary to adapt an old constitution to new conditions? If not, what can be done to secure governmental practices that are in close conformity with constitutional provisions?

Source: Glen Hahn Cope and Thomas M. Keel, "Texas Constitutional Spending Limits: Reality versus Perception," *Public Affairs Comment,* Vol. 36 (Summer 1990), pp. 1–5.

good government and honest, responsible officials. Nonetheless, given Americans' veneration of constitutions and their tendency to follow most of the constitutional rules most of the time, a restrictive and inflexible constitution can hinder a government from responding to public needs and demands.

Everyone does not agree, however, that the state's government has been unduly hampered by its constitution. It has been contended, for instance, that the "nature of the constitution of the state of Texas is only incidental to whether Texas has an honest, efficient, principled government. The caliber of the men who guide the state's affairs determines the type of government Texas has."[16] This viewpoint, while not without some validity, neglects two important considerations: (1) The constitution, directly through such matters as salary limitations and indirectly through its impact on governmental organization and practice, may affect the "caliber" of the people who hold public office. (2) Even "high-caliber" public officials can be hindered or frustrated by restrictive constitutional procedures and limitations that place many matters beyond change or current control or that fragment authority and diffuse responsibility. Particular allocations of tax funds and limitations on the governor's administrative authority are cases in point.

Constitutional Revision

Critics have long advocated that the Texas Constitution be either revised or replaced with a new constitution more in accord with the requirements of government in a modern urban society. Newspaper editorial writers, educators, the League of Women Voters, various political officials (including some recent governors), and others have spoken in support of revision.[17]

One impediment to revision has been the fact that until recently the constitution did not provide explicit authorization for calling a constitutional convention, although the power to call such a convention is widely considered to be inherent in legislative bodies. The situation was made murky in Texas by an attorney general's ruling in 1911 that an amendment authorizing a convention was necessary; some legislators have cited this as the basis for not calling a convention. Another question over which there has been controversy is whether a call for a constitutional convention would require approval by the voters. In 1919 the legislature, by simple majority vote, did pass a resolution calling for a convention. Referred to the voters for approval, it was rejected by a vote of 71,376 to 23,549 (representing about 10 percent of the eligible electorate).

Another means for constitutional revision is the use of a specially created constitutional revision commission (appointed by legislative or executive officials) to propose changes subject to legislative approval and the regular amending process; this could take the form of either article-by-article revision or a single, comprehensive amendment. Final approval by the voters would be required to put the changes into effect. Popular approval of a constitution (or changes therein) provides legitimation and distinguishes it from ordinary legislative enactment. Popular approval also symbolizes its status as fundamental law, an expression of "the will of the people," as some are wont to say.

A number of factors have contributed to the failure of efforts at constitutional revision.

First, there has been a lack of really strong public support for reform. The League of Women Voters is the only organized group that shows active and continued interest in revision. While many people have indicated that they are in favor of reform, they apparently do not feel intensely about it, and it is not a salient issue. The result is a kind of "permissive opinion" environment, which permits but does not compel action. Consequently, in the absence of strong political leadership (as by a popular governor) that could direct and lead it, public opinion seems unlikely to produce significant action.

Second, opposition arises because the Texas Constitution is a political document that affects the distribution of power in the political system. It does this by distributing power among participants in the processes of policy formation and administration and by incorporating policies that confer advantages to some while withholding them from others. Those who benefit from provisions in the existing constitution thus have a stake in its retention; revision might not remove or alter their advantages, but it does hold that risk. Respecting those who oppose revision on this ground, Professor J. William Davis suggests some illustrations:

> This category might include special business and financial interests that prefer the present somewhat irresponsible administration controls . . . teachers who have constitutionally protected pension provisions; construction firms and highway enthusiasts who can boast of the best roads in the country; agrarian interests that find themselves protected by special constitutional provisions [e.g., the homestead exemption]; recipients of, or participants in, special earmarked funds or taxes, who fear losing a favored position in the state financial scheme; policemen and firemen who have received some constitutional protection from their municipal employers. . . .[18]

Third, the legislature has not shown much enthusiasm for major constitutional change.[19] It tends to be the dominant branch of the state government, and legislative leaders are reluctant to permit changes that would significantly reduce legislative power or increase gubernatorial power. Although they are not apparently opposed to revision in principle, they have been concerned with retaining control over the revision process. Governors have been more strongly in favor of revision because the position of the executive, from their viewpoint, needs to be strengthened (see Chapter 6).

Fourth, many persons apparently do not find the present constitution seriously lacking in any major way and do not consider revision necessary. If they do perceive a need for some changes, they contend that this can be accomplished satisfactorily through the regular amending process. Thus, a few years ago the director of the Texas Legislative Council (see Chapter 5) argued that the Texas Constitution was "basically good," and any needed changes could be made by amendments. He went on to say that "our Constitution is too precious to be tinkered with just for the sake of change alone or to 'modernize' it in the interests of theoretical perfection. Neither do I subscribe to the idea that we should have a short 'model constitution.' "[20]

Partly as a consequence of the reform mood generated by the Sharpstown bank scandal (see Chapter 4), a major effort to revise the constitution got under way in 1971, when the legislature initiated an amendment containing the following provisions:

1. The members of the Sixty-third Legislature, elected in 1972, would meet as a constitutional convention in January 1974.

2. The legislature in January 1973 would create a Constitutional Revision Commission to make recommendations to the members of the legislature.
3. "The convention by vote of at least two-thirds of its members could submit for a vote of the qualified electors of this state a new constitution which could contain alternative articles or sections, or it could submit revisions of the existing constitution which could contain alternative articles or sections."
4. No changes were to be made in the Bill of Rights of the constitution. (Many regarded this as "sacred" and something the people would not permit to be altered.)

Opposition to the amendment came from conservatives, who opposed major revision of the constitution, and others, including many liberals, who questioned the wisdom of permitting the legislature rather than a specially selected constitutional convention to rewrite the constitution. However, only by having the constitutional convention composed of the members of the legislature could the two-thirds vote to propose the amendment be secured. The amendment easily won approval at the polls in November 1972 by a margin of 1,549,982 to 985,282. Apparently the voters were motivated by a desire for reform because they also approved amendments changing the procedure for amending the constitution and increasing the terms of office to four years for statewide elected officials.

In the spring of 1973, the Constitutional Revision Commission was appointed. After a thorough study of the existing constitution, and a series of public hearings throughout the state, the commission decided to draft a new constitution. The proposed new constitution drafted by the commission was much shorter and more generally phrased than the existing constitution.[21] It included such major changes as greater administrative powers for the governor, annual legislative sessions, gubernatorial appointment of appellate court judges, provision for county home rule, and elimination of much of the "statutory" material in the existing constitution.

In January 1974, the 181 members of the legislature met as the state constitutional convention to consider the revision commission's recommendations. As one might guess, in operation the constitutional convention looked and acted much like the legislature. The convention, by early July, had completed work on a proposed 11-article constitution that did not include some of the changes favored by the revision commission. Also, it was decided to submit some items separately to the voters, such as provisions prohibiting parimutuel betting, authorizing limited county home rule, and increasing the salaries of legislators. To be submitted to the voters, the new constitution had to be approved by two-thirds of the legislator-delegates. Minutes before the convention adjourned, the last version of the proposed constitution voted on received 118 votes, 3 short of the total needed for approval. Constitutional revision had failed again.[22]

Several factors contributed to the failure of the convention to submit a new constitution to the voters: (1) Because the delegates were also legislators, they were subject to pressure from interest groups because of the impact their votes might have on their political futures. Antagonism existed among some delegates because of past legislative conflicts. Moreover, the campaigning for speaker of the house, which went on during the convention, was a distracting and somewhat divisive influence. (2) Some of the delegates were opposed to constitutional revision of any sort. (3) The rule requiring a two-thirds majority vote to submit the proposed constitution to the voters proved to be an insurmountable obstacle. Only simple majorities had been required to approve articles and separate submission items as the convention proceeded in its work. (4) The governor, who is in the best position to exercise leadership on constitutional revision, chose to leave the convention to itself except when it proposed to reduce the gubernatorial veto power. He then readily got what he wanted. (5) Some emotional issues, especially that of right-to-work, served to polarize the delegates and exacerbate conflict.

The issue on which the convention ultimately foundered was that of right-to-work. Conservative delegates refused to vote for a constitutional package that did not include the right-to-work submission item, while many liberal or prolabor delegates refused to vote for one that did. The right-to-work issue was really symbolic because the guarantee has no more impact in the constitution than in statute law, and, in either case, its existence depends upon continued authorization in national labor legislation. Nonetheless, it became *the* labor issue in the convention, and no compromise proved possible. The final constitutional package, which included a right-to-work proposal, failed by a vote of 118 to 62. The 62 negative votes came mostly from liberal-labor delegates plus a few conservatives opposed to any constitutional revision.

When the legislature met in January 1975, however, the drive for constitutional revision was revived. Apparently stung by public criticism of the convention's failure and under the leadership of the speaker and lieutenant governor, the legislature went briskly to work considering a multitude of proposals for constitutional revision. The approach settled upon was article-by-article revision. In April, the legislature approved a series of eight propositions (which collectively contained ten articles) to be submitted to the voters in November. Each proposition took the form of an amendment to the existing constitution and, in total, provided a new constitution except for the Bill of Rights. There was little difference between the content of the ten articles and the proposed constitution that had been rejected by the convention the previous July. One authority stated that, if adopted, the new constitution would be "among the best, perhaps the best drafted state constitution in the nation."[23]

In November 1975, following a somewhat desultory and uninformative campaign for and against the proposed constitution, approximately 25 percent of the eligible voters went to the polls and overwhelmingly rejected all eight propositions by margins of three to one.[24] Whatever the reason for their decision—lack of understanding of the new constitution, opposition to various provisions, the governor's opposition to revisions, belief that revision should be done by a people's convention rather than the legislature, or whatever—it marked the end of this movement for comprehensive constitutional revision. Since then constitutional reform has not been an issue on the political agenda.

CONCLUDING COMMENTS

In its regular session in 1977, the legislature returned to its old practice of tinkering in piecemeal fashion with the Constitution of 1876. In every regular session and a couple of special sessions since then, the legislature has proposed several constitutional amendments. Almost all of them subsequently have won voter approval.

Detail continues to beget detail as efforts are made to adapt a rather antiquated constitution to the needs and interests of a modern society. Constitutional change produces less controversy when it is handled in a less salient, piecemeal fashion. This is even more the case because the amendments customarily authorize particular actions without any basic revision of restrictive provisions.[25]

NOTES

1. For discussions of federalism, see W. Brooke Graves, *American Intergovernmental Relations: Their Origins, Historical Development and Current Status* (New York: Scribner, 1964); and Daniel J. Elazar, *American Federalism: A View from the States* (New York: Crowell, 1966).

2. Cf. Minor B. Crager, *Legal Aspects of Fire Prevention and Control in Texas* (Austin: University of Texas, Institute of Public Affairs, 1969), pp. 16–18.

3. Most of the data in this paragraph are derived from *Statistical Abstract of the United States, 1989* (Washington, D.C.: Government Printing Office, 1989), secs. 8 and 9.

4. Citizens Advisory Committee on Constitutional Revision, *Interim Report to the 56th Legislature and the People of Texas,* March 1, 1959, as reprinted in *Governing Texas: Documents and Readings,* ed. Fred Gantt, Jr., Irving O. Dawson, and Luther G. Hagard, Jr. (New York: Crowell, 1966), p. 39.

5. Joe E. Ericson, "The Delegates to the Convention of 1875: A Reappraisal," *Southwestern Historical Quarterly* 62 (July 1963): 22–27.

6. Rupert N. Richardson, *Texas: The Lone Star State,* 2d ed. (Englewood Cliffs, N.J.: Prentice-Hall, 1958), p. 226.

7. Janice C. May, *Amending the Texas Constitution 1951–1972* (Austin: Texas Advisory Commission on Intergovernmental Relations, 1972).

8. For those desiring to read the constitution, a convenient place to find it reprinted is in *The Texas Almanac* (Dallas: Belo Publishing Co.).

9. T.C. Sinclair and Werner F. Grunbaum, "Personal Rights and Liberties," vol. 5, *Arnold Foundation Monographs* (Dallas: Southern Methodist University Press, 1960).

10. *Rose* v. *State,* 724 S.W. 2d 832 (1987).

11. Texas Legislative Council, *Laws Based on Population* (a report to the 58th Legislature, Austin, December 1962).

12. Janice C. May, "Constitutional Revision in Texas," in *The Texas Constitution: Problems and Prospects for Revision* (Arlington: University of Texas at Arlington, Institute of Urban Studies, 1971), p. 84.

13. Limitations in the constitution are well covered in George D. Braden, *Citizen's Guide to the Texas Constitution* (Austin: Texas Advisory Commission on Intergovernmental Relations, 1972), esp. pp. 61–72.

14. Duane Lockard, *The Politics of State and Local Government* (New York: Macmillan, 1963), p. 89.

15. There are, incidentally, two Section 61s in Article III because one was misnumbered when adopted. Another amendment would be needed to change this.

16. A. J. Thomas, Jr., and Ann Van Wynen Thomas, "The Texas Constitution of 1876," *Texas Law Review* 35 (October 1957): 917. This entire issue of the law review examines the Texas Constitution.

17. See Dick Smith, "Constitutional Revision, 1876–1961," *Public Affairs Comment* 7 (September 1961).

18. J. William Davis, "The Abortive Movement for Constitutional Revision, 1957–1961," in Gantt et al., *Governing Texas,* p. 63.

19. May, "Constitutional Revision in Texas," p. 88.

20. Quoted in Stuart A. McCarkle and Dick Smith, *Texas Government,* 6th ed. (New York: McGraw-Hill, 1968), p. 29.

21. Its recommendations are contained in three documents: (1) *A New Constitution for Texas;* (2) *A New Constitution for Texas: Text, Explanation, Commentary;* and (3) *A New Constitution for Texas: Separate Statements of Commission Members.* The second item contains biographical data on members of the commission. Also see Jay G. Stanford, "Constitutional Revision in Texas: A New Chapter," *Public Affairs Comment* 20 (February 1974): 1–6.

22. For a thorough account of constitutional revision activity in Texas, see Janice C. May, *The Texas Constitutional Revision Experience in the 70's* (Austin: Sterling Swift, 1975).

23. Janice C. May, "The Proposed 1976 Revision of the Texas Constitution," *Public Affairs Comment* 21 (August 1975): 1.

24. See Richard Murray and Curtis Forsback, "Anatomy of a Landslide: An Analysis of Texas Voters' Rejection of a New State Constitution," Institute for Urban Studies, University of Houston, 1976; and John E. Bebout, "The Meaning of the Vote on the Proposed Texas Constitution," *Public Affairs Comment* 14 (February 1978): 1–4.

25. An amendment providing for tax reduction and expenditure limitation was proposed by special session of the legislature in the summer of 1978 and approved by the voters in the fall. This was Texas's response to California's Proposition 13, which imposed a limitation on property taxes.

chapter 2

Political Participation and the Electoral System

Prospective voters at a registration drive.

Political systems define and attempt to implement policies deemed to be in the best interest of the society at large. The forms and means of definition and implementation have varied, but little effort was made in the past to significantly involve ordinary individuals in the processes through which political rules and decisions were made. That, of course, is no longer the case. As two leading scholars of modern politics note, "If there is a political revolution going on throughout the world, it is what might be called the participation explosion."[1] The belief that the ordinary person is politically relevant and ought to be an involved participant in the political system has taken firm hold throughout the world. People who have been outside of politics are demanding entrance into the political system; people who have been without influence or power are demanding a share of political control.

One might question the relevance of these general comments to Texas politics. Have not the United States and the state of Texas been committed to citizen participation since their beginnings? And do not most Americans, including Texans, support the values of democracy and citizen involvement? In the abstract, the answer is yes. The Declaration of Independence and the U.S. and Texas Constitutions all emphasize that government is an instrument to be wielded in the interests of the people. Similarly, evidence exists that the American public strongly prefers "democratic," as opposed to "nondemocratic," political systems. Nonetheless, a tension has existed through much of our history between our abstract commitment to democracy and popular participation and the practical implementation of these ideals.[2]

This discrepancy between democratic ideals and political realities is evident in the operation of the electoral system. Theoretically, it is the fundamental means by which citizens can control and direct their government. Parties and their candidates, officeholders and challengers, can present themselves for popular scrutiny, and the citizenry—via the ballot—can pass judgment on them. In this way, individuals, since they help to select their political leaders, are presumably obligated to accept and obey the government, pending another opportunity to vote their approval or disapproval. And political leaders, selected by the votes of the citizenry, are presumed to be legitimately entitled to their official positions.

Turning from the ideal to the historical record, one notes that large segments of the adult population in the United States, including Texas, were legally excluded from meaningful political participation until well into the twentieth century. Open legal exclusion has by now been virtually eliminated, but substantial numbers of the populace are still not involved in the electoral politics of their state or nation. This is especially true in Texas where, despite the presence of Houstonian George Bush at the top of the Republican ticket, only 5.4 million Texans voted in the 1988 presidential election. Since there were 12 million adults in the state, that translates into only 45 percent of those eligible actually participating, compared to 50 percent elsewhere in the United States.

Questions concerning the nature and extent of public participation in Texas politics thus remain relevant despite widespread abstract support for democracy and the present relative absence of legal barriers to individual involvement. This relevance is enhanced by the fact that electoral participation is selective; that is, those who regularly participate are not representative of the general Texas population. Some groups have been very active in Texas politics, while others have been only slightly involved. Because of the selective participatory patterns, state and local governments have often been especially responsive to certain groups' interests and demands and relatively insensitive to others. This remains substantially true today, despite the increasing efforts of new groups representing new interests to influence the political process.

The patterns of participation in Texas electoral politics are examined in the following sections. In discussing this topic, three groups are distinguished: (1) the adult population residing in the state, (2) those legally qualified to take part in the electoral process, and (3) those who actually involve themselves in electoral politics. The variations between the first group and the last two are of particular import to Texas political patterns. (The three groups are discussed under the headings "Characteristics of the Texas Population," "The Texas Electorate," and "Voter Participation.")

CHARACTERISTICS OF THE TEXAS POPULATION

Virtually all studies of politics have acknowledged a close connection between the demographic characteristics of large groups of people and their political behaviors. The racial, religious, occupational, educational, geographic, and class patterns characteristic of the Texas population are therefore worthy of our attention. In general, Texans are a diverse people. The land is, of course, vast and varied, ranging from western plains and mountains to central hills and eastern forests and the semitropical coastal plains of the south. And the diversity of the 17 million inhabitants is at least equal to that of the terrain.

Population Growth Patterns

In 1940 Texas had about 6.5 million residents. A half-century later the 1990 census counted 17,059,805 people in the state. Population growth in Texas has consistently exceeded national increases. Between 1970 and 1980, for example, Texas's population grew by 27 percent, while that of the United States as a whole grew by only about 10 percent. State growth slowed to 19.9 percent between 1980 and 1990, but this was still almost twice the rate of national growth (10.2 percent).

Birthrates in Texas typically exceed national levels, reflecting a high proportion of young adults in the state. However, most of the population gains in recent years resulted from the fact that more people moved to Texas than left the state. This was especially true between 1973 and 1982, when a tenfold increase in oil prices fueled a boom in many parts of the state. The declines in oil prices in 1982–1983 and 1986 resulted in massive job losses in the state and a significant slowing of growth rates. Growth continues, however, and Texas now ranks third behind California and New York in population; it should surpass the latter in 1994.

Not only have Texans increased in number, but they have also become much more concentrated in the major metropolitan areas. Over 80 percent of the population now lives in urban counties, with about 45 percent in the Dallas-Fort Worth and Houston-Galveston consolidated metropolitan statistical areas. In the 1950s and 1960s, the greatest growth was in cities such as Houston, Dallas, and Fort Worth. In the 1980s, growth slowed or stopped in the cities and shifted to suburban communities. Consequently, the great population gains in the 1980s were in suburban counties such as Collin and Denton (north of Dallas-Fort Worth) and Fort Bend (southwest of Houston). Meanwhile, most rural areas and small towns in Texas, which had half of the population in 1940, have struggled, often unsuccessfully, to maintain their existing population base.

The political implications of rural decline and urban and suburban growth have been great. Writing in 1949, V. O. Key, Jr., one of the most respected analysts of American state politics, noted that "the Lone Star State is concerned about money and how to make it, about oil and sulfur and gas, about cattle and dust storms and irrigation, about cotton and banking and Mexicans."³ These concerns doubtlessly continue, but as Texans have crowded into big cities and their suburbs, other issues have come to the fore. Foremost among these are heightened concerns about crime and law enforcement, mobility and transportation, public schools, and air and water pollution. These latter-day issues are often sharpened by an urban demography featuring poor inner-city minority communities surrounded by more affluent suburban whites.

Race, Ethnicity, and Religion

The population of Texas is more racially and ethnically mixed than those in most states. As Table 2.1 shows, about 60 percent of Texans are non-Hispanic whites, or "Anglos." Persons of Spanish origin account for about 26 percent of the state's population, blacks for about 12 percent; 2 percent are of Asian or other ethnic origin. In general, the Anglo percentage has been dropping, and the Hispanic population (which is largely of Mexican origin) has been growing.

This Hispanic growth reflects a relatively high birthrate and continued in-migration from Mexico. The political troubles in Central America are also causing a steady flow of immigrants from countries such as El Salvador. Many new migrants are "illegal aliens" or "undocumented workers," who enter the United States without complying with the immigration laws of this country. The increasing number of migrants, coupled with relatively high unemployment in the United States, has made their presence a major political issue in the United States and Texas. Estimates usually place the number of illegal migrants in Texas at between 0.5 and 1 million persons.

Presidents Carter and Reagan both proposed complicated programs to stem this in-migration, but opposition from some Hispanic groups and employer associations prevented passage of national legislation until 1986. The new immigration law included two controversial provisions. First, it extended legal residency to persons continuously in the United States since January 1, 1982, regardless of their previous legal status ("amnesty"). The law also provided for criminal penalties against employers who hire illegal aliens. Polls have shown that non-Hispanic Texans strongly support the employer sanctions provisions and tightening rules on future immigration from outside the United States.

The impact of the 1986 immigration law, which was modified in 1990,

Table 2.1   RACE AND ETHNICITY OF TEXAS POPULATION: 1980 AND 1990

	1980	1990	Change
Anglos (non-Hispanic whites)	65.6%	59.8%	−5.8%
Hispanics/persons of Spanish origin	21.0%	26.0%	+5.0%
Blacks/African-Americans	12.0%	12.1%	+0.1%
Asian-Americans/others	1.4%	2.1%	+0.7%

Sources: 1980 data are from *General Population Characteristics: Texas* PC80-1-B45 (U.S. Department of Commerce, Bureau of the Census, 1981), Tables 15 and 16. 1990 data are the preliminary totals provided to the Texas Legislature for redistricting purposes on Feb. 15, 1991.

remains in doubt; but few expect an end to the great immigration pressures arising from the population growth and economic problems of Mexico and Central America. These continuing pressures, coupled with a higher birthrate among Hispanic-American citizens and growing immigration from Asia, portend a continued shrinkage of the Anglo population that has dominated Texas since it achieved independence from Mexico. One 1986 report published by the Population Reference Bureau, for example, estimated that Anglos would account for just 43.4 percent of the Texas population by 2035, compared to the 39.3 percent estimated for Hispanic residents.[4] Such long-term projections are often seriously in error, but the trend toward a more diverse and Hispanic state population is not likely to be reversed.

Historically, the African-American and Mexican-American populations have been geographically concentrated in different parts of the state. Blacks generally resided east of an imaginary line running through Fort Worth, Austin, and Corpus Christi. Mexican-Americans generally lived south of a line running from El Paso to San Antonio to Corpus Christi. In recent years some dispersion throughout the state has occurred, especially among Mexican-Americans. In 1990, for example, more than 26 percent of the state's Hispanics lived the Houston-Galveston and Dallas-Fort Worth metropolitan areas.

The national pattern of blacks migrating to big cities holds true in Texas. In 1960, 41 percent of the African-American population lived in the four most populous counties. By 1990 more than 55 percent lived in these counties.

The religious preferences of Texans tend toward fundamental Protestantism and Catholicism. A January 1990 survey of registered voters in Texas by the Center for Public Policy at the University of Houston found that 31 percent were Baptists, 20 percent Catholics, 12 percent Methodists, 5 percent Church of Christ members, and 4 percent Lutherans. Another 4 percent were Presbyterians, 3 percent Episcopalians, 1 percent Mormons, and 1 percent Jews. Seven percent said they were not religious. In general terms, Texas Protestants are concentrated in the northern and eastern parts of the state, with a large Catholic population in South Texas and along the Gulf Coast.

This religious regional pattern becomes significant when public issues arise that involve regulation of community mores, such as permitting the sale of beer or liquor, legalizing bingo, allowing betting on horse races, or setting up a state lottery. Regarding issues like liquor and bingo where local option prevails, the Protestant areas tend to prohibit the sale or practice thereof, while the Catholic regions are more permissive.

Education, Income, and Occupation

Texas politics, in contrast to that of the other former Confederate states, has focused largely on socioeconomic rather than racial issues.[5] Since socioeconomic status is determined largely by an individual's education, occupation, and income, some discussion of these characteristics is warranted.

Historically, Texas and the South lagged behind the rest of the nation in economic development after the Civil War. The region was primarily a producer of commodities that commanded relatively low prices from the 1870s to the 1930s. Per capita income was about 60 percent of the national average at the turn of the century and improved only moderately until World War II. The immense national war effort directed at defeating Germany and Japan resulted in substantial investments in Texas to develop military and industrial facilities and integrated the state into the national industrial economy. After the war the nation's growing dependence on petroleum and natural gas for energy and petrochemical products provided a strong base for the state's economic growth. Expansion of trade, banking, insurance, and health care services further diversified the economy; and by the 1970s, the socioeconomic characteristics of the state's population differed little from those in the nation as a whole.

Table 2.2 shows that, in 1980, median family income in Texas was 98 percent of the national level, educational levels among adults were almost identical, and almost as many Texas workers held managerial or professional jobs as was the case nationally.

However, the same table documents the large differences among racial and ethnic populations within Texas. Black and Hispanic families in Texas, for example, earned less than 60 percent of the family income of Anglos. Blacks had 1.2 fewer years of formal education than did Anglos; Hispanics had 4.5 fewer years. And Anglo workers were far more likely to hold high-status jobs than were African-Americans and Hispanics. Interestingly, the small Asian-American community, which included a high percentage of professional workers, had the highest levels of education and income.

In summary, the 1980 census data showed that Anglo Texans were considerably better off than the state's large minority populations. Although 1990 census reports were not available when this book went to press, there is reason to believe that the gap widened rather than narrowed in Texas when the state's

Table 2.2   COMPARISON OF NATIONAL AND STATE SOCIOECONOMIC PATTERNS IN 1980: BROKEN DOWN BY RACIAL/ETHNIC POPULATIONS WITHIN TEXAS

	United States	Texas	Racial/Ethnic Groups in Texas			
			Anglos	Blacks	Hispanics	Asians
Median family income	$19,917	$19,618	$22,427	$13,042	$13,293	$23,719
Median years of education of persons over 25	12.5	12.4	13.3	12.1	8.8	14.0
Percent of employed persons with managerial or professional positions	22.7%	21.7%	25.7%	11.9%	10.7%	32.5%

Sources: U.S. data are from *General Social and Economic Characteristics: U.S. Survey* PC80-1-C1 (U.S. Department of Commerce, Bureau of the Census, Government Printing Office, Dec. 1983), Tables 83, 89, 96, 245. Texas data are from *General Social and Economic Characteristics: Texas* PC80-1-C45, Section 1 (U.S. Department of Commerce, Bureau of the Census, GPO, July 1983), Tables 66, 68, 72, 76, 78, 82, 86, 88, and 92.

economy experienced serious problems in the 1980s that hit hardest at low-income workers with little formal education.

THE TEXAS ELECTORATE

Political participation via the ballot is a right possessed abstractly by those who live in a democratic political society. In practice, however, no government extends this right uniformly to all persons within its jurisdiction. The necessity for some restriction seems obvious: Few would argue that children, foreign visitors, the mentally ill, or certain types of criminals should have access to the electoral system. Not only is exclusion practiced, but fear of fraud and manipulation has led to the development of an extensive regulatory process to supervise use of the ballot.

The individual states have discretion to regulate electoral participation within the limits defined by the U.S. Constitution and federal statutes. Texas, like other states, has established a process whereby citizens must present themselves in advance of an election, attest that they meet certain legal qualifications, and be enrolled on a list of qualified electors if they wish to vote. The procedure may sound trivial, but typically from one-half to one-third of the adult population never completes this preliminary process and thus is automatically excluded from direct participation in elections. The reasons for their failure are rooted in an interrelated pattern of historical discrimination, cumbersome registration processes, and a culture that does little to discourage political apathy.

The Historical Context

Historically, the state of Texas has acted to limit electoral participation. For 90 years, from 1876 to 1966, the state assessed a poll tax on individual electors. The tax was provided for in the Constitution of 1876 as a revenue measure but was later used as a device to restrict political participation, especially among poor whites, blacks, and Mexican-Americans. The fee was small—usually $1.75 in later years—but the bother of paying the tax probably exceeded its expense as a barrier to voter participation. Additionally, poll taxes had to be paid far in advance of most electoral activity. In its last years of operation, the tax for a calendar year was payable from October 1 of the preceding year to February 1 of the year in which it applied. The likelihood that individuals would forget or neglect to pay the fee was heightened considerably by requiring payment months before the May primaries and November general elections. Texans approved a constitutional amendment in 1966 abolishing the poll tax only after a federal court had ruled the tax invalid.

Another, and far more blatant, effort to reduce voter participation was the "white primary." This scheme was used by a number of southern states in addition to Texas to circumvent the Fifteenth Amendment to the U.S. Constitution, which prohibits a state's denial of suffrage because of race, color, or previous condition of servitude. The procedure was simple. The Democratic party dominated Texas politics after the post–Civil War Reconstruction period, so all that was required to exclude blacks from effective participation was to bar them from the party's nominating processes. This exclusion was justified on the grounds that a political party, as a private association, possessed the right to extend or deny membership to anyone for any reason it deemed sufficient. Registered blacks were still free to vote in general elections, but since the Democratic nominee always prevailed, this right was of little importance.

Legal challenges to the white primary were initiated in the 1920s. Finally, after 20 years of legal controversy and four major judicial decisions, the U.S. Supreme Court struck down this exclusion of black voters, reasoning, in *Smith* v. *Allwright,* that party primaries are an inseparable part of the total electoral process and thus come under the protection of the Fifteenth Amendment.

Registration and Voting Procedures

For several years after the poll tax was abolished, Texas retained the most cumbersome registration procedures in the United States. The 1966 constitutional amendment that removed the poll tax continued the system of annual registration far in advance of the party primaries and general election. Such a requirement placed a heavy burden on the ordinary adult, who was only marginally interested, informed, and motivated in political matters. The registration system was challenged successfully in federal court, and a more liberal law was passed in 1971. At present, one can register to vote in any election up to 30 days before polling day. Registration is for a period of two years, when new voter certificates are mailed to those on the rolls. If a person receives the new certificate, he or she is automatically continued on the rolls for another two years, but if the card is returned to the county voter registration office because the individual is no longer at his or her registration address, that person will be dropped from the rolls and must reregister to vote in future elections.

The potential electorate in Texas is defined by a set of restrictions that limits access to the ballot. The Texas Constitution denies the vote to "idiots" and "lunatics," "paupers" supported by the county (i.e., persons in county homes for the destitute, which does *not* include ordinary welfare recipients), and felons whose rights have not been restored. A constitutional provision denying the vote to persons under 21 years of age was rendered inoperative by the adoption of the Twenty-sixth Amendment to the U.S. Constitution in 1971, which lowered the voting age to 18. Until 1969 only qualified electors who owned property that had been rendered for taxation were eligible to vote in bond-issue elections, but the U.S. Supreme Court voided this practice as a violation of equal protection of the laws.

Traditionally voters were required to cast their ballots in the election precinct where they resided. Exceptions were made, however, in the case of qualified electors who expected to be absent from their county on the day of the election or who, because of illness or physical disability, could not appear at their precinct polling place on election day. Such persons could cast an absentee ballot at the county clerk's office from 20 to 4 days before the election or else secure and cast a mail ballot before election day. Provision was also made for Texas residents who were outside the state because of military service or outside the county in the employ of the federal government to cast ballots by mail.

In 1987 the legislature liberalized the absentee rules by removing the requirement that one claim a reason to vote early. Additional early polling places were also authorized. These rule changes have led to a sizable increase in absentee, or more properly now, early voting. In the 1990 general election, for example, more than 800,000 of the 3.9 million votes were cast prior to Tuesday, November 6.

VOTER PARTICIPATION

Voter registration and turnout in Texas traditionally have lagged behind national levels. The last ten presidential elections (1952–1988) attracted an average turnout of 57.4 percent among those of voting age across the country. In Texas, mean voter turnout in the same elections was 46.3 percent. Turnout in state and local elections is even lower. The last 15 general elections for governor drew an average of 33 percent of the state's adults to the polls. The combined vote in the Democratic and Republican primaries has been less than 30 percent since World War II and was just 22 percent of adult Texans in 1990. County and local races are usually even less popular with voters.

Voter participation, like income, educational attainment, and employment,

Reprinted by permission.

varies greatly among different segments of the Texas population. As one might expect, the poor and minority-group members are less involved in politics than are the more prosperous Anglos. Table 2.3 compares registration and voting levels within four demographically different areas within Houston in 1980.

These data make it strikingly clear how much variation in registration and voting there is along socioeconomic lines. In a solidly middle-class, Anglo neighborhood, registration was at 70 percent of the population in 1980, which meant that virtually all adults were on the voter lists. And there were 501 voters per 1000 population in the November 1980 presidential election. In an Anglo working-class area, there were just 420 persons registered per 1000 population, and only 250 voted. Registration in a black area was 501 per 1000 population, with 245 voting. The lowest levels of political participation are found in Mexican-American precincts. In the Canal-Navigation area, for example, there were only 256 persons registered per 1000 population, and just 108 per 1000 voted. This meant that the Mexican-American population had only about one-fifth of the voter participation of middle-class Anglos.

Some indication of the significance of these differences is evident when one looks at the righthand column in Table 2.3, which lists the vote percentage received in each area by the Republican presidential ticket of Ronald Reagan and George Bush. Obviously, there are great differences in voting patterns from area to area. The Reagan-Bush ticket got 74 percent of the Anglo middle-class vote, 42 percent of the Anglo working-class vote, just 20 percent in the Mexican-American area, and only 3 percent among blacks. Thus, variations in voter participation are of great practical significance. Generally, as in this case, differing rates of participation work to the advantage of Republican candidates in general elections.

Many observers felt that the elimination of the poll tax, followed by lowering the voting age to 18 and easing registration procedures, would result in a dramatic increase in voter participation. This did not happen. Voter registration did increase from 3 million to 4 million after the poll tax was eliminated in 1966,

Table 2.3   VOTER REGISTRATION AND PARTICIPATION IN FOUR HOUSTON-AREA NEIGHBORHOODS IN THE 1980 PRESIDENTIAL ELECTION

Area	Socioeconomic Characteristics	Registered Voters Per 1000 Population	Voters Per 1000 Population	Republican % of Two-Party Vote
West University	Anglo, middle class	701	501	74
Jacinto City	Anglo, working class	420	250	42
Acres Homes	Black, poor, and working class	501	245	3
Canal-Navigation	Mexican-American, poor, and working class	256	108	20

Source: Official returns, Office of County Clerk, Harris County.

and it rose another 2 million after the voting age was lowered to 18 and registration procedures were eased in the early 1970s. Actual voting has edged up more slowly, however. In 1964, for example, there were about 6 million adults of voting age in Texas, and 2.5 million voted in the Johnson-Goldwater presidential election. In 1988 there were 5.4 million voters in the Bush-Dukakis contest, but there were now more than 12 million adults in the state, so almost all the voter increase can be accounted for by population growth.

One can infer from such figures that while legal factors such as voting age and the existence or nonexistence of a poll tax affect voter registration and voter turnout, they do not alone explain participation patterns. Whether people vote is not simply a function of whether they *can* legally vote but also of whether they *want* to vote.

Empirical research into the behavior of the American electorate has shed some light on factors that are associated with voting and nonvoting. No such studies have as yet been done of the Texas electorate, but there is no reason to suspect that Texans differ substantially from other Americans in their general political behavior.

In general, we can say that a person votes or becomes politically active as a result of two sets of factors, one psychological, the other environmental.[6] Some people are "self-starters"; that is, they are moved to political action of their own accord. Ordinarily, they are so motivated because they think their activity will affect electoral or policy outcomes (a sense of political efficacy), or because they consider it their civic duty to be politically active, or both. Such individuals usually come from homes where political interest and participation are high. A disproportionately high number of them complete at least some college work, and they are often of middle or high socioeconomic status.

For others, political activity is much more a matter of immediate environmental factors. They are moved to political action by external stimuli—their friends, the news media, contact by a party worker, and so on. In such cases the social and political setting in which one operates is crucial. Of course, some people shut out or ignore political stimuli, but in general the more political information and stimulation people are exposed to, the more likely they are to be politically active.

Applying these general considerations to Texas politics provides some insight into the low participation patterns of state residents. Traditionally, the general environment did not encourage voter involvement. For the first half of the twentieth century a single political party dominated the political scene, restraining competition over political issues. Texas had few strong local political organizations or "machines" that were effective mobilizers of the vote in other areas of the country. And the individualistic political culture of the Southwest, in which people were expected to look out for themselves, left a legacy of political noninvolvement. When parents have been inattentive to politics, the likelihood of their children becoming politically apathetic adults is heightened. The patterns of the past are thus extended into the future.

The consequences of traditional apathy have been most severe among Texas blacks and Mexican-Americans. For generations they were legally or informally discouraged from political action. Breaking down their traditional nonparticipation has been a painfully slow process, as the political leaders of these groups can attest. The legal and social changes associated with the civil rights movement in the 1960s resulted in substantial increases in black registration and voting. By the late 1980s, black voter registration levels were proportionate to their share of the adult Texas population (about 10 percent), and actual voting was usually close to the Anglo level. Change has come more slowly for Mexican-Americans, many of whom came into Texas after 1900 and found an unfamiliar political culture transacted in a language they did not understand. Most attended inferior schools and faced a hostile Anglo establishment not disposed to share political power. Their Hispanic cultural background, with its stress on individual action and family commitment, hindered political activism and the development of effective political leadership. There are clear signs, however, that Mexican-Americans are making important political gains. Hispanic voter registration has more than doubled since 1978. Legislative representation has improved, with 25 of 181 senators and state representatives being of Hispanic origin in 1991. A major breakthrough came in the 1990 general election, when Dan Morales, a 35-year-old legislator from San Antonio, won the Texas attorney general contest. Morales, along with former San Antonio mayor Henry Cisneros, are among the brightest political stars in Texas politics.

Nevertheless, the progress made by African-Americans and Mexican-Americans should not be overstated. In 1991 blacks and Hispanics made up more than 38 percent of the Texas population but less than 25 percent of the registered voters in the state, and they cast less than 20 percent of the vote in the most recent general election. There are 30 statewide elected officials in Texas: only one is black, three are Hispanics. And few minorities have been appointed to the dozens of powerful boards and commissions that direct state agencies. Clearly, Anglos remain the dominant political group in Texas politics and will remain so for the foreseeable future.

THE ELECTORAL SYSTEM

Citizens lack means to control public policy directly in a democratic system, but it is expected that they will be given the opportunity to select key policymakers and to set general limits within which these policymakers operate. As we have seen, many adults do not qualify or, even if qualified, do not participate in the process. That aside, the practical implementation of this elective principle can be accomplished in many ways. A cursory survey of the 50 states would reveal that no two have devised electoral systems exactly alike, and a number have very little in common with each other. A basic difference centers on the degree of popular involvement in the selection of state and local officials. In some states only the governor and state legislators, among state officials, are chosen by public balloting. In others nearly all state leaders, including judges and key administrators, must stand for election. Texas—true to the spirit of Jacksonian democracy, with its stress on popular control—falls in the latter camp.

Changes in the Texas Constitution require majority approval by the state's voters, and voter approval is needed for a number of county and local policies (especially those involving new financial commitments). But more important are the rules and practices that allow qualified citizens to choose public officials. Three types of elections figure in this process: primary, general, and special.

Primary Elections

State statutes specify that most state and county public officials shall be chosen in a general election held every two or four years. But to be placed on the general-election ballot under the name of one of the major parties, a candidate must first qualify in a party primary. Texas political parties are discussed in Chapter 3, but since their primaries are an inseparable part of the election system and are extensively regulated by state law, this aspect of partisan politics is discussed here.

The importance of primary elections cannot be overemphasized. These preliminary contests narrow the choices presented to the general electorate from a potential of thousands to a very few. The importance of party nominations is reflected in the fact that Texas and most other states require that major parties choose their candidates in public elections. The longtime dominance of the Democrats made these primaries especially important in Southern states like Texas for most of the twentieth century.

State law requires that the major parties hold their primaries on the *second Tuesday in March of each even-numbered year,* which means that the party nominees are chosen eight months before the November general election. This extremely early primary date reflects a recent desire of Texas legislators to exert more influence in presidential nominations by participating in the "Super Tuesday" primaries held in 20 states in early March. Unlike the other states taking part in the presidential primary, however, Texas requires that nominees for all state and local positions also be chosen at this time. This means that in presidential years (1988 and 1992, for example) most voter attention is diverted to national candidate matchups, such as George Bush versus Robert Dole in the 1988 Republican primary, and away from state and local nominations. In years such as 1990 and 1994 that do not involve presidential elections, the very early primary generally works to the advantage of incumbent officeholders and/or candidates who have more funds to spend than their opponents.

If no candidate for state or local office receives a majority in the primary, the two contenders with the largest number of votes are matched in a runoff election held the second Tuesday in April. Texas voters do not identify themselves as members of a political party when they register and thus are free to vote in any party's March primary, but not in more than one. Voters are also prohibited from balloting in one party's March primary and switching over to another's April runoff.

To secure a position on the primary ballot, a candidate for state office must declare an intention of running by filing an application with the state party chair or, if a district or county office is sought, with the party's county chairperson. Applicants must either pay a filing fee, which ranges between $50 and $4000, depending on the office, or present a petition signed by a specified number of voters eligible to vote for the office the candidate is seeking.

Since filing fees are not sufficient to cover primary election costs, the state

A REDISTRICTING PRIMER FOR TEXAS

What is redistricting?　The periodic redrawing of the election districts from which various officials, including U.S. Congress members, state legislators, and many county officials, are elected.

When does it occur?　Most commonly after new U.S. census figures are released. Federal court rulings require that most districts be equal in population, so major readjustments are necessary when the final census count is made available. Most recently, that was in March 1991, which means that intense redistricting efforts were undertaken across Texas in 1991 and 1992.

Who does the redistricting?　The state legislature redraws the boundaries for U.S. Congress seats as well as the state Senate and House of Representatives. Local elected officials redraw county, municipal, and school district boundaries. However, at the state level, if the Texas legislature fails to redraw the districts in its regular session, the responsibility passes to a Legislative Redistricting Board made up of the lieutenant governor, attorney general, comptroller, land commissioner, and speaker of the house (note the absence of the governor).

Can their work be challenged?　Yes, and it almost always is. Federal and state courts can review, upon request of an injured party, the particular plans enacted. Plans must not only meet the "one person-one vote" standard of population equality but must also be drawn fairly in terms of the political interests of minorities. These court challenges often drag on for years after initial redistricting occurs and sometimes result in major changes.

Why is redistricting important?　Because the shape of districts greatly affects who can win and hold particular offices. Boundaries can be drawn

has assumed most of this obligation. A special fund was established by the legislature, and the secretary of state oversees payments from it to cover expenses incurred in holding the primaries.

General Elections

General elections are held on the first Tuesday after the first Monday in November of even-numbered years. Members of the Texas House of Representatives and the U.S. House must run every two years. The governor, state senators, and elected county officials run every four years, whereas U.S. senators serve six-year terms. Additionally, Texas voters ballot for presidential electors every other general election. In all cases the candidate who receives the most votes for an office wins; there is no runoff provision, as in the party primaries.

to favor Democrats over Republicans, Anglos over blacks, conservatives over liberals, or even specific individuals. There is an old and strong tradition in the United States and Texas of carefully drawing districts to produce such results. This is called "gerrymandering," after Massachusetts Governor Elbridge Gerry, who was an adept practitioner of the art nearly 200 years ago.

What does redistricting mean for Texas politics in the 1990s?   Because Democrats won the governorship, retained control of both the State Senate and House, and all five positions on the Redistricting Board in the 1990 elections, they controlled the realignment of districts for Congress and the state legislature.

In the case of Congress, this means the 3 new seats coming to Texas (increasing the delegation from 27 to 30), will likely go to the Democrats who already hold a 19- to-8 edge. In the legislature, it means Republican prospects for erasing the Democratic margin in the House and Senate before the twenty-first century are not good.

Blacks and Mexican-Americans, who generally support Democratic candidates in Texas, did better under the new plans enacted in 1991 compared to the 1981 lines. If state or local officials disappoint minority groups, the plans adopted may well be challenged in court.

What about the Republicans? Can they sue as well?   Minorities enjoy special protection under the Voting Rights Act; political parties do not. However, the U.S. Supreme Court has recognized that in some circumstances the federal courts have the power to overturn blatantly partisan gerrymanders. Texas Republicans strongly condemned the congressional and legislative plans enacted by the legislature in 1991 and immediately challenged them in federal court.

Places on the general-election ballot are quite restricted. Most serious candidates qualify via the Democratic or Republican primaries. Minor party candidates may qualify for the general election ballot via a primary or a convention procedure, depending upon the percentage of the vote their last gubernatorial candidate received. A number of candidates get on the ballot in this fashion, but save for a few Raza Unida party candidates in South Texas, minor party nominees have had no electoral success.

Independent candidates can get on the ballot via a petition process. For state office, a candidate must collect signatures equal to at least 1 percent of the total vote cast for governor in the last general election. Lower-level positions require a varying percentage of the gubernatorial vote, with the proviso that no more than 500 names are needed. The petition route has proven a difficult road to the general election ballot. From 25,000 to 40,000 signatures are needed for a state office, but the important thing is that signers must be registered voters who did not participate in a party primary that year. Candidates defeated in a party primary cannot avail themselves of the petition alternative to get into the November election. The last resort for an aspiring office seeker who has failed to qualify by party or petition is a write-in campaign. Texas law permits voters, in a general election, the option of writing in their personal choice if they are unhappy with the candidates on the ballot. But like the petition process, this has been of negligible importance in modern times. In 1977 the legislature tightened the write-in process by requiring such candidates to register with election officials prior to polling day for any votes they receive to be counted. In 1990, 19 write-in candidates for governor dutifully registered and had their votes recorded. Bubbles Cash, a retired Dallas stripper, led the pack with 3,287 out of a total of 11,700 write-in votes (or 0.3 percent of the total vote cast). In sum, those with a real chance of winning general elections in Texas must be listed on the ballot and, given the weakness of third parties, must be listed as the Democratic or Republican nominee.

Ballot procedures vary from county to county in Texas. Some rural areas still use paper ballots on which an individual votes by making a mark beside a candidate's name or issue option. Other areas use electronic voting machines in which one pulls levers to indicate vote choices. Urban areas are increasingly using punchcard ballots in which voters use a small stylus to punch out their votes on a card that will be tabulated by a computer.

Reprinted by permission.

State law provides for *straight-ticket* voting. This means a voter has the option of voting for all the candidates of a party by marking a single box, pulling a big lever atop voting machines, or punching out a single option on punchcard ballots. Paper ballots and voting machines utilize the *party-column ballot,* in which candidates for various offices are arranged in columns by party affiliation opposite the offices they are seeking. This system tends to encourage party voting and is thought to give some advantage to those listed in the first (left-hand) column. That position is given the party polling the largest vote in the governor's election. Ann Richards's victory in 1990 thus assured the Democrats first listing on the 1992 and 1994 ballots. Punchcard ballots use the *office-block ballot,* in which all the candidates for a particular office are listed, starting with federal offices and ending with county positions and propositions. Candidates are again ordered according to the size of the gubernatorial vote their party received in the most recent general election. If independent candidates qualify for the ballot, they are placed to the right of the party nominees (or below them on punchcard lists); their order is determined by lot.

Special and Local Elections

In addition to the biennial party primaries and general elections, special elections are occasionally required. The Texas legislature may schedule a vote on proposed constitutional amendments in a special election, and the governor is required to call special elections to fill vacancies in federal and state legislative offices and elective county posts. No party nomination is needed for a ballot position in a vacancy election. Anyone satisfying the office's legal qualifications can get on the ballot by making application and paying a filing fee, which varies from $10 for a local office to $1000 for a statewide position. This ease of access means special elections for important positions draw many candidates. For example, voters could pick from among 71 entries in the 1961 special election to fill the U.S. Senate seat vacated by Lyndon Johnson. The winner in a special election must get a majority. Failing this in a first balloting requires a runoff between the top two vote-getters. Candidates in a special election have the option of listing their party affiliation.

State law gives local government the option of scheduling their elections on any of four days during the year (the third Saturday in January or May, the second Saturday in August, or the first Tuesday after the first Monday in November). Most cities and school districts avoid the general election date in November of even-numbered years and use one of the other dates. Municipal and school elections are nonpartisan affairs in Texas, in that candidates run as individuals without party identification on the ballot.

The Texas Constitution, unlike several other state documents, does not provide for state issues to be placed on the ballot by citizen petition (the *initiative* process), or by legislative action (the *referendum* process). As a practical matter, however, Texans are increasingly being asked to decide various issue proposals at the polls. Most often this is done in the form of proposed constitutional amendments submitted for voter approval. On November 3, 1987, for example,

25 amendments were on the ballot. Some dealt with trivial issues (for example, abolishing the county treasurer position in Fayette County), others with important matters (such as issuing over $1 billion in bonds for state prisons, mental hospitals, and water development). The 1987 legislature also passed two "hot potatoes" along to voters by scheduling binding referenda on whether the State Board of Education should be appointed or elected (voters favored election) and on legalization of parimutuel wagering on horse and dog racing on a local option basis (it was approved).

Local governments also schedule frequent issue elections in addition to the required elections for municipal and school board positions held every two years. When local elections are added to the state primaries, general elections, and issue elections, Texans are often faced with three, four, or five elections in a given calendar year. Collectively, voters may have the opportunity to decide over a hundred issues or contests every year. Clearly, that overtaxes the abilities and interest of most voters. The great majority of Texans do not vote in state issue elections, or in local contests and referenda. Cutting back on this overworked electoral system seems impossible, given the popularity of "letting the people decide." Nevertheless, the reality is that relatively few voters take the time and trouble to involve themselves in the many opportunities available to elect candidates and decide policy issues.

Election Administration

State law regulates the electoral process in Texas, but actual administration of elections is largely the responsibility of county officials and local party leaders. A good deal of variation has resulted from this local control. We have already noted that some counties use paper ballots, others electronic voting machines, and still others punchcards.

The basic electoral unit in Texas, as in most states, is the precinct. There are about 6600 of these geographic units in Texas, with boundaries determined by county commissioners' courts. Some have as few as 100 voters, others more than 3000. A single polling place is required in each precinct, and all qualified residents, except those casting early or absentee ballots, must vote in the precinct where they live.

In party primaries the Democratic and Republican county executive committees appoint a presiding judge to run the election in each precinct, who then employs several clerks to assist in running the primary election. County commissioners' courts appoint the general election judge to oversee November voting. Traditionally, commissioners appoint members of their own party, which means that the election judges tend to be Democrats in Democratic areas and Republicans in GOP precincts. The Texas Election Code does, however, require appointment of at least one election clerk from each of the major parties. Further provision is made for parties and candidates to place poll watchers in such precincts as they desire. Perhaps because of these specifications, most observers feel Texas elections have been largely free of fraud in recent years. When charges of electoral corruption have been raised, they have usually not been in cities, as tends to be the case nationally, but in rural areas. South Texas, with its tradition of political machines, has drawn the most attention, and a number of officials have been prosecuted over the years for vote fraud in that area.

Apart from the mechanics of running the actual balloting, a number of officials are involved in the electoral process. The county tax assessor acts as registrar of voters and must, by March 1 of each year, prepare a list of registered voters and provide this list to election judges. The county clerk is responsible for preparing the ballot and conducting absentee voting in general and special elections. A county election board, which includes the county judge, clerk, and sheriff, plus the major party chairpersons, handles the technical problems of securing voting places and distributing necessary supplies.

In case of mechanical failure or if a demand for a recount arises, ballot boxes and voting machines are sealed and stored after the election judge determines and reports the vote count in the precinct. The county judge appoints a referee to supervise any recount, and representatives of the involved candidates may observe the process of reopening and tabulating the ballots or machine totals. Although state law guarantees a recount upon request to a candidate who came within 5 percent of winning an election or making the runoff, such requests are rarely made. Recounts have seldom changed election outcomes, and if recounting does not reverse the results, the seeker of the count must pay a small fee for each precinct involved.

While local party and governmental officials remain responsible for conducting elections, the 1967 legislature did provide for the secretary of state to become the chief election officer of the state. The original role of the secretary of state was limited to issuing detailed written instructions and directives concerning election laws, registration of electors, and voting. However, in recent years the importance of the position has increased, probably because court decisions have forced the state to take a more active role in administering elections. For example, the 1973 law providing for state financing of primary elections gave the secretary of state an important supervisory role in overseeing this process.

The U.S. Voting Rights Act

Of considerably greater importance than state supervision of Texas elections has been the recent role played by the federal government under the Voting Rights Act. Congress passed the Voting Rights Act on August 7, 1965, at the height of the civil rights movement. Certain general provisions of the VRA are permanent and apply throughout the nation. There are, however, special provisions that affect only certain parts of the country.

The general provisions of the VRA that apply to the entire country include the following:

> Prohibiting voting qualifications or procedures that deny or abridge
> a person's right to vote because of race, color, or inclusion in a
> language minority group

Making it a federal crime for a public official to refuse to allow a qualified person to vote or to threaten or intimidate any person to discourage that individual from voting

Abolishing residency requirements of more than 30 days for voting in elections for president and vice president

Granting federal courts the authority to appoint federal examiners and require "preclearance" of any electoral changes, where they think the circumstances warrant such action

Prohibiting the use of devices such as literacy tests and tests of "good moral character" that were historically used to discriminate against voters on racial or ethnic lines

These various national standards have forced Texas to make a number of adjustments in its electoral system. However, these general provisions have not proven especially difficult or irksome for the state in terms of compliance. Under the 1965 VRA, the special provisions were only applied to states of the deep South with a blatant history of racial discrimination against blacks, and Texas was not subjected to this coverage. But when the VRA was extended by Congress in 1975, Congresswoman Barbara Jordan of Houston successfully led an effort to apply the more strict special provisions to Texas.

The most important aspect of the special provisions is the *preclearance* procedure, whereby the state of Texas and all its political subdivisions and local governments must submit (preclear) any change in their electoral procedures to the U.S. Justice Department or to the U.S. District Court for the District of Columbia. The submitting authority has the burden of proof in establishing that the proposed change or changes do not have a racially discriminatory purpose or effect. The proposed change cannot be put into effect if the Justice Department or a federal court "objects" to it within a 60-day review period. Since electoral procedures have been broadly interpreted to include everything from municipal annexations to changes in polling places, the practical effect of this special provision has been to give the federal government a veto power over virtually every aspect of the state's electoral system.

Application of the VRA's special provisions to Texas has had considerable impact. Between 1975 and 1980, for example, some 16,208 proposed election changes from Texas were submitted for Justice Department review.[7] The Justice Department filed objections in only 85 of these cases, but they involved some of the most important elections and jurisdictions in the state. Many Texas counties have been forced to redraw their commissioner districts; adjustments were required in the 1981 congressional plan passed by the state legislature, and, most importantly, virtually every major city has had to abandon at-large systems of electing city councils. Such election changes have often led to shifts in political power, as in the case of San Antonio. This South Texas city has always had a large Mexican-American population (53.7 percent of the 1980 population was of Spanish origin), but most political power was held by affluent Anglos. In 1976 the U.S. Justice Department forced the city to abandon a council system in which all candidates ran citywide for a system based on single-member districts of equal population. The impact was immediate and dramatic, according to Charles L. Cottrell and R. Michael Stevens.

> Five Mexican Americans were elected to city council for the first time in San Antonio's history; geographically, seven persons were elected from areas within the city which had experienced little or no representation during the previous two decades. And with the election of one Black person to city council, minority group members composed a majority of city council for the first time in the city's history.[8]

After 15 years it is clear that federal involvement in state and local elections is not going to be a one-shot affair. For example, Dallas and Houston, like San Antonio, revised their city councils in the 1970s to give minorities better electoral opportunities. But in 1991 both cities were again under federal pressure to make additional changes in their electoral systems. A federal judge has ruled that the current Dallas system still violates the VRA and has ordered the city to enact a new plan or have one imposed by the court. Houston's Mexican-American community, unhappy after electing just one of 14 council members since the 1979 plan was approved by the U.S. Justice Department, is now threatening to sue the city unless Houston changes its electoral system.

MONEY AND THE ELECTORAL PROCESS

Mention has been made of the fees candidates must pay to get on the ballot in primary and special elections. Of far greater importance for candidates, however, are the enormous and increasing costs of getting oneself elected to office.

Present-day officeseekers in Texas have found there is no cheap way to win elections. With the electorate growing yearly and with weak party organization the rule, most candidates have tremendous problems in reaching the voters. Personal "stumping" is ineffective, save at the local level, because it touches so few voters. A candidate working 10 hours a day, 7 days a week, would need about 40 years to talk for 1 minute with every registered voter in Texas. Given the fact that campaigns usually last only 2 or 3 months, and that voters are not easily located and often not eager to chat with prospective officeholders, the limitations of personal campaigning become apparent. This is the case not only in statewide races but in most urban districts as well.

Of necessity, serious candidates must advertise themselves in newspapers and mailings and on billboards, radio, and television if they are to communicate with likely voters. Such advertising is very expensive. Consider the following examples:

- A large billboard on a heavily traveled urban freeway rents for $6,000 per month.
- A full-page ad in a Dallas or Houston newspaper can cost over $12,000.
- A 60-second television spot just before the evening news in Dallas and Houston sells for $15,000 or more.

- A first-class mailing to every household with a registered voter in Texas costs over $1 million in postage alone.

Campaign costs are rising well beyond inflation rates. For example, the major candidates for governor in 1982 spent over $25 million; in 1986 they spent about $30 million, but in 1990 total spending reached $53.8 million. The two serious candidates for the office of lieutenant governor spent more than $10 million in 1990, and the attorney general contestants another $6 million. The pattern persists down the ballot. Spending exceeded $1 million in five congressional races in 1990. Mayoral campaigns in Houston entail $3 million to $5 million in campaign costs.

Of course, spending the most money does not ensure victory. Clayton Williams spent $21.3 million in 1989–1990 but lost the governor's race to Ann Richards, who spent *just* $13.9 million. Still, outspending one's opponent clearly gives a candidate a big edge, as indicated by the fact that in every other major statewide race other than that for governor, the person who spent the most money won the position in 1990. Even in the cases such as Richards's, in which the winner spent less, it is clear that they had to raise a very large amount of money to stay competitive. The rule is that big money is *not sufficient* to win major elections in Texas, but it is *absolutely necessary.*

Where does the big money come from? Ideally, one would hope from ordinary citizens who share the views or philosophy of the individual candidates or their parties. In reality, financing most campaigns from small individual contributions is not possible. The sums needed are too great, and, since even interested voters are not easily persuaded to finance candidates, the cost of soliciting contributions from the general public is high. Since the stork does not bring political money, most candidates have to look to other sources for financing. In Texas, most campaign money comes either from the personal or family fortunes of candidates and wealthy friends or from groups or individuals who have business or professional interests affected by the office at stake.

The 1990 Texas governor's election provides ample evidence of both patterns. Clayton Williams used his great personal fortune (estimated at more than $100 million) to underwrite his dark horse race for the Republican nomination and to supplement his general election campaign spending. In all, Williams "loaned" his campaign $8 million. He raised another $13 million, mostly from groups such as contractors, businesspeople, and would-be appointees who had vital special interests in state government decisions.

Ann Richards had a larger base of individual contributors, but she also raised very large sums from interested parties such as trial lawyers. A single Port Arthur law firm, for example, loaned her campaign $200,000 in the closing days of the race.[9]

The increasing difficulty that men and women of modest means face in running for office and the great advantage enjoyed by those who possess wealth and are willing to invest it in campaigns has produced cries for reform. In the wake of the Watergate scandals in the early 1970s, the movement for fundamental reform gained momentum. Congress passed legislation limiting the size of contributions to federal officeseekers and provided for an income-tax checkoff plan to fund a large part of presidential campaigns. Congress also placed tight limits on the amounts that could be expended in congressional campaigns, but these limits were struck down by the U.S. Supreme Court in the *Buckley* v. *Valeo* decision. The Texas legislature also enacted the Political Funds Reporting and Disclosure Act of 1975, which made it much more difficult to hide political contributions and set stiff penalties for violators. But as the earlier discussion about campaign costs showed, these changes have not slowed the rush toward more and more expensive contests. The bottom line in Texas is that individuals, privately owned businesses or partnerships, and political action committees (PACs) may give any amount they wish (except in federal elections, where a limit of $1000 per person and $5000 per PAC prevails), and candidates are free to spend as much as they can raise or borrow.

CONCLUSIONS

A better perspective on the nature of Texas politics is gained if one keeps in mind that no existing "democratic system" lives up to the theoretical expectations often held about democracy. As the authors of an early study of American voting behavior conclude:

> The open-minded voters who made a sincere attempt to weigh the issues and candidates dispassionately for the good of the country as a whole exist mainly in deferential campaign propaganda, in textbooks on civics, in the movies, and in the minds of some political idealists. In real life, they are few indeed.[10]

In terms of political interest and motivation, knowledge of the issues, adherence to principle, and rational judgment in making political decisions, individual voters generally fail to satisfy requirements for a democratic system of government outlined by political theorists.

Texas politics, considered in this general context, does not represent some unique island surrounded by a democratic sea. The deviations from democracy found in the Lone Star State are rather typical of those in other states and the nation, only more severe than is usually the case. The low rates of political participation can be attributed to several factors: a registration process that for years discouraged citizens from qualifying for the ballot; an electoral system that places a heavy burden on candidates for public office; the absence of meaningful competition and alternatives in many instances; and a political tradition of non-participation among the poor, blacks, and Mexican-Americans. The financial problems Texas officeseekers face are little different from those confronting candidates in other states. These factors and the resulting lack of political involvement are changing, but slowly.

In the meantime, Texas politics has been basically an Anglo affair, often slanted in the direction of status-quo elements. White, middle-class Texans have possessed a disproportionate share of the politically relevant resources (income, leisure time, educational skills, political motivation), and the state's political system has, as it must, responded to this reality. Most political leaders are drawn from and supported by these active strata of the population, and their decisions as to who shall benefit by government and who shall pay for government inevitably reflect this. Reducing this to terms of liberalism versus conservatism (which is, one should be cautioned, only one of many legitimate ways of viewing politics), the selective participation patterns characteristic of the state have shifted the mainstream of Texas politics to the right of center somewhat more than one might expect, given the socioeconomic diversity of the population.

NOTES

1. Gabriel Almond and Sidney Verba, *The Civic Culture* (Boston: Little, Brown, 1965), p. 2.
2. For a discussion of the difference between abstract support for "democracy" and support for the practical application of democratic principles, see James W. Prothro and Charles M. Grigg, "Fundamental Principles of Democracy: Bases of Agreement and Disagreement," *Journal of Politics* 22 (Spring 1960): 276–294; and Herbert McClosky, "Consensus and Ideology in American Politics," *American Political Science Review* 58 (June 1964): 361–379.
3. V.O. Key, Jr., *Southern Politics* (New York: Knopf, 1949), p. 254.
4. *Houston Chronicle,* December 17, 1986, sec. 1, p. 20.
5. Key, op. cit., 254–261.
6. See Lester Milbrath, *Political Participation* (Chicago: Rand McNally, 1965), 39–141; and Bernard Berelson, Paul F. Lazarsfeld, and William N. McPhee, *Voting: A Study of Opinion Formation in a Presidential Campaign* (Chicago: University of Chicago Press, 1964), pp. 277–304.
7. U.S. Commission on Civil Rights, *The Voting Rights Act: Unfulfilled Goals* (Washington, D.C.: Government Printing Office, 1981), pp. 183–184.
8. Charles L. Cottrell and R. Michael Stevens, "The 1975 Voting Rights Act and San Antonio, Texas: Toward a Federal Guarantee of a Republican Form of Government," *Publius* (Winter 1978): 87.
9. Robert Cullick, "Days Before Election, Law Firm Loaned $200,000 to Richards," *The Houston Chronicle,* January 16, 1991, p. 9A.
10. Paul Lazarsfeld, Bernard Berelson, and Hazel Gaudet, *The People's Choice* (New York: Duell, Sloan and Pierce, 1944), p. 100.

chapter 3

Political Parties
in Texas

Delegates at a Texas state political party convention reflect the diversity of the state.

Direct popular control of government is impossible in large societies. Millions of citizens cannot inform themselves on the countless matters requiring public action, or assemble to debate and decide policy choices, or take time to see that specific public policies are executed. Even if it were technically feasible for people to do these things, most display little desire to assume such burdens. Public power and authority must therefore be delegated to legislators, executives, judges, administrators, and, occasionally, unofficial leaders. In an effort to connect the millions of individual citizens to the relatively few decision makers, intermediate structures have developed in democratic societies. Most important among these are political parties and interest groups.

Political parties perform three general sets of activities.[1] They select candidates who compete for political office; they help to publicize party programs or sets of political values; and they maintain some control over, and provide guidance to, elected officeholders in government. In doing these things, parties produce a number of unplanned consequences or latent functions. They acquaint members of the electorate with political values or information. They offer uninformed or poorly informed citizens a simplified map of the political world, help them form political judgments, and make it easier for them to be active politically. Competition between parties recruits political leaders and offers voters periodic choices between alternatives. Of course, as we shall see in the case of Texas, the extent to which any particular party or party system performs these activities or produces such consequences can vary greatly.

THE TEXAS PARTY SYSTEM

Except for the few days every four years when a national convention is in session, the major political parties in the United States are best thought of as loose coalitions of variously organized, virtually autonomous, state parties. The Texas Democratic and Republican parties are not, then, mere branches of encompassing national parties; rather, they exist primarily as state entities that make occasional contributions to national party affairs.

Considerable differences exist in interparty competition from state to state. Traditionally, Texas has been ranked as one of the least competitive partisan states. A study of a few years ago, for example, placed the Lone Star State forty-sixth among the 50 states in competition between parties.[2] But such was not always the case, and it is increasingly less so today. Two-party politics held sway in Texas from the end of the Civil War until the late nineteenth century, when bitterness over Republican-sponsored Reconstruction and blacks' place in politics and society wrecked the Texas Republican party. The result was more than a half-century, from 1900 to the 1950s, in which the Democratic party was seldom challenged and almost never defeated in electoral contests.

The one-party dominance had great significance for Texas politics. Most importantly, *one-party* politics dissolved into *no-party* politics.[3] With most voters and all serious candidates calling themselves Democrats, party labels became next to meaningless. Economic liberals and conservatives, racists and integrationists, flat-earthers and sun-gazers, wets and drys on the alcohol issue all crowded into the big Democratic tent. Instead of fights between well-defined parties for electoral support, a far more chaotic politics took hold in Texas. Cleavages among voters formed and reformed from campaign to campaign, depending on the specific issues and personalities involved. Flamboyant political personalities such as Miriam "Ma" and James E. "Pa" Ferguson and W. Lee "Pappy, Pass the Biscuits" O'Daniel often became issues in themselves. At the same time, matters of deep meaning to the people of Texas, such as the level of public services to be undertaken and the distribution of costs for these services, were seldom the basis for contesting elections. A politics of the status quo prevailed. Elected officials, lacking the support of a meaningful political party, were loath to raise basic and controversial issues. The absence of party support left them particularly vulnerable to pressures from such established economic interests as the state's oil, gas, and insurance industries.

Without political parties to channel and simplify political action in Texas, the latent functions of party activity mentioned earlier did not result. Individual voters, denied a choice between a "Democratic" and a "Republican" position, were left to their own devices and judgments in making political decisions. Nor could aspiring political leaders be recruited by or seek the support of established political organizations. In such a situation politics becomes a game of every person for himself or herself—a game well suited to those who begin play with ample economic resources and political influence and skills.

The era of fragmented, personalistic politics began to decline in the late 1930s, when the economic issues raised by the New Deal filtered into Texas politics. A political alignment along economic lines had progressed sufficiently by 1948 for V. O. Key, Jr., to note that "the terms 'liberal' and 'conservative' have real meaning in the Democratic politics of Texas."[4] In recent years the Democratic party has been increasingly unable to contain within itself this liberal-conservative split, and a resurgent Republican party has emerged in Texas.

The degree of competition provided by the Texas Republican party depends on what level of office is considered. In general, the higher the office, the stronger the Republicans run. In the eight presidential contests between 1960 and 1988, Republican candidates have outpolled Democrats, taking an average of 53.6 percent of the two-party vote. The GOP share of the two-party vote in the 12 U.S. Senate elections between 1960 and 1990 is 48.7 percent—with each party holding one seat throughout the period. In gubernatorial contests since 1960, the Republican vote share has been only 41.5 percent, but the victories of Bill Clements in 1978 and 1986 indicate the recent competitiveness at this level. The Republican party has also made considerable progress in congressional races, increasing its share of seats in the U.S. House of Representative from 2 of 24 in 1978 to 10 of 27 in 1987, before dropping back to 8 of 27 in 1991.

But Republican success in top-of-the-ticket and federal elections has not been matched in down-ballot and local contests. Prior to 1988, no Republican had won a statewide office other than governor or U.S. senator for over 100 years. After winning 3 of 6 Texas Supreme Court seats in 1988, Republican candidates filed for 16 statewide offices in 1990. However, as Table 3.1 shows, only 4 down-ballot candidates won despite the fact that U.S. Senator Phil Gramm led the ticket with 61 percent of the vote. Republicans have made gains in the Texas legislature but remain a minority in both houses. In 1991, 57 of 150 Texas House members were Republicans, as were just 9 of 31 state senators. Increasingly, Republicans are contesting and winning some county positions, but more than 80 percent of local officials are still Democrats.

These data show that Texas is no longer a one-party state. At the presidential level, Texas now leans Republican, and U.S. Senate and gubernatorial elections are very competitive. But Democrats still retain an advantage in most state and lower offices. Of course, party politics has been changing rapidly in Texas, and the thrust of change has been toward a more and more broadly competitive

**Table 3.1   STATEWIDE ELECTION RESULTS IN 1990:
DEMOCRATS VERSUS REPUBLICANS**

Office	Democratic Candidate	Republican Candidate	Republican % of Two-Party Vote
U.S. Senate	Hugh Parmer	Phil Gramm	61.7%
Governor	Ann Richards	Clayton Williams	48.7%
Lieutenant Governor	Bob Bullock	Rob Mosbacher	46.5%
Attorney General	Dan Morales	J.E. "Buster" Brown	46.5%
Comptroller	John Sharp	Warren G. Harding, Jr.	33.2%
Treasurer	Nikki Van Hightower	Kay Bailey Hutchison	51.7%
Land Commissioner	Garry Mauro	Wes Gilbreath	37.8%
Agriculture Commissioner	Jim Hightower	Rick Perry	50.6%
Railroad Commissioner	Robert (Bob) Krueger	Beau Boulter	41.7%
Chief Justice, Supreme Court	Oscar Mauzy	Tom Phillips	59.1%
Place 1, Supreme Court	Gene Kelly	John Cornyn	55.9%
Place 2, Supreme Court	Bob Gammage	Charles Ben Howell	43.3%
Court of Criminal Appeals, #1	Frank Maloney	Joe Devany	49.5%
Court of Criminal Appeals, #2	Sam Houston Clinton	Oliver S. Kitzman	49.4%
Court of Criminal Appeals, #4	Charles F. "Charlie" Baird	David A. Berchelmann, Jr.	49.7%
Court of Criminal Appeals, #5	Morris Overstreet	Louis E. Sturns	49.2%

Source: Unofficial returns, Office of Secretary of State, Austin, Texas.

system. Whether this trend will continue or be reversed is examined later in this chapter.

PARTY ORGANIZATION IN TEXAS

The Legal Structure

The organizational form of Texas political parties is prescribed by state law. Each party has a *permanent organization* that is legally responsible for managing the partisan process, and provision is made for *temporary organizations* to permit expression of membership views and fill certain party positions.

Figure 3.1 diagrams the relationship of individual voters to the party apparatus. In Texas, individuals do not register as members of a political party. Instead, they indicate their partisan preference by participating in the primary or

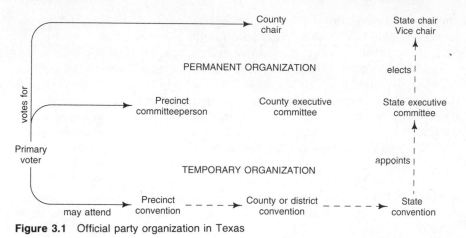

Figure 3.1 Official party organization in Texas

convention of the party of their choice. State law requires that political parties whose gubernatorial candidate received at least 20 percent of the vote in the last general election must nominate their candidates in primary elections. Practically, this means that the Democrats and Republicans have to choose their candidates by primary elections, while smaller parties are excluded from this requirement.

After voters have balloted in their party's primary (now held on the second Tuesday in March), they are eligible to attend that party's *precinct convention,* which is also held on the day or evening of primary voting. If one wishes to participate in the affairs of a minor party that does not hold primary elections, then one simply goes to the precinct or county meetings held by that party. One may vote in and/or attend the political convention of only one party in a given election year.

Precinct conventions offer interested citizens an opportunity for expressing their political views and values. These meetings entertain, debate, and pass on various public questions. More important, they select delegates to the next level of temporary organization, which meets two weeks after the precinct conventions. In the large urban counties that include more than one state senate district (Harris, Dallas, Tarrant, and Bexar), delegates convene in a *senatorial district convention.* In the other counties they assemble in *county conventions.* Each precinct is allocated a certain number of delegates based on that precinct's vote for the party's gubernatorial nominee in the last general election (one delegate for every 25 votes).

These county and senatorial district conventions also consider, debate, and pass resolutions on various political issues, but their major task is to select delegates to the *state convention,* which is held in June of primary years. State delegates are also apportioned on the basis of each county's or senate district's gubernatorial vote—the usual rate is one delegate for every 300 votes. The June convention certifies the party's nominees for the upcoming general election, produces a party platform, and chooses members of the state executive commit- tee. Prior to 1976, the state delegates also selected delegates to the national party conventions. Present law, however, requires that at least 75 percent of the presidential delegates be chosen by party voters in the March primary, so these June conventions now have only a modest role in the presidential nomination process.

Although the precinct, county, and state meetings are not of much importance in presidential politics, they are still the arenas in which control of the state and local party organizations is determined. As such, various factions within the major parties often do battle in these party gatherings. For years most of the intraparty fighting occurred among the Democrats, but more recently, as the Republican party has grown, it too has seen more internal turmoil. In 1986, for example, New Right religious activists took control of many county and senatorial meetings and passed strong resolutions on issues like home-schooling and abortion. In the process, they displaced many longtime party activists who had served as district and state delegates, generating a considerable amount of animosity in the process.

Like the temporary organization, the permanent organization of the parties breaks down into three levels. First, there is the *precinct committeeperson,* elected by the primary voters in each precinct or appointed by the precinct convention if no primary is held. The committeeperson (or precinct chairperson as he or she is sometimes called) occupies a pivotal position in the party, for it is at the precinct level that the party apparatus interacts with the individual voter. Besides running the primary election, he or she is expected to stimulate and coordinate party activities in the neighborhood. All precinct committeepersons are automatically members of the *county executive committee,* which is responsible for arranging the county primary election and the ensuing conventions. Much of the actual work at this level is performed by the chair of the county executive committee, who is elected in the primary if such an election is held, or appointed by the county executive committee. The *state executive committee* heads up the party. This group consists of 64 members: a chairperson and vice chairperson and a man and woman from each of the 31 state senate districts. The principal duties of the state committee include certifying statewide candidates for the primaries and setting up the state conventions.

THE IMPACT OF PARTY ORGANIZATION

Texas laws define the structure of political parties in the state, but legal rules tell us little about how party organizations actually work. The election code, for example, specifies a number of party positions, but in many cases these slots remain vacant. And even if people fill the legal party positions, they may or may not be active workers in the organization.

Historically, Texas has not been a strong party organization state. When David R. Mayhew rated the 50 states on a "traditional party organization" scale, he gave Texas a "2" on his 5-point scale [1 = lowest; 5 = highest].[5] A number of factors contribute to relatively ineffective party organization in Texas. Organizations, if they are to have much impact over time, require the investment of money, energy, and skills, but to attract these, they must offer something in return. Therein lies the weakness of party organization in Texas. According to a common conceptualization, partisan organizations recruit resources by offering three kinds of incentives or rewards to people—material, solidary, or purposive.[6] *Material* incentives are tangible goods and services such as money, property, jobs, and so forth. *Solidary* incentives include the enjoyment of social interaction, of being "where the action is," or of associating with important people. *Purposive* incentives come into play when an organization is a means of achieving some general social or political goal such as repealing the federal income tax, restricting abortions, or ending apartheid in South Africa.

Most of the strong party organizations in the United States, including the fabled big-city machines, were built primarily on material incentives such as patronage jobs, contract preferments, and direct aid to the needy. And most of the strong party organizations that have survived (like the Cook County Democratic organization in Chicago and the Democratic and Republican parties in Indiana) retain control of jobs and favors they can hand out to the faithful and deny the infidels. But in Texas, and especially in Texas cities, relatively few jobs and contracts can be used for party organizational purposes. There is a little federal patronage available when a party controls the White House, and public officials have some discretion in awarding favors such as architectural contracts for public projects, but, in general, the material cupboards are bare. About the only widespread source of regular patronage available is provided by the tradition of appointing precinct committeepersons as public election judges for their precincts. County commissioner courts (almost all of which are controlled by Democrats) have typically reserved these positions for local officials from their party. But the available rewards are small. Election judges typically work from 6:00 A.M. on polling day until late at night for $60 or so. They can also appoint a few clerks to assign in operating the polls, but they receive less than $50 for a long day's work. Such pay, offered two or three days a year, is not likely to attract many party laborers.

In many other states, big cities nurture party organizations, but not in Texas. Cities in Texas elect their leaders in nonpartisan elections and have placed most of the municipal jobs under civil service. Few rewards are available for distribution under this system, and urban party organization has traditionally been weak. More material incentives exist in rural areas, where "courthouse" jobs and favors can be dispensed more freely and with greater impact. It should come as no surprise that the most notable instances of machine politics in the state occurred in rural South Texas. Although recent state and federal pressure has weakened their hold, courthouse-based establishments in counties like Duval and Starr have used material incentives to control the votes of the mostly poor, unacculturated Mexican-American majority in the area.

This relative absence of material incentives means that party activists in Texas are recruited into party work primarily by solidary or purposive incentives. That is, they work because they enjoy the social life associated with political activity or because they see party work as a means of realizing political goals or values. A study of 140 Democratic and Republican precinct committeepersons in Houston in 1980, for example, found only 3 that indicated they were active because of personal, material reasons.[7] By contrast, 62 percent said they were active because they saw campaign work as a way of influencing the policies of the government, and 54 percent saw party work as a way of fulfilling a sense of community obligation. About a third of the people interviewed gave social reasons for their political activism. Motives such as these are usually acclaimed in civics texts, while materialistic motives are condemned, but organizations that rely almost exclusively on nonmaterial rewards are seriously hampered.

People who volunteer their time and effort to parties because they derive social satisfaction from the excitement of a campaign or working for a particular candidate tend to tire of the sport relatively quickly. The campaign and its attendant social life ends; the candidate is defeated and fades from view or is elected and goes off to Austin or Washington. For most who work in party organizations, the press of personal, nonpolitical matters eventually reasserts priority in their lives. Thousands of Texans labored to elect Ann Richards or Clayton Williams governor in 1990, but few continued to work for the Democratic or Republican parties after the election. Without material incentives to stabilize participation, party organizations face a problem of high turnover among activists. And, with their reliance on volunteers, the party organizations can generally function only during the few months of campaigning every two or four years.

Ideological rigidity is often associated with those who are drawn into party work because they have a deep desire to influence public policy. They are willing, nay eager, to invest their time, energy, and perhaps part of their fortune in partisan battles. But these workers exact a price. That price is rooted in the expectation that their party will remain true to the principles or causes they associate with it. Our interviews with Houston committeepersons in 1980, for example, clearly showed that the great majority of the party activists were much more committed to political principle than to party per se. Three-fourths of the sample felt no obligation to support party candidates with whom they disagreed on issues, and 80 percent thought that candidates should not compromise basic values to win elections.[8] By demanding that their party stick to the straight and narrow path of righteousness, these committed supporters often cripple its ability to make the sort of broad appeals essential to electoral success. We may personally admire party workers who would rather be right than win, but such attitudes undermine the effectiveness of party organizations over the long haul.

Part of the responsibility for the weak status of party organization in Texas and most other states rests with statutory provisions designed to ensure democracy in the partisan process. For example, the requirement that the major parties nominate their candidates by primary takes away the most crucial power a party organization can command: the power to give or withhold a place on the ballot under the party label for those contesting elections. More recently, parties have been further weakened by the tendency of major candidates to run their own campaigns independent of party operations. As a consequence, the $10 million campaigns Texas has had have often been of little benefit to the Democratic or Republican parties.

Despite these persistent problems, some factors have worked to improve party organizational performance since the early 1970s. In the wake of the

Watergate scandal and devastating defeats in 1974 and 1976, the national Republican party undertook a massive rebuilding effort. The GOP has developed effective fund-raising techniques (mostly by direct mail) and has used its expanded resource base to invest in modern organizational and campaign technologies. As a result of these efforts in Texas, the party has done a better job of recruiting and supporting candidates, registering voters, and getting out the vote on election day. Most observers feel the Republican party has had an organizational advantage over the Democrats both nationally and in Texas since 1978. Republican successes have not gone without notice, and Democrats have been struggling to get their house in order. While the Republican party retains a large financial advantage, the Democrats have narrowed the gap in other areas such as polling, voter registration, and the use of phone banks.

THE TEXAS DEMOCRATIC PARTY

The Sources of Democratic Hegemony

For most of the last 100 years, the Democratic party has been the dominant political force in Texas politics. Given that fact, we might best begin our discussion of the party by reviewing briefly the factors that led to and perpetuated this dominance.

First among these factors was the legacy of the Civil War, which branded the Republicans in the eyes of most white Texans as the "party of Yankee aggression." Texans, defeated and occupied after a bitter four-year struggle, instinctively pulled together to resist what they saw as a hostile external political environment. As V. O. Key, Jr., noted of the defeated South in general:

> The War left a far higher degree of southern unity against the rest of the world than had prevailed before. Internal differences that had expressed themselves in sharp political competition were weakened—if not blotted out—by the common experiences of the War and Reconstruction. And, however unreasonable it may seem, it follows . . . that a people ruled by a military government will retain an antipathy toward the occupying power.[9]

Under these conditions it is hardly surprising that the Democratic party easily established its political control in Texas after federal troops were withdrawn in the 1870s.

Some 20 years later a new movement—the Populist revolt—challenged Democratic dominance across the South in general and in Texas specifically. The Populist party arose from the bitter dissatisfaction of poor farmers squeezed between the high rates charged by banks and railroads on the one hand and low prices for their crops on the other. In 1892 and 1894 the Populists mounted strong bids for the governorship, and in 1896 took 44.3 percent of the vote for governor. But the Populists failed to break the Democratic hold on state politics. A principal reason was that in 1896 the national Democratic convention nominated a presidential candidate, William Jennings Bryan, who ran on an essentially Populist program. Within Texas, Democrats like Governor James Hogg (1890–1894) also co-opted many of the issue positions of the new party. The Democrats, once convinced of the seriousness of the Populist challenge, also outmaneuvered the Populists in a number of cases in the late 1890s.[10]

Once again in firm control, the Democrats in Texas and the rest of the South moved to ensure their political dominance by imposing devices like the poll tax and white primary to exclude blacks from the political process. The Democrats thus eliminated a somewhat unreliable element of the state's electorate and at the same time firmed up their image as the party of the whites in the region. Democrats now argued that a return to two-party competition was inherently dangerous because it would destroy southern solidarity in national politics and reopen the bidding for black votes, as had occurred in the 1890s. In Texas and the rest of the South these arguments were persuasive. The Populist party disappeared entirely within a few years, and the Republicans accepted a role as little more than a party in name only.

Why did this Democratic dominance, established in the early 1900s, persist so long into the twentieth century? Several reasons can be cited. First, with blacks excluded, the Texas electorate was relatively homogeneous until the 1960s in that most voters were native-born whites, of northern and western European ancestry, religious Protestants, and of ordinary economic means. Second, the lively competition that developed within the Democratic primaries provided something of an outlet for political differences within the state. Third, once in place, a dominant party tends to perpetuate itself. Lawmakers, elected under that one-party label, tend to adopt electoral rules favorable to the status quo. Financial backers restrict their contributions to candidates from the dominant party. Good candidates in Texas, understanding the political realities, chose to run as Democrats whatever their political views might have been. Finally, people who grow up in a one-party system tend to develop a set of political beliefs and values consistent with their environment. The traditional identification with the Democratic party was passed down from generation to generation of Texans with their mother's milk.

The Rise and Fall of Democratic Factionalism

The Emergence of Party Factions   Ever since Democratic dominance was established at the turn of the century, divisions and cleavages have plagued the party. Sometimes the divisions centered on issues, sometimes personalities, sometimes a combination of the two. In the last decade of the nineteenth century, Governor James Hogg fought for progressive reforms opposed by such powerful commercial interests as the banks and railroads. The flamboyant Fergusons divided Texas Democrats from the 1910s to the 1930s, for reasons of both personality and politics. James "Pa" Ferguson, a vigorous opponent of Prohibition and the Ku Klux Klan, was impeached and removed from the governor's office in 1917. Barred by state law from public office, he ran his wife, Miriam "Ma" Ferguson, for governor five times. She won twice. Such colorful characters aside, Texas Democratic politics remained conservative in tone and generally responsive to the established economic groups in the state through the first third of the twentieth century.

More permanent and pervasive differences within the majority party began to take shape in the 1930s. The severe hardships associated with the Depression and the controversy surrounding President Franklin Roosevelt's New Deal policies resulted in a national political realignment along economic policy lines. The Democrats, now identified as the party of the working person, or "little man," emerged as the new majority party in the country. Within Texas, the New Deal divided the existing majority party into two wings. One group supported Roosevelt and the national Democratic policies, the other opposed both. Support for the conservative, anti-Roosevelt group came primarily from the business and professional classes, the urban white middle class, and many public officials around the state. Aligned opposite them were political leaders, such as Congressman Sam Rayburn, whose first loyalty was to the national Democratic party; the state's small organized labor movement; some survivors from earlier Populist movements still dissatisfied with the power of special interests in the state; and segments of the black and Mexican-American population who were just beginning to enter, or reenter, Texas politics.

So long as Roosevelt lived, the intraparty dispute was muted, but after his death in 1945 the struggle for dominance within the party became open and bitter. The governor's election of 1946 was fought along clear-cut liberal-versus-conservative lines in the Democratic primary. The liberal standard-bearer, Homer Rainey, who had just been fired as president of the University of Texas, challenged conservative Beauford Jester in the primary. Rainey lost, and a pattern was established. The half-dozen hotly contested gubernatorial primaries from the late 1940s to the early 1970s all featured liberal Democratic candidates taking on conservative Democrats. The liberals continued to lose.

The Conservative Democratic Faction   Despite their long run of success, the impression should be avoided that the conservative Democratic faction was a well-oiled, disciplined political machine that periodically ground up liberal Democratic and Republican challengers at the polls. The faction can best be described as a loose coalition, drawing support from a multiplicity of mostly economic interests, citizens of a conservative ideological bent, and people eager to associate themselves with a winning team. There was no clearly defined power elite within the conservative Democratic group, and no single leader commanded the faction. There was one exceptional period in the mid-1960s, when Governor John Connally, a man of forceful personality and the possessor of substantial political assets, dominated Democratic conservatism in a way rarely seen in Texas. But even Connally could not perpetuate his influence beyond his term as governor. Preston Smith, a longtime conservative rival, followed Connally as governor in 1969, and Connally's protégé and heir apparent, Ben Barnes, was smitten at the polls in the 1972 Democratic primary.

The most striking thing about the conservative Democrats was their continuing political success. From the mid-1930s to the 1970s, every governor elected was supported by this faction. Most members of the U.S. Congress were elected with conservative support, as were a majority of the state legislature. Liberals achieved parity at times in one house of the legislature, but conservatives retained firm control of either the Texas Senate or House in all sessions.

Several interrelated factors contributed to the conservatives' success at the polls. Some have been alluded to before, but a summary list at this point is useful.

Low level of political participation. As mentioned in the previous chapter, participation is considerably higher in the conservative segments of the Texas population than in the liberal-leaning elements.

Superior access to resources. Electoral success requires money, the investment of certain skills, and media exposure. The conservative Democratic faction was fortunate in this regard because it enjoyed the support of those best able to supply these things—the well-to-do, major economic interests, and the owners of major media organs in the state.

Absence of party competition. So long as the Democratic party dominated Texas politics, political control could be maintained by winning the party primaries. This is somewhat easier to do than regularly winning general elections because (1) voter participation is lower in primaries than contested general elections, and (2) national party shifts to one party or the other do not have any effect or impact within a single party's primary.

Ability to define the rules of the game. Over the years, conservative Democratic governors, state legislators, and local officials drew up electoral rules to maximize their faction's advantage. Incumbent interests were protected by filing dates set far in advance of primary elections. Voters were not required to register by party, so that "presidential Republicans" could vote in the Democratic primaries without difficulty. In the last few years federal courts have reversed a number of the practices that worked to the advantage of the conservative Democrats, such as annual registration, high filing fees for those wishing to contest offices, and biased redistricting plans.

As in most cases, success breeds success. Because conservative Democrats usually won, they could recruit the candidates and financial backing necessary to continue winning. Conservatives could normally count on outspending liberal challengers in the primaries and Republicans in the general elections by margins of two or three to one. The self-perpetuating effect of winning was nowhere more evident than in the behavior of the South Texas political machines. Most of the machine-controlled votes came from impoverished Mexican-Americans, whose political interests were generally closer to liberal positions on issues such as minimum-wage legislation and welfare benefits. Nevertheless, these machines usually aligned themselves with conservative Democrats in party primary fights. The machines needed the rewards that came from supporting winners, and thus they hunted where the ducks were without much regard for ideological considerations.

Geographically, conservative strength in the primaries was greatest in central and western Texas. Liberals usually ran better along the Gulf Coast and in eastern Texas. Conservative Democrats also ran better in rural areas and small towns than in big urban centers. This reflected the fact that blacks and Mexican-Americans were concentrated in the larger cities, and conservatives usually had little success in appealing to these urban voters. Additionally, many urban conservatives began voting in the Republican primary in the 1960s, which reduced the vote potential for conservatives in the Democratic primary. Within cities, conservatives got most of their votes from middle- and upper-income whites, with much of the rest coming from blue-collar whites. Combined with their rural–small town support, this was usually enough to win.

The Liberal Democratic Faction If conservative Democrats have represented the better-off and status quo elements within Texas, who are the liberals? The liberal faction has been a loosely defined collection of officeholders, party activists, and voters. Lacking a state organization and denied control of the legal party structure in the state, Texas Democratic liberalism has been as much a state of mind as anything else. Just what that state of mind represents is not easily discerned.

Nonetheless, several general threads tie the liberal faction together. These would include the following:

Support for the national party and its presidential nominees. Since the days of Franklin Roosevelt, liberals have been party loyalists committed to supporting the Democrats' presidential ticket. This has often put them at odds with conservative party leaders who have preferred to be "flexible" in national party matters. Conservative Allan Shivers, governor from 1949 to 1957 and supporter of Republican Eisenhower in 1952 and 1956, was the favorite object of liberal anger in the 1950s and 1960s. Another former conservative governor, John Connally, became a bête noire for liberal Democrats when he headed up the national "Democrats for Nixon" movement in 1972 before formally switching to the Republican party the following year.

Expanding the role of state government, especially in the areas of welfare, education, health, and employment. Texas liberals, like their national counterparts, promote an activist government to help people who cannot manage for themselves. Examples of this orientation can be found in recent legislative sessions, where liberals led efforts to eliminate the constitutional limit on state appropriations for welfare and to improve workmen's compensation and unemployment insurance.

Shifting the tax burden so that it depends less on consumer taxation and more on corporate profits and high-income individuals. The liberal position on these matters was evident in the 1969 special legislative session, where senate liberals provided most of the votes to defeat extending the sales tax to food and drugs. In addition to fighting the extension of sales taxes, which fall most heavily on lower-income persons, legislative liberals have provided the few votes cast for corporate and personal income taxes. In recent years, liberals have argued that the state should collect higher taxes on oil and gas production (Texas assesses the lowest severance taxes of any major oil and gas producing state) and roll back property and/or sales taxes.

Defending individual rights against state power. While liberals generally favor governmental action in the social welfare sphere, they are usually opposed to laws that restrict individual behavior. Liberals have successfully opposed passage of any state abortion laws since 1973, when the existing statute was ruled unconstitutional by the U.S. Supreme Court. Liberals also led the fight to make possession of small quantities of marijuana a misdemeanor rather than a felony offense. And liberals provided most of the votes in a losing effort in the 1981 legislature to block passage of Governor Clements's bill authorizing wiretaps of private phones in investigations of drug dealers.

In contrast to other southern states, racial issues in Texas have not provided a major point of contention between the Democratic factions. Evidence of this can be seen in the fact that liberal Texas candidates such as Ralph Yarborough often ran well in inner-city black neighborhoods and among white voters in deep East Texas, a region where George Wallace polled a plurality in the 1968 presidential election. The absence of factional polarization along racial lines reflects several factors. The black population is relatively small, constituting about one-eighth of the state's residents, and poses little threat to the white majority in most parts of the state. Also, since the black and Mexican-American minorities are concentrated in different parts of Texas, there is no possibility of a minority coalition's endangering local Anglo political control in most cities and counties.

Probably more important is the fact that the issues that divide Texans along racial lines, such as school integration, fair housing, and equal opportunity in employment, have been primarily contested at the *federal* or *local* levels, rather than at the *state* level. Most of the controversial legislation and judicial decisions have come from the national government, and enforcement or implementation has fallen to local school boards, city councils, and county commissioners.

Liberal voting support came from the state's minorities, the rural poor (especially in East Texas), unionized workers, and a small but often vocal segment of the middle class. The liberal faction usually had trouble getting out its voters, who have been less likely to register and vote than other Texans. The liberal coalition, given its diversity, has been difficult to hold together. Ralph Yarborough, an outspoken liberal-populist, was most successful, winning three U.S. Senate elections and serving from 1957 to 1971. Otherwise, liberal victories in statewide races have been few and far between. The faction's best innings have come in presidential politics: Liberal Democrats helped hold off strong GOP challenges to John Kennedy in 1960, Hubert Humphrey in 1968, and Jimmy Carter in 1976.

Still, the liberal faction within the state has generally endured failure and frustration. For years it had great trouble winning the party nomination, especially for governor. More recently, liberals have improved their position in the

Democratic primary (largely because conservatives are no longer voting in it), but now when liberals win the nomination, they usually lose to Republicans in the general election. In 1984, for example, liberal State Senator Lloyd Doggett of Austin won a hard-fought U.S. Senate runoff against conservative Congressman Kent Hance. But Doggett was crushed by Republican Phil Gramm in the 1984 general election. The following comments by Billie Carr, a Democratic National Committee member and longtime liberal leader, reveal some reasons for the faction's problems:

> Well, of course, with the help of the McGovern-Fraser national Party rules, we get a much fairer shake today. The state party is reasonable, open, accessible. Liberals are now, to some degree, part of the party establishment. And, in some ways that makes things more difficult. Now we just can't criticize, we have responsibilities. Another problem is that we don't have the old clear-cut issues. In the 1950s and 1960s we had issues like civil and political rights for blacks and ending the war in Vietnam. There are still good issues around like women's rights, but it is harder to mobilize people, to get them interested and active about these problems. Texas liberals, like liberals all over the country, need a new agenda.[11]

Decline of Factionalism in the 1970s and 1980s Partisan politics are constantly changing in this country and the 50 states. Public figures come and go; new issues appear and old ones fade; voters come of age and die; people move from one part of the country to another. Texas is certainly no exception to this dynamic pattern. An analysis of change over time shows that one important recent development has been a decline in the importance of factional differences within the Democratic party.

The decline of factionalism is well illustrated by the hard-fought Democratic gubernatorial primary in 1990. Two of the three major contenders, State Treasurer Ann Richards and Attorney General Jim Mattox, had strong roots in the liberal wing of the state party. Former governor Mark White had been clearly identified with the conservative faction in the 1970s and early 1980s. One might therefore have expected that the contest would polarize along liberal-conservative lines as had primaries in the 1950s and 1960s. That did not happen.

Mattox, arguably the most liberal of state officeholders, ran as a conservative antitax candidate with a strong law-and-order record, boasting that he had attended 32 executions over the last seven years. White stressed his moderate ideological views and argued that he had made the hard choices for education reform and more tax revenues during his earlier term. Richards pointed out how much money she had earned for Texas during her tenure as treasurer and largely avoided specific tax or programmatic commitments.

Despite the candidates' early pledges to avoid personal attacks, the race quickly degenerated into name-calling and mud-slinging. Mattox said that White had lied by breaking his no-tax commitment to voters after being elected in 1982. Mattox also accused Ann Richards of having used illegal drugs while holding public office. White said that Mattox was the liar in the race who had misrepresented his record and, after failing to make a runoff, blasted Richards for using tactics reminiscent of Heinrich Himmler (a leading Nazi associate of Adolf Hitler). Richards said that Mattox was responsible for pulling the race into the gutter and accused White of "lining his pockets" with legal fees earned from boards dominated by his gubernatorial appointees.

In sum, the 1990 primary focused on personalities and personal attacks, not on the traditional ideological differences between the candidates.

The movement away from factionalism within the Democratic party involves more than clashing personalities. A fundamental shift has been occurring within the Democratic electorate and among party activists in Texas. The participating electorate within the Democratic primary has been getting much *smaller* in recent years. In the 1950s about 30 percent of the adults in Texas voted in Democratic primaries, but this figure fell below 20 percent in the 1970s. In 1986, 1988, and 1990, fewer than 15 percent of voting-age Texans voted in the Democratic primary. Participation has dropped sharply among self-identified Republicans and urban conservatives. In Harris and Dallas counties, the Republican primary often draws more voters than the local Democratic contest. At the same time, many conservative activists have left the Democratic party, further eroding the formerly dominant faction's intraparty strength.

On the other hand, as a result of registration and voting increases among blacks and Mexican-Americans, they have become a larger part of the Democratic primary electorate. This would, it might be supposed, be a boon to the liberal faction, given traditional voting patterns, but things have not quite worked out that way. As ethnic voter groups have grown in size and political sophistication, they have developed an acute sense of their special political interests. Black and Mexican-American voting patterns within the Democratic primary often reflect how particular candidates relate to these groups' special needs rather than to some general liberal or conservative label. Something akin to this has also occurred with organized labor, where support for broad liberal programs has often been replaced by a concern with special issues and appointments that relate directly to union leaders and members.

We thus see that while the conservative base in the primaries has shrunk, the liberal coalition has fragmented. The obvious result is a decline of bifactionalism and the emergence of more pluralistic, pragmatic politics within the Democratic party. Democratic aspirants for elective office find it much easier to operate in this environment by avoiding factional labels and assuming flexible positions on many public issues. This pragmatism is also a response to the necessity of dealing with more and more competitive Republican contenders in the general elections, a subject discussed in the following section.

THE REPUBLICAN PARTY IN TEXAS

The Republican Resurgence

After a half-century of dormancy as little more than a patronage-distributing group for national administrations, the Texas Republican party has again become a political force to be reckoned with. Republican presidential candidates have contested Democrats on more than an equal footing since 1948. John Tower and

Phil Gramm have held one of the state's U.S. Senate seats for the GOP since 1961, and Bill Clements's gubernatorial victories in 1978 and 1986 have further boosted party prospects. By 1991 about a third of the state's congressional and state legislative seats were held by Republicans. Republicans often run for, and frequently win, important local offices around the state.

The improved Republican performance reflects a number of social and political changes that have occurred in the last 30 years. One has been the steady movement of the national Democratic party toward a more liberal stance on economic and social issues. This shift, symbolized by presidential candidates George McGovern in 1972, Walter Mondale in 1984, and Michael Dukakis in 1988, has strained the loyalties of many traditional Texas Democrats, and some have left the ancestral party. Prominent among these is John Connally, who led the state Democratic party in the 1960s but declared himself a Republican in 1973. Congressman Phil Gramm switched in 1983 and was reelected to the U.S. House and then to the Senate as a Republican. State Representative Rick Perry changed parties in 1989, secured the Republican nomination for agriculture commissioner in 1990, and unseated veteran Democrat Jim Hightower in the general election. Other dissatisfied Democrats have adopted an independent stance in party politics, responding more to individual candidates than to partisan labels.

Changing socioeconomic conditions in the state have also worked to the Republicans' advantage. As noted in Chapter 2, Texas was a relatively poor state before World War II. The economic expansion that occurred between the 1940s and the 1980s supported considerable growth in the state's urban-suburban middle class, a group that has provided strong support for Republican candidates in the nation and state. Some of the expanded middle class were transplanted Texans who brought their Republican values from other parts of the country, but the greater number were natives whose changing income, status, and political views were increasingly more aligned with the Republican than the Democratic party.

The increasing political participation of fundamentalists and evangelical Christians has also benefited the Republican party in both the nation and the state. President Reagan drew strong support from the religious right in the 1980 and 1984 elections, as did George Bush in 1988. Texas GOP candidates have also had such backing. In 1986, for example, exit polls showed that Bill Clements got 79 percent of the votes from self-described "Evangelical Christians" in his gubernatorial contest with Democrat Mark White.

The strength of the national Republican party among young voters has also been reflected in Texas. In the 1960s and 1970s Democrats had a big advantage among voters under 30, but Ronald Reagan and George Bush won majorities of young adults in their presidential elections. The shift is evident in the Lone Star State. Republican candidates often win large majorities among young adults in Texas, as reflected in voting precincts at Texas A&M, SMU, North Texas State University, and Texas Tech. Most "college towns" in Texas (e.g., Denton, College Station, and Lubbock) are now represented by Republicans in the state House of Representatives.

One should also note that court-ordered reapportionment of congressional, legislative, and local governmental positions—usually at the behest of racial minorities—has benefited Republican candidates. Most of the GOP's voter strength is concentrated in large metropolitan areas, but these were, until the late 1960s, seriously underrepresented in most governmental bodies. Federal courts have forced a more equitable distribution of legislative seats, as well as requiring the adoption of single-member districts, which helps a minority party win local areas where it has voter strength.

Taken together, these elements have brought the Texas Republican party to a position of competitiveness in major state elections and many local contests. Having demonstrated electoral success, the party should have an easier time in the future recruiting good candidates, raising monies, and securing support from politically important groups than was the case when the GOP (like Texas liberal Democrats) was tainted by a "can't win" reputation. Some observers, impressed by recent elections, prophesy that Texas is becoming a strongly Republican state, much as it once was solidly Democratic. That possibility, along with others, is discussed later.

Patterns of Republican Electoral Support

The Primary Electorate   In the Democratic primary, the participating electorate has gotten smaller over the years, but it still draws a sizable number of voters (between 1 and 2 million) from something approaching a cross-section of the state's population. Matters are quite different on the Republican side. Recent GOP primaries have attracted between 350,000 and 850,000 voters—that is from *3 to 7 percent* of the state's adult population. Since this very small segment of voters determines half of the candidates who have a realistic chance of winning office in Texas, it behooves us to examine closely the primary electorate.

Almost all Republican primary voters are Anglos; fewer than 3 percent are black or Hispanic. Most have attended college, and half have graduated. Primary voters are usually from upper- or middle-income families and consider themselves to be political conservatives or, less commonly, moderates. Most live in or near large metropolitan areas. The Republican primary electorate also includes a disproportionate number of people who feel strongly about social issues (e.g., they oppose abortion or support Christian home schools).

Summarizing, we note that the Republican primary electorate is not only small but also a somewhat atypical slice of the Texas population. They are whiter, wealthier, better educated, more conservative, and more suburban than are Texans in general. Given their makeup, it is hardly surprising that the Texas GOP almost always nominates white, conservative candidates to carry the party banner in the general election.

Republican Support in General Elections   In the November general elections, far more people vote for Republican candidates than participate in the party's primaries. In 1984, for example, about 335,000 people voted in the primary that nominated Phil Gramm as the GOP U.S. Senate candidate. In November 1984, more than 3.1 million people voted for Gramm in the general election, or nearly 10 times the total primary electorate. Who are the general election Republican voters? We attempt to answer that question by looking at the geographic distribu-

Reprinted by permission.

tion of the party vote, at party voting by size of county, and at socioeconomic characteristics.

Figure 3.2 shows the areas of Texas where Republicans consistently run strongly. Most important are the Dallas-Fort Worth (1) and Houston (2) suburban areas, which usually contribute over 40 percent of the state GOP vote. Next is the Hill Country of Central Texas (3), which includes the northern and western suburbs of San Antonio and Austin. Republicans also run well in the Panhandle/ High Plains area that includes Lubbock and Amarillo (4); in the Permian Basin around Midland-Odessa (5); and the East Texas oil-field counties of Gregg, Smith, and Rusk (6).

Table 3.2 shows the vote percentage received by major Republican candidates between 1976 and 1990. In the six most populous counties (Harris, Dallas, Bexar, Tarrant, El Paso, and Travis), Republicans have historically run most strongly, followed by smaller urban counties (those with populations between 100,000 and 400,000). The rural counties have traditionally been the poorest for GOP candidates. In the last two gubernatorial elections, however, this pattern has been reversed. Bill Clements barely carried the large urban counties against Mark White but won by large margins in less well-populated areas. And in 1990 Democrat Ann Richards won in every large urban area in the state (even carrying normally Republican Dallas County) but lost most rural counties outside South Texas to Clayton Williams. This reversal suggests that major changes may be occurring in party voting patterns, a point we will return to later.

In socioeconomic terms, the Republican general election vote is highest in affluent white neighborhoods like Highland Park in Dallas and River Oaks in

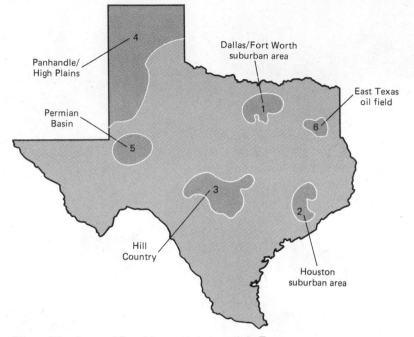

Figure 3.2 Areas of Republican voter strength in Texas

Houston, where GOP candidates customarily get over 80 percent of the votes cast. Republicans also run strongly in new middle-class suburban areas like The Colony (northwest of Dallas) and The Woodlands (north of Houston). Counties like Collin and Fort Bend that are dominated by suburban voters now vote Republican from the courthouse to the White House. In urban, white, working-class areas, GOP candidates usually get between 30 and 40 percent of the vote. The party's weakness is most evident among minority voters. Republicans can count on only 15 to 25 percent of the Mexican-American vote in most elections and on less than 5 percent from black Texans.

Exit poll data and precinct results from the 1990 gubernatorial election confirm the expected pattern of racial voting. Anglos supported Republican Clayton Williams by a margin of 57 percent to 43 percent for Richards, but Williams got only 20 percent of the Hispanic vote and less than 5 percent from African-Americans. Williams carried the suburban areas around Dallas-Fort Worth, Houston, and San Antonio, as well as traditional Republican counties in West and East Texas. He also ran well in blue-collar areas, taking nearly half the votes cast. However, he lagged badly in affluent areas. In River Oaks, for example, Williams got just 68 percent, about 15 points less than Republicans normally receive.

Williams's poor showing in up-scale urban areas reflected a huge "gender gap" among 1990 voters. The male, conservative, Republican nominee got 55 percent of male votes while running against a liberal, female Democrat. However, he garnered only 39 percent among women. Since there are slightly more female

Table 3.2 REPUBLICAN VOTE PERCENTAGE IN GENERAL ELECTIONS, 1976–1990, BY COUNTY POPULATION

County Population	1976 U.S. Senate Steelman (R) vs. Bentsen (D)	1978 Governor Clements (R) vs. Hill (D)	1980 Supreme Court Garwood (R) vs. Ray (D)	1982 Governor Clements (R) vs. White (D)	1986 Governor Clements (R) vs. White (D)	1990 Governor Williams (R) vs. Richards (D)
Over 400,000 (6)	48.0	52.4	54.8	49.6	50.2	45.8
100,000–400,000 (17)	41.6	50.4	50.4	46.0	53.7	49.7
30,000–99,999 (45)	39.6	48.8	45.2	44.2	56.8	51.6
Below 30,000 (186)	32.2	46.9	40.6	40.7	57.7	52.1
State Totals (254)	42.7	50.4	49.7	46.3	53.4	48.7

Source: Official returns, Office of Secretary of State, Austin, Texas. Population data is from 1980 census, and Republican vote percentage is of the two-party vote.

THE 1990 TEXAS GOVERNOR'S RACE: DOWN AND DIRTY ON THE CAMPAIGN TRAIL

Politics is a full-contact sport in Texas, but even veteran observers were struck by the meanness of the contest between Ann Richards and Clayton Williams. Mark McKinnon, a Democratic campaign consultant who worked in the hard-fought 1986 battle between Bill Clements and Mark White as well as in the 1990 race, found the latter to be much tougher. "Nineteen eighty-six was like *High Noon;* 1990 is like the *Texas Chainsaw Massacre.* One is a gunfight. The other is a slaughter."[12]

The viciousness of the 1990 election reflected several factors. To begin with, negative campaigning has become more common throughout the country, as candidates find that 30-second attack ads on opponents often score more points with voters than recitations of their own good qualities. Even so, the Williams-Richards race stood out as perhaps the dirtiest campaign in the country. What made the Texas campaign such a mud fight?

First, let us examine the campaign strategies adopted by the Richards and Williams camps. Richards entered the general election contest after being battered in a hard-fought Democratic primary (see p. 61) that left nagging questions about past drug use and highly negative assessments of the candidate. Richards's strategists felt that they could do little to change these perceptions; they felt that she would win the November election only if voters formed an equally low opinion of her opponent, about whom most voters knew little beyond the information provided in Williams's television commercials. Accordingly, the Richards camp relentlessly attacked Williams's political competence and his business ethics and accused him of insensitivity to women, minorities, recovering alcoholics, and so forth. Williams, as an outsider with little knowledge of state politics, felt that his best route to victory lay in reinforcing the negative perceptions many Texans had already formed about Richards. Consequently, his well-funded campaign attacked Richards as a big-spending liberal and hinted that she had a lifestyle not accepted by most Texans.

Williams entered the general election contest with a large lead in all published polls. His advantage was threatened, however, by a propensity for gaffes. During the primary, he had joked to reporters about similarities between bad weather and rape ("If it's inevitable, relax and enjoy it.") Such comments drew national and state attention to the race and emphasized the personal and increasingly bitter tone of the race.

Despite Williams's tendency to shoot from the lip, he was still the clear frontrunner as the campaign entered its final weeks. His advantage, to a great degree, reflected the fact that while most voters were turned off by the negative quality of the campaign, more blamed Richards than Wil-

Clayton Williams calls Ann Richards a "liar" and refuses to shake her hand at a campaign appearance in Dallas.

liams for this. Williams changed that attitude, however, by a series of major blunders. Foremost among these was a highly publicized confrontation in Dallas on October 11, 1990. The candidates' paths crossed at a law-enforcement awards luncheon each was to address. Williams, angered by a new charge that a bank he controlled was involved in laundering drug money, sought out Richards, and the following exchange occurred:[13]

Williams: "I'm here to call you a liar today."
Richards: [Clearly taken aback] "I'm sorry, Clayton."
Williams: "That's what you are. You've lied about me. . . . I'm going to finish this deal, and you can count on it."
[Williams then spurned Richards's extended hand and walked away.]
Richards: "Clayton, that's not very gentlemanly."

Videotapes of the incident led every major television news story that evening, and a wirephoto of Williams refusing Richards's handshake was front-page news across Texas and in many national papers. Williams was badly damaged by the 20-second encounter, as voters shifted the blame to him, not Richards, for the nastiness of the race. Combined with other fumbles in the last week of the campaign, Williams turned a 15-point poll lead into a 100,000-vote electoral defeat on November 6, 1990.

than male voters, this gender difference was disastrous for Williams and the Republican party.

THIRD PARTIES IN TEXAS

From time to time in Texas, new political parties have emerged and sought a role in the political system. The Populist party was a significant force in Texas in the 1890s. More recently, supporters of George Wallace launched a major bid for Texas electoral votes in the 1968 presidential election under the banner of the American Independent party. Wallace's party garnered 584,269 votes (18.3 percent), led in 22 counties, and finished second in 38 others. The Raza Unida party was active in Texas in the 1970s, electing several county officials in South Texas and putting up a few statewide candidates. Their most successful statewide candidate, Ramsey Muniz, got 214,118 votes for governor in 1972, or 6.3 percent, and helped to make the contest between Dolph Briscoe and Republican Hank Grover very close. In 1980 John Anderson got on the Texas presidential ballot as an independent and took 111,613 votes.

The Libertarian Party is the only third party currently active in Texas politics. It ran candidates for all major statewide offices in 1990 and contested a number of local races. The strongest Libertarian candidates (Jeff Daiell for governor, Suzanne Love for treasurer) won less than 4 percent of the total votes cast in statewide contests.

Why have third parties fared so poorly in Texas? At first glance, the Lone Star State would seem likely to support a multiparty system. Texas is large and has a diverse population, and there is little evidence of an enduring consensus on issues among voters. Yet after more than a century of trying, third parties have not been able to break the Democrats' and Republicans' monopoly on electoral success in the state. The reasons for this include the following four factors:

1. *The electoral rules of the game.* The "winner-take-all" quality of elections in Texas and the United States, as opposed to the proportional representation systems common in Europe, makes it difficult for third parties to establish a political base. Having 10 or 20 or even 30 percent of the vote usually elects no one to office in Texas, so minor parties usually achieve significance only as "spoilers" by taking votes from major party candidates. Additionally, the major party candidates are assured the best places on the ballot, and they have their primaries paid for by the taxpayers of Texas. Minor parties do not share in such largesse. And since Democrats and Republicans will continue to write the rules under which state politics is played, the major parties' advantage is likely to continue.
2. *The nature of the major parties.* American political parties tend to be loose, decentralized entities capable of adapting to different state electorates and to changing public opinions on issues. They are not highly organized, nor often committed to any firm set of principles. Such characteristics certainly apply to the dominant party in Texas, the Democrats, and are reflected in Democratic candidates who follow flexible,

pragmatic courses. This flexibility of Democrats and, to a lesser degree, of Republicans, tends to undercut the potential of third parties because if new issues arise or opinions shift on old issues, the major party candidates can usually adapt to the new realities.

3. *The nature of the minor parties.* Ironically, it has often been the small parties, not the big ones, that have been inflexible in their approach to voters in Texas. Many of these parties are comprised of small groups of individuals strongly committed to political goals or positions that command little support among the state's voters. In most cases, these parties disdain compromises made to win votes because such a "sellout" would, in the members' eyes, be but an imitation of the corruption they associate with the major parties.

4. *The natural advantages enjoyed by the major parties.* The rule in electoral politics, as elsewhere in life, is "Them that has, gits." Put less crudely, those who enjoy current benefits are usually in the best position to ensure the flow of future rewards. The case of political parties competing for candidates, money, media attention, and votes illustrates this point. Most able, serious, and politically experienced officeseekers in Texas (along with, to be sure, many lacking in ability, seriousness, and experience) choose to run as Democrats or Republicans because they think only major-party candidates can win. Television, radio, and newspapers cover Democrats and Republicans because media editors think no one else can win. Financial contributors invest their dollars in Democrats and Republicans because they think one or the other's candidates are bound to win. Voters usually narrow their choices to Democrats or Republicans because they do not want to throw their votes away on losers. Under these conditions, they are all right to act this way—no one but the Democrats and Republicans *can* win. The expectation ensures the result.

In light of these factors, the prospects for significant third parties are bleak in Texas, as indeed they are in most American states. A popular national political leader denied a major-party nomination for the presidency might launch a serious bid for Texas's presidential votes, as George Wallace did in 1968 and John Anderson attempted in 1980. Or special local conditions might enable a third party based on a distinctive segment of the state's electorate to enjoy local success briefly, the way Raza Unida did among Mexican-Americans in Zavala County in the mid-1970s. Such special conditions aside, there is virtually no chance for the establishment of stable, influential third parties within Texas. That should hardly be surprising, given the great difficulties the Republicans have had in becoming a competitive *second* party.

If third parties are not in the future, what lies ahead for the state's party system? The following section speculates on that subject.

THE FUTURE OF PARTY POLITICS IN TEXAS

This concluding section focuses on two questions. Is Texas now a truly two-party state? And given that partisan politics has changed enormously here over the past

20 years, where is Texas party politics heading over the next 20 years or so? Opinions naturally differ on such matters (and they change over time, as readers of earlier editions of this book can attest), but we offer up our speculative judgments on these matters and the consequences of what we see and foresee in Texas.

THE COMING OF TWO-PARTY POLITICS TO TEXAS

In reviewing recent election results, it seems clear that Texas is now a two-party state when it comes to major elections. The Republican party has the advantage in presidential voting and competes on an equal footing in gubernatorial and senatorial elections. These electoral gains are reflected in a major shift in party identification patterns among Texas voters in the last ten years.

Since 1978 the Center for Public Policy at the University of Houston has polled state voters a number of times. Figure 3.3 summarizes partisan identification patterns in seven surveys taken between 1978 and 1990. These show a sharp erosion of the Democratic advantage over this period. In 1978, 48 percent of Texans said they were Democrats and just 19 percent said they were Republicans. By 1986 this ratio had fallen to 40 percent Democratic versus 26 percent Republican. A September 1990 poll showed virtually no difference, with 34 percent saying they were Democrats and 33 percent Republicans. The number of self-identified independents was more stable, ranging between 31 and 38 percent.

Republican gains reflect the advantage the GOP has enjoyed among "party-switchers" and its strong performance among young voters. The party-switching pattern is evident from some questions asked in the September 1986 survey. About a third of the people interviewed said they had changed their party identification over the years, with most shifting from Democrat to Republican or

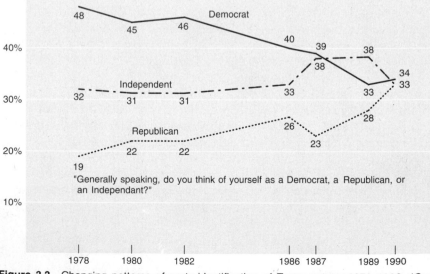

Figure 3.3 Changing patterns of party identification of Texas voters, 1978–1990. (*Source:* Surveys conducted by the Center for Public Policy, University of Houston.)

Democrat to independent. For example, just 13 percent of the 1986 Democrats said they had once been Republicans, but 43 percent of the Republicans reported they were former Democrats. Similarly, only 11 percent of the independents were former Republicans, but 42 percent had once been Democrats. In addition to picking up a majority of party-switchers, the Republican party also did well among new voters entering the electorate in the 1980s (Ronald Reagan got over 60 percent of the vote from Texans under 30 in 1984). And the GOP did very well among voters who moved to Texas during the boom years from 1973 to 1982.

If recent election results and party identification data confirm the two-party system in Texas, what are the broader consequences of this development? Some have been mentioned before, such as the shift in voter interest and participation from the party primaries in the spring to the November general elections. Increased party competition has also contributed to the higher costs of running for public office. Major candidates not only have to win the primary nomination but must also prevail in a very expensive general election contest. The 1990 gubernatorial contest is a good case in point. Ann Richards spent $4 million to win the Democratic primary, and another $10 million in the general election campaign. Clayton Williams spent $8 million in the GOP primary and another $15 million in the general election. Together, the seven major candidates spent more than $50 million running for governor in 1990, making it *the most expensive state election in U.S. history.* The escalation in costs is evident in down-ballot races. The Republican and Democratic candidates for a commissioner seat in Harris County spent about $600,000 each in 1990.

Two-party politics also makes a difference after elections are over. The Texas legislature traditionally operated in a rather nonpartisan manner, with Democrats and Republicans working together on many issues. Partisan conflict within the legislature became much more pronounced in the late 1980s, especially in the House, where Republicans and Democrats became sharply polarized over taxing and spending issues.

LOOKING TO THE FUTURE

Are Texas Republicans going to continue to make gains at the Democrats' expense? Will the GOP become the dominant state party as the Democrats were 30 years ago? Although the future is unpredictable, our best educated guess is that neither party is likely to gain a decisive advantage over the other in coming years.

We have noted the Republican party has some significant advantages—better organization and funding, and strength among party-switchers, new voters, and in-migrants. Having a Texas Republican in the White House does not hurt, either. But Democrats still have some good cards, as their strong performance in the 1990 elections indicated. One major advantage the Democrats have is better "bench strength" in terms of potential candidates. With most local and state elective offices held by Democrats, that party has a generally stronger group of future nominees than is available to the Republican party. The 1990 governor's race is again instructive. Democrats could choose between three veteran campaigners who had all won statewide offices before. Republicans could choose from among a former congressman who had lost two recent statewide elections and three candidates who had never run for elective office before. As noted, the GOP primary voters selected Clayton Williams, a wealthy businessman who impressed voters with a number of effective television ads. The dangers of running an inexperienced candidate who has little knowledge of state issues and campaign realities did not become evident until late in the race, when Williams made a number of mistakes that a more seasoned nominee would likely have avoided.

In brief, in an era in which voters are looking more and more at individual candidates and less at party labels, good candidates are essential. By almost any measure, the Democrats retain an advantage in the available candidate pool.

The demographic factors that favored Republican growth in the 1970s and early 1980s have also shifted. The severe economic problems Texas experienced in 1982–1983 and 1986–1987 slowed the growth of the urban middle class and reversed migration patterns. By the late 1980s more adults were leaving Texas in some years than were moving in. The fastest-growing segment of the Texas electorate in the early 1990s is Mexican-American voters, who remain decidedly Democratic in party preference.

National factors that benefited Republicans in the 1980s are less evident in the 1990s. George Bush is popular with Texas voters, but less so than was Ronald Reagan. The national leadership of the Democratic party has a more moderate image than was the case in the 1980s, and Republicans cannot count on having relatively weak presidential opponents like Walter Mondale or Michael Dukakis in the 1990s. National deficits, economic concerns, and a growing national pessimism make it difficult for either party to generate much new support.

If short-term factors no longer seem to be working for the Republicans, can the Democrats regain their dominant position of the 1950s and 1960s? Our answer is no. The Texas Republican party has far too large a base of voter and organizational support to be pushed back to its minority status of the 1960s. Looking ahead 20 years or so, we expect a continuation of partisan patterns in which Democrats retain an advantage in congressional and legislative elections (partly because they hold most of these seats, and beating incumbents is difficult), but in which Democrats and Republicans will continue to contest major state offices on an equal footing. Specific election outcomes will largely turn on short-term factors unique to each contest and not on some underlying party advantage.

A final look at the 1990 results reported earlier shows the absence of party voting. The strongest Republican candidate (U.S. Senator Phil Gramm) got 61.7 percent of the two-party vote; the weakest Republican candidate (comptroller nominee Warren G. Harding, Jr.) got 33.2 percent. In other words, more than 1.2 million Texans voted for Mr. Gramm, but not Mr. Harding. Those "swing" voters now decide every election contest between the party nominees.

NOTES

1. Frank Sorauf, *Party Politics in America,* 4th ed. (Boston: Little, Brown, 1980), p. 11.
2. Austin Ranney, "Parties in State Politics," in *Politics in the American States,* 3d ed., ed. Herbert Jacobs and Kenneth Vines (Boston: Little, Brown, 1976), p. 61.

3. V.O. Key, Jr., *Southern Politics* (New York: Knopf, 1949), pp. 298–311.
4. Ibid., p. 255.
5. David R. Mayhew, *Placing Parties in American Politics* (Princeton, N.J.: Princeton University Press, 1986), pp. 132–142.
6. See Robert Salisbury, "An Exchange Theory of Interest Groups," *Midwest Journal of Political Science* 13 (February 1969): 1–32.
7. Richard Murray and Kent L. Tedin, "The Emergence of Two-Party Competition in the Sunbelt: The Case of Houston," in *Political Parties in Local Areas,* ed. William Crotsy (Knoxville: University of Tennessee Press, 1987), pp. 39–62.
8. Ibid.
9. Key, *Southern Politics,* p. 7.
10. Roscoe Martin, *The People's Party in Texas: A Study in Third-Party Politics* (Austin: University of Texas Press, 1970), pp. 230–251.
11. Interview with Billie Carr by Richard Murray, January 14, 1980.
12. Quoted in David Elliott, "Voters' Refrain: Richards, Williams, None of the Above," *Austin American-Statesman,* September 22, 1990, p. B-1.
13. Quotes from Gerald Volgenau, "Texas Campaign Gets Even Hotter," *Philadelphia Inquirer,* October 13, 1990, p. A-1.

chapter 4

Interest Groups in Texas Politics

Protest demonstrations are a common form of political pressure activity.

In every democracy, interest groups emerge to press political demands. The reasons are simple enough. In any political system, the institutional structure, composition of political leadership, and policies adopted generate conflict, dissatisfaction, and frustration among people. These lead to demands for different political actions. Some of these demands can be aggregated and processed through political parties. Parties, by their nature, are limited vehicles for transmitting a multiplicity of citizen demands. Major parties must make broad appeals, shy away from firm commitments to specific groups, and subordinate virtually all else in pursuit of their first priority—winning elections. That being the case, many people turn to specific associations or organized groups to promote certain governmental actions or policies. It is such organized associations pursuing political goals that we call *interest groups*.

Interest groups are of special importance in Texas; because, as noted earlier, Texas was without a competitive party system for most of its history.

Paradoxically, scholars have paid little attention to interest groups' contribution to Texas politics except for certain groups that lobby in the legislative, executive, and administrative branches of state government to secure favorable policy decisions. Lobbying represents an important aspect of group activity, but other activities are also of great significance. A Dallas business group pours funds into a favored candidate's race; families of persons killed in alcohol-related automobile accidents write to Texas trial judges and appear in court to protest what they consider to be extremely light penalties for driving while intoxicated; fundamentalist Christians provide legal support to parents educating their children in "home schools" across the state; and the possibility of casino gambling divides Galvestonians into pro and con groups contesting local referenda. All such activities contribute to the sum of interest-group involvement in Texas politics.

Any discussion of Texas interest groups is handicapped by the relative inattention they have received and by the fact that much group political activity is purposefully hidden from public view. These factors limit the following discussion of the bases of group organization, the tactics used by such organizations, and interest groups' general impact on Texas politics.

THE BASES OF GROUP ORGANIZATION

Interest groups are organized aggregates or, more simply, groups of people who have joined together for some common purpose. This purpose might be protection or advancement of the group's economic interest, as is the case with trade associations, professional groups, and labor unions. Or it might be more general in nature, as with groups that oppose environmental pollution or wish to eliminate corruption from government. Generalization is difficult. Some groups pursue long-term objectives (e.g., bettering employee working conditions or arresting a perceived Communist influence in American politics), while others seek short-term goals (e.g., preventing a specific tax increase or purging sex education courses from the public school curriculum).

Given the complexity of purposes that distinguish groups, a more basic issue must be dealt with: Why do some groups that share interests organize and engage in political action, while others do not? Why are doctors, lawyers, and steelworkers in Texas well organized for protection of their economic interests, while secretaries, janitors, and farm laborers are hardly organized at all? Why do residents of one area in the path of a proposed freeway organize a vigorous protest against losing their property, while citizens in another place accept relocation without complaint? There is virtually an infinite number of common purposes that could serve as organizational bases, but only a limited number of organized groups do in fact exist.

Several general factors promote or retard the degree of collective political action engaged in by a group with common interests.

Size of the Group   Contrary to what one might think, the *smaller* the group, the more easily it can be organized. Large groups are cumbersome and hard to coordinate. Each individual's contribution to the collective enterprise is small, and "letting George do it" is a persistent problem.[1] With small groups, each person's contribution is important to group success, and one's share of the group benefits is larger; thus organizational participation is more rational from the individual's viewpoint. A practical illustration of the size principle can be seen in the fact that it is far easier for the few oil-exporting nations to organize than it is for the many oil-importing nations to do so.

Group Concentration   The more concentrated the potential group, the more easily it can be organized. The organizational costs of communication and coordination increase sharply when a group's membership is scattered. Four thousand young people concentrated on a college campus can be combined for political action with a great deal less effort than it would take if the same number were scattered in 100 different places.

Membership Resources   Organization entails costs, especially if the group is too large for face-to-face interaction. Means for communicating with members are usually necessary in all but the simplest organizations, and employment of a permanent staff is often necessary. Since organizational costs are usually borne by group members, the more resources they possess the more easily they can afford organization. Resources include not only money but also such things as leisure time and skills useful for organizational activities.

Organizational Resources   People join organizations because they perceive membership to be in their best interest. Organizations must thus provide inducements or incentives to prospective members.[2] Sometimes the incentive is simply that the individual agrees with the goals or purposes of the organization; but this is often insufficient, especially when the group is large. Mass organizations usually develop selective incentives that help them attract individuals into their folds. To work, one may have to join a union; to enjoy good social relations, one may have to become a member in a neighborhood civic club; to achieve career status or prestige, one may have to join a professional association.

Climate for Organization   The constitutional guarantees of speech, assembly, press, and petition should equally protect all groups' rights of organization, but circumstances make it easier for some groups to associate formally than others. A group that reflects general community values, like a veterans' organization, will likely encounter no opposition; but a group that supports legalizing marijuana might face harassment. An association that challenges a local power structure may find in its path a series of legal and illegal barriers that do not obstruct those who go along with the powers that be.

Applying these considerations to Texas helps one understand variations in group organization. The 40,000 or so doctors can organize far more easily than can the hundreds of thousands of clerks in the state. Urban blacks can build up an organizational infrastructure that surpasses that found among dispersed rural blacks. Trial lawyers can afford group organization; janitors cannot. Unions that control selective incentives for members, like admission to apprentice programs

for the skilled trades, have little difficulty in recruiting members. Unions representing workers not qualified through apprentice programs (e.g., auto mechanics)
are not so fortunate. Organizers of a Committee to Restore Prayer in the Public
Schools would face few problems in a conservative city like Amarillo; the same
could probably not be said for a Gay Liberation or Young Socialists League
chapter.

Business Groups

In the first pages of his book, *Politics and Markets,* the noted economist Charles
Lindblom states:

> Not a myth but a misunderstanding is the common view of how liberal demo-
> cratic government works. Except for some analysis of interest groups, demo-
> cratic theory makes no place for the business enterprise. In American law the
> corporation is a "person" and in all the democratic market-oriented systems,
> corporations and other business enterprises enter into politics. Their needs and
> preferences are communicated to lawmakers no less urgently than those of
> other citizens. But these fictitious persons are taller and richer than the rest of
> us and have rights that we do not have. Their political impact differs from and
> dwarfs that of the ordinary citizen.[3]

Texas business enterprises are indeed "taller and richer" than others involved in state politics. The economic boom Texas enjoyed after World War II
was rooted in its emergence as the center of the national and international energy
industry. A number of oil and gas behemoths such as Exxon, U.S.A., Shell Oil,
and Tenneco are headquartered in Texas; others, like Texaco and Chevron, have
sizable managerial and technical staffs based in the state. In addition to the major
oil companies, hundreds of independent energy firms are based in Texas as well
as some of the largest oil service companies like Halliburton and Baker-Hughes.
    Although the energy-based boom ended in the early 1980s, it did support
a general expansion of state corporate interests. Bank-holding companies with
assets up to $20 billion emerged in Dallas and Houston. Privately owned utilities,
real estate, and development firms thrived as people and capital flowed into Texas.
The new prosperity spread to those offering professional services to corporate
clients, like large law and accounting firms. In sum, the business sector in Texas
expanded enormously between 1946 and 1982.
    Quite obviously, the largest of Texas's corporate enterprises possess enor-
mous resources. The managers at Exxon, Southwestern Bell, Shell Oil, and Halliburton have access to numerous lawyers, accountants, public relations experts,
full-time political lobbyists, and millions of dollars in advertising or public affairs
budgets. No other interested parties can enter the political arena with such assets.
These economic goliaths can usually take care of their own political needs without
relying on collective action.
    Most business firms, however, do not have the resources or the interest to
operate independently in political matters. Joining with other businesses is not

only economical, it also tends to increase the impact these firms can have on political decision makers. Some of these associations, like the Texas Association of Business or local chambers of commerce, represent general business interests, but most represent particular segments of the business world. Beermakers have the Texas Brewers Association; oil operators have the Texas Independent Producers and Royalty Owners Association; highway contractors have the Good Roads Association; and so on into the hundreds. The reasons for such collective activity in Texas are easily understood. State government collects over $10 billion a year in taxes; business firms want to pay as little of this as possible. State government has regulatory power over virtually every type of economic activity in Texas; businesses want regulation that, at a minimum, does not interfere with their ability to operate profitably and, at a maximum, enhances their profitability. Finally, state government spends billions of dollars for goods and services; many businesses, such as highway contractors, could not survive without selling their services to the state.

In general, one can say that the business sector is better organized than any other set of interests to advance or protect its political interests. But that reality should not obscure important facts. First, the business sector is not monolithic. Deep conflicts often divide corporate interests like railroads and pipelines, big oil companies and independent producers, and bankers as opposed to savings and loan associations. Second, by no means are all businesses well represented in the political arena. For example, there are several hundred thousand independent retailers in Texas whose numbers, diversity of interests, geographic dispersion, and relative lack of resources preclude effective organization.

Finally, the economic problems Texas experienced after 1982 have taken a toll on the corporate sector. Many companies that were politically active in the 1970s have disappeared owing to bankruptcies or mergers (e.g., Braniff Airlines, Getty and Gulf Oil, and Republic National Bank). Others, like the H. L. Hunt family businesses in Dallas and T. Boone Pickens's Mesa Petroleum, survived in much weakened condition. Business lobby groups like the Houston Chamber of Commerce and the Association of General Contractors have suffered substantial losses in membership and dues. Consequently, the advantage of superior resources that big business brought to the political table for most of the twentieth century has been reduced somewhat in the last ten years.

Occupational Groups

In contrast to the situation in most industrialized states and at the national level, business groups in Texas do not have to contend with a strong organized labor movement. Only 300,000 workers are members of unions in Texas, which represents less than 5 percent of the state's work force, as compared to 15 percent in the country as a whole. Despite vigorous organizing efforts by a number of unions, the percentage of unionized workers in the state has been declining in recent years.

The weak status of organized labor in Texas reflects several factors. Public attitudes in the South generally stress individualism rather than collective action, and there is a considerable amount of antiunion feeling, even among blue-collar workers. Many employers in the state, such as Brown and Root, the huge construction firm, are ideologically opposed to unions and fight with great determination efforts to organize their workers. Organized labor also operates under severe legal handicaps. Texas is one of 20 states with a "right-to-work" law that prohibits union-shop arrangements. Under this law no worker can be required by a majority-approved, company-union agreement to join a union to get or keep a job. The principle sounds admirable, but unions argue that it creates a "freeloader" problem, in that many workers will enjoy the fruits of having a union represent them but will refuse to pay their share of the cost of such representation. Other restrictions on unions include an anti–check-off law that prohibits an employer from deducting union dues without prior written permission from the employee concerned, a prohibition of mass picketing and secondary boycotts, inclusion of unions under the state antitrust laws, and a provision that labor unions are liable for damages resulting from strikes in breach of contract.

About half of the 150,000 farmers in Texas belong to one of several farm groups. The traditional lack of consensus among farmers is reflected in the fact that prominent organizations like the Texas Farmers Union and the state branch of the American Farm Bureau disagree on virtually every issue affecting agriculture. Periodic efforts have been made to organize farm workers in Texas, particularly in the lower Rio Grande Valley. However, these efforts have met with little success, and farm laborers remain unorganized.

Most high-status professional workers in Texas, such as medical doctors and lawyers, have long had effective associations protecting their public-policy interests. In the 1960s and 1970s other white-collar workers, such as teachers, nurses, and public employees, turned to group organization to promote their interests.

Nevertheless, no more than one-quarter of the 8 million employed persons in Texas are represented by any sort of occupational association. Since organization is common only among white-collar professionals and skilled blue-collar employees, this means that virtually all lower-paid workers are not represented by groups in the political arena. This has, as we shall see, significant implications for public policy in Texas.

Ethnic and Racial Political Groups

One of our popular literary traditions maintains that the United States is a "melting pot" in which persons of diverse ethnic origins are assimilated into the mainstream of American life and culture. Certainly, there is some evidence to support this view. For example, Irish-Americans and German-Americans have become highly assimilated in the last half-century, and Polish and other Slavic-Americans seem to be in the process of doing so at the present time. Nevertheless, there is considerable evidence that for many racial or ethnic groups, assimilation has progressed at a much slower pace. This has especially been the case with Americans of African or Hispanic origin. The reasons for their continuing distinctiveness reflect not only high degrees of ethnic consciousness within these populations, but also the effects of centuries of political, social, and economic discrimination that Americans of darker skin have endured in this society.

In Chapter 2 we emphasized that Texas has both large black and Hispanic populations that account for more than a third of the state's residents. Stress was also placed on the fact that in terms of almost every objective measure—income, educational levels, occupational patterns—blacks and Hispanics rank far behind the Anglo majority in Texas. Given the distinct socioeconomic status of black and brown Texans, plus the political discrimination that each population has been subjected to, it is hardly surprising that a number of politically active groups are rooted in these communities.

These groups tend to be of two general types. The first are organizations concerned with the general social and political problems facing the minority populations; the second focus on more specific problems or political tasks. A number of groups in the first category are affiliated with national associations. There are, for example, chapters of the National Association for the Advancement of Colored People (NAACP) active in every large metropolitan area in Texas. Similarly, the League of United Latin American Citizens (LULAC) and the American GI Forum represent Mexican-American interests around the state. Such organizations are active on a range of problems: school desegregation, employment and promotion practices, securing more political appointments, for example. The specialized groups include the Mexican-American Legal Defense and Education Fund (MALDEF), the Harris County Council of Organizations (HCCO), and the Progressive Voters League (PVL). MALDEF is principally concerned with research and litigation relevant to the needs of the Mexican-American community. The other two are black voter groups (the first in Houston, the other in Dallas) that screen candidates for public office, issue endorsements, and work to deliver the minority vote to the endorsed officeseekers.

Despite the fact that there are several hundred black or brown organizations in Texas that do get involved in politics, only a tiny fraction of the black and Mexican-American populations are members of these groups. Low membership reflects the situation of many adults in these populations. They are poor, lack leisure time, have limited access to political information, and have more than enough to do in facing the everyday problems of survival. It is difficult for many blacks and Hispanics to invest their time, energy, and money in political efforts that usually have no immediate payoff.

The impact of ethnic political groups in Texas is difficult to assess. Politically, blacks and Mexican-Americans have made obvious headway over the last 30 years. Discriminatory legislation has been erased from the statutes; both groups are reasonably well represented within the Democratic party structure; more minority legislators are getting elected; and a few more political appointments are coming to minorities. Still, there has been only modest progress in closing the socioeconomic gap that separates blacks and browns from Anglos in Texas. One problem these disadvantaged minorities face is the great difficulty they encounter in uniting around a common political program. A current example concerns the way the government should deal with nonlegal immigrants from Mexico and Central America. LULAC and other Hispanic groups have stressed that the problem should be approached from the perspective of the human rights of the individuals involved. Accordingly, they supported the amnesty provisions in the 1986 immigration law, while strongly condemning the employer penalties for hiring undocumented workers. African-Americans, on the other hand, were opposed to amnesty and supportive of employer sanctions because they saw Hispanic.immigrants as competitors for a limited number of jobs.

Tensions between Hispanic and black groups have also arisen over sharing political power in major cities. In 1989, for example, many Hispanics in Houston were bitter when former city controller Leonel Castillo lost an at-large council runoff election to Sheila Jackson Lee, a black attorney. Mexican-Americans were particularly aggrieved because this outcome gave African-Americans five council seats, with only one held by a Hispanic.

Ethnic diversity in Texas is growing as immigration from the Pacific rim increases. The new waves of Asian immigrants (predominately Chinese and Vietnamese) have encountered significant discrimination, as depicted in the movie *Alamo Bay* and the fatal beating of a Vietnamese teenager in Houston by neo-Nazi "skinheads" in 1990, but little political organization is yet evident in these populations. Many Asian-American adults are not yet U.S. citizens, and their traditional cultures have not emphasized collective political action, so meaningful group politics may be some time away.

There are, of course, other identifiable ethnic populations in Texas. Most notable among these are the approximately 100,000 Jews in the state. Though relatively small in number, Jews tend to be active in many social and political groups, and they can bring considerable political pressure to bear on issues of great interest to the Jewish population. The Texas legislature found this out in 1977 when it was pressed to pass legislation making it illegal for any Texas firm to cooperate with the Arab economic boycott of Israel.

Finally, we should note that while many Texans retain a sense of their German, Polish, Czech, or other European heritage, there is virtually no meaningful political organization along these lines in the state.

RELIGION-BASED ACTIVISM

Most Texans, like other Americans, think of themselves as religious—a majority as Christian Protestants, a large minority as Roman Catholics. About half the state's residents report they attend religious services on a fairly regular basis. Historically, most religious groups in Texas have not been noted for their political activism except under unusual circumstances. One such instance occurred in 1928 when the Democratic party nominated Al Smith, the Irish-Catholic governor of New York, for the presidency. Texas Protestant leaders, rallied by the president of Baylor University, worked vigorously for Smith's defeat. Church leaders have also been occasionally stirred into action by state issues like authorizing the sale of liquor-by-the-drink or legalizing charitable bingo games (Catholics for, Baptists against). The Christian Life Commission, a political arm of the Texas Southern Baptists, led the 1991 fight against authorizing a state lottery.

In the 1960s and 1970s, a number of church-based groups actively supported "liberal" causes like civil rights for blacks, ending the Vietnam War, and organizing farm workers. Occasional liberal activism was evident in the 1980s, as in Catholic Bishop Leroy Matthiesen's opposition to manufacturing nuclear weapons in Amarillo. And some church leaders were front and center in protesting the American decision to declare war on Iraq in 1991. Despite such examples, the greater amount of recent political activity rooted in religious groups has been by evangelical and fundamentalist Christians backing "conservative" causes.[4] This upsurge in evangelical activism is national in scope but has been especially evident in the South and Texas.

According to observers like A. James Reichley, the rise of the religious right reflects several factors.[5] Specific governmental actions like the U.S. Supreme Court decisions prohibiting prayer in the public schools (1961) and legalizing abortion (1973) deeply offended many evangelicals. Also contributing was a dissatisfaction with the public schools in general, and specifically with the teaching of biological evolution as opposed to biblical creation in science courses. More important than these specifics was a general sense among evangelicals that the moral foundations of American society were crumbling. The resulting growing commitment to political action was reflected in the formation of groups like the Moral Majority, founded by the Reverend Jerry Falwell in 1979.

These national trends have had a significant impact in Texas, with its relatively large percentage of evangelical and fundamentalist Christians, led by outspoken leaders like the Reverend Criswell of the First Baptist Church in

Reprinted by permission.

Dallas and the Reverend Ed Young at the Second Baptist Church in Houston. In the 1980s and early 1990s, such religious leaders were in action against abortion, gay rights, pornography, and including the theory of evolution in textbooks, and in favor of prayer in the schools, backing our troops in the Persian Gulf, and making America great and moral again.

POLITICAL-INTEREST GROUPS

Interest groups rooted in political agreement per se, rather than some kind of economic, ethnic, or religious interest, tend to be of two kinds. The first are narrow-range groups that concentrate on a single issue or a related set of issues. Single-issue groups are now active in Texas to reform marijuana laws, toughen laws against drinking and driving, stop the construction of nuclear power plants, and so forth. The proliferation of these groups reflects the fact that they can organize rather easily because they typically require a modest short-term investment by supporters (e.g., writing a check, writing a legislator, going on a sponsored trip to Austin). In addition to single-issue groups, Texas has a number of organizations that focus on specific areas of public policy. For example, the Sierra Club is concerned about a range of environmental issues, whereas the Texas Research League is especially interested in taxing and spending patterns.

General political interest groups active in the state are often spin-offs of national associations. Typical of this genre are Common Cause of Texas, the Texas Conservative Union, and the Texas Women's Political Caucus. Common Cause is the largest "public interest" group operating at the national level, with more than 200,000 dues-paying members. They have been active in support of a number of reform measures, like campaign finance changes, since the early 1970s. The Texas Conservative Union and Women's Political Caucus have only a few thousand members in the state, but they have been prominent representatives of conservative and feminist perspectives.

The combined impact of these various political groups is hard to assess, partly because they often oppose each other. One can safely say their influence does not approach that of economic associations in state politics, but they certainly add diversity to the Texas interest-group scene.

TACTICS AND STRATEGY OF GROUP POLITICS

Interest groups usually rely on four methods of securing favorable public action: lobbying, mass propagandizing, electioneering, and litigation. Additionally, unorthodox and sometimes illegal tactics have occasionally been used by groups in pursuit of their objectives.

Lobbying

Lobbying is the process wherein group representatives interact with public decision makers in the hope of influencing policy. Most of the publicized lobbying in Texas occurs in the state legislature, but lobbying is by no means restricted to the legislative process. Wherever decisions are made that affect group interests—be it city hall, the governor's staff, the courts, or administrative agencies—one finds lobbying activity.

Lobbying, at least successful lobbying, involves a transfer of benefits between groups and decision makers. A lobbyist may dispense material benefits, but often he or she offers political support or information to the public official, who in turn takes the lobbyist's position into account in making policy decisions. Outright bribery, public suspicions to the contrary, is rare.

At every session of the Texas legislature, one can find hundreds of lobbyists in attendance or around the capitol at various times, serving as representatives for various groups. Many lobbyists are longtime political actors, often having served as legislators themselves, and many are quite knowledgeable about legislative issues and the operation of the legislative process. They may draft bills, mastermind legislative campaigns, help line up support for or against given bills, and otherwise work to secure their goals.

Lobbyists typically do a goodly amount of wining, dining, and entertaining, although some observers (note the comments of George Strong in the Box on page 88) claim the importance of such efforts have declined. Nevertheless, legislators and other public officials are often taken to dinner, invited on hunting and fishing trips and other junkets, and provided with liquor or entertainment. What the lobbyist seeks to secure by these activities is not so much direct commitments for favorable votes, but "access" and "goodwill." Lobbyists must be able to talk with legislators when the need arises, and that is obviously much easier if they have established friendly relations prior to discussing specific business.

Many legislators who are lawyers are employed by corporations and groups and are paid retainer's fees for their efforts. Nonlawyers are sometimes employed in "public relations" positions by banks and other businesses. Such arrangements are legal, although many question their propriety. When a bill affecting a corporation or interest group comes before the legislature, does a legislator employed by that group act as the representative of the client or of the constituent? Although the answer is a matter of conjecture, apparently groups believe that employing legislators holds some benefit.

Lobbyists and interest-group representatives often appear at committee hearings and present oral or written statements on the need for, the merits of, and possible effects of given bills. In so doing, they provide legislators with much useful, if self-serving, information on legislation—some of which would not otherwise be available. Also, lobbyists occasionally encourage the attendance at hearings by persons favorable to their position in an effort to create the impression that they have wide public support.

Because of the many forces that play on legislators and the legislative process, it is not possible to determine with precision the impact of lobbying efforts. The success of a particular group will depend on such factors as its size, status, resources, cohesion, and position on issues and the attitudes of legislators, public opinion, and so on. Groups are likely to claim substantial power and success for themselves. This, among other things, helps create the impression that they are a force to be reckoned with and at the same time impresses their members and supporters.

Whatever their actual impact, lobbying groups do perform a number of useful functions: (1) They are a major source of demands for legislative action in that they pressure public officials to act in response to their interests. (2) They provide a great deal of useful, if sometimes biased, information to public officials, much of which is of a specialized or technical nature. (3) They help keep their members and the public informed as to what the legislature is doing and how they may be affected by proposed legislation. (4) In a broad sense, group pressures provide a sort of functional representation that supplements the regular system of geographic representation.

The discussion thus far should not be taken to mean that there has been no criticism of lobbying. On the contrary, there has been much criticism of interest groups as being selfish, greedy, corrupt, and undemocratic, especially if their views or interests are in conflict with the person doing the criticizing. Although demands have often been made for the regulation of lobbying on behalf of special interest groups to prevent abuses and corruption, lobbyists have been unregulated for most of the state's history. A 1907 statute did prohibit efforts to influence legislation "by means other than appeal to reason" and provided that persons guilty of lobbying were subject to fines and imprisonment. This rather stringent statute was never enforced.

In 1957 mounting criticism of some lobbying activities and some legislative scandals, such as the taking of a $5000 bribe by a legislator, culminated in the adoption of the Lobby Control Act. Unlike the earlier statute, the 1957 law made publicity rather than prohibition of lobbying activities its purpose. Lobbyists were required to register and provide certain information about themselves, the legislation in which they had an interest, and their expenditures incurred while engaged in "direct communication" with legislators. In general, the law did little to control or modify lobbying activities. Numerous loopholes in the act restricted its effect, and its provisions were not vigorously enforced. A tougher law was enacted in 1973, which seems to have, if nothing else, made lobbyists more circumspect. Traditional practices, such as showering selected legislators with expensive gifts on "governor for a day," have disappeared. It would now be surprising to find lobbyists paying for legislators' apartments in Austin, a common practice a few years ago.

Fear of adverse publicity is probably as responsible as new laws are for limiting lobby abuses. The good old days when "gentlemen of the press" did not write critically about "gentlemen of the legislature" have passed. For example, *The Texas Monthly,* a magazine with more than 200,000 subscribers, rates legislators after each session. A good way to make the "ten worst" or "furniture" list (this includes members who are neither good nor bad, just around) is to be overly responsive to lobby pressures.

Caution on the part of state officials is also well advised because law enforcement agencies have become more aggressive in seeking out wrongdoing in the legislative process. In the early 1980s the Federal Bureau of Investigation ran a

A VETERAN LOBBYIST COMMENTS ON THE 1991 LEGISLATURE

George Strong has lobbied the Texas legislature since 1976. But unlike most of his colleagues, he also works as a campaign consultant in elections. This combination of "inside" and "outside" knowledge uniquely equips him to analyze the current lobby scene in Austin. We spoke with him early in the 1991 session.

George, how has lobbying changed since you came here?   Fifteen years ago it was a looser, free-wheeling environment. Half the members would be over at the Quorum Club late at night, and some of the old-timers relied on the three "Bs"—beef, bourbon, and pardon the term, "broads,"—to get things done. Now most members are home in bed by 10 o'clock. They're up early jogging, or crewing on the lake. Today lobbyists stress the three "Fs"— facts, footwork, and finances. Facts because with 4000 bills introduced each session, a lobbyist's best resource is accurate information that members need before making decisions. Footwork because you have to get to know most of the 181 members, make friends, stay in touch, if you want the chance to make your case. And finance because the first duty of everyone here is to get reelected, and that can cost a lot of money. I make contributions and help members raise money because if they get defeated, they can't do me any good.

It sounds like lobbyists are tied to incumbents in elections?   Generally, yes. Even when members vote against you, you try to stay friendly with them, and that means you do not support their election opponents. Some members of lobbying groups don't play it that way, like the trial lawyers. They're the Israelis of this place, an eye for an eye. If you don't go with them on their bills, some of them will threaten you, try to beat you in the next election. That works with some members, but not all, and the trial lawyers have had some problems as a result.

series of "sting" operations aimed at corrupt state and local officials. The "Brilab" sting ensnared several Texans, including House Speaker Billy Clayton. A Houston jury eventually found Clayton innocent of bribery charges, but his elective political career was ended (Clayton is now one of the more prominent Austin lobbyists).

More recently, House Speaker Gib Lewis has run afoul of both the press and prosecutors. The *Austin-American Statesman* first ran a series of articles in 1990 raising questions about the ethics and legality of the speaker's actions. Then, on December 28, 1990, Travis County District Attorney Ronnie Earle secured two indictments charging that Mr. Lewis had violated state ethics laws by accepting and not reporting a gift from a law firm holding lucrative contracts regulated

Who are the most effective lobby groups? I'd say the auto dealers, the realtors, the medical doctors. They've all got great grassroots support. There is an auto dealer in every legislative district, and their lobbyist makes sure the dealers know and befriend their local legislators. That makes their lobbyist's job a lot easier here in Austin.

Who are the least effective? Organized labor can be highly effective on one or two issues, but they are spread too thin. They take positions on too many issues. The Chambers of Commerce look good on paper, claiming to represent business interests in Texas, but there are too many different interests within the business community, so it's hard for them to get their act together. Anti-abortion and consumer groups spend too much time singing to the choir and too little on building grassroots support out in member districts.

Right now the legislature is under a cloud because two indictments are pending against House Speaker Gib Lewis, and other legislators are rumored to have legal problems. How will this affect lobbying this session? Well, everyone is nervous. People will be more careful. But I think the great majority of members have not abused the process. If something does not pass the smell test, they don't do it.

How many legislators lack olfactory glands? A few, very few, but they have brought everyone under suspicion. We need, and will pass, a stronger lobbying law this session. In addition to having to register and file monthly reports on general activity and amounts of money spent, we will have to specify with *whom* we did what. Other restrictions on gifts and trips will be added.

by state legislative action.[6] Lewis denied the charges and was reelected speaker in January 1991 with only one dissenting vote, but his indictment and rumors of others to follow placed the legislature under a very dark cloud. The principal reason for that cloud is evident from state records that show that, for the regular session of the legislature in 1989, some 800 registered lobbyists spent more than $1.8 million on gifts and entertainment for the 181 members of the Senate and House.[7] That represents almost four times the salary ($600 per month) each member drew from the state during the session.

Interestingly, the leading lobby spenders in the 1990s are no longer the "Big Four" representing the oil, petrochemical, railroad, and manufacturing industries, but the "Hired Guns." The latter are described by journalist Paul Burka

Reprinted by permission.

as "a dozen or so Capitol veterans, most of them former legislators or top staffers, who specialized in single-shot issues with major economic implications, like tort reform or opening Texas to interstate banking."[8] They represent many clients, enabling them to raise huge sums of money, a goodly portion of which is redistributed to members of the House and Senate. Hiring these lobbyists does not ensure passage or defeat of legislation (they often work against each other), but many feel that someone from this group must be employed in order to play on a level field in Austin.

Electioneering

Interest groups often involve themselves in the electoral process. Organized groups have found they get more favorable responses from public officials they have helped elect to office. Organized labor in Texas has relied heavily on electioneering as a group tactic. Unions, with their large memberships and staffs, can offer candidates campaign workers as well as financial contributions. However, labor union influence is restricted largely to a minority of legislative districts that have substantial numbers of unionized workers. Business groups cannot match labor's personnel, but they can provide financial assistance and technical expertise in selected candidates' campaigns.

The electioneering rule is simple: Elect one's friends and defeat one's enemies. Of course, there are risks involved. Backing a loser does little to ingratiate one with the winning candidate. Large economic interests sometimes avoid this problem by giving aid to competing candidates. In the 1978 U.S. Senate contest between John Tower and Robert Krueger, both received substantial support from the oil industry. Law firms hedge their bets by having some partners support one side while others go with the opposition. In most cases, however, interest groups paly it safe by giving generously to incumbents and ignoring challengers. That helps create and sustain a closed system in Austin of veteran legislators and experienced lobbyists who can scratch each other's backs.

There are legal restrictions on group financial involvement in Texas elections. Corporations and labor unions are both prohibited from contributing to political races, but this law has little practical effect. Labor unions long ago set up "political education" committees that collected money from members apart from union dues and used these funds to back candidates friendly to organized labor. Business firms, on the other hand, traditionally relied on large monetary contributions from owners or corporate officers as a means of ensuring access to the political process. However, in the aftermath of the Watergate scandal in the early 1970s, disclosure laws about contributions have been strengthened, and strict limits have been placed on the amount of money an individual can contribute in presidential and congressional campaigns. Under these conditions, business firms have followed labor unions in setting up political action committees (PACs) to collect and distribute funds. A firm or professional association forms a PAC, which then solicits contributions from stockholders (or members) and executives or managers and parcels out the money to favored candidates. By 1991 there were more than 4500 PACs in the United States, and several hundred were active in Texas.

A *Houston Chronicle* study of PAC activity in the 1986 elections found that these groups contributed $4.7 million to Texas legislators, or 61 percent of the cash raised by the lawmakers during the election season.[9] Huge contributions were channeled to powerful members. House Speaker Gib Lewis, who faced a tough reelection campaign in Fort Worth, received $653,407 in special-interest money during 1986, or 96 percent of all the contributions he received. A number of other legislators received up to $250,000 in PAC money. As a consequence of PAC activity, state elections are increasingly not just contests between candidates and political parties, but PACs versus PACs. That pattern was evident in the 1990 State Senate District 11 contest where incumbent Chet Brooks spent $600,000 to fend off a Democratic primary challenge from State Representative Lloyd Criss who also spent $600,000. Most of Brooks's money came from the medical doctors, defense lawyers, and insurance interests. Criss was largely funded by the trial lawyers.

Critics of this new pattern of campaign finance worry that monied interests may be buying privileged positions in our state and national political systems. John Hildreth, Texas director of Common Cause, argues there should be meaningful limits imposed on special-interest contributions. In Hildreth's view, "the more we rely in our political process on special interests, PACs, the less control citizens have over the political process."[10] An underlying problem with growing PAC funding of elections is public accountability. Political action committee contributions have to be reported when the amount is $100 or more, but very few voters follow such reports closely, and there is little public understanding of which PACs are backing particular candidates. Compounding the accountability problem is the fact that many PACs have innocuous names that disguise the interests they represent. For example, very few voters know that TEXPAC represents the Texas Medical Association, or that LIFT is the political action arm for Texas trial lawyers.

When elections are scheduled on constitutional amendments or local issues, interest groups often become directly involved in campaigning for one side or the other. Horse racing interests spent over $1 million dollars securing passage of a 1987 amendment allowing pari-mutuel wagering in Texas. The Houston Chamber of Commerce and religious right groups squared off against the Houston Gay and Lesbian Political Caucus in a heated 1985 referendum on employment rights in the city (the gay-backed position lost). And in Corpus Christi, pro-life groups, backed by the local Roman Catholic bishop, forced a charter election proposing that human life begins at conception. They were countered by Citizens United for Charter Integrity, and the proposed change was voted down 62 percent to 38 percent.[11]

MASS PROPAGANDIZING

Groups use mass propagandizing to influence public opinion in the hope this will result in some desired political action. A classic, though unsuccessful, example of this approach was the American Medical Association's radio and television campaign of the early 1960s against federal Medicare legislation.

Mass propagandizing requires extensive use of mass media. Sometimes advocacy groups get free access, as on radio talk shows or TV interviews, but these opportunities are limited and often unavailable to those pressing for specific policies. This means mass propagandizing usually requires the use of expensive paid media. Groups with resources thus have more options in this area than others. Most can afford continuing programs to improve their public image. The National Rifle Association, for example, placed a series of "We Are the NRA" ads in Texas magazines in the late 1980s. The advertisements profiled, in flattering tones, individual members of this powerful interest group. Their opponents bought counterads in Houston and Dallas newspapers featuring Sarah Brady, wife of former White House press secretary James Brady. Mrs. Brady argues for controls on handguns like the one John Hinckley purchased in Dallas just before shooting President Reagan and her husband (who remains severely disabled) in April 1981.

Groups occasionally use direct mail to promote their cause. In 1989 a pro-life organization mailed a graphic anti-abortion tabloid to several hundred thousand households in Houston.

The impact of such efforts is questionable. Polls taken before and after the anti-abortion mailing in Houston showed no movement in public opinion (which tends to be pro-choice in the Houston metropolitan area). Given the difficulties of changing minds, and the great costs of media advertising, interest groups in Texas use mass propaganda techniques sparingly.

Litigation

Americans have become a very litigious people. We have thousands of judges, hundreds of thousands of lawyers, and millions of pending lawsuits clogging a massive judicial system. Almost every important political dispute eventually ends up in the courts. The NAACP pioneered the national use of litigation to secure interest-group objectives by bringing a long series of challenges against segregation laws and practices in the various states. Following the national trend, Texas groups have increasingly turned to the courts to resolve political issues. Sometimes they win, as was the case with black-supported challenges to many aspects of Texas election laws and with pro-choice groups' assault on the Texas statute outlawing abortions that was overturned by the U.S. Supreme Court in *Roe* v. *Wade* (1973). Sometimes they lose, as was the case with an initial challenge to the state's system of financing public schools that was rejected by the U.S. Supreme Court in 1971 *(Rodriquez* v. *San Antonio Independent School District).*

Losers can try again, as the school finance case demonstrates. Rebuffed in the federal courts, Mexican-American plaintiffs brought suit in state courts in the late 1980s and eventually won a unanimous verdict from the Texas Supreme Court in January 1991 holding that the state's system of funding public schools can no longer depend on local property tax values.

Seeking a solution to political problems via litigation has disadvantages. It takes time, some financial backing, legal expertise, and reasonably good cases (courts require real cases to make rulings; hypothetical situations are of no value). And there is no assurance that those who bring matters into court will prevail. Still, there are notable advantages, particularly to groups that have standing in many constitutional areas (e.g., blacks), to groups that are unpopular (e.g., gay political associations), or to those who have already been rejected by nonjudicial decision makers in the political system.

Unorthodox Tactics

Interest groups use tactics that are available to them. And what is available depends on the nature of the group and the context in which it is operating. Groups, such as the Texas Brewers Association, that possess ample material resources and enjoy access to elected political leaders are well suited for lobbying. Those that have high community standing and sufficient resources, as does the Texas Medical Association, may well rely on a media campaign to generate favorable public opinion. The Texas AFL-CIO invests its personnel in electioneering.

However, there are groups very much interested in policy outcomes and political decisions that do not enjoy abundant material resources, access to political leaders, high community standing, or considerable numbers. Their situation dictates the use of unconventional tactics. Some of these tactics strain the bounds of legality; others are clearly illegal.

Historically, extralegal or illegal tactics are not new in Texas politics. Populist farmers of the late nineteenth century sometimes resorted to violence against their visible enemies, the railroads and the banks. The various Ku Klux Klan organizations that appeared in Texas after the 1870s had little compunction about breaking laws when it suited their purposes. Labor unions in Texas, as elsewhere, have relied on picketing, boycotts, and occasional violence in securing their position in the state.

In the 1960s reliance on unconventional political tactics increased in Texas, as in the rest of the country. Organizations or groups of college students, poor people, blacks, Mexican-Americans, and others often felt they could have no influence on state or local political decisions if they relied only on socially acceptable methods. So unorthodox means were utilized. Mothers of dependent children receiving welfare disrupted operations in county welfare offices around the state to protest a cutback in their monthly allocations. College students in Austin had to be forcibly removed from trees that were to be cut so a football stadium could be enlarged. Mexican-American high-school students in Crystal City staged a school walkout to dramatize opposition to school policies that favored the Anglo minority in the community. The Black Panther party in Houston announced it had "liberated" an area in the Third Ward ghetto and warned city police not to enter the section. This led to a confrontation with the police in which one Panther leader was killed and others were wounded.

As these examples indicate, most of the groups using unorthodox tactics in the 1960s were on the liberal or left side of the political spectrum. In the 1970s and 1980s, the use of radical tactics spread across the political spectrum. Texas farmers, pressed by falling agricultural prices and foreclosures, staged disruptive "tractorcades" around the Capitol in Austin. Pro-life Texans harassed persons entering Planned Parenthood facilities and picketed the homes of physicians who performed abortions. Religious conservatives showed little respect for the "sacred property rights" of X-rated bookstores and movie-house owners.

The pendulum may be swinging back to the left in the 1990s. Act-Up Against AIDs has used aggressive tactics to demand more public response to the growing toll from this epidemic. When U.S. forces engaged Iraq in 1991, peace demonstrations on a scale not seen since 1972 were held in Austin and other Texas cities.

THE IMPACT OF GROUP POLITICS IN TEXAS

The preceding sections should have convinced the reader that there are many political groups active in Texas and that they rely on a variety of methods to influence the political system. The important question remains: What difference do interest groups make in Texas politics? Would things be substantially different if such associations did not exist, did not enter the political arena? An answer can be sought in two ways: first, by looking at the specific impact groups have on particular decisions; second, by assessing the overall effect of group activity on public policy in Texas.

In the first instance, one usually proceeds by examining the track record of lobbying groups because their activities are fairly visible. A problem here, as mentioned earlier, is that most groups are prone to exaggerate their own signifi- cance. For example, after the 1973 legislative session, Common Cause of Texas claimed credit for the enactment of a number of "reform" measures, including lobby-control legislation, campaign financial disclosure, an ethics bill, an open meetings law, and legislation providing for public access to government records. Given the mood of the legislature that year and the commitments of the speaker of the house, it is likely most of this legislation would have passed without the assistance of Common Cause. At the other end of the spectrum, the Texas Association of Business releases a list after each session of the bills it killed that were inimical to its members' interests. Again, most of these measures would have likely failed irrespective of specific lobby pressures.

Perhaps the best way to get a reading on the relative clout of specific groups in the legislative process is to see what transpires when there is a head-on collision between lobbies on an issue on which most legislators have not formed a prior opinion. An example of such a clash in the 1977 session was the slurry pipeline fight between the railroads and private utilities. The issue was whether the rail- roads would be forced to give the right-of-way to a pipeline from Colorado that would bring crushed coal, mixed with water, to power plants in Texas. Railroads currently haul this coal, and they would not voluntarily allow competing pipe- lines to cross their property. After one of the most spirited lobby efforts in recent years, the utilities prevailed over the railroad association. In 1989 a coalition of business groups, medical doctors, and insurance interests pushed through major revisions in workers' compensation law that were bitterly opposed by trial lawyers and organized labor.

Examining such cases can be instructive, but too-close attention to detail can obscure the general role of interest groups in the state. The basic point to keep in mind is that *the generally conservative, status quo forces in Texas enjoy an overwhelming advantage in group politics.* These forces are rooted in the business and high-status associations of the state. They are highly organized, employ skilled political operatives, possess unrivaled financial resources, and have access to virtually all policymakers in state government.

These privileged groups do not have to contend with effective counterforces, given the weakness of organized labor and public interest associations. They are further advantaged because they are usually cast in the role of defending existing policy or practice. The American and Texas political systems, with their great complexity, favor those who want to block, rather than initiate, new policies. Established groups in Texas basically want to preserve the low tax–low service state, to keep economic regulation at a minimum, and to make sure that such regulation that is required continues to be in the best interests of those being regulated.

The success of these groups is reflected in the broad outlines of public policy in Texas. The cost of living for middle- and upper-income Texans is among the lowest in the country, primarily because of the favorable tax treatment such individuals receive. Comparative assessments usually rate Texas as one of the most hospitable states in the country for business and industry. This is reflected by the fact that more insurance companies are chartered in Texas than in any other state. Texas was also the last of the 50 states to establish a commission to regulate private utilities. That delay may have been no great loss, since most of the already existing 200 boards or commissions in Texas have been "captured" by the industry they are supposed to regulate. An example of such is provided by the Railroad Commission, which has regulated the oil and gas industry since the 1930s. The Commission has always sought to maintain a close and friendly relationship with the industry. This is hardly surprising since it started its regulatory activities at the behest of oil and gas companies that wanted production controlled to prevent price fluctuations rather than in response to some general public need.

There are a few counterexamples of organized group successes on behalf of noneconomic elites in Texas. MALDEF's court victories have been mentioned. And in San Antonio, the COPS group (Communities Organized for Public Service) has forced local business and public officials to deal with some of the pressing needs of the poor Mexican-American neighborhoods in that city. These occasional exceptions do not, however, detract from the fundamental reality that public policies in Texas are tailored to the needs of the business and corporate interests within the state. The result, as Neal R. Peirce and Jerry Hagstrom concluded in *The Book of America: Inside 50 States Today,* is that "Texas political life has been directed by a single moneyed establishment. In no other state has the control been so direct and unambiguous."[12]

CONCLUSIONS

Twenty years ago, E. E. Schattschneider, a respected analyst of American politics, took issue with the pluralist view that all segments of the population in the United States are represented through interest group politics.

> The vice of the groupist theory is that it conceals the most significant aspects of the system. The flaw in the pluralist heaven is that the heavenly chorus sings with a strong upper-class accent. Probably about 90 percent of the people cannot get into the pressure system.[13]

The general tendencies Schattschneider pointed to are unusually manifest in Texas. Electoral participation is low in the state, and it too is biased toward upper-class and conservative interests. Political parties, organizations that Schattschneider thought were essential counters to the class bias of group politics, are weak in Texas. Nor is effective political power vested in the hands of elected public officials in the state.

What this adds up to is a situation that gives organized interests unusual influence. Political leaders must have support for themselves and their policies, and such support is most readily available in Texas from established economic interest groups. Public policy with regard to taxing, spending, and apportioning the benefits of government has long reflected that reality and likely will continue to do so for the foreseeable future.

The severe economic problems Texas experienced in the 1980s deeply affected interest groups. With the state facing difficult budget choices, groups dependent on state spending (schoolteachers, highway contractors, state employees) mobilized strong efforts to protect their share of public resources. On the other side of the budget crisis, the need for billions of dollars in additional revenues to replace declining oil and gas receipts forced current and potential tax-paying groups to become more politically active.

The hard choices (basically, to cut state services or raise taxes) have produced some shifts in traditional political alignments. During the long and bitter 1987 and 1989 legislative budget battles, the case for raising state taxes was most forcefully made by conservative business leaders like H. Ross Perot. He and other corporate executives had become convinced that Texas's long-term economic future required more, not less, public investment in education and other state services. Labor and liberal groups that led the charge for more state revenues in the 1950s and 1960s have become less significant in the late 1980s and early 1990s.

NOTES

1. This thesis is fully developed in Mancur Olson, *The Logic of Collective Action* (Cambridge, Mass.: Harvard University Press, 1965).
2. See Robert Salisbury, "An Exchange Theory of Interest Groups," *Midwest Journal of Political Science* 13 (February 1969): 1–32; also James Q. Wilson, *Political Organizations* (New York: Basic Books, 1977).
3. Charles E. Lindblom, *Politics and Markets* (New York: Basic Books, 1977), p. 5.
4. See Kenneth D. Wald, *Religion and Politics in the United States* (New York: St. Martin's, 1987), pp. 182–219; also A. James Reichley, *Religion in American Public Life* (Washington, D.C.: Brookings, 1985), pp. 311–331.
5. Reichley, *Religion in American Public Life,* pp. 315–317.
6. Roberto Suro, "Powerful Texas Politician is Indicted," *New York Times,* December 29, 1991, Sec. 1, p. 7.
7. *Ibid.*
8. Paul Burka, "Is the Legislature for Sale?" *Texas Monthly,* February, 1991, p. 122.
9. R. G. Ratcliffe, "PACs Put Up $4.7 Million to Push Issues," *Houston Chronicle,* January 4, 1987, Sec. 1, p. 1, 29.
10. *Ibid.,* p. 29.
11. "Anti-Abortion Measure Rejected in Corpus Christi," *New York Times,* January 21, 1991, Sec. 1, p. 8.
12. Neil R. Peirce and Jerry Hagstrom, *The Book of America: Inside 50 States Today* (New York: Norton, 1983), p. 625.
13. E. E. Schattschneider, *The Semi-Sovereign People: A Realist's View of Democracy in America* (Hinsdale, Ill.: Dryden Press, 1975), pp. 34–35.

chapter 5

The State Legislature

Citizens and lobbyists in the gallery observe a session of the Texas House of Representatives.

The primary task of the legislature, viewed from a traditional, legal perspective, is to "legislate," to enact statutory laws governing the people and territory over which it has jurisdiction. It is more useful, however, to describe the primary task of the legislature as participation in the formation of public policy. This is so because the form and content of public policies depend not only on statutes passed by the legislature but also on actions by the governor, administrative agencies, and the courts. All help shape public policies, which are the actual courses of action followed by government on topics of concern, such as the regulation of petroleum production, the licensing of barbers, or the rights of the criminally accused. Moreover, there are also many unofficial participants in the policy-formation process, including political parties, pressure groups, the communications media, and private citizens.

In addition to policy formation, the Texas legislature may variously engage in a number of other activities. These include supervising the administrative agencies, approving gubernatorial appointments, conducting legislative investigations, impeaching or otherwise removing executive officials from office, proposing amendments to the state constitution and approving or disapproving amendments to the U.S. Constitution, handling congressional districting within the state, and deciding election contests for legislative seats. In 1981, for the first time in its history, the House of Representatives voted to deny a seat to the winner (a Republican) of a contested seat on the ground that there were voting irregularities in the election. The person denied the seat was subsequently reelected in a special election held to fill the vacancy.

Much has been written in recent years concerning the decline in importance of state legislatures and, concomitantly, the shift of initiative and power in legislative activity to the chief executive. It is indeed probably fair and accurate to depict the state governor, like the president, as playing the role of "chief legislator" in the legislative process. However, whatever the actual relationship between the governor and legislature in a given state, and whatever one might think the relationship should be, it is only the legislature that, in the final analysis, can enact laws or legislation. The governor and others can recommend and urge the enactment of new laws, taxes, or expenditures, but only the legislature can enact them into law, into legitimate and binding public policy. These generalizations are especially apt in Texas, where the legislature is widely regarded as being the dominant branch of state government.

The power to enact legislation is highly important in a modern society, especially when one recalls the discussion in Chapter 1 of the wide range of matters dealt with by the state. In 1989, for example, the legislature passed 1317 bills in the regular session and 46 more in two called sessions. The governor vetoed 53, with the other 1310 becoming law. Their subject matter ranged from the important (creation of the Texas Department of Criminal Justice, regulation and aid for *colonias,* and revision of public school finance) to minor changes in local government authority.[1] In all, what the legislature does or does not do is of much consequence for the people of Texas.

LEGISLATIVE PERSONNEL

Representation

The Constitution of 1876 set the maximum size of the Texas House of Representatives at 150 and the Texas Senate at 31, with the members to serve two-year and four-year terms, respectively. In comparison with other states, the Texas legislature appears about average in size. Membership of state senates ranges from 17 in Nevada to 67 in Minnesota, while the range for lower houses is from 35 in Delaware to 400 in New Hampshire.

Little is known conclusively about the significance of the size factor, but there is no shortage of theory regarding it. For example, a larger legislature will provide better representation of the people, a smaller legislature will be more efficient, and so on. A long-standing generalization in social science literature holds that the larger an organization or group, the more likely it is to be controlled or dominated by a few of its members. This seems borne out by the Texas legislature; most observers would agree that the House has been more tightly controlled by a leadership group than the Senate. In larger groups, relationships tend to become more formal and hierarchical.

The *geographical district* (an electoral unit based on the number of people living in a defined geographical area, such as a county or portion thereof) has been the standard device for selection of members of the Texas legislature. As in the rest of the nation, the belief (but not always the practice) has been that these districts should be roughly equal in population.[2] Such alternative schemes of representation as *functional representation* (whereby representatives are selected by specified social and economic groups) or *proportional representation* (whereby each political party gets legislative representation in ratio to its share of the total popular vote in an area) have never been used at the state level in the United States. In establishing geographical districts, Texas and the other states have usually followed the boundary lines of counties and other existing governmental units.

The Texas Constitution of 1876 stated that members of the House were to be elected from districts as nearly equal in population as possible. It also provided that senators were to be elected from districts having an equal number of qualified voters, with the limitation that no county could ever have more than one senator. In nineteenth-century Texas these rules, and practices thereunder, permitted substantial equality in representation on the basis of the "one person-one vote" criterion. But as the state increased in population and became more urbanized, the one-senator limit came to have a restrictive impact on populous counties. Then in 1936 the constitution was amended to limit the number of representatives to the House from urban counties. No county could have more than seven representatives until its population reached 700,000; a county that exceeded that figure would receive one additional representative for each additional 100,000 population.

These constitutional limitations, legislative failure to redistrict after every federal decennial population census as required, and refusal of the legislature to provide as much equality under the rules as possible when it did act all resulted in substantial disparities in the populations of legislative districts. Thus, in 1961 the populations of senatorial districts ranged from 157,000 to 1,243,000. The four most populous counties (Harris, Dallas, Bexar, and Tarrant) contained 35.7 percent of the state's population but elected only 4 senators, or 12.9 percent of the Senate. Another example: In accordance with the limitation on House representatives, Harris County had 12 representatives even though on a strict population basis it was entitled to 19. (Ideally, in 1961 each House member would have represented about 64,000 people, a figure obtained by dividing the state's population of 9,580,000 by 150.) In short, the situation was one of substantial inequality in legislative representation, with urban areas being underrepresented and rural areas overrepresented—again using equal population size of districts, or the one person-one vote criterion, as the standard of judgment.

The Texas situation was not unique. Overrepresentation of rural areas was a nationwide phenomenon, and indeed was much more severe in some other states, such as Florida and Georgia. In no state, it should be noted, were urban areas overrepresented. Many complaints were registered against this condition.

It was argued that rural overrepresentation made state legislatures unresponsive to the problems and needs of urban areas, contributed to conservatism in public policy, gave an unfair electoral advantage to the political party or party faction dominant in rural areas, produced cynicism and distrust toward state government, and was generally unfair.[3] Those who benefited from rural overrepresentation were neither much disturbed by the situation nor convinced by the arguments levied against it. Redress would have required giving up some of their power, and those who possess power rarely yield it willingly.

For many years the efforts of those seeking to reform this situation were unavailing. In 1946 the U.S. Supreme Court held that legislative reapportionment was a "political issue" and hence was not something to be decided by the courts.[4] Other courts followed this lead, and the state legislatures were unwilling to act, being controlled by majorities that benefited from or approved of rural overrepresentation. Then in 1962 a breakthrough occurred for the proponents of reform. The U.S. Supreme Court, in deciding *Baker* v. *Carr,* overturned its 1946 rule and held that state legislative malapportionment raised an issue of equal protection (or treatment) of the laws under the Fourteenth Amendment and could properly be heard by the federal courts. (*Baker* v. *Carr* originated in Tennessee, where the state legislature had not been reapportioned since 1901 despite a constitutional provision requiring that it be done every ten years.[5])

As a consequence, many cases involving legislative malapportionment were rapidly brought to the federal courts. Two years later, in another case, the Court ruled that both houses of state legislatures had to be apportioned according to population (i.e., one person-one vote). The Court specifically rejected the federal analogy, or "little federal system," in which one house of the state legislature is based on population and the other on geographic units in the fashion of the U.S. Congress.

These decisions were brought home to Texas in 1965 in the case of *Kilgarlin* v. *Martin,* which originated in Harris County. A federal district court in Houston declared unconstitutional the provisions of the Texas Constitution that limit representation for urban areas, and the legislature was in effect directed to reapportion itself on a population basis. Its first effort at reapportionment in 1965 contained some substantial disparities in House districts and subsequently had to be revised in 1967 to meet constitutional requirements. (*Districting* refers to the drawing of the boundary lines of districts, while *apportionment* involves the allocation of representatives to districts. Although these terms are often used interchangeably with no great intellectual hurt, it is useful to keep in mind the two types of activity involved.)

Equality in representation has now become an established feature of the American constitutional system. It creates little controversy, unlike the situation of a decade ago. Determining the boundaries of districts, however, is still a matter of much controversy.

Redistricting in the 1970s and 1980s: Law and Politics

In 1971 the legislature was confronted with the task of having to redistrict itself to reflect the population shifts revealed by the 1970 census. It is traditional for each house of the Texas legislature to redistrict itself without interference by the other. The Senate, for reasons that are not fully clear, never got around to redistricting itself before the 1971 legislative session was adjourned. The House redistricting was controlled by Speaker Gus Mutscher and his allies, who drew new district lines to the electoral disadvantage of as many members as possible of the "Dirty Thirty," a rather strange alliance of liberal Democrats, Republicans, and a few conservative Democrats who steadfastly opposed the speaker. The chairman of the House committee handling legislative redistricting was later quoted as saying that he had done his "dead-level best to eliminate liberal House members" and prevent reelection of many of the Dirty Thirty.[6] In the process many counties were split between legislative districts.

The House Redistricting Act of 1971 was immediately challenged in the state supreme court by some Republican party officials on the grounds that it violated the Texas Constitution by unnecessarily dividing counties between legislative districts; their contention was upheld by the court.[7] Subsequently, the court ruled that new House districts would have to be drawn by the state Legislative Redistricting Board.[8]

As a consequence of the House's unconstitutional action and the Senate's inaction, redistricting of both houses became the responsibility of the Legislative Redistricting Board. Authorized by a constitutional amendment in 1949, the board is composed of the lieutenant governor, speaker of the house, attorney general, comptroller of public accounts, and commissioner of the general land office. If the legislature does not complete the task of redistricting in the first regular legislative session following the federal decennial population census, the board takes over the task. The year 1971 was the first in which action by the board was required; in 1951 and 1961 the mere threat of board action was apparently sufficient to produce legislative action.

The board, which was dominated in its proceedings by Lieutenant Governor Ben Barnes, had little difficulty in producing a redistricting plan for the Senate. It protected the seats of most incumbent senators, a not uncommon practice in legislative redistricting. For the House, the board devised a plan providing for 11 multimember districts electing a total of 60 representatives and 90 single-member districts. Harris County was awarded single-member districts, as was demanded by most of the county's legislative delegation, while the other populous counties were given multimember districts.

Some words of explanation are in order here on the use of single-member and multimember districts. The members of the Senate have always been elected from single-member districts. The House used a combination of single-member and multimember districts; in recent decades, as the state's population became concentrated in a few counties, it relied more heavily on multimember districts and the place system. In a multimember district, a candidate ran for a particular seat, designated as Place 1, Place 2, and so on on the ballot, and each voter could vote for a candidate for each place in the district. To illustrate: Under the redistricting board's House plan, Dallas County, with its population of 1,327,321, was set up as a single district with 18 representatives (or one for each 74,645 persons, which was the ideal figure for a representative on the basis of the 1970 census). In the 1972 election Dallas County voters were entitled to vote for a candidate for each of the 18 seats (or places). The constituency of each representative was the entire county.

The use of multimember districts became increasingly controversial. Critics contended that multimember districts restricted electoral competition by necessitating large campaign expenditures and made districts so large that representatives could not be really responsive to their constituents. Further, the majority that elected one representative could elect all of them. This had the effect of denying representation to ethnic and political groups—blacks, Mexican-Americans, Republicans, liberal Democrats—who might be minorities on a countywide basis but would be majorities in some residential areas. The defenders of multimember districts contended that such districts promoted strong, united, civic-minded legislative delegations who would act for the good of the entire community. Moreover, single-member districts would polarize counties along racial lines.[9] In practice, multimember districts favored the election of conservative Democrats, and they usually controlled the redistricting process, which thus became a source of political power.

The redistricting board's 1971 House plan was promptly challenged in the federal courts by Republicans, liberal Democrats, blacks, and Mexican-Americans on two grounds: (1) Multimember districts unconstitutionally discriminated against blacks and Mexican-Americans; the districts for Dallas and Bexar counties were especially criticized. (2) The deviation in population size was too great to be constitutional. With an ideal size of 74,645, districts ranged from 71,597 to 78,943 per representative, or from 5.8 percent overrepresentation to 4.1 percent underrepresentation. In January 1972, a three-judge federal district court agreed with both contentions, ordered single-member districts immediately for Dallas and Bexar counties, and directed the legislature to redistrict the entire House at its 1973 session.[10]

The state appealed the district court's ruling to the U.S. Supreme Court, which partly upheld and partly overruled the lower court.[11] The deviation in the population size of House districts was ruled not sufficient to make the redistricting unconstitutional because, in the Court's view, the constitutional standards for state legislature districts are not as strict as those for the U.S. Congress. (In another case, the Court upheld a districting scheme for Virginia that involved a population variance of 16 percent.[12]) The Court also said that multimember districts are not unconstitutional per se but must be shown to have a discriminatory effect. To sustain a claim of discrimination, it is not enough to show that the racial groups allegedly discriminated against do not hold legislative seats in proportion to their voting potential; rather, it is necessary to show that the potential process leading to nomination and election is not equally open to participation by particular racial groups. In sustaining the district court, the Supreme Court held that the lower court's order directing the abandonment of multimember districts for Dallas and Bexar counties was justified "in the light of the history of political discrimination against Negroes and Mexican-Americans residing, respectively, in those counties and the residual effects of such discrimination upon these groups."[13] The case was remanded to the federal district court for further action.

On the basis of the Supreme Court's decisions, single-member districts, as drawn by the federal district court, were put into effect in Dallas and Bexar counties, as well as Harris County, for the 1972 elections. No action was taken concerning the constitutionality of multimember districts for the other nine counties, although the district court did retain jurisdiction over the matter.

The Texas legislature, in its 1973 session, took up the question of House redistricting but adjourned without taking any action. Conflict existed over what the legislature should do. Some especially wanted single-member districts for Tarrant County (Fort Worth), which—with a nine-member House delegation— seemed especially likely to be the subject of future court action; others wanted single-member districts on a statewide basis. Liberals were not strongly in favor of legislative action, believing that redistricting would be more in accord with their interests if done by the judiciary. As a consequence of the legislature's inaction, the judicial proceedings concerning the constitutionality of representative districts were pushed toward completion. In January 1974, the federal district court ruled that multimember districts for most counties that still had them were unconstitutional because they discriminated against the electoral opportunities of minorities.[14] Then in 1975 the Texas legislature enacted a law providing for the election of all 150 House members by single-member districts. Although multimember districts still survive in some other states, they now are a relic of the past in Texas.

In 1981 the legislature was again confronted with the task of drawing new legislative districts for the 31 Senate and 150 House members, on the basis of the 1980 census. This touched off a major struggle, as various interests contested for advantage. Liberals, conservatives, Democrats, Republicans, blacks, Mexican-Americans, incumbent legislators—these and more were involved. Two legislative "rules of thumb" gave some guidance to the struggle: The House and Senate were each responsible for drawing up their new districts, and, to the largest extent possible, the interests of incumbent legislators in reelection should be protected. A third consideration was imposed on the redistricting process by the national Voting Rights Act: Changes in election rules must not discriminate against or dilute the voting strength of blacks and Mexican-Americans. A fourth consideration was partisan advantage. Whereas previously the Republicans had had little impact on redistricting, by 1981 their numbers had increased to where they were of importance, especially in the House. Moreover, once redistricting legislation was passed, it would have to secure the approval of Republican Governor Clements. A fifth consideration, of course, was that districts would have to be approximately equal in population size to square with the one person-one vote standard. The outcomes of the redistricting struggle were sets of House and Senate districts that provided some additional representation for minorities (but not as much as some preferred) and urban areas; tried to protect the seats of most Democratic incumbents; and left the Republicans unhappy, as the plan sought to minimize their future gains in representation.

The legislature's redistricting bills quickly ran into difficulty. The Senate redistricting plan was vetoed by the governor, who said it was unfair to Republicans and minorities. The House districting bill was signed into law by the governor, only to be challenged in the state courts by minority groups. Ultimately the

Texas Supreme Court declared the House plan unconstitutional because it need-lessly disregarded county boundary lines in setting up new districts. These guber-natorial and judicial actions meant that round two in the redistricting struggle would be handled by the Legislative Redistricting Board.

The Board, which was composed of five Democratic state officials, com-pleted action on new districts in October 1981. Challenges to the Board plan were quickly raised in the state and federal courts and before the U.S. Department of Justice. In January 1982, the Department of Justice held that the new districting plans violated the Voting Rights Act because they diluted the political strength of Mexican-Americans and blacks. This argument had been presented to the Department of Justice by, among others, the Texas secretary of state, who was a Republican official.

Round three in the districting struggle was played out before a three-judge federal district court (all three judges were Democrats) as a consequence of a suit against the districting plans filed by a group of Republican state legislators and joined by the Mexican-American Legal Defense and Education Fund. (This suit was in progress at the same time as the proceeding before the U.S. Department of Justice.) The federal court in March held that the importance of holding the state's primary elections as scheduled on May 1 overrode the objections of the Department of Justice to the Legislative Redistricting Board's districting plans. The court, however, did go on to redraw some of the districts' lines and to hold that the modified plans would be in effect only for the 1982 elections.

As a consequence of their ruling, round four in the districting struggle occurred when the legislature met in the spring of 1983. This round was affected by some new considerations. Republican Governor Clements had been replaced by Democratic Governor White. The Republican secretary of state was also gone. Finally, in 1981 the Voting Rights Act had been changed to make it easier for minorities to challenge districting plans. Where previously intent to discriminate had to be proved, now it was adequate to show that the *effect* of new districts was discriminatory. The legislature made changes in the boundaries of some House and Senate districts during its 1983 session. Whether these would be sufficient to protect the districting plans against judicial challenges was not clear.

Round five occurred when the Mexican-American Legal and Defense Fund (MALDEF) challenged the Dallas County districts on the grounds that they discriminated against Hispanic voters. In January 1984, a three-judge federal district court upheld the legality of the Dallas districts. This decision was not appealed by MALDEF, and the redistricting struggle ended.

Legislative redistricting in 1991 was somewhat less contentious than previ-ously because the rules governing the process were more settled and because the Democrats were in full control. There were some sources of controversy, how-ever. For one, there were questions about the accuracy of the 1990 census figures. Also, there were efforts by Hispanic groups to secure more urban representation; the Republicans wanted more districts created in urban areas, where the most population growth had occurred and where they were politically strongest; and incumbents generally wanted to protect their chances for reelection.

The redistricting bill adopted by the legislature compressed Republican voters into the fewest possible districts. When two incumbent legislators were "paired" in a district, it usually involved two Republicans, or a Democrat with an apparent edge over a Republican. Nineteen counties were divided between House districts. Also, Hispanic groups thought some district lines were drawn to their disadvantage.

The governor permitted the redistricting bill to become law without her signature, although some Hispanic organizations had urged a veto. This did not mark the end of the redistricting struggle, however. Lawsuits challenging the constitutionality of the law were initiated by the Republican party and Hispanic groups. Approval by the Department of Justice under the Voting Rights Act was also needed. For these reasons, there was uncertainty as to whether the legislature's handiwork would prevail.

In sum, this discussion indicates that legislative redistricting is at once a legal, technical, and political task. It arouses strong feelings among various political participants because it involves the allocation of political power. In the future it will likely become more partisan given the political strength of the Republican party.

As noted earlier, many contentions have been made concerning the past impact of rural overrepresentation and multimember districts on state politics and policies. What, now, have been the consequences of reapportionment and redistricting in line with the one person-one vote criterion and the exclusive use of single-member districts? One clear result is that urban counties now have more legislative representation than they had under the old system. In 1987, six populous counties (Harris, Dallas, Bexar, Tarrant, El Paso, and Travis) elected 71 members (46 percent) of the House.

Second, representation has been brought into line with the ethical standard of equality of representation by population, which many people have regarded as proper and desirable in itself, regardless of other effects. Third, single-member districts in large counties have contributed to the election of more black, Mexican-American, and Republican representatives. Those districts are the primary reason, for example, for the increase in black representatives from 2 in 1971 to 14 in 1979. Fourth, in populous counties, single-member districts have contributed to increased electoral competition, both in primary and general elections.[15] Fifth, so far as the nature of public policy is concerned, no drastic changes from past practices and policies appear to have been made by the legislature since 1967. Some before-and-after studies are needed to indicate with some precision what, if anything, has changed. It is our impression, however, that as of now the legislature has not become markedly more responsive to urban needs and problems.

Membership

The formal constitutional qualifications for membership in the legislature can be easily stated. To be eligible for the Texas House, one must be 21 years of age, a citizen, and a resident of his or her district for one year and the state for two years. For the Texas Senate, the standards are 26 years of age, citizenship, and one year of residence in the district and five in the state. These are only the formal, minimal qualifications for legislative office, and few would contend that all who meet them really have an equal chance to be elected to the legislature. Many are eliminated by the unstated, informal qualifications that also exist. One formulation categorizes these informal qualifications under the headings of motivation, resources, and opportunity.[16] Some will in effect be disqualified because they are not motivated to seek a legislative seat, being uninterested in politics, unwilling to campaign for elective office, or whatever. Others who may be motivated may lack such necessary resources as money, time, or knowledge to campaign for office realistically. Still others may lack a meaningful opportunity to seek legislative office because of their socioeconomic characteristics. In many districts a person's race, sex, religion, or party affiliation may effectively disqualify him or her. For example, persons who are Republicans and who run for office as Republicans still operate at a decided disadvantage in many areas of the state, although change is occurring. Racial barriers severely limit the opportunity for blacks to gain office, and many people still do not regard politics as a proper sphere for women.

With respect to socioeconomic characteristics, the "typical" Texas legislator, like his counterpart in many other states, is a male, white, Anglo-Saxon Protestant—or WASP, to use the popular acronym. In 1991, of 181 members of the legislature, there were only 22 women, 13 blacks, and 24 Mexican-Americans. Sixty-five members were Republicans, which represented a substantial increase in their numbers from recent years. Over four-fifths were Protestants, and most were native-born Texans. Occupationally, lawyers were the largest group (about two-thirds of the Senate and one-third of the House), followed by businesspersons (including insurance and real estate agents) and farmers and ranchers. Industrial workers and union officials were scarce. Most of the legislators were between 30 and 45 years of age, with comparatively few under 30 or over 60. Most were also college graduates, with only a handful who had never attended college.

What is the significance of all this? For one thing, it indicates that the legislature is clearly not comprised of a cross-section of the state's population. Such groups as whites, Protestants, and persons with higher socioeconomic status are overrepresented in proportion to their numbers in society; while such groups as Catholics, blacks, women, and working-class people are underrepresented. Second, the data indicate that there are indeed informal qualifications for office. Other things being equal, a Texas-born, white, college-educated lawyer has a better chance of being elected to the legislature than does, for instance, a person born outside the state who has a high-school education and is employed in a factory. If he or she is a black or Mexican-American, the chances diminish even further. Third, its composition probably helps give a broadly "conservative" orientation to the legislature: Most legislators are "successful" according to existing social standards and have a "stake" in existing social and economic structures. Consequently, they are indisposed toward making sweeping or radical changes in the existing order of things.

There has often been a substantial turnover in the membership of the legislature from one session to another. This has been a persistent characteristic of most state legislatures. On the average, in a given session of the Texas state legislature a quarter to a third of the members will be serving their first term. The rate of turnover has usually been lower in the Texas Senate than in the Texas House, perhaps because of the longer term of office and greater prestige of Senate service and because many representatives view a House seat as a preliminary step toward another office.

The tenure (length of service) of members is fairly short, as the rate of turnover would lead one to predict. In a given session of the legislature, most members will have served six years or less, although senators tend to serve longer than representatives. In 1991 only a small fraction of the legislators had served ten years or longer. An exceptional case was Senator A. M. Aikin, Jr., of Paris, who served continuously in the legislature from 1933 until he retired in 1978.

Partly as a consequence of rather rapid turnover and short tenure, many members of the legislature may be viewed as "amateurs." They lack the experience in the complexities of legislative procedure and in the rough-and-tumble of legislative politics, the knowledge of legislative issues, and the contacts and friendships necessary to get things done—all of which are more likely to come with continued service in the legislature. This general condition probably serves to strengthen the position of the elected leadership, especially in the House, and of lobbyists, who are often quite knowledgeable about procedure and policy matters.

LEGISLATIVE STRUCTURE

Sessions and Compensation

The state constitution provides that the legislature will meet in a regular biennial session, to last no longer than 140 calendar days, beginning on the second Tuesday in January in odd-numbered years. A particular legislature runs for a term of two years. Since Texas entered the Union, these terms have been numbered consecutively; thus, the legislature organized for the two-year term beginning in January 1991 was officially designated the "Seventy-second Legislature."

Until the last decades of the nineteenth century, annual legislative sessions were the rule in the American states. However, growing public distrust of and dissatisfaction with the legislatures, which is well chronicled in histories of the late nineteenth and early twentieth centuries, led to the imposition of limits on the length and frequency of their sessions. A common notion was that the less time the legislature was in session, the less damage to the public welfare it could cause. (A cynical definition during this era held that an "honest" politician was one who, once bought, stayed bought.) By the mid-1940s only four states had annual legislative sessions. Since then the pendulum has swung in the opposite direction, and now nearly all of the states have annual sessions, although many continue to regulate their length. Constitutional amendments authorizing annual sessions for the Texas legislature were defeated soundly by the voters in 1969 and 1972, however. Some assert that the legislature cannot deal adequately with the state's needs and problems on a limited, biennial basis, but others argue that it indeed can and, further, that annual sessions would lead to unnecessary legislation and increased costs for operating the legislature.

In addition to its regular biennial sessions, the legislature can be called by the governor into any number of special sessions, each limited to 30 days' duration. During special sessions the legislature may consider only legislation relating to topics specified by the governor. Special sessions have been called during most of the biennial terms of the legislature since 1930, and their frequency has been increasing in recent years. During 1965–1990, 27 special sessions were held. Governor Mark White called special sessions in 1984, 1985, and 1986 to deal with the problems of educational reform, indigent health care, and the budget deficit, respectively. The divisive issues of workers' compensation and public school finance required two special sessions in 1989 and four special sessions in 1990, respectively, for their resolution. Many observers take the increasing use of special sessions as evidence that the legislature cannot adequately perform its work on a biennial basis.

The salaries of Texas legislators, which historically have been low, are specified in the state constitution. An amendment adopted in 1975 raised salaries to $7200 annually (up from $4800). Legislators also receive an expense allowance of $30 a day during regular and special sessions. Comparatively, among large urban states, Texas legislative salaries rank quite low. For example, in 1990, state legislators in New York, Michigan, and California received annual salaries of $57,500, $45,450, and $40,816, respectively.

Legislators also receive allowances, set by the memberships of the two houses, for staff, office, and other expenses. Texas was one of the first states to provide year-round staff assistance for individual legislators. House members are allocated $6500 a month during legislative sessions and $5500 a month when the legislature is not in session. Senators are permitted to spend up to $13,500 monthly on staff. These funds enable members to hire administrative assistants or secretaries, researchers, or other full- and part-time staff aides. Office space in the capitol building is also provided. This level of staff assistance helps legislators better meet the legislative, constituent, and other demands on their time.

Legislative Leaders

The principal leaders in the legislature are the presiding officers of the two houses: the speaker of the house and the lieutenant governor. Although they are selected in quite different ways, both have available a substantial range of formal powers and informal means by which they can seek to control and direct the actions of their respective houses. Included among their formal powers, which—it should be emphasized—are derived from rules adopted by a majority of each house, are the following:

1. Appointment of members to standing, special, and interim committees and designation of committee chairpersons.
2. Appointment of members to conference committees.
3. Acting as presiding officers, which includes interpretation of their house's rules and decisions on points of order, recognition of members who want to speak on the floor, the putting of motions to a vote and deciding voice votes, and so on.

4. Referral of bills to committees, which is especially significant when a bill comes within the jurisdiction of two or more committees.
5. Participation in debate and, for the speaker, voting on issues; the lieutenant governor can vote only in case of a tie.
6. Substantial control of the agendas of their houses, that is, determination of what matters will be considered when, if at all.

These two leaders also benefit from the prestige attached to the positions they hold. Although they do derive much influence from their official positions, their influence also depends importantly on how skillfully they use their formal powers, their ability to bargain with and persuade both influential and rank-and-file members, the confidence they are able to evoke in their leadership, and the ideological composition of their respective houses. The last item is especially important for the lieutenant governor. A conservative lieutenant governor will undoubtedly have more influence and power in dealings with a conservative rather than a liberal majority. During the last two decades, a period during which much has been written about the power of the lieutenant governor, this condition has prevailed. During the 1973 legislative session, Lieutenant Governor William Hobby, Jr., elected the previous fall as a reform candidate, early developed close relationships with the veteran, mostly conservative, senators who dominated the Senate. Among other things, this helped him protect his formal powers against an effort at reduction by some liberal senators. Over the years Hobby displayed much skill in sensing the moods of the Senate and was an effective and respected leader until he voluntarily retired in 1990.

The lieutenant governor is elected by the voters in a statewide election for a four-year term (as of 1974). Most lieutenant governors have served in the Senate prior to their election, Hobby being a recent exception. Historically, the lieutenant governor has not always been an influential legislative leader. Professor J. William Davis, a careful student of the office, states: "A weak lieutenant governor was anticipated by the framers of the Texas Constitution. . . ."[17] Even as late as the 1930s, it was considered a position of honor and prestige but not one of power and influence. During the 1940s and 1950s the office was transformed into one of substantial power, especially during the tenures of Allen Shivers and Ben Ramsey, although the processes by which this happened remain unexplained. Thus, the Texas lieutenant governor stands in sharp contrast to the vice president at the national level. Both preside over bodies to which they were not elected and of which they are not members. However, while the lieutenant governor has become a very influential legislative leader, the vice president is still essentially an outsider who has little impact on the operation of the U.S. Senate.

The speaker of the house is elected by the members of the Texas House at the beginning of each biennial session by majority vote on a public ballot. The formal election of a new speaker is usually the culmination of a lengthy campaign for the speakership and may only ratify what has already been determined by informal means. In 1969, for example, Representative Gus Mutscher had clearly lined up enough votes to win the speakership before the session met. The other candidates had no real chance to be elected. In 1972, however, when Rayford

Price was elected speaker at a special session following the resignation of Mutscher, the issue was in doubt until the formal House vote was taken.

Campaigns for the speakership usually begin at least two years before the time a candidate hopes to be elected and involve the expenditure of much time and many thousands of dollars. In the session preceding the one in which election will occur, candidates begin trying to obtain pledges of support from the present legislators. Since some of the legislators will not be in the legislature two years hence, speaker candidates may also involve themselves in the primary and general-election campaigns, seeking to help candidates favorable to their position to get elected and perhaps aiding the opposition of those who are unfavorable. The governor, lobbyists, pressure groups, and other political actors also become involved in the speakership contest because their political fortunes may be affected significantly by whoever is elected speaker. The important role played by the speaker in shaping House legislative action makes it clearly desirable to have a friend rather than an opponent in this position. It is not altruism that makes lobbies a major source of campaign funds for speaker candidates. Most persons selected as speaker since 1959 have served two terms or more, if they so chose.

An incumbent speaker, because of the powers and prerogatives of the office, has a great advantage when seeking reelection. Members will be reluctant to "cross" the speaker and support another candidate because of the adverse consequences that may befall them if that candidate loses. The fact that the speaker is chosen by a public roll call vote means that members must openly indicate their preference, which works to the incumbent's advantage. Representative Bill Clayton effectively used the power of the office, after his initial election in 1975, to win election to a then unprecedented four terms as speaker. After winning by a landslide in 1981, he announced he would not seek another term. This set off an intense campaign among several members to succeed him two years later. Representative Gibson Lewis, a conservative Democrat, was elected speaker by a large majority in 1983. Even before he made committee assignments for the 1983 session, he began collecting pledges of support from members for reelection in 1985. In 1991 he was elected to his fifth term as speaker.

Apart from the speaker and lieutenant governor, there are no other formally elected or designated leaders in the legislature. In each house, the presiding officer does have some trusted lieutenants—often referred to as "the team" or, less elegantly, "cronies"—who assist in the leadership role, as well as a number of staff aides. Several representatives act as floor leaders for the speaker, helping to ensure that things happen on the floor when the speaker wants them to happen (e.g., a motion being made at a propitious time or information being conveyed to supporters as to the speaker's position on a given issue) and to line up votes in support of the speaker's position. In both the House and Senate, the chairs of the powerful State Affairs committees will be close to the leadership, as will some of the other more influential committee chairpersons.

The Committee System

Much of the legislative work of the Texas legislature is handled by the permanent standing committees in the House and Senate. On the basis of reform rules adopted in the early 1970s, the number of Senate committees was drastically reduced from 27 to 9, and the number of House committees from 46 to 21. By 1989, however, Speaker Gib Lewis had increased the number of House committees to 36. Senate committees numbered 12. About a third of the committees in each house have permanent subcommittees that perform some of their legislative work. The committees in existence during the Seventy-first Legislature are listed in Table 5.1.

The size of House committees is set by the House rules, with most committees having 9 or 13 members. In the Senate, the determination of committee size is left to the discretion of the lieutenant governor when appointments are made.

Table 5.1   MEMBERSHIP OF TEXAS LEGISLATIVE COMMITTEES, 1989

House Committees		Senate Committees	
Agriculture and Livestock	9	Administration	12
Appropriations	23	Criminal Justice	7
Business and Commerce	9	Economic Development	11
Calendars	9	Education	11
Corrections	9	Finance	13
County Affairs	11	Health and Human Services	9
Criminal Jurisprudence	9	Intergovernmental Relations	11
Cultural and Historical Resources	9	Jurisprudence	7
Elections	9	Natural Resources	11
Energy	9	Nominations	7
Environmental Affairs	9	Rules	5
Financial Institutions	9	State Affairs	13
General Investigating	5		
Government Organization	9		
Higher Education	5		
House Administration	9		
Human Services	9		
Insurance	9		
Judicial Affairs	9		
Judiciary	9		
Labor and Employment Relations	9		
Liquor Regulations	9		
Local and Consent Calendars	9		
Natural Resources	9		
Public Education	9		
Public Health	9		
Public Safety	9		
Redistricting	9		
Retirement and Aging	9		
Rules and Resolutions	9		
Science and Technology	9		
State Affairs	13		
State, Federal, and International Relations	9		
Transportation	9		
Urban Affairs	11		
Ways and Means	13		

Source: Texas State Directory, 1989.

Their size ranges from 7 to 13. Along with the reduction in the early 1970s of the number of committees came a reduction in the number of committee assignments for legislators. House members are now limited to assignment on two committees, and they may chair no more than one committee each since 1981. This represents a substantial reduction from 1971, when committee assignments averaged 5 for House members and 11 for Senate members. This was criticized frequently as an impossible workload. It is not possible to say whether the reduction in committee workload has produced more careful and thorough committee action on legislation because of problems in measurement, but it is reasonable to assume that it should facilitate that end. A fact to be kept in mind here is that some committees have a much heavier workload than do others.

In making committee assignments, the presiding officers and their top aides may take a variety of factors into consideration: for example, whether the legislator is a friend or supporter of the presiding officer; the legislator's preferences for assignments and positions on major issues that may come before the legislature; whether the legislator is of the same ideological bent (liberal or conservative) as the presiding officer; the legislator's preferences and support of or opposition to lobbyists; the desire to maintain a geographical or rural-urban balance in assignments and provide ethnic-minority representation; and the apparent willingness of the legislator to cooperate with the presiding officer's "team." Experience indicates that a legislator who is a trusted friend or supporter and shares the presiding officer's ideological leanings is likely to fare much better in getting desired committee assignments or chairs than is the legislator who is not and does not. Thus, in 1969 and 1971 Speaker Gus Mutscher, a conservative, appointed conservatives to chair nearly all the committees and largely ignored liberals, who constituted a substantial minority of House members. By contrast, Price Daniel, Jr., distributed committee chairs fairly evenly among liberals and conservatives and, on the whole, was evenhanded in making committee assignments. In the 1981 Senate, dominated by conservatives, most committee chairs went to conservatives. When Gib Lewis became speaker, he replaced many of the House committee chairs with his own appointees, even though some of those replaced shared his political perspective. In 1991, eight of the committee chairs designated by Lewis were Republicans.

The House rules provide for a limited seniority system. Under this system, up to half of the members of most committees are selected on the basis of seniority (years of consecutive service in the House). At the beginning of a session, in order of seniority, each member designates a preferred committee. If half of the committee seats have not already been filled by seniority, the member gets a position on that committee. This continues until each member has picked a committee. The remainder of the positions on the committees, including the committee chairs and vice chairs, are appointed by the speaker. (In 1985, Lewis also acquired authority to dismiss committee chairs at his discretion.) Exempted from the seniority system are the committees on Appropriations, Human Services, Calendars, Local and Consent Calendars, General Investigating, House Administration, and Rules. All of the members of these committees are selected by the speakers. Most of these committees have important internal legislative management duties;

hence, control of them helps the speaker control the House. In the Senate there is a modified seniority rule that provides that three or four members of each committee, depending on the committee's size, must have served on it during the previous session. The use of seniority is intended to limit the power of the presiding officers, but, because of its restricted scope, it has had limited impact.

From one session of the legislature to another, there has been substantial turnover of both committee members and chairs, even when they are reelected to the legislature. In the U.S. Congress, by contrast, the seniority system, which is based on continuous service on a particular committee, provides for much stability in committee membership. Instructive here are the findings of Professor William Oden on assignments to nine important House committees and eight important Senate committees for a 12-year period. In the House, "70 percent of the committee members had no previous experience on that committee, while 22 percent had one previous experience [or term] on that committee." In the Senate, "35 percent . . . had no previous assignment on the committee while 31 percent of them had only one previous experience on that committee."[18] Another study for a later period found that 70 percent of the members of all committees had no prior experience on their committees.[19] Committee chairs are more likely to have had previous experience on the committees they chair, and this holds better for Senate than House chairs.[20]

The various House and Senate committees differ significantly in terms of their importance, prestige, and legislative work loads. Some, such as the State Affairs, Appropriations, Finance, and Ways and Means committees, are powerful and prestigious, handling most of the important legislation coming before the legislature. Others, such as the House Agriculture and Livestock, Liquor Regulation, and Transportation committees, handle few bills and rank low in prestige. In one session four House committees (Judiciary, Intergovernmental Affairs, State Affairs, and Education) handled over 52 percent of all bills dealt with by the House.[21]

Although some committees are not very important in the handling of legislation, they may still serve useful purposes when viewed from other perspectives. An appointment as chair or vice chair, even of a relatively inactive committee, may be desired by members for prestige and to aid their reelection. From the leadership's point of view, committee assignments and chairs are, to use Oden's phrase, "coins of the political realm" that can be used in promoting its programs. Lesser committees may be used as "dumping grounds" for those out of favor with the leadership.

The fate of bills introduced in the legislature depends greatly on the committees and their chairpersons. The committee chairpersons have significant power over the operation of their committees, including the appointment of subcommittees (except permanent Senate subcommittees, whose members are designated by the lieutenant governor); the conduct of committee meetings; determination of the committee agenda and whether public hearings will be held on bills; referral of bills to committee; and selection of the committee staff. The power exercised by chairpersons over their committees is what makes their selection such an important prerogative of the leadership. In exercising their power, chairpersons have customarily been responsive to the leadership; an indication by the speaker that a particular bill should be killed, for example, usually is sufficient to cause it to be forgotten in a subcommittee. In 1981, Lieutenant Governor Hobby stacked the Senate Judiciary Committee with opponents of electronic surveillance and wiretap legislation and appointed a liberal senator to chair the committee. Such legislation, which was a leading feature of the governor's "anti-crime" proposals, was opposed by Hobby.

Committee stacking, however, may also have unintended consequences. Thus, in 1985 Speaker Gib Lewis stacked the House Ways and Means Committee with representatives opposed to tax increases, a majority of whom were Republicans. When it became apparent during the 1986 special session that a tax increase was necessary to alleviate the state's fiscal crisis, Lewis (who had come reluctantly to support a tax increase) was unable to get a tax bill out of the committee. Somewhat embarrassed, he had to send the tax bill to the State Affairs Commission for action. In 1987 he replaced many of the recalcitrant members of Ways and Means with legislators more favorably disposed toward tax increases, given the state's continuing financial difficulties. Some saw this as an act of reprisal on Lewis's part.[22]

All bills are referred to a committee following introduction, and there they are discussed, evaluated, amended, sent to the floor for action, or killed. Much of the deliberative work on legislation is done by the committees, floor action often being perfunctory. Of course, committee action on bills may also be perfunctory, with only a few minutes, or less, being spent in consideration of some bills. The committee system permits a division of legislative work and should facilitate the development of specialization, so that the legislature will have its own policy experts or specialists to handle the various types of legislation that come before it. Also, it is obviously not physically or intellectually possible for each member of the legislature, or the legislature as a whole, to examine fully and master the hundreds of bills considered in a single session.

Although the Texas committee system provides for a division of legislative work, it is conjectural as to what extent it actually does provide the legislature with policy experts or specialists. The short duration of legislative sessions, the lack of adequate professional staff assistance for most committees, and the rather large turnover of members all work against the growth of expertise. Consequently, the Texas legislative committees lack the expertise and influence of their counterparts in the U.S. Congress. Their lack of expertise, the high turnover of members, appointment by the presiding officers, and the lack of a seniority system also prevent them from becoming independent sources of power in the legislature. To put it another way, the committee system does not disperse and decentralize political power, as does the committee system in Congress.

Legislative Aides and Assistants

The modern legislator is harried for time, confronted by a variety of demands and pressures, and faced with the task of having to consider, make sense of, and vote on hundreds of issues, many of which are quite complex or technical. To act

HAVE YOU EVER HEARD THIS THEORY THAT IF YOU GAVE A BUNCH OF MONKEYS TYPEWRITERS, THEY COULD WRITE "HAMLET" IF YOU GAVE 'EM LONG ENOUGH?

BUDGET SESSION TODAY

BEN SARGENT

Reprinted by permission.

somewhat rationally, the legislator sorely needs information, advice, and assistance in the performance of duties. Some sources of assistance for Texas legislators are surveyed in this section.

Personal and Committee Staffs   As has been noted, each legislator is given funds for hiring a personal staff. Although much of a staff's time is devoted to secretarial and clerical work (e.g., handling mail from constituents), many legislators do have assistants to help them keep track of legislation, brief bills, research particular problems, and perform other duties related to the business of legislating. Because such jobs are often of a part-time nature, given the legislature's limited sessions, they may not attract really professional people or afford good opportunities for professional development.

A loosely knit coalition of representatives (mostly liberals and Democrats) known as the House Study Group was formed in 1975. Members contributed some of their expense funds to hire staff to analyze legislation and thereby increase their legislative effectiveness. In a decade, the membership of the House Study Group expanded from a few dozen to over 100, including some members of the Senate. Some members of the House and its leadership, however, became disgruntled with some of the staff's reports and with the staff's lobbying against what it considered bad legislation. Consequently, in 1986 the House Administration Committee ruled that legislators could not use their expense accounts to support the House Study Group.

Many House members complained about this action to Speaker Gib Lewis and his aides. Negotiations led to the creation of the House Research Organization to take the place of the study group. The House Research Organization is funded by the House and is under the direction of a 15-member steering committee that is selected independently of the speaker. Its research reports and bill analyses are provided to all House members.

Most of the committees have clerks but not professional staffs, that is, staff members who have special knowledge or skill in particular substantive policy areas. (Notable exceptions are the House Appropriations and Senate Finance committees, which receive assistance from the staff of the Legislative Budget Board, and the House Committee on Revenue and Taxation, which draws on the staff of the Texas Research League, a private, business-supported organization.) Thus, the average legislator can expect little aid from committees in the performance of legislative duties. The committees' lack of professional staff is probably another factor reducing their legislative importance, in that it deprives the committees of the power that staff knowledge and expertness could bring to their dealings with lobbyists, administrators, and others.

The Texas Legislative Council   Created by legislation in 1949, this council is headed by a joint committee of ten representatives and five senators; the speaker of the house and lieutenant governor, who appoint the members from their respective houses, serve ex officio. The lieutenant governor serves as chair of the council, which has a full-time executive director, a research staff, and an annual budget of several hundred thousand dollars. The council's principal purpose is to conduct studies of public problems, prepare reports thereon, and make pertinent legislative recommendations. In recent years the council has studied such topics as constitutional revision, local legislation, county government, municipal annexation, juvenile delinquency, and state insurance laws. In addition to its research activity, its staff does much of the drafting of bills and resolutions for legislators. Also, for a few years now the council has conducted a short orientation program for new legislators to help inform them on such matters as legislative organization and procedure.

The Legislature Reference Library   Perhaps the major task of this library is to maintain an up-to-date, computerized legislative history of all bills and resolutions introduced in the legislature. Run by a professional library staff, it also maintains a large collection of state documents and other materials pertinent to the legislative process. Although the library is an invaluable source of information, it should be emphasized that it is primarily a place in which to do research rather than a source of research assistance, producing studies of public problems for harried legislators.

The Legislative Budget Board   This board is given detailed consideration in Chapter 10. Composed jointly of members from the House and Senate, the board, with the assistance of a full-time director and staff, prepares a state budget for legislative consideration. It also is authorized to make evaluations of state programs. During sessions, members of the board's staff serve as the staffs of the legislative appropriations committees.

Interim Committees   During each legislative session a host of interim committees, each consisting of a few House or Senate members, or both in the case of joint committees, are appointed at the behest of legislators and others. So named because they meet between legislative sessions, interim committees are set up to examine particular policy problems such as tax-exempt charitable foundations, water districts, public school finance, or workers' compensation.

Interim committee studies can be a fruitful source of information on public problems, and on occasion they have recommended important legislation.[23] For instance, the legislature in 1965 passed a series of antipollution bills recommended by an interim committee on land use and environmental control. The Select Committee on Public Education, which included gubernatorial and legislative appointees, contributed substantially to school reform legislation enacted in 1984 that included the famous "no pass-no play" rule. The attention of an interim committee many also be a means of keeping an unsuccessful piece of legislation "alive" from one session to another. Nonetheless, the usefulness of these committees can be restricted by poor planning of their activities, insufficient staff assistance, and poor attendance by members (although they do receive travel and per diem expenses when attending committee sessions.) Some committees have appeared to be mostly a means for the political benefit of individual legislators or, as has been alleged, an excuse to be in places like Austin and College Station on football weekends.[24] The validity of this allegation is disputed, especially by legislators.

LEGISLATIVE PARTICIPANTS AND THEIR INFLUENCE

In addition to those officially elected as legislators, there are many other participants in the legislative process. Although the formal power of decisions on proposed legislation resides with the legislators and the governor by virtue of veto power, various individuals and groups interact with and seek to influence or control legislative decision making. They provide advice and information, exert pressure, and otherwise seek to influence the conversion of demands into policy outputs. Collectively, the legislators plus these individuals and groups make up the legislative system. While it is impossible to state precisely how much impact particular groups or participants may have, we can at least indicate their patterns of activity.

Political Parties

Because of the almost total domination of the Texas legislature by the Democratic party until the 1970s, party influence in the legislative process has been practically nil. (The vote on the contested election in 1981 was one of the few times the Texas House has divided along party lines. See page 99.) It is difficult to be partisan when there are few if any persons against whom one can be partisan. This situation is beginning to change as the number of Republican legislators increases, especially in the House. In 1969 there were 2 Republicans in the Senate and 7 in the House; in 1991 there were 8 in the Senate and 57 in the House. (See Table 5.2.)

The Texas tradition of nonpartisan legislative organization continues in that currently neither house is organized along party lines for the consideration of legislation. The House Study Group initially drew most of its members from the ranks of moderate and liberal Democratic representatives and often opposed the conservative speaker on legislative issues. By 1979, however, it had largely abandoned its opposition role. In 1981 a House Democratic Caucus was organized with the intent of mobilizing all Democratic representatives against the Republicans. Although the Caucus continues in existence, it has never become a major legislative force. Speaker Lewis and members of his team have remained apart from it.

The Republicans in the House have followed two different strategies in seeking to gain influence. In 1977 they acted generally as a cohesive voting bloc but without being formally organized. Then, two years later, they became part of the mostly conservative coalition supporting Speaker Clayton. Two Republicans were rewarded with assignments as House committee chairs, and others got good committee positions. Partisanship was avoided because, as one Republican representative put it, "Anything smacking of partisanship might land us right back where we were under Gus Mutscher and his predecessors: junior members of the Poet Laureate selection committee, not even able (in the Texas legislative idiom) to pass gas."[25] This has continued to be the strategy of the Republicans in every legislative session since 1979. Speaker Lewis appointed nine Republicans to head committees in 1987. Informal communications and meetings rather than formal organization help tie the Republicans together.

Although a Republican Caucus was organized at the beginning of the legislative session in 1989, it did not become a major player in the legislative process. If Republican strength persists or increases in the Texas legislature, however, it seems unlikely that Texas will remain among the small handful of states where the legislature is not organized along partisan lines. A harbinger of the future may be the unity Republicans have displayed in opposing increased taxes in recent years. In 1987, in order to gain the 100 votes needed to put a tax bill into immediate effect, Speaker Lewis had to craft a strategy that permitted the House Republicans first to vote against the tax bill and then to vote for another bill making the taxes immediately effective.

Table 5.2   PARTY STRENGTH IN THE TEXAS LEGISLATURE, 1975–1987

	1975	1977	1979	1981	1983	1985	1987	1989	1991
House									
Democrats	133	132	126	114	115	98	94	93	93
Republicans	17	18	24	36	35	52	56	57	57
Senate									
Democrats	28	28	27	24	26	25	25	23	23
Republicans	3	3	4	7	5	6	6	8	8

To date, the absence of meaningful party organizations and partisanship in the legislature has probably had the effect of increasing the impact of pressure groups in the legislative process. In one-party systems the party loyalties and influences that would compete with and lessen the influence of pressure groups are largely nonexistent, leaving groups with a more hospitable context in which to operate.

There are liberal and conservative factions within the Democratic party, with most legislators being identified with one or the other. Since 1950 the conservative faction has been dominant, except in the Senate for a couple of sessions; its ratio of strength has varied from two-to-one to three-to-two. These factions are rather loose and amorphous, however, and tend to lack continuity and leadership. Moreover, many issues that come before the legislature do not lend themselves to liberal-conservative conflict: for example, liquor regulation (where wets and drys struggle), highway construction, fish and game regulation, and most local legislation. Factional alignments are most likely to be visible and important on such matters as taxation, civil rights, welfare, and labor legislation. Even on these, the individual legislator may be influenced by gubernatorial pressure, constituency interests, public opinion, or the leadership of his house to vote on other than ideological considerations. Factionalism, in short, appears important on only a portion of the legislation considered in a session, albeit an important portion, and even then it may be only one of many factors that help shape the legislator's voting decision.

Nonideological factions may also develop, perhaps forming around a major issue or in opposition to the leadership. An illustration of the first is a grouping known as the "Immortal 56," which blocked the enactment of a sales tax in the early 1940s. The Dirty Thirty of 1971, held together by its distaste for and opposition to the heavy-handed leadership of Speaker Mutscher and his team, is an example of the second. Each displayed considerable unity in voting.

In recent years a number of nonparty organizations, or "caucuses," have developed in the House. These include the Mexican-American Caucus, the Black Caucus, and the Texas Conservative Coalition. With the approval of the House Administration Committee such groups can occupy state office space, use state supplies, and receive financing from their members' office and staff funds.[26] These groups provide research services for their members and may also facilitate the development of voting blocs or coalitions. A report on the Mexican-American Caucus in 1985 stated that its power came partly from its ability "to deliver 30 votes" on legislative issues.[27] Groups of this sort have not emerged in the smaller, more clubby Senate, although some senators do support and draw on the services of the previously mentioned House Research Organization.

The Governor

The twentieth-century Texas governor has become an important source of major policy proposals and initiative in the legislative process. What the governor recommends will usually receive serious consideration, and what the governor opposes will often not be enacted. Although the Texas legislature clearly does not serve as a rubber stamp for gubernatorial initiatives, legislators are typically concerned to know the governor's position on major issues (if, one must add, the governor has one). This is one clue they can use in assessing the importance of legislation and evaluating the support or opposition for it.

The governor's formal powers are more appropriate to the role of legislative leader than chief executive. Further, the public's evaluation of the governor depends more on successes and failures in the legislative arena than on skill or finesse as an administrator. Both the public and the legislature have come to expect the governor to lead; this is part of the official role. The office possesses a variety of tools for leadership, some authorized by the constitution, others informal in origin.

The constitution authorizes the governor to send messages to the legislature recommending the enactment of legislation. The "State of the State" message at the opening of a regular legislative session is customarily delivered in person to a joint meeting of the two houses and is well reported by the press. In this message the governor appraises the problems confronting the state and recommends a general program for dealing with them. The details of the program will subsequently be spelled out in written messages sent to the legislature as the session moves along. The impact of these messages will depend on such factors as the popularity of the governor, the timeliness and political acceptability of the messages, the governor's relationship with the legislative leadership, and the skill and effort with which the governor works for their adoption. One of the most prolific users of the message power was Governor W. Lee "Pappy" O'Daniel (1939–1941).[28] He enjoyed comparatively little success, however, because of sharp political differences between him and the legislature. Professor Fred Gantt, Jr., has commented that, over the years, "Results would seem to indicate that the legislature resents too frequent a display of 'gubernatorial influence' through exercise of the message power."[29]

The constitution also empowers the governor to call special sessions of the legislature. Each special session is limited to 30 days' duration, but there is no limit on how many can be called. The governor's influence is enhanced during special sessions, as the legislature can consider legislation only on topics specified. The legislature does possess all of its other powers during these sessions. In fact, it was during a special session called in 1917 to deal with appropriations for the University of Texas that the legislature impeached, convicted, and removed Governor James E. ("Pa") Ferguson from office.

The items most frequently specified for consideration by special sessions include appropriations, taxation and revenue, education, and liquor regulation.[30] A call for a special session, after indicating the main tasks for which it is being called, usually includes as a final item "to consider and act on such subjects and questions as the governor may submit from time to time." This open-ended item lays the basis for bargaining by the governor with the legislature. The governor may seek to win support for certain measures in return for agreeing to open the session for consideration of matters of interest to legislators. Variations in the use of this power are illustrated by Governor Price Daniel, who called eight special sessions during six years in office, and Governor Dolph Briscoe, who called two special sessions during an equal period in office. In 1959, following the regular session, Governor Daniel called three consecutive special sessions and kept the legislature in Austin the entire summer before it was induced to pass a tax bill to meet a large budget deficit.

The governor also has the veto power. The constitution provides that before any bill passed by the legislature can become law, it must be submitted to the governor for consideration and approval. While the legislature is in session, the governor has 10 days after receiving a bill in which to exercise the veto. If a bill comes during the last 10 days of a session or after the legislature has adjourned, the governor has 20 days in which to take action. In either instance, action must be taken in order to veto a bill; otherwise it will become law without the governor's signature. The governor has no pocket veto, unlike the president. If the veto power is exercised while the legislature is in session, the governor must return the bill—along with a veto message setting forth objections—to the house that first passed it. If the bill is repassed by a two-thirds vote in each house, the governor's veto is overridden, and the bill becomes law. Of course, when the legislature has adjourned before the governor acts, the veto is absolute because there is no opportunity for the legislature to reconsider. This is when a large portion of the bills passed by the legislature reach the governor's office.

In practice, however, the governor's veto in recent decades has been final, no matter at what point it is exercised. During the long period from 1876 through 1968, only 25 out of a total of 936 vetoes (or less than 3 percent) were overridden by the legislature.[31] Moreover, since 1941 only one veto has been overridden by the legislature. This happened in 1979. Involving as it did a relatively minor local bill, it was apparently intended as an object lesson to Republican Governor Clements. Forty-seven other vetoes by Clements that year stood up.

Among the reasons given for vetoes are that the bills are variously uneconomical, unconstitutional, unnecessary, defectively worded, or against public policy. If one cuts through the verbiage, this often means that essentially the governor disagrees with the legislature's judgment. Thus, in 1987, with little opposition, the legislature passed a bill that permitted cities other than Houston to adopt and enforce ordinances against vicious dogs, so long as the ordinances were not breed-specific (e.g., aimed at pit bulls). Governor Clements vetoed the bill on the grounds that this was a local issue and that the legislature should not dictate how cities should regulate animals.

Included in the veto power are the item veto and the threat to veto. On appropriations bills, the governor can veto particular items while accepting most of the bill's provisions. This serves to enhance gubernatorial power in the area of finances. It has been held by the attorney general, however, that the item veto is limited to "line-items" in appropriations bills. It does not extend to legislative materials in the form of "riders" attached to such bills.

Probably at least as important as the actual use of the veto is the potentiality of the threat of a veto. The enactment of some bills can be prevented by the governor's indication that they will be vetoed if passed. More positively, the governor may seek to influence the content of a bill by threatening to veto it should it contain, or not contain, particular provisions. Such action, if skillfully done, will often produce the desired changes because legislators are often more interested in passing bills than provoking vetoes. Thus, many observers believe that the legislature in 1969 would not have passed a one-year appropriation bill, which was vetoed, had Governor Smith clearly indicated he would veto it if passed. In 1971 he confounded the legislature by vetoing the entire second year of the Appropriation Act, which required a special session of the legislature to reenact the second-year appropriations.

These three constitutional powers—messages, special sessions, and veto—constitute only a portion of the total legislative power available to the governor. Many informal or extralegal means are open to use. For one, the governor may seek to influence the selection of the speaker of the house in order to have a speaker with whom it is possible to work effectively. This must be done circumspectly, as too strong or overt action could antagonize the legislature. Second, the governor may use the power of appointment to reward or bargain with legislators for support of legislative goals. An alternative use of this device was made in 1965, when Governor Connally appointed Speaker Byron Tunnell to a Texas Railroad Commission vacancy; he thereby seemingly cleared the way for selecting his friend and supporter, Ben Barnes, as speaker. Third, informal conferences, breakfast meetings, social gatherings, and other meetings may be used to win legislative support. Professor Gantt reports that "without exception, governors, staff members, and legislators say they consider a conference to be one of the most successful and most frequently used techniques in the legislative process."[32] Fourth, the governor can use the communications media, especially radio and television, as a means of appealing directly to the public for grass-roots support for legislative proposals. Fifth, executive liaisons may be used to lobby, communicate with, and persuade legislators. Sixth, the governor may use influential persons to bring pressure to bear on legislators. These can include pressure-group representatives or important residents in the legislator's district (e.g., bankers, business people, local party leaders, or important campaign contributors). Contacted by the governor or the staff, such persons may act to urge or otherwise induce legislators to do the governor's bidding. Lastly, the influence the governor enjoys as the state's chief elected official should not be ignored. The office confers high status upon its occupant.

The governor thus has available a considerable bag of leadership techniques. Much of an individual's success will depend, however, on personal and political standing and the deftness with which the tools available are used. Heavy-handedness or excessive timidity in their use may diminish one's influence, as may an inadequate sense of what is politically timely or possible. Governor John Connally is generally regarded as having been more successful as a legislative leader in his second term than in his first, an important difference being the skill and experience he had acquired in this role. In contrast, Governor Dolph Briscoe often seemed uninterested in acting as a legislative leader. Party affiliation became a more important factor in 1979, when Republican Bill Clements became governor.

Interest Groups

Although interest groups have already been discussed at length, reiteration of their importance in the Texas legislative process is appropriate. Scores of organized groups use a variety of methods to influence legislative activity. Group representatives lobby, or communicate directly, with legislators in an effort to secure desired policy decisions. Besides providing selective information to legislators, lobbyists reason, persuade, exhort, cajole, and occasionally threaten in trying to bring legislators around to their position. Organized groups wine, dine, and entertain; provide opportunities for legislators to supplement their meager public salaries legally, as by retainer fees for legislators who are lawyers; and frequently intervene in the electoral process in support of friends and in opposition to enemies. Though it is difficult to measure with precision, interest-group activity undoubtedly has a substantial impact in the legislative arena. The consequences of that impact are in dispute.

Defenders of interest groups and their lobbying tactics point out that any group in Texas is entitled to bring its views to the attention of the state legislature. Group activity provides a two-way channel through which citizen demands can be presented to public leaders and leadership positions can be communicated to the members of various groups. Additionally, these groups make available much needed, if sometimes biased, information to underinformed legislators and stimulate public interest and participation in politics.

Critics rejoin that the tactics that groups utilize in securing influence in the legislature are expensive and thus usually available only to the more affluent or well-organized groups. They argue that the host of favors, preferments, and campaign contributions available to legislators inevitably obligates the members who accept them and undermines their independent judgment on public issues that are of special interest to those bestowing the favors. The ultimate result is that the legislature, which is publicly responsible for making policy decisions, ends up rubber-stamping policies covertly decided on by group representatives outside the legislative halls.

Achieving a balanced view of the role of interest groups is difficult. There are cases, such as the 1969 Workmen's Compensation Act, in which the legislature simply approved a bill that had been worked out in advance by representatives of business, labor unions, and plaintiff attorneys. Bills creating local water districts may be quietly passed, with little public awareness, in response to requests from real estate developers. But there are many instances where the legislative output is determined by a complex set of factors, of which interest-group activity is only one. Comparatively, interest groups are probably more important in the Texas legislative process than they are in the U.S. Congress or most other state legislatures. The absence of a strong state executive and a competitive party system, coupled with underpaid, understaffed, part-time legislators and little media publicity on lobby activities, all combine to increase the impact of interest groups.

Administrative Agencies and Officials

State agencies and officials become involved in the legislative process if for no other reason than because it is the source of their legal authority and appropriations. Bills introduced in the legislature frequently originate in the agencies, and agency officials appear before legislative committees to defend or oppose legislation in which they are interested. The bill that eventually became the Texas Clean Air Act was drafted by two employees of the State Health Department, the agency that had responsibility for pollution control at the time; it was introduced by a state representative acting at their request. The two employees said they wanted to both make state pollution control more effective and avoid federal control, as provided by the national Clean Air Act.[33]

Agencies may also engage in lobbying, legislative liaison, and related activities on behalf of their legislative goals. The University of Texas has attracted considerable attention to its lobbying activities in recent years in support of larger budgets and expanded operations. To a great extent, agencies have to take care of their own interests before the legislature as best they can. Because of their substantial independence from the governor, because of the many demands on the governor's time, and because the governor may hesitate to become embroiled in some controversies, agencies do not depend very greatly on gubernatorial support. Indeed, they may oppose the governor on some legislative matters.

Two officials of notable importance to the legislative process are the attorney general and the comptroller of public accounts. The attorney general's department gives legal assistance to legislators in bill drafting and, upon request, provides legislative committees and others with opinions concerning the constitutionality of actual or proposed state legislation. Although these opinions are not legally binding, the legislature almost always complies with them. In 1987 the attorney general made life easier for the legislature by ruling that a billion-dollar budget deficit could be made up in the next fiscal biennium (1987–1989) rather than the remaining few months of that year. The comptroller has a constitutional duty to certify whether funds are available under existing laws to finance appropriations. Appropriation acts cannot be passed until it is certified that funds are available. (See Chapter 10 for further discussion.) In sum, these two officials help provide the legal framework within which the legislature operates and, in so doing, affect legislative outputs.

The Courts

The state courts, particularly the appellate courts, must be counted as occasional participants in the legislative process. Through exercise of their powers of statutory interpretation and judicial review, they help determine the meaning and impact of laws and, upon proper challenge, their constitutionality. We have already seen how the Texas Supreme Court declared the 1971 Legislative Redistricting Act unconstitutional. As another illustration, the state courts have declared a number of *bracket laws* unconstitutional. These are specific laws dealing with local governments that are so drafted as to have the appearance of generality and thereby avoid the state constitutional prohibition on local legislation. A bracket bill might be drafted to apply to all counties falling between specified upper and lower population limits, while in actuality only *one* county does so. Many such laws are passed at the request of local officials and groups; they continue in effect because they are needed and no one tests them in the courts.

The legislature may be influenced in the drafting and enactment of laws by anticipation of what the courts may do in interpreting their meaning or passing on their constitutionality. Long a commonplace reflection of this was the *severability clause* that was included as a matter of routine in many laws. The clause provides that if one part of a statute is declared unconstitutional, the validity of the remainder of the statute will not be affected. In 1973 the legislature sought to deal generally with this "problem" by adopting a statute that declared all statutes, past or future, "severable" unless otherwise specially provided.

The federal courts may also affect the state legislative process, as by the chain of decisions from 1962 to 1976 that led to and provided guidelines for the reapportionment of state legislatures. Sometimes, too, substantive state laws are declared unconstitutional, as was one that levied a tax on natural gas sold in interstate commerce. The appeal of such a tax was that its burden would be "exported" to the citizens of other states. Generally, considerations of constitutional authority are more significant for the state legislature than the U.S. Congress.

LEGISLATIVE PROCEDURE

The primary concern of this section is the formal rules and procedures by which bills become law. (Technically, when introduced, a legislative proposal is called a *bill;* after its passage, it is designated as an *act.* Unless vetoed, it becomes law and is legally binding on those affected.) For purposes of brevity and ease of understanding, only the major stages in the process will be sketched, beginning with action in the Texas House of Representatives.

Introduction of Bills

The Texas constitution provides for "split" legislative sessions. The first 30 days of a legislative session are reserved for the introduction of bills, the second 30 days for committee consideration of bills, and the remaining 80 days for floor debate and disposition of bills. (This is a good example of the detail included in the constitution.) This order of business can be suspended by a four-fifths vote, which is regularly done by both houses. Consequently, customary procedure in the House and Senate permits unlimited introduction of bills during the first 60 days of a session.[34] After that period, only local bills, emergency appropriations, and bills designated as emergency matters by the governor can be introduced, and only then by a four-fifths vote to suspend the rules. The formal introduction of bills and resolutions is a privilege reserved for members of the legislature. (Resolutions are used mainly for formal expressions of legislative opinions, as on busing or a legislator's birthday, or for internal legislative matters; however, joint resolutions are used to propose amendments to the state constitution and to ratify amendments to the U.S. Constitution.) Customarily, a bill is introduced in the House when a representative gives four copies of it to the clerk of the House. There is no limit on the number of bills that representatives can introduce, but realistically only a few will probably have much chance for consideration. (A Dallas legislator in 1979 introduced 105 bills, of which only 4 or 5 were passed.) Constitutionally, bills concerned with taxation or revenue can originate only in the House, and resolutions for the approval of gubernatorial appointments are solely a matter for the Senate. Bills and resolutions dealing with all other matters can be introduced initially in either the House or the Senate, or they can be introduced concurrently in both houses in an attempt to speed their adoption.

According to constitutional prescription, no bill may deal with more than one subject. This may seem like a technical detail and, in a sense, it is. However, those who cannot block the passage of a bill may subsequently challenge its constitutionality on the ground that it deals with more than one subject. A successful challenge renders it null and void. This is another illustration of how formal rules can be used for political advantage.

What has been said thus far relates to the formal introduction of bills. Their actual origin or birth is another matter. Probably few bills are conceived by the legislators who introduce them. Most will trace their origins elsewhere—to the governor, state agencies, local governments, interest groups, private citizens—and will be introduced as an accommodation to such parties. Whether the legislator actually works for their passage is another matter. Not infrequently, bills are introduced and then quietly forgotten. Given their subject matter, this is often just as well. Or perhaps, for example, there really is a need for a law requiring teaching of the Declaration of Independence in the public schools.

Bills not passed during the session in which they are introduced die when it ends. To be considered during the next session, they would have to be reintroduced and started again at the beginning of the process. Some controversial bills may be dealt with in several sessions before they are finally enacted into law. Bills concerning state regulation of public utility companies were before the legislature for many years prior to the enactment of legislation in 1975 setting up a Public Utility Commission. For some bills, their "time" never seems to come. Legislation authorizing parimutuel betting on horse races has been a perennial nonfinisher.

Committee Action

Once introduced, all bills are referred to a committee for consideration. If there is a question as to which House committee should receive a bill, the speaker makes the assignment on the basis of the rules defining committee jurisdictions. These leave the speaker considerable discretion, which may be exercised to the advantage of the interest the speaker favors. In the Senate, the lieutenant governor has similar power; moreover, the Senate rules make no attempt to define committee jurisdictions. Once referred to a committee, the fate of a bill depends greatly on the actions of the committee chair and members. Many bills are pigeonholed and never heard from again. In one session, House committees failed to report out 481 of 1184 bills (40.5 percent) referred to them. In comparison, Senate committees did not report out 138 of 584 Senate bills (23.7 percent).[35] Legislative commit-

HOW A BILL *REALLY* BECOMES A LAW

In your government textbook you've read that the legislative process works a certain way. It doesn't. The following is a true story about the real legislative process.

HB 1705 began before the session at a bill drafting meeting I had with two civic leaders from the Southgate-Rice University area. They are home-owners and title lawyers who fear for the future of their neighborhood once deed restrictions expire in a couple of years. Since Houston has no zoning, deed restrictions are the only means available for preserving neighborhoods. In new subdivisions most deed restrictions provide a method for extending their effective period before they expire. Some older neighborhoods like Southgate have no such provisions.

Once deed restrictions lapse in these older areas, homeowners are often faced with commercial encroachment, apartments, and a decline in property values and the residential quality of the neighborhood. HB 1705 provided a procedure to give homeowners the opportunity, through a peti-tion process, to extend the term of their deed restrictions for 25 years. To prevent "unconstitutional taking of property," nonconcurring property owners were allowed to opt-out and other property uses begun after restric-tions expired were exempted.

As a strong believer in private property rights, I introduced HB 1705. The first step in making it law involved taking our draft to Legislative Council lawyers for redrafting into bill form compatible with all existing laws. A complex, 14-page bill resulted.

The bill was heard April 13th by a House committee of which I am a member—having your bill assigned to one of your own committees expe-dites the process. A Southgate area lawyer–civic leader testified for it; no one opposed it. HB 1705 unanimously passed committee unamended.

On April 23rd and 24th, HB 1705 was debated on the House floor. I offered corrective amendments and answered questions from other mem-bers. One colleague's question indicated a potential problem with the bill. Thanks to his insight we corrected the problem in Senate committee. Such useful exchanges often occur among legislators who have different back-grounds and areas of expertise. The bill passed 117–6 and went to the Senate.

Since Senate rules require a two-thirds vote to take up a bill for floor debate, selection of a good Senate sponsor is critical. Since 11 Senators can kill a bill, I was careful to select a sponsor who could steer HB 1705 through the thousands of bills in the end-of-session logjam. I had a good working relationship with several Senators from past years when I worked on a Senate committee staff, enabling me to secure a sponsor who chaired the powerful committee to which HB 1705 was referred, whose home city had no zoning, and who has a reputation for his effectiveness. Unfortunately, such interpersonal relationships often play as much or more of a role in passing bills than do the merits of the issue.

On May 11th, the day of the Senate committee hearing, the Senate sponsor was suddenly confronted by several lobbyists for developers, mortgage bankers, realtors, and title-insurers. They had waited to oppose HB 1705 in the Senate, where the rules make it easier to kill, although no one had contacted us previously to oppose the bill and it had received no public opposition. The Senate sponsor agreed not to kill the bill and I began a series of meetings with lobbyists, staffpersons, Senators, and Houston civic leaders. For 10 days there was an endless series of phone calls, apparent compromises, breakdowns in negotiations, and several redrafts of the bill all during 16-hour work days which included appropriations and redistricting bills.

In working out a "compromise" I encountered two types of lobbyists' objections. On one hand were technical objections from persons with expertise in their area of specialization. Experienced lobbyists commonly provide good information this way and these objections were easily resolved.

One lobby group tried to kill the bill. Since some Senators told us they would vote against the bill if that group opposed it, we had to delete or change some areas of HB 1705 objectionable to them and they accepted some important aspects of HB 1705. After three postponements, the "new HB 1705" passed Senate committee on May 21st in a scene resembling a calf-scramble.

It was near the end of the session and our committee hearing was in the Senate chamber while 4 other committees met simultaneously in rooms adjacent to the chamber. Senators serve on more than one committee and were dashing from room to room through a sea of lobbyists, legislators, staff people, press, and befuddled tourists. My staff and I had to "round up" Senators to get our votes on committee, with 4 Senators stepping out of other meetings to cast "aye" votes from the far corners of the chamber. We could've used a lariat.

Next I met with the original supporters of the bill and we determined that, although the "new HB 1705" was substantially narrower in scope than the original, the bill would still help their neighborhood. Once I assured the Senate sponsor we had the needed 21 votes, he passed the bill 24–1 on May 29th, 3 days before the session ended. The House accepted the Senate changes two days later.

But a funny thing happened to HB 1705 on the way to making it law. I had worked with the Governor's staff and interested lobbyists to be sure he knew this was a compromise bill. However, he apparently did not heed this information and instead called two large contributors about the bill. As a result of these calls he vetoed the bill.

I later contacted one of these contributors who supports the lobby group that once tried to kill the bill. He cited opposition to parts of the bill that had long since been removed in negotiations. Apparently he advised the Governor to veto HB 1705 without ever seeing the final compromise version.

I plan to return to Austin and pass this bill again next session.

Source: Reprinted with the permission of Representative Paul Colbert, from his constituency newsletter, Spring 1981.

tees in several other states, unlike Texas, are required to report on all bills sent to them.

Quite a few bills, because of the importance of their subject matter, the controversy they create, or the influence of their proponents, are given a public hearing at which witnesses (e.g., lobbyists, officials, private citizens) may appear and give testimony on their merits, possible impact, and the like. Hearings are often poorly publicized and poorly attended. A notice tacked on a bulletin board five days prior to the hearing often constitutes "public notice." The House rules provide for the electronic recording of testimony, but often no printed transcripts are readily available; this obviously reduces the value of hearings as a source of information for those not in attendance.

It is not necessary, however, for a bill to be given a hearing before it is reported out of committee, and many are not. Committee action, but not necessarily a committee hearing, is part of standard legislative procedure. Sometimes committee action can take such perfunctory form as a hastily called meeting of committee members in a corner of the legislative chamber. In other cases, committees may simply ratify decisions made by the leadership of their house.

The House committee (or subcommittee thereof) considering a bill may make changes in it during the *marking-up process,* as detailed treatment is called. All changes or amendments in a bill made at the committee stage must be approved by a majority vote of the House when the bill comes before it. A committee can circumvent this requirement by adopting and reporting out a complete committee substitute (a *clean bill,* in legislative parlance) in place of the original bill. It may possess little similarity to the original bill, and legislators have been known to disown or abandon bills after committee treatment, or floor amendment for that matter. Bills are reported out of committee and sent to the floor of the House for consideration either by a majority vote favoring the bill or by a minority report signed by two to four members, depending on the size of the committee (a majority vote on the floor is subsequently needed to place it on a calendar). The minority-report procedure is infrequently used because a bill that cannot get majority support in committee will usually have little chance of passage.

Calendar Stage

Bills reported favorably from a House committee go to the Calendar Committee for assignment to one of the House calendars. The speaker, who appoints and controls the Calendar Committee, can have the final say here. (There are also calendars for resolutions and for minor and congratulatory resolutions; these are not included in this discussion.) The six calendars, listed in the order of their priority, are these:

1. *Emergency calendar:* all bills requiring immediate action, bills submitted as emergency matters by the governor, all tax bills, and the general appropriations bill
2. *Major state calendar:* all bills of statewide effect that involve major developments or changes in state policy, excluding any on the first calendar
3. *Constitutional amendments calendar:* all joint resolutions proposing amendments to the Texas Constitution or ratification of amendments to the U.S. Constitution
4. *General state calendar:* bills of statewide effect and secondary importance and bills that apply to more than one, but not all, counties
5. *Local calendar:* bills that apply to single-named counties, such as those involving game or fish regulations, excluding bracket bills
6. *Consent calendar:* bills that are not expected to have opposition regardless of their extent or scope, as recommended by the appropriate standing committees.

Bills are usually placed on the appropriate calendars in the order in which they are received from the committees, although the Calendar Committee has "full authority to make assignments to calendars in whatever order is necessary and desirable . . . to insure adequate consideration by the House of important legislation." The Committee may also act to kill legislation, as in 1979 when it refused to place on the debate schedule nearly 200 of the 890 bills sent to it, thereby preventing their floor consideration. The rules further provide that the calendars, except those for local and consent matters, be taken up in the order we have listed. The Calendar Committee prepares and distributes printed calendars at least 24 hours before they will be considered. (The lead time is 48 hours for the state and local calendars, which are under the jurisdiction of a separate committee on Local and Consent Calendars.)

Under House rules, Senate-passed bills and resolutions are given priority on Wednesdays and Thursdays. As the House usually does not meet on Fridays and Saturdays, this leaves Mondays and Tuesdays as the main days for consideration of House bills and resolutions. This schedule is fairly flexible, however; on Senate days when no Senate bills are pending, the various House calendars can be taken up. Local and consent bills may be taken up as the volume of business warrants and convenient openings in the schedule appear. Toward the end of a session, as the volume of floor business increases, the House may meet on Fridays, and perhaps even Saturdays and Sundays. Also, a suspension of the rules procedure permits a bill to be brought up for consideration out of its regular order. The speaker has discretionary authority to recognize a member to make a motion to make the bill a special order, which then requires an affirmative two-thirds vote of the members.

Floor Action and Debate

Once a bill comes out of committee and reaches the floor for consideration, its chances for passage are fairly good. Much of the real consideration and screening of bills, to the extent that such takes place, is handled by the committees. On the other hand, this should not be taken to mean that once a bill clears a committee the worries of its sponsor are largely over. Support must be actively sought to ensure passage, especially if a bill is of major importance, and amendments intended to cripple or substantially alter the bill must be fought off. Some amendments may have to be accepted to pick up support for the bill. Occasionally a bill will be so altered by floor amendments that its sponsor withdraws it from consideration.

When debate occurs on "major" bills (i.e., those on the first four calendars listed above), it is restrained, at least in duration, by the House rules. Each speaker is limited to 10 minutes, except that the representative in charge of the bill is permitted 20 minutes to open and 20 minutes to close debate. Under the rules, debate can be terminated by majority vote (on a motion to call the previous question), which enables a majority to forestall filibustering easily. Some delaying activity, called "chubbing," may be permitted when the speaker desires to delay a vote or consideration of a matter for some reason. Commentators seem agreed that the debate on bills is often not of high quality and that it may do little to inform or enlighten on the merits of legislation; but it may generate some heat, as evidenced by the fact that physical altercations are not unknown on the floor of the Texas House.

One should not assume, however, that the debate on bills is unimportant because it may lack focus on the "merits" of legislation and appeals to reason. An eloquent speech may change a few minds and win a few votes. However, speeches are often more important because of who is talking than because of what is said. Such factors as personal popularity, debating style, and courtesy shown other members by the debater may influence votes. On the other hand, a "smart-aleck" response to a question or a personal attack on a fellow legislator may do harm to one's cause. Also, a member who is widely disliked, because of personality, style, or other factors, can jeopardize a bill merely by getting up to speak in favor of it.

Many bills, especially those on the local and consent calendars, are quickly and quietly passed with little or no debate, and many representatives will be uninformed as to their content. In a single session in May 1977, the House passed some 150 bills listed on the local and consent calendars. (The Senate surpassed this record in 1981 by passing 189 bills in less than two hours on the next to the last day of the regular session.) A state representative provided the following description of the House in action on "local and consent calendar day":

> Facing us is a long list of bills that are theoretically "uncontested"—though several are at least as important as others we've debated for hours on the regular calendar. The impetus is to move the bills through all the necessary motions—fast—with members lining up to give only one-sentence "explanations" of each measure.
>
> Clayton is a master of the auctioneer's patter required for this show, and he has developed a rhythmical slapping of the gavel that almost demands that the pace not be broken. Once today when a colleague was a little slow in coming to the front mike (in the House chamber), the Speaker barked unhappily, "C'mon members! Let's keep rolling!"
>
> As well as I can make them out, these are the magic words that the Speaker intones to move bills on "L & C" to third reading and final passage:
>
> "Clerkill readabill." (The clerk starts to read the bill's title but is interrupted a split-second later by the smack of the gavel.) "Izzair jection? Passterd reading."[36]

The legislature tends to move at a somewhat leisurely pace during the early weeks of a session. Daily sessions are short, and adjournments for three-day weekends are not uncommon. Activity picks up as the end of the session looms, and a substantial portion of the bills passed by the legislature are put through during the closing days. During this end-of-the-session rush, lack of time and pressure for adjournment (which must occur by midnight on the 140th day of the session) causes even major bills to be considered often in a perfunctory manner, or to fail of enactment.

The Texas Constitution requires that a bill must be "read on three several days" before it can be passed by either the House or the Senate. The first reading, by caption only, takes place after introduction and before referral to committee. The second reading occurs when the bill is taken up for consideration on the floor, at which time the bill is subject to debate and amendment. Approval of the bill, together with any amendments made to it, is by majority vote at this stage. The third reading takes place when, on a different legislative day (which may or may not coincide with a calendar day), the bill is taken up for final passage; this also requires a majority vote. As a consequence of a constitutional provision obviously intended to help ensure adequate consideration of legislation before adoption, all of this means that each house must formally give its approval to a bill twice before passage. The formal requirement is often complied with in mechanical fashion. Also, it is possible for the House to suspend the rules by a four-fifths vote and vote on the final passage of a bill immediately following the second reading.

Voting in the House is done electronically. Each representative's desk has a voting button that is connected to a large electronic board at the front of the House chamber. This records whether a legislator votes yea or nay on the issue at hand and permits quick and visible, if not always fully accurate, votes to be taken. Although it is in violation of House rules, members occasionally cast votes for other members who are absent from the floor temporarily, or even out of Austin, by merely pushing their voting buttons. This has become an accepted practice, and it may be done with or without the permission of the absent member. Despite the publicity sometimes given the practice by the press, nothing has been done to discipline those involved. Questions to ponder are whether it is ethically or politically desirable for a representative to cast votes for another and whether the practice is justifiable, given our beliefs about representation.

Senate Procedure

As some comparisons between House and Senate procedures have already been made, only a few unique features of Senate procedure are commented on here.

Bills can be reported out of Senate committees only by a favorable majority vote of the committee members unless the Senate directs otherwise. Once reported out, bills are placed on a single Senate calendar in the order in which they come out of committee and without regard to their content or importance. The Senate rules provide that bills shall be taken up for consideration in the order listed on the calendar. However, the rules also permit the suspension of the calendar by a two-thirds vote to enable bills to be considered out of their regular order. This has become the customary manner in which bills, especially those of some importance, are brought before the Senate. The lieutenant governor has considerable discretion in deciding whom to recognize to make a motion to suspend the calendar and take up a bill. Those wanting to make such motions usually informally arrange to do so in advance with the lieutenant governor, who is more likely to favor friends or supporters than others in making such agreements. Thus, while a bill can be passed by majority vote, it normally takes a two-thirds majority vote to bring it to the floor. Conversely, one-third of the Senate can block consideration, thereby making possible minority control over which bills are considered. In 1973 a mandatory oil and gas field unitization bill, strongly backed by the major oil companies, was killed because its Senate supporters, while in the majority, were unable to muster the two-thirds vote needed to take it off the calendar.

Debate in the Senate is conducted under looser rules than in the House. Senators are generally permitted to talk on a bill as long as they desire or are physically able to keep talking. In 1977, Senator Bill Meier (Euless) spoke for 43 hours against a bill, which was passed as soon as he quit the floor. (For those interested in such matters, this set a Texas and world record for a one-person filibuster.) Debate can be limited by simple majority vote, which eliminates the possibility of lengthy filibusters like those that occasionally occur in the U.S. Senate, where a two-thirds vote is required to close off debate. Filibusters in the Texas Senate are thus comparatively short-lived. They are most likely to be effective in the closing days of a session, when every hour counts and a few hours' delay can prevent consideration of important matters. Then a filibuster may have the desired effect of preventing consideration of a bill or getting agreement from the leadership to bring up a particular bill.

Except for filibusters, and in contrast to the House, where debates may go on for hours or days, long floor fights are uncommon in the Senate. Senators rarely bring bills up for floor consideration unless they know in advance they have the votes to pass them. Usually senators work out disagreements on a bill before it is brought to the floor. This may be done in committee or with the assistance of the lieutenant governor, who tries to get senators to resolve conflicts by bargaining and compromise. On the whole, "floor life" is much more sedate in the Senate than in the House.

During the first 60 days of a legislative session, a four-fifths vote is required to pass most bills in the Senate; after that, a simple majority suffices. Voting is usually done by roll call.

Conference Committees

Different versions of a bill are often passed by the House and Senate for various reasons: for example, the interests of particular members, different constituency interests, and response to pressure groups. When this happens, the house that first passed the bill is usually requested to accept the changes made by the other house. If this is done, the bill is sent on to the governor. If this tack fails, the house that made the changes may be asked to reconsider its changes. Customarily, however, the differences between the two houses will be resolved through the use of a conference committee to devise a compromise version of the bill acceptable to both.

A conference committee is an ad hoc committee composed of five members from each house, who are appointed by the presiding officers. Usually a conference committee's members are drawn from the standing committees that originally handled the bill; a majority of the conferees are supposed to represent the majority position on the bill in their respective houses. Nonetheless, it is not unknown for a presiding officer to appoint a majority of conferees hostile toward a bill passed by their house. A conference committee deals only with a single bill and, during a session, there will be as many conference committees as bills in dispute. A single member, especially one in favor with the leadership, may serve on several conference committees.

In adjusting the differences on a bill, the conferees from each house act as a unit, which means that anything done by the conference committee must be acceptable to a majority of the conferees from each house. Conference-committee action well illustrates the dealing and bargaining characteristic of the legislative process. Once the conference committee agrees on a compromise version of a bill, it is sent to the two houses for approval. If the conference committee cannot reach agreement, a new conference committee may be appointed, or the bill may simply be abandoned. Although a conference-committee bill can be disapproved by either house, this rarely happens. The pressure of time (conference-committee reports often come up near the end of a session), the desire "to have a bill," and the lack of ready alternatives all work toward acceptance of the conference committee's handiwork. (The rules prohibit amendment of conference-committee bills.) The alternatives, in short, are often the conference-committee bill or no bill,

and to many the latter is unacceptable. Because of the pressures of time and the
fact that the rules prohibit amendment of conference committee versions of bills,
the conference committees have a major impact on the content of legislation
enacted by the legislature.

Final Action

A bill that has been passed in the same form by both houses is then enrolled (put
into final, official form), signed by the presiding officers, and transmitted to the
governor for action. Gubernatorial approval or disapproval marks the final stage
of the formal legislative process. With the exception of general appropriation acts,
which become effective at the beginning of the fiscal biennium, acts go into effect
90 days after the legislature adjourns. If, however, an act is deemed an "emergency matter" (by virtue of a statement to that effect included in it) and if it is
passed by a two-thirds vote of those elected to each house, it goes into effect as
soon as it is signed by the governor.

Logjams and Workloads

A frequent criticism of the legislative process in the American states is that it
often results in end-of-the-session logjams during which harried legislators enact
large quantities of ill-considered legislation in order to dispose of their work-
loads.[37] The Texas legislature has not been exempt from this complaint. Evidence
for it appears in such data as the following: In 1985, of the 4021 bills introduced
in the legislature, 1024 were passed by the legislature, and 980 became law (44
having been vetoed by the governor.) Final floor actions were taken on nearly 900
bills during the final 12 legislative days.

   The situation may not be as grim as it initially appears, however, given
Professor Harvey Tucker's findings. Although decisions to pass bills are concentrated in the final weeks of a session, most bills introduced are not passed.
Decisions to kill bills—whether made in subcommittees or committees, at the
calendar stage, or on the floor—occur throughout the course of a session. The
later in the session a final decision is made on a bill (i.e., the longer it survives),
the more likely it is to be approved. Moreover, about half of the bills passed in
the closing days of a session appeared on the local and consent calendars. Special
procedural requirements apply to such bills. Notice of a legislator's intention to
introduce a local bill must be published in a newspaper in the affected locality
at least 30 days before its introduction. It must then receive the unanimous
agreement of the committee handling it and survive the scrutiny of the Committee
on Local and Consent Calendars. Once placed on a local or consent calendar, it
must be removed if contested by five members, or if floor debate on it exceeds
ten minutes. These requirements help protect against the adoption of inappropri-
ate local bills.

   All of this does not deny the existence of a logjam of sorts at the end of a
Texas legislative session. It appears somewhat less pernicious, however, when it
is viewed as the culmination of a reasonably systematic legislative process, and
not as something akin to the spontaneous feeding frenzies of bluefish. Quite a bit

of deliberation may have preceded the decisions made in the final days. Its adequacy is a matter of both empirical and normative judgment.

The Importance of Procedure

The ostensible purpose of the formal rules and procedures by which the legislature operates is to make the legislative process fair, orderly, and predictable. Without stable, agreed-on rules, it would be difficult for legislators to make decisions on the hundreds of bills and resolutions coming before them during a session. In the absence of rules, chaos would reign. Although the rules of the Texas legislature are not as complex as those of the U.S. Congress, they contain many technicalities and ambiguities and may prove to be quite baffling, especially to new members. Other things being equal, more experienced members are likely to have greater knowledge of and ability to use and manipulate the rules and consequently have an advantage.

Knowledge of rules and procedure is one skill a legislator must have to be effective in passing bills. But, as a former member of the legislature has written, a legislator soon "learns that a knowledge of the formal steps that a bill must go through between introduction and final passage merely provides him with a road map. It is not a means of transportation." Each of the formal steps required by the constitution and rules is "more like a roadblock than a gateway for the author of the bill."[38] Eleven major points or "roadblocks" through which a bill must pass before becoming law can be listed: committee (and perhaps subcommittee) action, scheduling, and floor action in the House; committee action, scheduling, and floor action in the Senate; conference committee; House and Senate action on the conference report; and gubernatorial approval. At any one of these points, a bill can be killed by its opponents (or perhaps die of indifference). When a bill passes any one of these points, it may mean only that its supporters can go on and try to navigate the next point, or "roadblock," in the legislative process.

Bargaining, compromise, and modification of a bill are often necessary to clear it through the various points. The legislator who wants to get bills passed must actively work to garner support for them. This includes getting a member of the other house to serve as their sponsor and work for their passage in that body. Nothing much happens "automatically" in the Texas legislature.

A major conclusion that can be drawn is that current legislative procedure tends to give an advantage to those seeking to prevent the enactment of certain legislation or bring about a weakened version of it. This, indeed, is the desire of many pressure groups, especially business and conservative groups, operating in Texas politics. Those who are skilled in the manipulation of procedures have an added advantage. Still, nothing beats having the skill and influence needed to round up the votes to win.

NOTES

1. Texas Legislative Council, *Accomplishments* (Report to the Sixty-fourth Legislature, Austin, 1975).

2. Gordon E. Baker, *The Reapportionment Revolution* (New York: Random House, 1966), p. 20.
3. Ibid., for further discussion.
4. *Colegrove* v. *Green,* 328 U.S. 549 (1946).
5. *Baker* v. *Carr,* 369 U.S. 186 (1962).
6. William C. Adams, "The Introduction of Single-Member House Districts in Harris, Dallas, and Bexar Counties: Some Implications for Texas Politics" (Paper presented at the annual meeting of the Southwestern Political Science Association, Dallas, March 1973), p. 4.
7. *Craddick* v. *Smith,* 471 S.W. 2d 375 (Tex. 1971).
8. *Mauzy* v. *Legislative Redistricting Board,* 471 S.W. 2d 570 (Tex. 1971).
9. *Houston Post,* January 9, 1972, Sec. A, p. 9.
10. *Graves* v. *Barnes,* 343 F. Supp 704 (W.D. Tex. 1972).
11. *White* v. *Register,* 412 U.S. 755 (1973).
12. *Mahan* v. *Howell,* 410 U.S. 315 (1973).
13. *White* v. *Register.*
14. *Graves* v. *Barnes,* Civil Action No. A71CA142 (1974). U.S. District Court.
15. Adams, "Introduction of Single-Member House Districts."
16. James D. Barber, *The Lawmakers* (New Haven, Conn.: Yale University Press, 1965), pp. 10–15.
17. J. William Davis, *There Shall Also Be a Lieutenant Governor* (Austin: University of Texas, Institute of Public Affairs, 1967), p. 92.
18. William E. Oden, "Tenure and Turnover in Recent Texas Legislatures," *Southwestern Social Science Quarterly* 65 (March 1965): 373.
19. Melvin Hairell, "The Politics of Committee Assignments in the Texas House of Representatives" (Master's thesis, University of Texas at Austin, 1971), pp. 173–180.
20. Ibid., pp. 177–180.
21. Citizens Conference on State Legislatures, *A New Order of Business* (A Report to the Texas Legislature, April 1973), pp. 26–27.
22. *Houston Chronicle,* January 22, 1987, p. 22.
23. For a description of the operation of the 1971 Senate Interim Committee on Urban Affairs, see Delbert A. Taebel, "Administering the Interim Committee: A Case Study," *Public Affairs Comment* 17 (January 1971): 1–4.
24. *Houston Post,* September 20, 1978, sec. A, p. 4. Some two dozen legislative committees were scheduled to meet in Austin on the same weekend as the University of Texas–Wyoming football game.
25. *Texas Observer,* June 17, 1977, p. 11.
26. *Houston Post,* January 25, 1985, p. 6A.
27. Juan J. Hinojosa, "The Mexican-American Caucus," *Texas Journal of Political Studies* 7 (Spring–Summer 1985): 27.
28. Fred Gantt, Jr., *The Chief Executive in Texas* (Austin: University of Texas Press, 1964), p. 212.
29. Ibid., p. 218.
30. Fred Gantt, Jr., "Special Legislative Sessions in Texas: The Governor's Bane or Blessings," *Public Affairs Comment* 16 (November 1970): 2.
31. Fred Gantt, Jr., "The Governor's Veto in Texas: An Absolute Negative?" *Public Affairs Comment* 15 (March 1969): 1–4.
32. Gantt, *Chief Executive in Texas,* p. 245.
33. G. Todd Norvell and Alexander W. Bell, "Air Pollution Control in Texas," *Texas Law Review* 67 (June 1969): 1089–1092.

34. House Research Organization, *How a Bill Becomes Law: Rules for the 70th Texas Legislature,* Special Legislative Report No. 131 (Austin: January 28, 1987).

35. Wayne Odum, "The Functions of Standing Committees in the Texas Legislature" (Paper presented at the Southwestern Political Science Association Convention, Dallas, March 1967).

36. Chase Untermeyer, "The House Is Not a Home," *Texas Monthly* (September 1977): 112.

37. This discussion draws on two articles by Harvey J. Tucker: "Legislative Logjams: A Comparative State Analysis," *Western Political Quarterly* 30 (March 1986): 67–78; and "Legislative Workload Congestion in Texas," *Journal of Politics* 49 (May 1987): 564–578. See also House Study Group, "Major Issues of the 69th Legislature," Special Legislative Report No. 119 (Austin: August 12, 1985).

38. Dick Cherry, "The Texas Legislature from Within," in *Governing Texas: Documents and Readings,* ed. Fred Gantt, Jr., Irving O. Dawson, and Luther G. Hagard, Jr. (New York: Crowell, 1966), p. 119.

chapter 6

The Chief Executive

Ann Richards on the campaign trail in 1990 in her successful quest for the governorship.

The twentieth century is sometimes called the "century of the executive." Americans traditionally have thought of their governments as consisting of three branches—the executive, legislative, and judicial—with the executive consisting of those institutions that comprise the administrative, or "doing," side of government, in direct contact with the populace in carrying on the day-to-day work of government. The executive branch is ordinarily headed by a chief executive—the president, governor, or mayor. However, this concept of the executive branch is of limited value in understanding modern politics and is not very descriptive of political reality. A more realistic view of modern government in the United States might describe it as consisting of four branches, with the chief executive and administrative team comprising a separate entity from the administrative agencies that conduct the programs of the government. The twentieth century has witnessed an increase in the prestige and power of both the chief executive and the administrative agencies, with the focus of attention in the political process centering increasingly on the chief executive.

140

The foundation of the position of chief executive is the authority to direct the administrative apparatus of the government. Article II of the U.S. Constitution establishes such a position for the president by vesting the executive power in the office and then providing it with tools designed to make the power effective. The president, however, has become much more than the administrative head of the government and may appropriately be referred to as chief legislator, commander-in-chief of the armed forces, ceremonial head of the government, leader of the political party, and leader of public opinion. The presidency has become the center of the process through which policy is formulated, adopted, and executed. The same is true for most chief executives throughout the world, for the position has become the focus of attention and the major center of power in most governments.

Three factors have combined to contribute to the increased importance of chief executives in modern governments. First, the development of the welfare/regulatory state has tended to make the programs of government more complex, requiring that legislation be adopted in general terms, leaving more discretion in the hands of those who carry out policy. This strengthens the chief executive vis-à-vis the legislative body because the chief executive usually has first call on the loyalty of the administrators. Second, the long series of crises that have characterized every decade of the twentieth century have contributed to the enhancement of the chief executive because crises usually result in at least temporary increases in executive power. Third, the decline in power and influence of legislative bodies has been a contributing factor; with their divided and fragmented patterns of leadership, legislatures have tended to have trouble mastering the complexities of modern policy and programs.

The preceding comments on chief executives have been couched in general terms more relevant to chief executives in nation-states than in the states of the United States. But despite the existence of formidable obstacles, the development of a broad and inclusive role in the policy process for the chief executive has also occurred in the American states. The evolution of the governorship has been described aptly as moving from figurehead to leadership.[1]

A trio of factors combined to make governors of the eighteenth and nineteenth centuries resemble figureheads more than chief executives. First, the colonial experience left Americans with a fear of excessive executive power; the result was that the early state constitutions generally provided for a dominant legislature and a weak governor. The legacies of the colonial years were short terms in office, restrictions on reelection, and restraints on the governor's power to appoint and remove. Second, the Jacksonian era of popular democracy resulted in the election of a multiplicity of administrative officials over whom the governor potentially had little influence. Third, a widely accepted goal of depoliticizing administration resulted in the creation of boards and commissions to head agencies. The governor's influence over such agencies often was quite limited, for the members usually served overlapping terms and were removable only for narrowly specified causes.

The enfeeblement of governors began to end in the latter years of the nineteenth century, as they began to assert themselves as the political leaders of their states; and the growth of the importance of the governorship has continued into the twentieth century. Several factors contributed to its rise. In addition to the general factors that contributed to the rise of chief executives, an "administrative efficiency" movement, supported by good-government reform groups, became active in the states. Efficiency was equated with coordinated government having central administrative responsibility in the hands of the chief executive. Constitutional revisions and administrative reorganizations supported by the movement resulted in increased powers for many governors. Finally, the development of universal suffrage and political parties strengthened the governors' political positions by virtue of their being heads of the political parties in their states. The consequence was that the governors' roles as chief executives expanded.

THE OFFICE OF GOVERNOR

The constitutional framework for the office of governor is provided by Article IV of the Constitution of 1876, which states:

> The Executive Department of the State shall consist of a Governor, who shall be the Chief Executive Officer of the State, a Lieutenant Governor, Secretary of State, Comptroller of Public Accounts, Treasurer, Commissioner of the General Land Office, and Attorney General.

Of the constitutionally established offices, all except the secretary of state are elective. The constitution, in a reflection of the distrust of gubernatorial leadership existing in 1876, named the governor chief executive officer of the state and then established an executive branch of which the governor was only first among equals in a group of elected officials. It then proceeded to limit gubernatorial authority further by not allowing the governor to exercise various tools commonly granted chief executives.

The Formal Office

The Constitution of 1876 provided for the selection of the governor by the qualified voters of the state for a two-year term, with the winner required to receive only a plurality of the votes cast. However, the constitution was amended in 1972 to provide four-year terms for the governor and other elected state officials, and in 1974 the gubernatorial term became four years. The governor must be at least 30 years old, a citizen of the United States, and a Texas resident for at least 5 years preceding the election.

The salary and fringe benefits of the governor of Texas are, in comparison with other states, moderately attractive; the salary during fiscal year 1992 was $93,432, and other benefits include a residence and an allowance for operating it, offices in the capitol building, a limousine, and use of an executive-style airplane.

The governor is also provided a staff to assist in performing the duties of the office. Although staff organization varies from governor to governor, there are certain essential functions staffs perform: program development, media relations, scheduling appearances and otherwise planning the governor's schedule, coordinating appointments to office, handling political and party affairs, maintaining liaison with other governmental bodies, and supervising of staff services. Governor Bill Clements's staff, for example, was organized under two coequal assistants. One was responsible for legislation and budget matters, the general counsel, and the special planning/coordinating divisions. The other coordinated office administration and was responsible for the press secretary, appointments to office, and political and party affairs.

In addition to the general staff, special tasks that also require staffs occasionally are assigned to the governor. The nature of the tasks varies widely, and sometimes they simply represent an interest of a particular governor; more commonly they are of a planning/coordinating nature. The planning/coordinating adjuncts have little to do with the essential functions of executive leadership and eventually tend to be separated from the office, as occurred in earlier years when defense and disaster relief and comprehensive health care were transferred to state agencies with similar responsibilities and federal-state relations was made into a separate agency. At the beginning of 1991, major divisions concerned with equal employment opportunity and criminal justice were part of the governor's office, and the office was responsible for several lesser activities. Incoming governor Ann Richards recommended, and the legislature approved, the transfer of almost all such activities to state agencies with related responsibilities.

The governor of Texas may be removed from office only through the process of impeachment and conviction. The process specified by the Texas Constitution provides that impeachment (indictment) must be by a majority vote of the House of Representatives, and conviction by a two-thirds vote of the Senate. Impeachment is not as restricted under the Texas Constitution as under the U.S. Constitution: The Texas Constitution does not specify grounds, whereas the U.S. Constitution states that impeachment may be only for treason, bribery, or other high crimes and misdemeanors. Even so, a Texas governor has been removed only once.

The constitution provides that the lieutenant governor will exercise the power and authority of the governor in case of death, removal from office, inability or refusal to serve, or impeachment of the governor. If the lieutenant governor is unable to serve, the president pro tem of the Senate is next in line of succession, and succession beyond that point is determined by statute. At present the order of succession is the speaker of the house, attorney general, and the chief justices of each of the 14 courts of appeals, based on the numbers assigned to the courts for purposes of identification.

As a legal matter, the lieutenant governor becomes governor when the governor is out of the state. Governors ordinarily arrange their excursions to avoid the possibility that important gubernatorial decisions will be made during their absence, a policy attributable to the rivalry that ordinarily exists between two influential and ambitious politicians with differing interests. The constitutional framework of separation of powers and checks and balances has the consequence of encouraging conflict between the legislative and executive branches, and, although the constitution provides that the lieutenant governor is a member of the executive branch, the important functions of that office are legislative. Consequently, conflict inevitably occurs between the lieutenant governor and the governor. A classic example of such conflict and of the triumph of political realism (the lieutenant governor as legislative official) over constitutional formalism (the lieutenant governor as executive official) was Governor John Connally's veto in 1965 of a bill making the lieutenant governor a member of the board of an administrative agency on the grounds that the separation of powers would be violated by making the presiding officer of the Senate a member of an executive agency.

Gubernatorial Responsibilities

The office of governor of Texas is a product of the framework established by the Texas Constitution as modified by statutes, traditions, and popular expectations. The duties of the governor are varied and complex, leading to such diverse activities as shepherding policy proposals through the legislature, naming the members of the boards that make policy for economic regulatory agencies, promoting the state's agricultural and industrial products, and heading the party's delegation to a national convention. For purposes of analysis, the duties can be grouped into five types: administrative, legislative, political, intergovernmental liaison, and ceremonial. But beyond the five there exists a miscellany of responsibilities.

Administrative Responsibilities   The Texas Constitution provides that the governor will be the chief executive officer of the state and will cause the laws to be faithfully executed. This constitutional provision has combined with popular expectations to place responsibility on the governor for the operation of the agencies that constitute the executive branch of government.

Legislative Responsibilities   Popular expectations and constitutional provisions also combine to give considerable responsibilities to the governor in the area of legislation. The constitution establishes the governor's legislative responsibilities through five provisions: (1) The governor may present information to the legislature on the condition of the state at the beginning of each session and at the close of the governor's term of office. (2) The governor may recommend legislation. (3) The governor is required to present to the legislature at the beginning of each regular session an estimate of the amount of money required to be raised by taxation. (4) The governor may veto bills (and items of appropriations within appropriation bills) that have been passed by the legislature. (5) The governor may call the legislature into and specify the purpose of special sessions. Beyond the constitutional provisions, expectations have developed that the governor will pursue the office by presenting a program designed to improve the condition of the populace or the operations of state government. As a consequence, the governor is expected to present an extensive program to the legislature for its consideration.

Political Responsibilities While the legislative and administrative responsibilities of the governor have a constitutional basis, the governor's political responsibilities, although just as real, derive from tradition and practice. The governor is the political leader of the state, often serving as representative of the state on national issues of special importance to the state by holding press conferences at governors' conferences or in Washington. If the governor's relations with the presidential nominee of the party are good, the governor usually plays a major role in the presidential campaign within the state. The most significant aspects of a governor's political responsibilities, however, revolve around the political party.

Democratic governors traditionally dominated their political party, although there were occasional exceptions, such as in 1948 and 1956, when forces loyal to the national party won control from conservative governors Coke Stevenson and Allan Shivers. In both instances the governors were leaving office, and the incoming governor did not enter the contest. Since 1968 changes in party rules designed to ensure more proportional representation have weakened, if not eliminated, the governor's party control, but the importance of such control is minimized by the decline of liberal/conservative bifactionalism, which reduces the probability of opponents using the party as a forum to embarrass a governor, and the negligible role that political parties play in the policy-making process.

Texas has less experience with the relationship between the Republican party and Republican governors, but the relationship is similar. After his election in 1978, Governor Bill Clements did not attempt to dominate the selection of the state executive committee, but the state chairman was selected with his approval, and relations between the governor and the party leadership were friendly. After Clements's defeat in 1982, critics charged the party with placing too much emphasis on the gubernatorial campaign to the detriment of other Republican candidates, many of whom were unexpectedly defeated. The chairman resigned, and a replacement was chosen who was acceptable to Clements's supporters and critics. During his second term, Clements's influence over the party organization increased, and he benefited more from shared partisan identification than have contemporary Democratic governors. The larger Republican contingent in the House of Representative, which shared his conservative ideology, increased his bargaining power with the Democratic legislative leaders by ensuring that vetoes could not be overridden.

Intergovernmental Liaison Responsibilities The constitution provides that the governor will, in the manner prescribed by law, conduct all intercourse and business of the state with other states and with the United States; and by tradition the governor often serves as liaison officer with political subdivisions of the state. Although some of the liaison activities are not new (for decades governors have had responsibilities for extradition of fugitives and have served on interstate boards and commissions), the growth in the 1960s and 1970s of national programs of grants-in-aid has increased the importance of this role. Texas governors have assumed these responsibilities, and special units responsible to them have been created to handle federal/state relations and community affairs.

Ceremonial Responsibilities   Probably every government has a ceremonial figure who symbolizes the government, ideally bestowing dignity and majesty. In the United States this responsibility is usually given to the chief executive, and Texas is no exception. The governor as the symbol of state government issues decrees and proclamations, signs documents, issues certificates of office, acts as the state's goodwill ambassador, and greets notable visitors (often making them honorary Texans or even admirals in the Texas navy).

Miscellaneous Activities   The governor undertakes many additional activities that over the years have accumulated around the office. Some of the more important involve military and judicial responsibilities. The Texas Constitution makes the governor commander-in-chief of the military forces of the state: As such, the governor may call out the national guard to execute the laws, repel invasions, and suppress insurrections and may assume command of the state police during public disasters, riots, and insurrections. Judicial responsibilities include the power to appoint some judges to vacant positions, but only to serve portions of terms, and the authority to grant clemencies in certain instances and one 30-day reprieve in capital cases.

Gubernatorial Powers

The Texas Constitution declares that the governor is chief executive. The governor is identified by the public as responsible for the administrative activities of state government and as leader of one of the two major political parties and is expected to develop a legislative program that will become the focus of attention in the legislature. To operate effectively as the chief executive, however, the governor must have the necessary tools of a political and legal nature, for a chief executive needs both formal authority and persuasive ability to accomplish objectives. Political scientists believe that the formal tools should include the power to appoint, remove, and direct the activities of lesser executive officials and to prepare and oversee the execution of the budget.

Appointive Powers   The constitution provides that, unless otherwise provided by law and with legislative positions excluded, vacancies in state and district offices are filled by appointment of the governor with the consent of the Senate. The governor appoints the boards that head most of the administrative units, including those dealing with the essential governmental functions of transportation, health and welfare, and higher education. An exception is public education, which is headed by an elective board, but Governor Mark White was given temporary appointive authority over that board when it was reconstituted in 1984 with responsibility for implementing major changes in the public schools. Although the exact number of positions filled by gubernatorial appointment is not known, one estimate places the number made during a four-year term at 4000.[2]

   While governors appoint the boards of most of the state agencies that are essential to their interests, three important factors serve to dilute considerably the influence they derive from that authority. First, the requirement of confirmation by the Senate may constitute a formidable barrier. The two-thirds majority required for senatorial confirmation, when combined with the traditional senatorial courtesy that allows senators to veto appointments of residents of their districts who are personally objectionable, forces governors to consider the probability of rejection prior to making most appointments.

Second, the necessity of considering the desires of an agency's clientele before making appointments serves to limit a governor's choice. The governor may be politically indebted to the clientele, or the clientele may be able to muster the necessary votes in the Senate to prevent confirmation.

Third, the administrative structures of most of the state agencies, which are headed by boards whose members serve six-year staggered terms, limit the governor's influence. Ordinarily, one-third of the membership is appointed at two-year intervals. A governor potentially could serve for two years and still have appointed only a third of a board's members, and until recently that third may have been appointed at the end of the two years, not the beginning. The terms of many board members expired on December 31, and new governors are not sworn in until mid-January. An outgoing governor thus had an opportunity to fill those positions, and from John Connally onward governors did so for appointment to the Board of Regents of the University of Texas, perhaps the most prestigious position filled through gubernatorial appointment, and occasionally other positions. After his defeat in 1982, Bill Clements made numerous "lame duck" appointments that the Democratic majority in the Senate refused to approve.

Reprinted by permission.

Considerable confusion resulted, and one member of the Board of Dental Examiners served a year without realizing that her appointment had not been approved. In an attempt to resolve the matter, legislation was enacted that established February 1 as the date upon which the terms of most board members begin. Incoming governments now confront the problem of lame duck appointments only in the case of appointments to unexpired terms.

Removal Power   The Texas Constitution imposes crippling limitations on the governor's authority to remove administrative officials. Article XV provides for the removal of elected state officials and judges of state district and appellate courts through the process of impeachment and trial; it also provides for removal for actions not sufficient for impeachment of the judges by the governor on address after a two-thirds vote of each house. The article also states that the legislature will provide by law for the trial and removal from office of all officers of the state for whom a removal process is not specified in the constitution. The terms *trial* and *removal* are of great importance; the requirement of a trial means that the removal by executive action of a state official is prohibited. This does not mean that all employees of the state must be tried in a judicial proceeding before removal, for the legislature can classify most jobholders as "employees" rather than "officers." It can also provide that an appointee holds office at the pleasure of the appointing authority, rather than for a fixed term.

　　While the constitution does not confer removal authority on the governor, the legislature could confer such authority by allowing appointment of administrative officials or board members to serve at the governor's pleasure. The legislature, which usually has no desire to increase the power of the governor, has not done so; and, with a few minor exceptions, governors have been without authority to remove executive officials outside their own staffs. Under prodding from Governor Bill Clements, the legislature in 1979 submitted, and the voters in 1980 approved, a constitutional amendment giving the governor power to remove, with the consent of the Senate, appointees the governor had selected personally for membership on boards and commissions. This extremely limited authority has not been used.

Directive Power   While the Texas Constitution provides that the governor is the chief executive officer of the state and is to cause the laws to be faithfully executed, it does not provide the powers to carry out its imperatives. The constitution further provides that the governor may require reports from all administrative officials, but it grants the governor no authority to direct their activities beyond the limited authority in the law enforcement field during emergency situations. Even the governor's power to compel reports is somewhat meaningless, for the governor has no means to compel compliance and is not authorized to take any action on whatever might be reported. Other governors have undoubtedly shared John Connally's lonely lament: "Nobody works for the governor. They all work for their boards. Administrators won't volunteer anything—I never know anything except by hearsay. They volunteer nothing."[3] A governor who desires action from administrative officials must resort to political maneuvering rather than the issuance of administrative directives.

Budgetary Powers   The Texas governor's role in budgeting is discussed in greater detail in Chapter 10, but for the moment it is necessary to note that the influence derived from budgetary responsibilities is quite restricted. While the governor is authorized to prepare a budget encompassing a spending plan for state government, the legislature has diluted this influence by establishing a Legislative Budget Board to prepare a competing budget. This reduces legislative dependence on the governor for information. Additionally, while the president and many state governors have authority to oversee the execution of the budget, until recently Texas did not provide the governor with any such authority. Some authority was granted the governor in 1987, but it is limited and circumscribed, and its impact on the governorship is as yet unclear.

The Political Governorship

The weakness of the formal powers of the Texas governor means that the influence of the office varies with the occupant. Past occupants have been white, mainstream Protestants, and most have been males; when Ann Richards became governor in 1991, her only female predecessor was Miriam Ferguson, who was elected as a proxy for her husband. Governors ordinarily have extensive political experience, and only Mrs. Ferguson and W. Lee O'Daniel were newcomers to politics.

Historically, the successful candidate for governor often was the governor. From the end of Reconstruction through 1990, only 4 of 30 governors were not elected to at least one additional term, and only Miriam Ferguson's and Bill Clements's terms were not consecutive. Traditionally the governor served only two terms, but after Allan Shivers was elected to a third full term in 1954, the next two governors also successfully sought third terms. The pattern of rewarding the governor with a second term was established when the term of office was two years, but potential opponents and the voters are less willing to concede a second term to a governor who has served four years. Dolph Briscoe, Bill Clements, and Mark White, the first governors to serve such terms, unsuccessfully sought reelection, although Briscoe had served the final two-year term and Clements was reelected after four years out of office.

In partisan and factional terms, Texas governors have tended to be conservative Democrats. An analysis of the governors from 1906 to 1964 indicates the pervasive dominance of Democratic conservatives. All 17 governors were Democrats, only one was considered liberal, and 3 were moderately liberal; the remainder were conservatives.[4] The liberals all served prior to World War II. Over the next decade both governors were conservative Democrats. Conservative dominance was challenged regularly by liberals after 1950, but a liberal was never elected governor during the period of liberal/conservative bifactionalism.

A Republican gubernatorial candidate first presented a serious challenge in

1962, and from 1968 onward the general elections were as closely contested as the Democratic primary, and often more so. As described in Chapter 3, the Republican challenge and other developments eventually resulted in a decline of liberal/conservative bifactionalism; as a consequence, Democratic governors increasingly have leaned toward ideological moderation.

The election of 1978 marked the culmination of the transition from bifactionalism to two-party competition. In the Democratic primary, Governor Dolph Briscoe, originally elected as a conservative, received significant support from organized labor and ethnic minorities, and his opponent, Attorney General John Hill, was supported by many white liberals. Both enjoyed significant conservative support, and the issues that ordinarily divide liberals and conservatives did not play a major role in the campaign. Bill Clements's victory in the general election over Hill marked the election of the first Republican governor since Reconstruction.

The 1990 campaign marked another major transition. The Democratic primary featured a run-off between Attorney General Jim Mattox and State Treasurer Ann Richards. Both were long identified with the liberal faction of the party, but again liberal/conservative issues did not play a major role in the campaign. Richards may be the first liberal to gain the governorship since Jimmy Allred (1935–1939), but her campaign did not emphasize a broad array of liberal issues, and the fiscal difficulties of her governorship make pursuit of a liberal agenda difficult.

THE EVOLUTION OF THE GOVERNORSHIP

Although the Texas governor does not possess formidable formal power, real power is not always formally conferred by constitution or statute. Formal power may be little more than a legal clerkship, while real power may be exercised through political leadership rather than legal delegation of authority. Since Texas governors are dependent upon political influence for whatever success they enjoy in exercising leadership, the impact of the governor varies with the personality and political skills of the incumbent. Nevertheless, every governor works within a set of expectations and traditions and an overall political context that establish parameters outside of which a governor operates only with great difficulty. An examination of the evolution of the governorship is necessary for an understanding of the parameters within which contemporary governors operate.

The most significant factors influencing the leadership role of the governor appear to be the factional/partisan situation and the method of electing the governor. In terms of partisan divisions and electoral methods, four gubernatorial eras are identifiable. The first, or formative, era spans the years from independence to the end of Reconstruction. The second, designated the Confederate colonel era, begins with the end of Reconstruction, stretches into the first decade of the twentieth century, and ends with the adoption of the direct-primary method of selecting the Democratic nominee for governor. The third, or one-party Democratic, era—encompassing the period that began with nomination by direct primary and ended after World War II—was one in which politics was highly personalized and victory in the Democratic primary was tantamount to election. The fourth, or contemporary, era covers the evolution of liberal/conservative bifactionalism into two-party competition.

The Formative Era

The Texas governorship historically traces back to the office of President of the Republic of Texas.[5] The constitution of the republic was modeled on the Constitution of the United States, but with modifications common to the constitutions of the southern states from which most of the early Texans emigrated. The president was granted powers similar to those of the president of the United States, but with important exceptions: the term of office was only three years, consecutive terms were forbidden, and the vice president was elected separately. The presidency of the republic was a significantly weaker office than the office of president of the United States.

The problems faced by the republic were overwhelming and were never adequately dealt with during the era of independence. The treasury was perenially exhausted, and an adequate revenue base was never developed; defenses against Mexican and Indian attacks were inadequate, and battles developed over the disposal of the country's only significant asset, public lands. Political divisions to some degree mirrored political divisions in the United States between Democrats and Whigs, but political parties did not develop. Individual loyalties to the two most important presidents provided what coherence there was to the politics of the period. Sam Houston, the dominant political figure of the republic, was a Jacksonian Democrat who favored economy in government and peace with the Indians, and Mirabeau B. Lamar supported territorial expansion, a national bank, and protective tariffs. The politics of the period was tumultuous, as might be expected from a group that had made a revolution, and Houston's fractious personality did not make for smooth legislative/executive relations. Houston, who served in or was president during the term of office of every congress of the republic, was often at odds with Congress and vetoed many bills.[6]

After the U.S. Congress approved annexation, a convention was called to write a state constitution. The Constitution of 1845 created a strong chief executive: Only a governor and a lieutenant governor were elected by popular vote; the governor was allowed successive terms in office; and most of the important officials, including judges, were appointed by the governor with the approval of the Senate. The gubernatorial term, however, was only two years.

The period from annexation until the Civil War was also characterized by problems with finance and peace on the frontier, and the resources of the state were not adequate to solve the problems. The republic left a sizable debt, much of it secured by pledges of customs revenues, which states constitutionally cannot collect. On the frontier Mexico was no longer a problem, but attacks by Indians continued. The governors, for the most part veterans of the struggle for independence who had emigrated from the southern states, struggled with the problem ineffectually. Sam Houston remained the dominant political figure (all but two of the six elected governors were his friends or political associates) and as United

States senator actually did more toward solving the debt problem than did the governors. Houston arranged for Texas to give up land claims on its disputed northwestern frontier in return for funds to pay the debt. The governors were not dominating political figures (only two were elected to second terms), but the problems were largely beyond the ability of state government to control. (See Table 6.1 for a list of the governors of this period.)

In a reflection of the southern background of most Texans and support of the party for annexation, pre–Civil War Texas was Democratic, but there was little party organization. Gubernatorial elections usually were not partisan, although by the mid-1850s the sectional tensions that led to the Civil War were becoming important in Texas politics and national party politics became of significance. Senator Houston voted against the Kansas-Nebraska Act, which opened new territories to slavery, and thereby made his reelection impossible. In a search for vindication he returned to run unsuccessfully for governor in 1857. But in 1859 he ran again as an independent supporter of the national union, or unionist, on a platform based on opposition to reopening the African slave trade and better frontier protection against Indian attacks, and he won. After Abraham Lincoln's victory in 1860, secessionist sentiment increased, but Houston resisted calling the legislature into special session to consider secession. The secessionists called their own convention, which, after endorsement by the legislature, submitted secession to a successful public vote. Houston was forced from office after he refused to swear allegiance to the Confederacy.

Most white Texans, including some prewar unionists, fought for or supported the Confederacy. The three Confederate governors were secessionists who devoted most of their time to raising men and supplies for the Confederate armies

Table 6.1 GOVERNORS OF THE
              FORMATIVE ERA

Governor	Term of Office
Pinckney Henderson	1846–1847
George Wood	1847–1849
Hansborough Bell	1849–1853
J. W. Henderson[a]	1853
Elisha Pease	1853–1857
Hardin Runnels	1857–1859
Sam Houston	1859–1861
Edward Clark[b]	1861
Francis Lubbock	1861–1863
Pendleton Murrah	1863–1865
A. J. Hamilton[c]	1865–1866
James Throckmorton	1866–1867
Elisha Pease[c]	1867–1869
E. J. Davis	1870–1874

[a] Lieutenant Governor Henderson became governor and served for a month when Bell resigned to serve in the U.S. House of Representatives.
[b] Lieutenant Governor Clark became governor when Houston refused to take an oath of allegiance to the Confederacy and was deposed.
[c] Provisional governor named by military authorities.

and to defense of the frontier against Indians. The end of the war marked the beginning of a period of disorder and confusion for Texas government, which the bankrupt state government was helpless in confronting. Governor Pendleton Murrah and several other officials left for Mexico, and for two months there was effectively no state government.

A. J. Hamilton, a former United States congressman who had joined the Union army, was appointed provisional governor. Working without a legislature or other appendages of government, he appointed hundreds of officials, began operation of the government, and called for the election of a constitutional convention. The 1866 convention was dominated by former Confederates but recognized political reality by nullifying the ordinance of secession and granting limited rights to blacks. With some modification, the Constitution of 1845 was presented to the voters for approval, and the new officials it authorized were elected. James Throckmorton, a unionist who fought for the South, was elected governor over E. M. Pease, a unionist former governor and postwar Republican who refused to participate in public affairs during the war. After the inception of military rule in 1867, Throckmorton was removed and Pease appointed provisional governor to serve until an acceptable constitution was written and the new offices it created were filled. A new constitution featuring a strong executive was adopted in 1869, and new officials were elected. Pease resigned in protest against the alliance of the military commander with the radical reconstructionists, and for several months the military ruled the state without a governor.

The new governor, E. J. Davis, was the leader of the radical Republican faction. Constitutionally, statutorily, and politically, Davis was a governor of great power, and during his four-year term he dominated the largely inexperienced legislature. A state militia and a state police force, both commanded by the governor, were created, and the governor could declare martial law whenever he desired. Davis appointed most public officials, including local offices. He was plagued by vehement opposition from a majority of the state's white population and a variety of intractable problems, including frontier protection, lawlessness, and widespread refusal to pay taxes. The opposition charged extravagance and gross abuse of power, especially in use of the state police and declarations of martial law.

In 1872 Democrats regained control of the legislature, and in 1873 Democrat Richard Coke won the governorship from Davis. The Democrats reversed many Republican policies and called for a constitutional convention to meet in 1875. The convention was dominated by Democrats who favored decentralized government, white supremacy, and states' rights and were intent upon preventing the alleged excesses of state government during Reconstruction. The constitution the convention drafted, which was submitted to popular vote in 1876 and was approved, generally limited and restrained government and specifically was designed to limit the authority of the chief executive.

The Confederate Colonel Era

The governorship of Richard Coke and the adoption of the Constitution of 1876 marked the end of one era and the beginning of another for the Texas governorship.[7] (See Table 6.2 for a list of the governors of this period.) From independence through Reconstruction the norms and expectations associated with governmental institutions were flexible and the influence and role of governors varied, but more often than not the governor was expected to provide policy leadership in state government. The Constitution of 1845 provided for a formal office that was reasonably adequate for this role. During Reconstruction, and especially during the Davis administration under the Constitution of 1868, the governor dominated state government.

Coke was reelected governor in 1876 in an election typical of gubernatorial contests until 1906. The key decision was made by the Democratic state convention, and the Democratic nominee was then elected governor. Coke was a Virginia-born lawyer and former Confederate officer with strong support from rural interests. He favored retrenchment in government, but with a touch of progressivism that recognized the need for improved transportation facilities. Of the nine men who served as governor from 1876 until 1906, seven had served as Confederate officers, and six of those had been born in southern or border states.

The Democratic party was a powerful force, and the governors nominated by the party were effectively the leaders of state government; even though the office was constitutionally weak, the party and its platform provided a unifying force around which the governor could rally support in the legislature. From the late 1870s into the 1880s the major political issues revolved around state finances and the sale of public lands, with differences over whether sales should be made only to settlers or should include sales to speculators in order to raise money to pay the state debt and finance public education. Only the impingement of national issues threatened Democratic gubernatorial nominees. Hostility to tight credit and limitations on the money supply led first to the rise of the Greenback party, then an independent movement, and finally, in the 1890s, to a major challenge from the Populist party, but not even the most serious challenges resulted in Democratic defeats. The third-party movements were to some extent useful to the governors in that they emphasized the need for Democratic unity.

**Table 6.2   GOVERNORS OF
THE CONFEDERATE
COLONEL ERA**

Governor	Term of Office
Richard Coke	1874–1876
Richard Hubbard[a]	1876–1879
Oran Roberts	1879–1884
John Ireland	1884–1887
Sul Ross	1887–1891
Jim Hogg	1891–1895
Charles Culberson	1895–1899
Joe Sayers	1899–1903
Samuel Lanham	1903–1907

[a]Lieutenant Governor Hubbard became governor when Coke resigned to serve in the U.S. Senate. He served over two years but was never elected to the office.

By the mid-1880s a new set of issues was arising, and Texas Democrats began to divide along conservative and progressive lines. Conservatives continued to emphasize states' rights and decentralized, nonactive government. Progressives were less inclined to fear governmental action; they opposed economic domination, especially in land ownership, by out-of-state corporations; and favored vigorous antitrust laws and a railroad commission with strong regulatory authority. By 1900 most progressives favored prohibition of the sale of alcoholic beverages.

The progressives captured the governorship in 1891 with the election of Jim Hogg, and the change was not only philosophical but generational.[8] Hogg was the first native-born Texan to be elected governor and the first governor since Reconstruction not to have served in the Confederate army. As Texas's attorney general he had emphasized enforcement of antitrust laws and had filed lawsuits that eventually recovered 1.5 million acres of land railroads had improperly acquired as subsidies for their construction costs. Hogg and his fellow progressives had supported planks in the Democratic platform calling for a railroad commission, stronger state antitrust laws, state financial support for lengthening the school term to six months, greater financial support for the state university, and restrictions on large landholdings by non-Texans. He had encouraged young progressives throughout the state to become candidates for the legislature, and after his nomination he continued to make speeches calling for the people to send legislators to Austin pledged to carry out the instructions of their constituents as expressed in the Democratic platform.

Hogg's battle for a railroad commission was not won easily, as a combination of business interests opposed to governmental interference in the economy; western interests not yet served by railroads; constitutional strict constructionists opposed to the merging of legislative, judicial, and executive powers in one body; and the politically powerful railroads united in opposition. His supporters were narrowly successful in electing a progressive speaker of the house, and in his initial address to the legislature Hogg appealed to Democratic loyalty in urging creation of the commission, reminding the Democratic members that they were committed to enactment of the Democratic platform. He argued that the platform of the dominant political party should be carried into effect because responsible government required that party pledges should not be slighted when fundamental principles were not violated. During negotiations over the authority of the commission and the method of choosing its members, he threatened to veto unacceptable legislation and go to the people prior to a call for a special session. He emphasized his determination that Democratic lawmakers not default on their obligation to write a strong regulatory law. Eventually a commission was created that resembled what he desired.[9]

In the nineteenth century governors did not have extensive staffs; consequently, they had to use personal and political associates for assistance in designing and carrying out their policies and programs. Hogg's biographer contends that one of his outstanding characteristics was his ability to attract able men.[10] Hogg took an interest in the careers of his friends and protégés and was actively involved in their candidacies. Indicative of his ability was his persuasion of John

Reagan, a legendary figure in Texas politics who was a contemporary of Sam Houston and who had served in the Confederate cabinet, to resign from the United States Senate to chair the railroad commission.

During Hogg's governorship the legislature enacted a variety of progressive reform measures, including an alien (non-Texan) land law (an 1891 version was overturned by the courts and an 1893 version not effectively enforced), court reform, improvements in the civil and criminal codes, and controls to ensure the soundness of railroad, municipal, and county bonds. The railroad commission and other progressive legislation produced a split in the Democratic party in 1892 that resulted in a dissident group of conservatives supporting the candidacy of longtime Democrat George Clark in the gubernatorial general election. Demands by more radical agrarian groups for stronger governmental programs than the Hogg progressives would support produced a major challenge from the Populist party, which nominated Tom Nugent for governor. Hogg was comfortably reelected, but both Clark, who was supported by the Republicans, and Nugent received more votes than normal for non-Democratic candidates; Hogg was reelected with less than a majority of the total vote.[11]

The split in the Democratic party that resulted in a competitive general election in 1892 was an indication that the convention system for selecting the Democratic nominee for governor was becoming inadequate for the changing nature of Texas politics. As long as the Democratic party could unite behind white supremacy, states' rights, and limited government, conflicts among personalities could be decided at the convention, and Democrats could repel Republican and inflationary fiscal policy challenges. The broadening of the scope of political debate by the progressives created a situation in which the stakes were great enough that the losers were unwilling to accept the decision of the convention and insisted on taking their position to the voters.

The convention system for selecting nominees did not end immediately but persisted for over a decade. The progressive/conservative conflict was muted as the Hogg reforms were accepted and the Democrats supported easy-money policies in an effort to repel the Populist challenge. The governors at the turn of the century enjoyed broad support. Hogg was succeeded by Attorney General Charles Culberson, a fellow progressive who also had been too young to serve in the Civil War, but Joe Sayers and Samuel Lanham, the final two governors elected without use of party primaries, were nonnative Confederate veterans who, like most of the governors of the Confederate colonel era, were business-oriented conservatives.

The resurgence of traditional conservatism after Hogg is attributable to three factors. First, business and industrial elements were becoming more important in what had been an overwhelmingly agricultural economy; this importance was magnified by the rise of petroleum production around the turn of the century. Second, the decline of the Populist party, which failed to attract meaningful support beyond its rural Protestant base and which found some of its more popular proposals embraced by the Democrats, removed the challenge to the Democrats from the left. Finally, the basic rules of political participation were changed.

The Populist/Democratic rivalry of the 1890s resulted in appeals by both parties to black voters as well as in campaigns and elections that were tainted with illegalities. After Populist voters returned to the Democratic party a variety of measures were adopted that, when combined, had the dual purpose of reducing black influence and making elections honest. Payment of the poll tax was made a prerequisite for voting. In many counties the Democratic party had begun using primaries, usually with participation restricted to whites, to nominate local officials. In 1903 and 1905 laws were enacted that in effect made primaries the mandatory method for selecting Democratic nominees for all offices, and from 1906 onward primaries were conducted to select the Democratic nominee for governor. Linkage of the poll tax to voting, complex election laws requiring primaries for parties polling over 100,000 votes in gubernatorial elections, and the exclusion of blacks from the Democratic primary eliminated the Republican party from contention and made future development of radical parties difficult. The Democrats for all practical purposes eliminated all opposition.[12]

The One-Party Democrats

Texas governors of the Confederate colonel era were on the whole competent executives who were the leaders of state government. Most were conservatives, committed to white supremacy, states' rights, and limited government, but those who were committed to progressive reforms were able to use the resources of the office, especially the leadership of the Democratic party and appeals to party loyalty, to achieve their objectives. Successful gubernatorial candidates had to be widely known within the party, and the requirement of a two-thirds vote at the convention ensured broad support. The political strength of the office is indicated by the success rate in achieving reelection; from Richard Coke through Samuel Lanham, every elected governor was reelected to a second term.

The early 1900s experienced a resurgence of progressives in Texas politics that was part of the national progressive movement. The Texas progressives focused on honesty and efficiency in government, especially in elections, and on enactment of Prohibition. In 1906 there were four major candidates for the Democratic nomination, and the eventual winner was Tom Campbell. Campbell's election marked a transition from one era to another. His predecessor was the last Confederate veteran to serve as governor, and Campbell was the first governor to run in a primary and the last to be nominated by a state convention (in effect, if no candidate received a majority in the primary the state convention chose the nominee from among the primary contenders). (See Table 6.3 for a list of the governors of this period.)

Campbell was a progressive who favored Prohibition and campaigned as a friend of laborers and small farmers and an enemy of corporate influence in politics. In his first term of office he was moderately successful in achieving progressive objectives. A variety of relatively minor educational, labor, and health reforms were enacted; corporations were prohibited from contributing to political campaigns; the leasing of convict labor to private entrepreneurs was ended; and one of Hogg's objectives was finally realized with the passage of legislation restricting the issuance of free passes by railroads.

Campbell's second term, however, was much less successful. Business and

**Table 6.3   GOVERNORS OF THE
ONE-PARTY ERA**

Governor	Term of Office
Tom Campbell	1907–1911
Oscar Colquitt	1911–1915
Jim Ferguson	1915–1917
William P. Hobby[a]	1917–1921
Pat Neff	1921–1925
Miriam Ferguson	1925–1927
Dan Moody	1927–1931
Ross Sterling	1931–1933
Miriam Ferguson	1933–1935
Jimmy Allred	1935–1939
W. Lee O'Daniel	1939–1941
Coke Stevenson[b]	1941–1947
Beauford Jester	1947–1949

[a]Lieutenant Governor Hobby became governor with the impeachment of Ferguson and then was elected to the 1919–1921 term.

[b]Lieutenant Governor Stevenson became governor when O'Daniel resigned to serve in the U.S. Senate and then was elected to two terms.

commercial interests believed that his policies discouraged investment of out-of-state capital, and they helped secure the election of a conservative majority in the legislature. Additional progressive measures favored by Campbell were not enacted, and he was unable to secure legislative approval for a statewide prohibition amendment to the constitution despite approval in the Democratic primary of 1908 of a referendum calling for such an amendment. Campbell criticized the legislature for failing to implement the party platform and blamed the failure on the influence of lobbyists for selfish interests.

Campbell's difficulties with the legislature in his second term contrasts sharply with the effectiveness of Hogg. The elimination of non-Democratic opposition and the use of primaries for selecting nominees had changed the nature of political conflict in a manner that made appeals to party loyalty and party platforms much less effective. More candidates competed for Democratic nominations, and individuals were able to rise in state politics more readily without the support of extensive political organizations. The electoral changes designed to eliminate blacks and irregularities drastically reduced the size of the electorate, and the persons who became nonparticipants were disproportionately likely to respond to appeals from progressive candidates on economic issues.[13]

Campbell was succeeded by Oscar Colquitt, a conservative who in his campaign advocated a policy of "legislative rest." Colquitt united the antiprohibitionist forces against three other candidates who favored Prohibition in a year in which the only other major political issue was the integrity of United States Senator Joe Bailey. The primary election law had been changed, and the candidate receiving the most votes in the primary was the nominee. Colquitt won the nomination with only 41 percent of the vote, and the legislature had a prohibitionist majority. Colquitt's relations with the legislature, which over his objections submitted an unsuccessful prohibition amendment to the voters, were unfriendly, but he did not present an extensive legislative program, and little was lost. Colquitt did not receive the customary routine renomination but was opposed by a prohibitionist candidate who received 45 percent of the vote.

The trends that were to dominate Texas politics and the governorship throughout the one-party era were already evident in Colquitt's administration. There was an absence of influence on the part of political parties, legislative/executive relations were characterized by conflict, and policies revolved around the personalities of key leaders and emotional issues such as Prohibition. The most important of these personalities during the second and third decades of the century was introduced to Texas politics with the successful gubernatorial candidacy of Jim Ferguson in 1914. From 1914 through 1940 either Ferguson or his wife, Miriam, ran for the Democratic nomination for governor eight times and were successful on four occasions. In most of the other six elections Ferguson-backed candidates contested the nomination, and on two occasions Jim Ferguson sought other offices.

Jim Ferguson was an antiprohibitionist who promised to veto any law passed by the legislature relating to the liquor question, a position that endeared him to many Mexican-Americans in South Texas and, especially, to the German-Americans of Central Texas. Claiming to be in the Jim Hogg tradition of support for the poor and less powerful, Ferguson pledged increased state aid to rural schools and promised to support laws limiting the rent charged tenant farmers for land. Poor tenant farmers and laborers in the commercial logging areas of Southeast Texas always constituted important bases of support for Ferguson.

Ferguson's first term of office was quite successful because the legislature, with some members still identified with the progressive resurgence of the first decade of the century and others elected as Ferguson supporters, was quite supportive. A tenant law was passed (but later held unconstitutional). Several state colleges were created, a program of financial assistance to rural schools was enacted, and a constitutional amendment was adopted authorizing the state to furnish free textbooks to public school students. Roads traditionally were the responsibility of counties, but the need of the developing economy for reliable transportation combined with the availability of federal grants led to the creation of a state highway system.

Ferguson was easily reelected in 1916, but his second term was cut short. His political appeal was similar to that of Hogg, Culberson, and Campbell but did not include the progressive emphasis on integrity, honesty, and efficiency in government. Instead, he acted upon the axiom that to the victor belong the spoils. As governor, and later as the governor's husband, he took an active interest in awarding highway and textbook contracts, even sitting with the highway commission during deliberations. He also used the governor's power to issue pardons to criminals as a form of patronage.

Ferguson took an active interest in matters of the internal administration of the University of Texas and demanded that the president fire several professors. The president refused and was supported by the regents, and in 1917 Ferguson vetoed the university's appropriation. Although the veto was not the stated reason for his eventual impeachment and removal, it mobilized a large number of influential enemies who undertook a close scrutiny of his activities. The House of Representatives undertook an investigation that resulted in 21 articles of impeachment being brought against him, and the Senate found him guilty of ten of the charges, the most important of which involved misapplication and diversion of public funds and the acceptance of $156,000 from sources he refused to identify.[14]

Jim Ferguson's first term as governor remained the last effective progressive or liberal gubernatorial administration in the one-party era, and he was the last governor with an extensive and successful legislative program in that era. Ferguson resigned from office the day before Senate action on his removal was completed, thereby futilely hoping to make ineffective the permanent disability from holding office that constitutionally accompanies removal through the impeachment process. He ran unsuccessfully for the Democratic nomination for governor in 1918, but in later years his candidacy was successfully challenged, and his wife ran as his surrogate. After his initial term in office he seemed more interested in patronage than programs, and Miriam Ferguson's administrations not only were marred by charges of corruption but also were largely bereft of accomplishment.

The governors of Texas who served between Ferguson's impeachment and the Great Depression were for the most part economic conservatives who did not propose extensive programs. The primary political issues in Texas of the second and third decades of the twentieth century other than Fergusonianism were Prohibition and its enforcement and the Ku Klux Klan. Ferguson, who enjoyed strong support among Catholics and German-Americans, was anti-Klan and did not favor strict enforcement of the prohibition laws. The Klan enjoyed numerous electoral successes, but a Klan-supported candidate never captured the governorship. The strongest Klan challenge was in 1924, when Miriam Ferguson defeated the Klan-supported candidate. Under Ferguson leadership the legislature enacted an anti-Klan law that, among other provisions, prohibited the wearing of masks in public. After 1924 the Klan rapidly declined in influence.[15]

Two of the governors in the 1920s were reformers who advocated programs designed to increase accountability and efficiency in government. Pat Neff, who otherwise was a conservative known for his advocacy of strong enforcement of the prohibition law and use of the Rangers and National Guard in invoking antiunion laws against striking railroad employees, supported adoption of a new constitution and urged revision of the tax laws, which he called inefficient and unfair. The legislature did not follow his recommendations.

Dan Moody was also a "good government" reformer. As attorney general during Miriam Ferguson's first term, he undertook an investigation after charges of corruption arose in the letting of construction contracts by the Ferguson-controlled highway commission and successfully sued to have several contracts canceled. In 1926 he defeated Miriam Ferguson for the Democratic nomination for governor in an election in which the chief issues were the road contracts and pardon policy of the governor.

Moody led the only progressive administration of the 1920s, advocating regulation of public utility and transportation companies, increased state support for public schools, concentration and modernization of the prison system, improvement of the eleemosynary institutions, reform and modernization of the system of taxation, and the most extensive system of governmental reorganization and reform ever proposed by a Texas governor. His reorganization program featured consolidation of the many state agencies into a small number of departments, use of the merit system for state employees, shortening the ballot by eliminating the election of several state officials, and the adoption of a unified system of accounting for all state departments.

In a period of prosperity the legislature responded to some of Moody's suggestions for improving public services: State support for public schools was increased to allow an academic term of six months, a goal of progressives since Jim Hogg; minimum salaries guaranteed by the state for public school teachers were increased; and a construction program was undertaken at the eleemosynary and correctional institutions. The proposals for administrative reorganization were almost entirely lost. Moody called five special sessions of the legislature, but at the conclusion of his two terms in office the only administrative reform of significance to be enacted was the creation of the office of state auditor with authority over the accounting system.

Moody's lack of success in securing enactment of his program contrasts sharply with the successes of Hogg, Ferguson, and, to a lesser extent, Campbell. Although they were not always successful and experienced greater difficulty in dealing with the legislature during their second than during their first terms, all three were able to secure the enactment of meaningful legislative programs. Moody could not build legislative majorities for his proposals, and the reasons for his failure appear not to have been personal. A popular, handsome politician who first became known for prosecuting members of the Klan as a district attorney and then attained wide recognition as attorney general for his battle with the Fergusons, Moody received national attention and was mentioned as a possible Democratic vice presidential nominee. Hogg had the prestige and influence of the Democratic party and its platform to call upon, and Campbell also used appeals to party loyalty, although the effectiveness of such appeals had declined greatly by the end of his second term. By the time of Moody's administration the one-party system was thoroughly developed, and Moody did not find appeals to party loyalty of any benefit.

Jim Ferguson's personality inspired intense loyalty on the part of poor sharecroppers, laborers, and small farmers, and he developed personal political contacts throughout the state. Candidates were identified as either Ferguson or anti-Ferguson; in effect Ferguson made himself the dominant political issue. In his successful electoral efforts enough Ferguson supporters were elected so that he could achieve sufficient support to enact desired legislation. Ferguson's influence on the legislature is demonstrated by action on his disability from holding office. After Miriam Ferguson was elected governor in 1924, the legislature approved a law removing the disability, but after her defeat in 1926 the legislature repealed the law. Attorney General Moody had ruled the law unconstitutional, and, after Jim Ferguson brought suit to be placed on the ballot in 1930, the Texas Supreme Court agreed. Ferguson's success in dealing with the legislature seems unique to his personality and appeal and was not a model that could be emulated by later governors.

The Great Depression began in 1929 during Dan Moody's second term, but dealing with its effects was left to his successors, Ross Sterling and the Fergusons. Ultimately the problems created by the economic collapse were beyond the ability and resources of state governments to deal with, and the national government undertook the responsibility, either directly or through aid to state and local governments.

By 1934 economic issues were paramount in national politics. Recovery from the Depression was not yet underway, but President Franklin Roosevelt's New Deal programs, designed to ameliorate the suffering and promote recovery, had begun. There were six candidates in the Democratic primary to succeed Miriam Ferguson, who did not seek reelection. A Ferguson-supported candidate campaigned for the abolition of the state property tax, the right of labor to bargain collectively, state programs to provide widespread home ownership and to prevent foreclosure in time of distress, and a shorter work week so that employment could be provided for all persons. The more conservative candidates favored reductions in governmental expenditures and increased use of taxes on natural resources to provide relief from property taxes.

The winner was a moderate, Attorney General Jimmy Allred. Allred is sometimes referred to as Texas's first liberal governor, but that reputation is based as much on his close allegiance with the Roosevelt administration and the national Democratic party as on his policies as governor. Allred's campaign emphasized regulation of lobbyists and reform of the pardoning process, which the Fergusons again were accused of using as a form of political patronage. His platform also called for the creation of a public utilities commission and a modern state police force by combining in one department the existing Highway Patrol and Texas Rangers. He was opposed to racetrack gambling, which recently had been authorized by the legislature, and, while personally a prohibitionist, pledged to abide by a popular vote on that issue. He called for a decrease in tax rates with improvements in tax administration to increase collections, and he favored enactment of a chain-store tax as a curb on monopolies. These positions placed Allred in the older progressive tradition of Hogg, Culberson, and Campbell, and he did not emphasize the contemporary liberal positions favoring progressive taxation, collective bargaining for workers, welfare programs, and racial equality.

Allred began his governorship with a notable failure when he attempted unsuccessfully to influence the outcome of the contest for speaker of the House of Representatives. He never enjoyed support from a majority in either house of the legislature but instead had to battle to build coalitions on every issue. Although he had offended the House leadership by opposing the election of the speaker, the more conservative Senate blocked more of his legislative program than did the House. Allred's relations with the House improved somewhat in his second term after an ally was elected speaker.

Allred had some real accomplishments during his two terms: The system of pardons and paroles was changed to reduce the role of the governor; the Rangers were converted from a patronage-ridden organization in which thou-

163

sands of persons held special commissions into a professional law enforcement agency; a Department of Public Safety was created that included the Rangers and the Highway Patrol; statewide prohibition was repealed and replaced by a local option system; and racetrack gambling was made illegal. Perhaps his greatest accomplishment, however, was to bring New Deal antidepression programs financed primarily through federal grants to Texas. The most important of such programs successfully supported by Allred were a state employment service and pensions for the needy elderly, popularly called old-age pensions.

The old-age pension program was something less than a full success for Allred. Throughout his administration the state treasury experienced deficits, and he and the legislature were unable to agree on tax legislation. Pensions were funded only for nominal amounts, and legislation enacted during his second term to provide aid to the needy blind and dependent children was not funded until later administrations. Allred eventually recommended increased taxes on inheritances and natural resources, enactment of a selective luxury tax, and consideration of an income tax. Only the chain-store tax was enacted, along with taxes on alcoholic beverages, which produced considerable revenue after Prohibition was repealed.

Allred became governor at a time when conditions seemed ideal for a liberal reformer. Poverty and deprivation were widespread, there was disillusionment with the political order, and populist and radical appeals found receptive audiences throughout the country.[16] The problems of the Depression were compounded in Texas by an agricultural recession that extended through much of the 1920s and the existence of a large class of tenant farmers who lived in perpetual poverty. These conditions produced the Fergusons and their populist rhetoric, interest in patronage, and modest accomplishments; Allred and his moderately liberal but unfunded programs; and Allred's successor, W. Lee O'Daniel.

A large field of candidates entered the Democratic primary after Allred, in keeping with tradition, announced that he would not seek a third term. Several experienced politicians were included among the candidates, but the eventual winner was O'Daniel, a Fort Worth milling-company executive and host of a country music radio program. O'Daniel campaigned with his band and vocalists and won the nomination without a runoff. His platform was the Ten Commandments and his motto the Golden Rule. As governor he did not have an extensive legislative program, and he was unpopular with legislators, many of whom resented his repeated attacks on professional politicians. His appointments were regularly rejected as unqualified or inopportune. On one occasion O'Daniel, a prohibitionist, had four nominees to the Liquor Control Board, including a prohibitionist minister, the president of the Anti-Saloon League, and a past president of the Women's Christian Temperance Union, who were rejected before a fifth nominee was approved. Veteran journalist Richard Morehead describes O'Daniel as having a "basic ignorance of politics and government," and that judgment does not seem unfair.[17]

O'Daniel was not popular with Texas politicians, but he enjoyed immense popularity with the voters and was easily reelected in 1940. In 1941 a vacancy occurred in a Texas seat in the U.S. Senate, which O'Daniel successfully sought in a special election. He allegedly received support from opponents identified with beer and liquor interests, who wanted him out of the governorship and were friendly with his successor, Lieutenant Governor Coke Stevenson.[18] Stevenson was one of Texas's ablest governors, but he left little impact on the governorship and state government. His background equipped him admirably for the governorship—he had been a county attorney, county judge, and a member and speaker of the House of Representatives prior to his election as lieutenant governor. He was effective in dealing with the legislature and accessible to and friendly with newspaper reporters, and he had a reputation for honesty and integrity. Nevertheless, an admiring journalist cites as the most significant achievement of his administration the adoption of the constitutional amendment designed to prevent deficits in the state treasury by making the comptroller of public accounts responsible for estimating revenue available for appropriation.[19]

Two factors account for Stevenson's minimal impact on state government. First, he was psychologically and philosophically a conservative who was neither committed to expansion of state services nor inclined toward aggressive leadership. Had he been so inclined, however, it is doubtful that he could have accomplished much, for a more decisive factor limited his opportunities. He was governor during the wartime years when the country's attention and resources were devoted to the war effort.

In 1947, Texas state government was confronted with a backlog of problems or demands for services that had accumulated during the Depression and World War II. Prisons, mental hospitals, and schools for the mentally retarded were old, decrepit, and often run by nonprofessionals, and secondary roads were of poor quality. In an era in which public education had become quite popular but also more expensive, state aid to local schools was small and not related to need. The makeup of the system of colleges and universities had not changed since 1929, despite population shifts and growth. Managerially, the highest levels of government were equally backward: The legislature did not have any significant staff assistance, the governor had only a small staff of personal assistants, and the state budget was prepared by the Board of Control, an independent agency responsible for such housekeeping functions as central purchasing and maintenance of state buildings. The budget, moreover, was merely a tabulation of selected requests (highways, aid to public schools, and welfare were not included), and the sources of revenue necessary to finance the expenditures were not included.

In 1947–1949 important policy and structural changes occurred that shaped Texas politics, state services, and executive/legislative relations for the next four decades. Beauford Jester, who was elected governor in 1946, was an unlikely person to preside over a modernization program that resulted in major changes in state government. He was a courtly, conservative southern gentleman who left the Railroad Commission to run for governor in a race that foreshadowed the liberal/conservative struggles of the next two decades. After an academic freedom struggle of several years between the president, Homer Rainey, and the regents of the University of Texas, the regents fired Rainey, who in a search for vindication ran for governor with the support of what became the party's liberal faction. Rainey became the chief issue in the campaign, with several candidates lambasting him for alleged socialistic, anti-Christian behavior. Jester, who was supported by moderates as well as conservatives unhappy with the policies of the national Democratic party, stayed out of the controversy and defeated Rainey decisively in the second primary.

The programmatic and policy changes that occurred during Jester's governorship and with his support were quite impressive and, considering his base of political support, surprisingly progressive. An antilynching law was adopted, and constitutional amendments were approved by the legislature (although eventually defeated by the voters) to repeal the poll tax and to provide for annual sessions and salaries for the legislature. Of greater lasting significance were the programmatic changes: A Board for State Hospitals and Special Schools to operate the mental hospitals and schools for the retarded was created, and a movement to provide the impetus for increased appropriations for both construction and operating funds was begun; a Youth Council was created to operate juvenile correction and orphan facilities; the higher education system was expanded, and increased appropriations for existing schools were provided; and the State Board of Education was created to administer a newly approved minimum foundation school program.

Three changes in the context in which the governor and the legislature make policy were as momentous as the policy changes. The first of the changes occurred in 1947, when the relationship between the Senate and the lieutenant governor underwent an important transformation. In 1945 Lieutenant Governor John Lee Smith decided to run for governor, and the senators, meeting in executive session, settled on Senator Allan Shivers as his successor and helped secure Shivers's election in 1946. Lieutenant governors had long possessed the authority described in Chapter 5 to make committee appointments and to control the agenda of the Senate but had rarely used that authority to exercise power. Shivers used it very skillfully, leading one of the senators to comment, "When John Lee Smith was lieutenant governor the Senate ran the Senate. But Shivers began to take things over, and soon was running the Senate, with the Senate's consent."[20] Shivers was a supporter of the modernization program and played an instrumental role in its passage in the Senate.

The second change did not occur until 1949, when under Shivers's leadership the legislature created the Legislative Council to perform research and draft bills and the Legislative Budget Board to prepare a budget for legislative consideration. The two boards and their professional staffs have made the legislature less dependent on the executive for information and have thereby strengthened the legislature in its relations with the governor.

The creation of the Legislative Council and the Legislative Budget Board contributed to the third change. The chair and vice chair of each were the lieutenant governor and the speaker of the House of Representatives. The speaker had long been influential in the proceedings of the House, but the added duties and perhaps the necessity for stronger centralized leadership to prevent the House from being outmaneuvered by the Senate resulted in a strengthening of the speakership. Like the lieutenant governorship, the speakership became essentially a full-time position, and the occupants henceforth have been influential rivals of the governor.

Beauford Jester died in July 1949 after serving less than three years in office.

His programmatic accomplishments were quite substantial, but he bequeathed a governorship that was, vis-à-vis the legislature, considerably weakened and that has largely survived in that weakened condition. He was succeeded by Lieutenant Governor Allan Shivers, who had contributed greatly to the weakening of the governorship through his actions in strengthening the lieutenant governorship and his leadership in the creation of the Legislative Council and Legislative Budget Board. Shivers began what can be considered the modern or current era in the development of the Texas governorship.

THE CONTEMPORARY GOVERNORSHIP

Joseph Schlesinger has developed a general rating of the formal powers of the governors of the 50 states based on four measures of strength: budget powers, appointive powers, tenure potential, and veto powers. Governors are rated on each of the four measures and assigned a score from one to five. Under the rating system in 1971 the governor of Texas was rated the least powerful governor in the nation. Since that time the term of office has been increased to four years, and in 1983 the Texas governor rated only next to last.[21]

The Texas governorship, weak in formal power and confronting a legislature with a tradition of independence, does have potential bases of power, for inherent in the office are factors that enable the occupant to influence others without possessing legal authority over their actions. The prestige of being chief executive and the most widely known official in the state allows the governor to command public attention and build support that exerts pressure on other officials, and the more successful Texas governors have resorted effectively to public appeals for support for their programs. The power to make appointments to the boards that are responsible for the operation of the administrative system enables a governor to obtain support from groups interested in appointments, a source of influence more important to contemporary governors than to the governors of earlier eras when the state did not regulate as many activities and provide as many services. Governors of the Confederate colonel era could use their position as party leader to rally support for their programs, but this source of support was largely lost in the one-party era.

Dependence on such sources of influence as patronage and appeals for public support and partisan loyalty means that governors have the power to persuade, not to direct. They must secure legislation that will make their objectives law, for their position in the executive branch does not allow them to direct the activities of administrative officials. The real importance of the Texas governorship thus lies in its legislative role. The evolution of the office has been such that governors are expected to assume leadership in securing the enactment of programs presented in their campaigns. The success or failure of a governor's administration, therefore, is likely to be determined by success or failure in dealing with the legislature and, consequently, is more dependent on variations in a governor's political skill than on legal powers.

Many things determine the success of Texas governors, but four factors seem to be of predominant importance. First, the successful governor needs a considerable store of personal political skills, including articulateness and persuasiveness with both small groups and mass audiences; knowledge of when to offer rewards or threaten punishment and when to push on or retreat; and the ability to attract and utilize a capable staff. Second, the governor's standing with the electorate may determine success in office. Margin of victory may be of importance, but current popularity is probably of greater significance. Third, relations with the legislature, especially its presiding officers, are of great importance, for a recalcitrant legislature can thwart a governor almost completely. Fourth, the governor's attitude toward the office may contribute to success or failure.

With respect to the last factor, two attitudes are identifiable. An aggressive attitude on the part of a governor leads to the development of an extensive legislative program, broad and intensive interest in the policies of administrative agencies, and pursuit of objectives with all available tools. The successful aggressive governors have held well-defined plans for improving either the condition of the populace or of state government. A deferential attitude leads to a more passive role; a limited legislative program, with what is offered treated merely as suggestions that others are free to accept or reject; and independence of the administrative agencies. Of course, a particular governor would never be aggressive at all times on all issues and, given the expectations that have arisen around the office and the drive necessary to become governor, wholesale adoption of a deferential attitude is improbable. Nevertheless, some governors are much more aggressive than others, and in some a tendency toward a deferential attitude is detectable. Generally, a governor who adopts an aggressive rather than a deferential attitude is more likely to be considered successful. A governor such as Coke Stevenson who sets out to accomplish little and does so might be considered a success, but expectations of the public and political analysts require a record of positive accomplishment.

Nine persons have served as governor during the contemporary era of the Texas governorship. (See Table 6.4.) Probably all would classify themselves as aggressive rather than deferential in their approach to the office, and at times all

Table 6.4 GOVERNORS OF THE CONTEMPORARY ERA

Governor	Term of Office
Allan Shivers[a]	1949–1957
Price Daniel	1957–1963
John Connally	1963–1969
Preston Smith	1969–1973
Dolph Briscoe[b]	1973–1979
Bill Clements	1979–1983
Mark White	1983–1987
Bill Clements	1987–1991
Ann Richards	1991–

[a] Lieutenant Governor Shivers became governor when Jester died, and then was elected to three terms.

[b] The term became four years in 1975.

displayed behavior that would justify that classification. Allan Shivers, John Connally, and Bill Clements had general programs, broad conceptions of the role of the governor, and the requisite personalities that led them to pursue their objectives aggressively. Price Daniel held a broad conception of gubernatorial responsibilities but lacked the personal characteristics that make for consistent, aggressive pursuit of gubernatorial objectives. Mark White's governorship resembled Daniel's, not because of an unaggressive personality but because of indecisiveness and an unwillingness to confront the state's financial problems. Preston Smith and Dolph Briscoe were, on the whole, deferential in their approach to the governorship.

The Governor as Aggressive Leader

The three governors who were most consistent in the aggressive approach to the governorship spanned the three decades of the contemporary era. All were business-oriented conservatives, and, although they differed sharply in background, philosophy, and success, all were leaders to be reckoned with in any significant development in state government during their tenures.

Allan Shivers: Aggressive Ex-legislator   When Allan Shivers became governor in 1949 he was only 41 years old but had an extensive background in Texas government.[22] He had been elected to the state Senate in 1934 and, at age 27, became the youngest state senator in Texas history. Shivers represented a Southeast Texas district that included highly unionized Jefferson and Orange counties, and during the 1930s he supported numerous liberal measures, including, in his first term, such New Deal measures as old-age pensions and unemployment compensation. He quickly became one of the more influential members of the Senate, and when he left in 1947 to become lieutenant governor he was the senior member in length of service.

As lieutenant governor, Shivers changed in his political philosophy. The young senator who had been supported by labor unions and supported early New Deal welfare measures became a strong supporter of states' rights and an opponent of labor unions. In his first term as lieutenant governor, he used his power to appoint committees and to influence floor action to secure the passage of nine antiunion bills. But Shivers did not simply become a negative conservative, for he believed in an active government. The antiunion measures were part of an overall strategy to promote economic development. His inaugural address as lieutenant governor had the theme of state responsibilities and expressed his philosophy, which his biographers characterize as the belief that the national government had become so big and costly because state and local governments had failed to do their jobs.[23] He called for reforms in state government to make it more responsive and responsible, including four-year terms for executive officials and constitutional revision to make more positions appointive. Throughout his career Shivers acted upon that philosophy. He joined with Governor Jester in supporting increased expenditures for public welfare, public schools, colleges and universities, prisons, state hospitals and schools for the retarded, farm-to-market roads, and soil and water conservation.

The primary problem remaining in the modernization program revolved around the state's mental hospitals and schools for the mentally retarded. Jester had vetoed their appropriation for the second year of the biennium because money was not available to finance the general appropriations act if the entire act became law, and because he regarded their appropriation as inadequate. Upon becoming governor, Shivers undertook an extensive public relations campaign pointing out the horrors of the existing system prior to calling a special session to provide funding for a construction program.

The enactment of authorizing legislation with funding essentially completed the postwar modernization of state government. In the remainder of the 1950s, the importance of programs or services as a political issue receded, and political conflict revolved around how to finance existing programs, many of which were experiencing rapid growth, and national political issues. There were few programmatic innovations during the remainder of Shivers's governorship.

In 1950 the United States Supreme Court issued a momentous decision for Texas politics, holding that coastal states did not own the submerged lands, which became known as *tidelands,* off their coasts. Shivers worked out a compromise with Sam Rayburn, Speaker of the national House of Representatives and a Texan, and President Harry Truman, which provided that the states and national government share in oil and gas revenue produced on such land. The compromise was not effectuated, however, largely due to the opposition of Texas Attorney General Price Daniel, who insisted on an all-or-nothing strategy. Shivers never forgave Daniel for his opposition to the compromise. Texas and other coastal states supported legislation in the Congress giving the states the lands, but it was vetoed by Truman. Adlai Stevenson, the Democratic nominee to succeed Truman, also pledged to veto such legislation, leading Shivers to break with the Democratic party and support Republican Dwight Eisenhower for president in 1952 and 1956 and, in the process, earn himself the permanent enmity of the state's liberal and loyalist Democrats.

Shivers's support for Eisenhower marked an increasingly conservative turn in his political position. His speeches began to contain attacks on the coddling of communists in government, and his attacks on unions became much stronger. One of the features of his difficult campaign for reelection in 1954 was a famous film entitled "The Port Arthur Story." The film pictured a communist-tainted retail clerks' union as paralyzing the city with its strike; one scene was of the industrial city with smokeless smokestacks. Critics alleged that it took hours on a Sunday morning to get the few seconds of film. A campaign folder distributed in an area of East Texas where segregationist sentiment was thought to be strong showed a picture of a black carrying a picket sign that also had a sticker supporting Shivers's opponent, Ralph Yarborough. This was representative of an increasingly antiblack, segregationist position that began after the United States Supreme Court declared separate but equal schools unconstitutional in 1954. Shivers supported local control of schools and promised to use every legal means at his disposal to maintain segregation. He used the Texas Rangers to prevent black children from entering all-white schools; opposed the use of federal troops to enforce court orders; helped revive the pre–Civil War doctrine of interposition, which claimed the right of the states to interpose their sovereignty between their citizens and improper actions by the national government; and labeled Yarborough a captive of the National Association for the Advancement of Colored People.

Shivers's accomplishments in modernizing state government are quite substantial, although he made many of them as lieutenant governor during Jester's governorship, and he achieved most of his political objectives, although many of them remain quite controversial. Shivers was a masterful politician, and his record of success as governor is primarily attributable to his skills in dealing with the legislature. His relations with the presiding officers were quite good; he worked especially well with longtime friend and former Senate colleague Ben Ramsey, who served as lieutenant governor from 1952 onward.

In his relations with the legislature, Shivers employed several strategies. He bargained with individual legislators, to whom he was very accessible. A favorite ploy was to postpone issues until special sessions, where he had control over which legislation could be considered, and then bargain for votes for measures he supported by allowing consideration of measures favored by particular legislators. On other occasions, Shivers chose to influence the legislature through outside pressure. Perhaps the best example of this strategy was his campaign to secure financing for improving the mental hospitals and schools for the retarded. His task was not easy, however, for the legislature was divided, with one faction opposing any tax increase, another favoring an omnibus approach that increased numerous existing levies, and a third favoring utilization of a new, broad-based tax, either sales or income.

Shivers undertook an extensive public relations campaign pointing out the horrors of the existing institutions; he made speeches to business and financial groups and sent a series of columns to newspapers under his byline. A tax plan (an increase in 25 business and commodity taxes and a one-cent increase in the cigarette tax earmarked for construction at mental hospitals and schools for the retarded) was worked out with friendly legislators. Shivers then called a meeting of the 30 most prominent lobbyists, to whom he indicated that the liberals in the house would attempt to tax the interests they represented even more heavily. Most of the lobbyists eventually announced support for the increases affecting their clients. In deference to legislative sentiments for independence (and perhaps to avoid public opprobrium), Shivers never formally recommended the plan; instead, he just allowed it to emerge from the legislature.

On other occasions, however, Shivers chose to lead openly. In 1953 salary increases for public school teachers had been postponed until a special session, which he called in 1954. He adopted a similar tactic of securing support for his tax plan from the business and financial interests of the state prior to the beginning of the session (an indication of the change in his status since 1950 was that the business leaders, and not their lobbyists, were invited to the meeting) but presented the plan in a speech to the legislature with the comment that a governor who recommends the spending of money has a responsibility to recommend the means to raise it.

Shivers's influence and success were not limited to the legislative arena. His lengthy service, combined with an ability to inspire personal loyalty and careful selection of appointees to boards and commissions, allowed him to wield a degree of influence over the executive branch enjoyed by few, if any, other Texas governors. His staff was characterized by frequent shifts between the official staff and his campaign organization, since he insisted that state employees not be involved with the campaign; but it was characterized by high ability, and many of its members became protégés who eventually held higher state offices.

Shivers's biographers contend that he was the strongest governor in Texas history, but in his attempts to strengthen the governor's office he failed completely. The voters defeated the amendment increasing the term of office to four years, and he was unable to secure approval from the legislature of measures to increase the governor's appointive powers, a failure he lamented in 1955 during a scandal involving the veterans' land program that resulted in the imprisonment of Land Commissioner Bascom Giles, an elected official. Shivers claimed to have received over 1000 letters blaming him for appointing Giles. Another major scandal occurred in 1955, which involved state regulation of insurance companies, and the two scandals resulted in a decline in influence during his final two years in office. Shivers left the governorship weaker than it had been at the beginning of Jester's governorship; but because of his great personal ability and influence he enjoyed great influence. Less capable governors enjoying less favorable circumstances have been unable to exert comparable influence.

With the completion of the reform program, much of Shivers's time and energy were devoted to battling the liberals and securing financing for the growth occurring in improved state services. In the 1950s Texas was one of the few states utilizing neither a general sales tax nor an income tax, which are broad-based taxes that tend to grow with the economy and population. Instead, the state relied on collection of selective sales, commodity, and natural-resource taxes. Shivers opposed both broad-based taxes and repeatedly and successfully recommended increasing existing taxes. In consequence, he bequeathed a tax system that was inadequate to finance state government; that system bedeviled his successor throughout his terms of office and ultimately contributed to an unsuccessful campaign for reelection.

John Connally: Aggressive Patrician   After leaving the governorship, John Connally served as secretary of the treasury, left the Democratic party to become a Republican, was considered for appointment to the vice presidency of the United States, was acquitted of Watergate-related bribery charges, and conducted an unsuccessful campaign for the Republican nomination for president.[24] However, when he began his campaign for governor in 1962, he was unknown to most Texas voters. Connally had not previously sought elective office, and his only official position had been a short term as secretary of the navy. He was politically experienced, however, having been active in the campaigns and political endeavors of Lyndon Johnson and having worked to influence the activities of the Texas legislature and the United States Congress.

Connally was considered a moderate during his first campaign for governor, in which he defeated liberal Don Yarborough in the Democratic runoff and faced a tough Republican challenge from Jack Cox in the general election. Connally's governorship was characterized by commitment to economic development, but his concept of economic development was primarily attractive to business interests and seemed to liberals to offer little immediate benefit to the underprivileged. Connally believed in an active government and supported increased expenditures for economic development. During his first term in office, he successfully supported legislation to create a Tourist Development Agency, improvement of state parks to attract tourists, and increased funding for the Texas Industrial Commission, which worked to attract new industry to Texas. The cornerstone of his program, however, was increased spending on colleges and universities; he believed that in a technological society dollars followed knowledge, and that improvement in the higher education system would attract economically desirable high-technology industries to Texas.

Connally's first term as governor was at best only modestly successful. Despite his other successes, including creation of a committee to study education beyond the high school, he failed in his most important objective. He called for sharply increased appropriations for the state's colleges and universities, and the legislature insisted on appropriating less than he recommended in order to appropriate more for construction projects at mental hospitals and schools for the retarded. The members of the conference committee on the general appropriations act offered and Connally rejected a compromise; Connally then made extensive use of the item veto to eliminate numerous appropriations, including several projects at the hospitals and schools.

Overall, Connally's relations with the legislature were not friendly. Part of the difficulty was his conception of the executive and legislative functions, which was not in keeping with the Texas experience. Connally favored a strong chief executive; his biographers characterize his administration as focusing on strengthening the authority of the governor and on making the chief executive the originator of both programs and legislation.[25] He was not an admirer of the legislative process (he chose not to run for the United States Senate on several occasions when his election was probable), and he did not care for intimate, day-to-day contact with legislators. He preferred to work through the presiding officers and key members, but his influence over those figures during the 1963 session was not great. Additionally, he did not like dealing with lobbyists, whom other governors have found to be useful intermediaries in dealing with the legislature. Instead, he preferred to deal with their employers, especially the industrial and financial leaders of the state.

Some factors that were to account for his later success were already identifiable in Connally's first term. He demonstrated his tenacity by refusing an unacceptable compromise on appropriations and his willingness to exact a price for opposition through the use of the item veto. Throughout the dispute he insisted that the proper role of the governor in budgeting be recognized. His explanation of the vetoes on statewide television was articulate and persuasive. During the remainder of his first term, he moved to extend his influence over the bureaucracy, even becoming involved in a minor scandal when he prevented the University of Texas regents from selecting a Republican architect to design a building.

Many, but not all, of the conditions necessary for success were present during Connally's first term. Some observers thought that his staff, while bright, was a bit inexperienced and occasionally guilty of errors and cavalier treatment of legislators, although this was not of decisive importance. An example of poor staff work was Connally's explanation of his appropriation vetoes. He said that the vetoed expenditures would provide a contingency fund for higher education, should additional money be badly needed. Since some of the items vetoed were constitutionally or statutorily "earmarked" for specific purposes, his statement was misleading, in that the money could not be diverted to the colleges and universities. Good staff work would have prevented the misleading explanation, which was seized upon by critics.

More importantly, Connally was not an overwhelming political figure; he had been elected by a narrow margin, and he confronted a legislature presided over by strong and independent politicians who were not inclined to look to the chief executive for leadership.

Events between 1963 and 1965 were to change Connally's political position drastically. First, he took the opportunity presented by the debate in the U.S. Congress on civil rights legislation, which was to become the historic Civil Rights Act of 1964, to separate himself from the liberalism of the national administration by denouncing the public accommodations section of the bill, thereby firmly establishing himself as the leader of the state's conservative Democrats. Second, President John Kennedy was killed and Connally wounded by an assassin in Dallas in November 1963. The two developments combined to improve Connally's electoral standing, and he was overwhelmingly renominated and reelected in 1964. As the legislative session of 1965 approached, his position was improved, but he faced, as he had in 1963, a legislature in which each house was headed by a strong and independent presiding officer who was expected to oppose major portions of his program. A vacancy suddenly occurred on the Railroad Commission, and Connally appointed the speaker of the house, Byron Tunnell, to the position. Ben Barnes, who had been a Connally campaign worker in 1963 and was considered a protégé of the governor, was then elected speaker, thus ensuring that at least one of the two houses would be led by an ally.

Connally enjoyed great success in securing desired actions by the legislature in 1965. He secured approval of the main features of his budget proposals, including generous appropriations for the colleges and universities. Other legislative successes included reorganization of the state's programs for coordinating higher education, tuberculosis control, and water resources, and the authorization of comprehensive community mental health programs. His staff, with some changes in personnel and two years of experience, seemed to work almost flawlessly (several were later to join President Johnson's administration in important positions), and the House—under Barnes's leadership—did not present any obstacles. Lieutenant Governor Preston Smith, who was eyeing the governorship and definitely was not a political ally, seemed hesitant to oppose Connally; he did not even create the expected havoc when Connally vetoed a prized medical school for his hometown of Lubbock.

By the beginning of his third and final term in 1967, Connally had established his reputation as a successful and aggressive governor. Many of the policy initiatives during the final term, however, seemed to belong to Barnes, who continued to serve as speaker. Smith became a major obstacle, forestalling a Connally-Barnes attempt to have the Senate accept without change the House version of the appropriations bill, which would have prevented Smith from appointing and influencing the Senate conferees. Smith also prevented the Senate from giving its consent to a constitutional revision effort, forcing Connally and Barnes to proceed with only the approval of the House. Even the House largely ignored his budget and revenue proposals, but his overall influence remained so strong that he was able to dominate the Texas delegation to the 1968 Democratic National Convention, even though his successor as Democratic nominee for governor had been chosen.

There is room for disagreement about the accomplishments of John Connally as governor. Professor Clifton McCleskey considered Connally a strong, skilled political practitioner who frittered away his talents and finally wrought nothing more majestic than a circumscribed coordinating board for higher education.[26] Admirers claim a more substantial list of accomplishments, most involving organizational and managerial changes, not initiation of new programs or alteration of power relationships. Critics question how successful many of the changes have been: The water agencies were again reorganized in 1977 and 1985; the Parks and Wildlife Department has had a stormy existence; and the coordinating board at times appears ineffectual. The limited success of the reorganizations may be attributable to Connally's tendency, alleged by some critics, to become interested in a challenge, arrive at a solution, and then lose interest rather than provide the continuing support necessary for long-range accomplishments.[27]

Bill Clements: Aggressive Outsider   When Bill Clements left the governorship in 1991, his eight years in office over two nonconsecutive terms constituted the longest service of any Texas governor, but, like John Connally, when he began his campaign he was unknown to Texas voters. Clements's long and successful business career had been in the oil-drilling business, and he had not been active in politics until he became a major contributor to Richard Nixon's presidential campaigns. In 1973 Nixon appointed him deputy secretary of defense, a position he held until the Republicans lost the presidency in 1976. He was considered an underdog in both the Republican primary and the general election in 1978, but with massive spending of personal funds he successfully overcame lack of voter identification; in doing so he broke a Democratic monopoly on the governorship that had lasted over a century. Clements was defeated by Mark White for reelection in 1982, but in 1986 he defeated White to recapture the office.

In his campaigns Clements emphasized conservative, antigovernment issues, presenting an image of an outsider who would relieve the voters of governmental oppression. In his first campaign he promised to reduce taxes and to support a constitutional amendment to allow the passage of legislation through the initiative and referendum process in Texas state government. He also pledged to reduce the number of state employees by 25,000. His second campaign was less specific, but he criticized White for supporting tax increases during a fiscal crisis, indicated that he had a plan to eliminate a budget deficit, and promised that tax increases would not be necessary during his governorship.

Clements's promises proved difficult to keep. In his first legislative session in 1979, his legislative program seemed hastily formulated, and in most instances he simply endorsed legislation others had introduced, rather than presenting drafts prepared by his staff. The program presented, however, was quite broad; the major features were a $1 billion tax reduction, initiative and referendum, a budget execution system controlled by the governor, and wiretapping authority for the police in suspected drug trafficking cases. None of his major proposals succeeded. Constitutional amendments providing for legislation through initiative and referendum and executive budget execution were not approved. The Legislative Budget Board budget, which proposed spending more than the governor favored and which he labeled a "Christmas wish book," was adopted essentially as prepared. While the legislature did provide more aid to local schools and presumably thereby allowed reductions in local property taxes, the legislature spent much more than Clements recommended and did not provide for a reduction in the number of state employees.

Clements's initial lack of legislative success was not surprising. He was not experienced in state government, and he personally knew few legislators, including the legislative leadership. There was no core of experienced Republicans whom he could recruit as staff assistants; his assistant in charge of legislative liaison, a former conservative Democratic legislator, was not appointed until the day before the legislative session began. At times Clements seemed almost to invite friction with the legislature. His "Christmas wish book" reference was certain to offend the influential members of the budget board, and even in minor matters his actions occasionally were abrasive. A notable example was his veto of a bill approved on the local and uncontested calendar removing the regulatory authority of the Parks and Wildlife Department over hunting and fishing in a specified county. Such laws were routinely approved by legislators out of deference to the legislative sponsor. Clements objected that policy should be consistent throughout the state but did not make that objection known during legislative consideration. The legislature, in an usual action, overturned the veto, with several Republicans voting with the majority.[28]

In his second legislative session in 1981, Clements was somewhat more successful in dealing with the legislature. His staff and program were better prepared; his relations with the presiding officers of the two houses were better (he often was allied with Speaker Bill Clayton, a conservative who later became a Republican). He knew more legislators and even occasionally entered the floor of the legislature to lobby for his proposals; the number of Republican legislators who could be counted upon to support his position had increased. The most important factor in the improvement of his legislative record, however, was that his goals were more limited. Although nominally he still supported his grand proposals, in effect he abandoned all of them. The focus of his legislative program was an antidrug, anticrime package of legislation featuring a proposal, repeatedly defeated in previous legislatures, authorizing the Department of Public Safety to employ wiretaps in suspected drug cases. Wiretapping legislation was approved, as was most of the remainder of the anticrime legislation. Clements had some success in legislative redistricting, and he supported a constitutional amendment (which was defeated by the voters) for financing a water development program.

Clements's program during his second term in office resembled his program during the final two years of his first term. His campaign in 1986 essentially was an attack on the fiscal competence of Mark White and did not feature an extensive platform. Once in office he did not develop an extensive legislative program. His staff, which was in place much earlier than in his first term and included several veterans of that term and others active in Republican politics, was quite experienced and considered better organized than White's staff. His budget director, a key appointment given the fiscal situation, was Bob Davis, a former Republican legislator with a reputation as an able, experienced Republican partisan.

The legislative program the governor developed did not receive much attention, but the budget was widely publicized. Allegedly it allowed for moderate growth over existing spending levels without requiring a new tax increase. Critics charged that it contained numerous questionable accounting transactions, and it became known as the "funny money" budget. Perhaps its most widely publicized proposal was the sale of a state mental hospital to the Highway Department in order to divert funds earmarked for highways to general revenue. Legislative leaders insisted that several of the transactions were unconstitutional and that others would never be approved by the legislature. Clements continued to insist that all his proposals were legitimate, and private meetings repeatedly failed to resolve the differences when the principals could not agree on how the executive and legislative budgets differed.

Early in the legislative session Clements agreed to extension of several temporary tax increases enacted in 1986, but throughout the regular session he refused to accept additional revenue-raising legislation, and the legislative leadership refused to approve appropriations without additional legislation. Finally, in a summer special session, Clements relented and agreed to legislation that would generate almost $6 billion, about half of which involved making permanent the temporary legislation. This reportedly was the largest state tax increase in United States history.[29]

Clements declared victory, claiming that he had stopped the growth of state government and that the tax increase was really White's, who had bequeathed to him not only the temporary taxes but also an increased spending level. As part of the acceptance of the tax increase, Clements did secure a significant concession. Democratic legislators had refused to approve enabling legislation that gave effect to a constitutional amendment adopted in 1985 authorizing a budget execution system. In return for his acceptance of the tax increase, the legislative leadership successfully supported creation of such a system.

The final two years of Clements's second term were the quietest of his governorship. Clements had indicated that he did not intend to seek reelection, and by the beginning of the 1989 legislative session, potential successors had begun their campaigns. Clements agreed with the legislative leadership to meet and discuss factual matters in order to agree at least on the substance of their disagreements, a problem two years earlier. A budget was adopted that did not require the enactment of revenue-raising legislation, but a court decision declaring the state's system of aid to local schools unconstitutional resulted in a special legislative session in 1990 that increased taxes and fees by over $500 million for the biennium. Clements did not play a decisive role in shaping the legislation, but after vetoing one plan he accepted another, slightly revised version.

Clements's leadership style has been described in terms such as aggressive, confrontational, brash, and outspoken. Throughout his governorship he demonstrated a zest for being governor and attempted to provide policy leadership for state government, and his rhetoric may often have been designed to establish strong bargaining positions. His personal image of outspokenness was a source of both popularity and unpopularity. The most prized accomplishment of his governorship was that he slowed the growth of state government.[30] Yet government, as measured by spending and the number of employees, was larger when he left office than when he entered. Clements called for the greatest change in Texas state government of any of the governors of the contemporary period. If he had been successful, he would have reversed the tendency toward growth of state government (by limiting the growth of state revenue and the number of state employees), and he would have made government more responsive (through permitting legislation by initiative and referendum) and better managed (through management audit teams and a budget execution system). In his first term management improvement was effected in several state agencies, and during his second term a budget execution system was adopted, but its impact is uncertain. After failure in his first legislative session, Clements abandoned his great vision; his legislative accomplishments afterward did not have a great and lasting impact on state government because of their limited scope and not because of lack of achievement.

In his first term Clements experienced some real success in areas not related to legislation. His appointments to boards and commissions generally were of high quality, the product of an extensive talent recruitment program, and appointees were not closely identified with agency clienteles. The appointments were nonpartisan in that Clements did not insist that appointees be or become Republicans. In his second term appointments became more partisan (perhaps because there were more Republicans available for appointment) and more closely identified with agency clienteles.

Clements's political accomplishments were more impressive than his governmental successes. In his first term he was an influential figure in national Republican politics, directing Ronald Reagan's presidential campaign in Texas and serving on Reagan's transition team, but his involvement in national politics declined during his second term. Prior to his election as governor, the Republican party had won numerous local offices and positions in the Texas legislature and the United States Congress, but the Democratic party was the dominant party; lobbyists, trade association executives, and influential individual campaign contributors who wanted to influence the policies of state government identified with and contributed to the Democrats. Clements changed the perception that Democrats would always govern. Republican political consultant Karl Rove, for example, contends that Clements's performance as governor, by convincing conserva-

ANN RICHARDS: CONSENSUS AND INCLUSION

Incoming governors always seem to face an imposing array of problems; but in 1991, when Ann Richards became governor, that was especially true. In addition to unusual fiscal difficulties, Richards was confronted with a crisis brought on by court decisions declaring unconstitutional the system of state aid to public schools. Richards assumed office after a campaign that had featured personalities and not issues and programs, but that did not mean that expectations for her governorship were low. She was the first governor from the liberal wing of the party since the 1930s and the first since John Connally to articulate a vision of a better life for ordinary Texans. The means for accomplishing that vision were centered on making good education and equal opportunity available to all members of society.

Throughout her political career, which began with volunteer campaign work, advanced to campaign management, and included service as a county commissioner and state treasurer, Richards has maintained friendly personal relations with opponents and members of opposing parties and factions. As a policymaker she emphasizes inclusiveness and consensus; she wants all affected persons and groups interested in a policy involved in its development and prefers that her staff develop a consensus on the policy before it is brought to her for approval. If a consensus has not been achieved, she tends to delay decisions until one can be developed.

Richards began her governorship by displaying a subtle, diplomatic aggressiveness in pursuit of her objectives, and she experienced some success. She took control of two troubled agencies, the Board of Insurance and The Department of Commerce, from her predecessor's appointees; and an important campaign promise was fulfilled when a revision of the statutes regulating the insurance industry was enacted. However, she did not present proposals for revising the system of state aid to local schools and raising revenue to fund the state budget, although she did exert some influence and signed the school finance and general appropriations legislation. Her success as governor will probably depend on success in those areas, and preliminary results are inconclusive. Even if constitutionally acceptable, the school finance measure may be politically unpopular because of associated increases in property taxes. The broadening of the franchise tax to include profits of non-capital intensive corporations and the establishment of a lottery, contingent on voter approval of a constitutional amendment, may not be adequate to prevent debilatating battles over taxation in future legislative sessions.

tive Democrats and independents that a Republican could be trusted to provide responsible leadership, gave Republicans a credibility they had not previously enjoyed.[31]

Aggressive Conceptions and Ambivalent Leadership

Allan Shivers, John Connally, and Bill Clements did not always achieve their objectives, but on matters of importance in state government they had a position they supported with vigor. Their personalities matched their conception of the office, and in most instances they had the courage and commitment to fight for their policies. If the personality, courage, and commitment are not all present, an aggressive conception of the governorship can become an abstract ideal that is not converted into strong executive leadership. This was the case with Price Daniel and Mark White.

Price Daniel: Indecisive Confrontationist   In 1955 Price Daniel announced that he would not seek reelection to a second term in the United States Senate in 1958 amid speculation that he would run for governor in 1956.[32] Positions in the United States Senate are often more prized in modern American politics than state governorships, but Daniel's interests had focused on state issues, and his interest in the governorship was not a surprise. When he announced his candidacy, which was delayed until only a few days before the filing deadline in an example of the indecisiveness that critics perceived throughout his career, Daniel said that he would rather be governor of Texas than president of the United States.

Daniel's background seems to make him one of the most qualified persons ever to become governor of Texas. His family had deep roots in Texas history (one of his ancestors had founded his hometown of Liberty and served as the first *alcalde,* or mayor, during Spanish rule, and his wife was a descendant of Sam Houston); and Daniel had great experience in public office, first serving as a member and eventually speaker of the state House of Representatives, and then as state attorney general. In 1952 he successfully sought election to the United States Senate in a campaign emphasizing his commitment to secure the ownership of the tidelands for Texas and, in support of the same issue, followed Governor Shivers in supporting Eisenhower for president. He was a leader in the enactment of legislation giving the coastal states title to some of the tidelands, but after that battle was over he did not have many other issues to pursue. He was an unassuming, unpretentious, and allegedly unsophisticated person; neither Daniel nor his family was happy in Washington.

Daniel's major opponent in the Democratic primary was liberal Ralph Yarborough. Daniel had avoided much of the bitterness that Democratic loyalists held for Shivers and had even earned some liberal respect by opposing an effort by conservatives to place Eisenhower on the Democratic ballot in 1952. In his 1956 campaign, however, he aroused lasting enmity with the emphasis of his campaign, which, besides stressing integrity in government and states' rights, focused on preventing radicals from gaining control of the governor's office (the radicals identified most often were labor unions, the Americans for Democratic

Action, and the National Association for the Advancement of Colored People).
He also pledged support for local efforts to maintain segregation.

The 1956 campaign culminated in a narrow runoff victory over Yarborough, but the bitterness did not reach its peak until September, when Daniel,
who did not participate in the struggle between Shivers and Democratic loyalists
for control of the delegation to the national convention, seized control of the state
Democratic executive committee.

Daniel's 1956 campaign, however, had other emphases that reveal the
moderate nature of his political outlook. Programmatically, he promised increases in pensions for the needy elderly and improvements in hospitals for the
mentally ill, greater support for public education at a time when the postwar baby
boom was beginning to increase enrollment in public schools, and a water conservation and development program. As a part of his emphasis on honesty and
integrity in the aftermath of the insurance and veterans' land scandals, he supported strict lobbyist registration and legislative financial disclosure laws. In what
was perhaps the most important pledge of the campaign in terms of impact on
the governorship and state government, he announced unalterable opposition to
a general sales tax and support for taxes on natural resources to provide revenue
for his program.

Daniel's governorship was a troubled period for Texas government. The
system of taxation was inadequate, and throughout his three terms as governor
he fought politically debilitating battles over tax legislation. His firm opposition
to either a sales or income tax left him with the difficult task each fiscal biennium
of putting together an omnibus plan that increased a broad array of existing taxes
and occasionally found new items to tax. Shivers had successfully followed this
strategy, which required consummate political skill because it tended to arouse
a broad range of interests in opposition; but business interests, organized through
the Texas Manufacturer's Association, began to argue that they could not afford
further increases in selective levies and as an alternative supported enactment of
a general sales tax.

The taxation issue arose in Daniel's first term and overshadowed the remainder of his program. He eventually fought off a sales tax but in doing so did
not achieve enactment of much of his legislative program; critics charged that
during the session he was initially inactive, indecisive, and ineffective. The taxation and spending legislation was largely shaped by the legislature, and this
remained the pattern throughout his governorship. Daniel did not use or even
perceive the budget process as an effective planning and management tool, and
the legislature became dominant in financial matters.

When he did not secure the enactment of the most important features of
his legislative program, Daniel called the legislature into special session, where
the water development and lobbyist registration measures were enacted. The
water development program was largely shaped by the legislature, however, and
the law requiring lobbyists to register was so sweeping and general as to be
ineffectual; a bill requiring disclosure of the financial interests of legislators was
not approved. In statewide radio addresses during the regular session and at the
beginning of the special session, Daniel appealed for public support of his program and lambasted the legislature as the tool of selfish interests. Many legislators

were alienated, and overall his relations with the legislature were unfriendly. Allen Duckworth, the experienced and respected columnist of the *Dallas Morning News,* characterized his first term as one of timidity and confusion; no governor in years had been subjected to so much abuse. Duckworth attributed some of Daniel's difficulty to his rivalry with Shivers, whose many friends regularly acted to oppose Daniel.[33]

Although Daniel was unpopular with legislators and regarded as timid and indecisive by political observers, he remained popular with the voters. His only opponent for renomination in 1958 was liberal State Senator Henry Gonzalez of San Antonio, who received only 18.7 percent of the vote, and he defeated a token Republican opponent in the general election even more overwhelmingly. As he began the second term, however, he seemed much changed from the timid and indecisive governor of his first term. He proclaimed himself the protector of the common people against the unfair sales tax favored by special interests. The state, which had collected much less in oil and natural gas taxes than had been antici-pated and was accumulating a sizable deficit in its general fund, faced a need for large increases in revenue. Daniel proposed a variety of measures to raise revenue; the most important and controversial suggestions were an "escheats" bill requir-ing banks and utilities with abandoned money to give it to the state and a tax on natural gas being shipped in pipelines.

Daniel remained adamantly opposed to a general sales tax, but his task in preventing its adoption was more difficult than in 1957. He was confronted with not only a Senate dominated by Shivers loyalists but also a House whose speaker favored a sales tax. Daniel again lambasted the legislature, charging that the power of special interests was much greater in Austin than in Washington.[34] Ultimately he was successful in preventing passage of a sales tax, but it took three special sessions to enact the necessary revenue measures and an accompanying teacher pay raise.

Daniel emerged from the 1959 sessions of the legislature with a different image from that acquired during his first term as governor. He had adopted a confrontational stance toward the legislature and had prevented the enactment of a sales tax, but he had not been very influential on revenue legislation; the escheats bill had failed, and opponents succeeded in writing the natural gas tax in such a manner that it was quickly declared unconstitutional by the Texas Supreme Court.

Although unpopular and not respected in the legislature, Daniel remained popular with the voters and prepared to seek a third term as governor, a feat accomplished previously only by Allan Shivers. Daniel had moderated his image to such a degree that a liberal challenge was not forthcoming, but he was chal-lenged in the primary by Jack Cox, a conservative supported by Shivers. Daniel received almost 60 percent of the vote, and in the general election again defeated his Republican challenger by an overwhelming margin. Although he attributed some of the lack of harmony with the legislature to his own stubbornness and insisted that he would not tell the people whom they should elect, he did admit that matters would be better if some of the more unharmonious legislators were not reelected.[35]

Daniel began his third term in a seemingly strong political position. He had been overwhelmingly reelected, his first two terms were free of scandal, and the new House of Representatives chose a speaker who was ideologically compatible and personally friendly. The state faced another financial crisis, however, and a consensus developed that manipulation of the existing tax structure would not produce adequate funds and that a fundamental change in the revenue system was necessary. Revenue problems had confronted Daniel since the beginning of his governorship, and he had been forced to expend his political resources preventing enactment of a general sales tax. He presented the 1961 legislature a plan featuring the escheats legislation and a 1 percent payroll tax, but the payroll tax proved so unpopular that it was quickly withdrawn. Daniel continued to oppose a sales tax during the regular session but did not propose a viable alternative. When the regular session did not enact a revenue plan, he called a special session in which, after spending his career opposing a general sales tax, he recommended one to the legislature. Eventually a somewhat different sales tax was approved by the legislature, and Daniel allowed it to become law without his signature. He unsuccessfully sought reelection in 1962, when he ran third in the Democratic primary.

Daniel's governorship was not characterized by major innovations or accomplishments he initiated. The financial problems of the state were such that perhaps not even the most able governor could have accomplished great things, however, for funds were not available for improvements in services to a growing population without enactment of major new taxes, and the governor in office when that occurred undoubtedly had to suffer in popularity. A forthright support of a sales tax in 1957, however, might have been more acceptable to the voters than long and adamant opposition and then eventual acceptance in 1961, and it would have freed Daniel to work on other matters.

Although he often presented an image of an aggressive confrontationist representing the people against special interests, Daniel was unwilling to provide leadership for fundamental change in the revenue system, and he often changed his recommendations for piecemeal change. His indecisiveness and confrontational tactics led to unfriendly and ineffective relations with the legislature, which became much more dominant during Daniel's tenure as governor. The dominance was most apparent in the taxing and spending process, but it was also evident in other legislative matters. At the conclusion of his governorship, Daniel claimed that, of 151 recommendations to the legislature, 131 were enacted, but many were shaped primarily by the legislature and were enacted in forms substantially different from what the governor had recommended. This was true of the major policy developments during his governorship—a water development program, paid parole and probation systems, reorganization of the juvenile offender program, regulation of lobbyists, and a code of conduct for state officials.

Mark White: Bedeviled by Finances   Mark White defeated incumbent Bill Clements in the 1982 gubernatorial election in a year of great Democratic political success in Texas. White, a former secretary of state during the administration of Governor Dolph Briscoe, had unexpectedly won election as attorney general in 1978 on a platform of reducing utility costs. He won the Democratic gubernatorial nomination without a runoff but was not expected to defeat Clements, whose campaign was well financed and organized. He benefited greatly from Democratic voter registration and turnout programs largely funded through the reelection campaigns of U.S. Senator Lloyd Bentsen and Lieutenant Governor Bill Hobby.

In the closing weeks of the 1982 campaign, White again found utility costs a popular issue by promising to abolish the fuel adjustment charge that utilities had been authorized to pass on directly to customers as a separate item in utility bills. White received strong support from public school teachers, pledging to support salary increases for them. He indicated that he did not believe that it would be necessary to raise taxes, a position different from that of Clements, who said he would not veto an increase in the gasoline tax, which is earmarked for highways and schools. White indicated that he also favored increased spending on highways.

In January 1983, Comptroller Bob Bullock announced a decrease from earlier estimates of the revenue available for expenditure in the upcoming biennium. The decrease was attributed to a national economic recession that affected the Texas economy, a drastic devaluation of the peso that adversely affected the economies of areas bordering Mexico, and a downturn in the oil and gas industry that resulted in a moderate decrease in the price of petroleum. Clements had presented a budget that recommended spending almost $1 billion more than the estimate of available revenue, which was reduced twice more during the 140-day legislative session. Obviously increases in teachers' salaries and highway construction could not be funded from the existing revenue system if existing programs were financed at current levels.

White did not present his budget for two months, or until almost half the legislative session had been completed. It recommended additional funds for highways and teachers' salaries and exceeded the estimate of available revenue but did not include a plan for increasing revenue. Instead, it suggested alternative approaches for legislative consideration. White's alternatives were widely interpreted as an abdication of leadership. After another month he announced his support for a specific revenue plan based on increases in "luxury" and "sin" taxes and an increase in the gasoline tax, which would be devoted to retiring bonds whose proceeds would be used for highway construction. The leadership of the House of Representatives opposed increases in taxes, and White's plan, with the proposal of highway construction bonds being labeled deficit financing, received little support in the legislature. Under the leadership of Lieutenant Governor Bill Hobby, appropriations were approved that were financed by increases in numerous fees and accelerated collection of several taxes, but increases for highway construction and teachers' salaries were not included. White was left with major campaign commitments unfulfilled.

The pledge to abolish the fuel adjustment charge included in utility bills was fulfilled. White recommended making the members of the Public Utility Commission elective, a move his critics interpreted as an attempt to pass responsibility for utility rates from himself to the voters, but the legislature did not act on his recommendation. The term of one member had expired, and White's criticism led to the resignation of the other two. Thus, during the first months of his administration White appointed all three members of the commission, and they instituted procedures requiring utilities to justify to the commission increased costs attributable to increases in the price of fuel.

In lieu of salary increases for teachers, a special committee was created to study the state's system of public education. Under the leadership of Dallas businessman H. Ross Perot, the committee recommended major changes in the system. White called a special session of the legislature, and legislation was enacted that reallocated funds to poorer districts, required competency tests for teachers and graduating students, set more stringent requirements for participation in extracurricular activities, and made numerous other changes. The state-funded minimum salary for beginning teachers was increased, and a career ladder plan, which provides additional pay for teachers meeting merit standards, was created. Funds were provided for the additional costs by increasing taxes on gasoline, tobacco products, and alcoholic beverages, and by raising the general sales tax by an eighth of a cent. Additional money was also approved for highway construction. The educational reforms became White's proudest accomplishment, and their approval, along with the tax increases that financed them, improved his reputation for legislative leadership.[36]

In the final two years of Mark White's term he continued to have difficulty with state finances. Weakness in the oil and gas industry resulted in only slight annual increases in revenue, and it was obvious before the 1985 legislative session began that the existing revenue system would not provide funds that would maintain services at existing levels for a growing population. White, Bullock, and the Democratic leaders of the legislature decided, however, that additional tax increases following those of 1984 would endanger Democratic control of the governorship and perhaps of the legislature; thus, tax increases were not considered in 1985. To prevent reductions in services, Lieutenant Governor Hobby developed a plan for raising fees. Almost all fees charged by the state were increased, with tuition charged students at state-supported colleges and universities constituting the most important source of additional revenue.

The fee increases proved to be only a temporary solution to the state's financial problems. As the increases became effective in late 1985 the price of petroleum began to decline drastically. Bullock announced that revenue collections would not reach expected levels, and the state would experience a considerable deficit in its general revenue by fiscal year 1987. In early 1986 White directed all units of the executive branch to reduce discretionary spending by 13 percent. An analysis by the comptroller of public accounts staff indicated that if spending were lowered by that amount the deficit would only be halved, and it quickly became evident that most units would not reduce spending as directed, although some reductions did occur. Cash-flow difficulties eventually forced White to call the legislature into special session, and tax increases were enacted that, while not eliminating the deficit, allowed the treasurer to meet the state's obligations on a day-to-day basis. White was defeated by Clements in the 1986 gubernatorial election, thus bequeathing the financial problems he had inherited to his predecessor/successor.

Deferential Leadership and Legislative Domination

The Texas legislature, regardless of the governor's approach to leadership, is a strong and independent body. Decisive, aggressive governors do not dominate the legislature, and indecisiveness leads to legislative assertiveness. The absence of both an aggressive concept of executive leadership and an aggressive personality leads to legislative dominance of the chief executive in policy initiation, as is illustrated during the administrations of Preston Smith and Dolph Briscoe.

Preston Smith: Deferential Ex-legislator   Preston Smith became governor in 1969, after serving 12 years in the legislature and 6 years as lieutenant governor. He contrasted sharply with his predecessor, John Connally, in that he was not as articulate or photogenic. The center of his political strength was in the rural areas, towns, and small cities. He was not particularly popular with the middle-class voters of the larger cities and their suburbs, and he did not enjoy the close relationship experienced by Connally with the major business and financial leaders of the large cities.

Smith was able to assemble a very experienced staff, drawn largely from former legislators, campaign aides, and associates in state government. His staff was competent and diverse, and he tended to grant its members considerable discretion. On some occasions the discretion may have been too great, for in some instances he was badly served by his staff. For example, in 1969 Smith appointed two campaign contributors to the Board of Examiners of Psychologists; he quickly withdrew the appointments after the nominees were criticized as not having the required qualifications. One nominee, the operator of a marital counseling service, was accused of being a medical quack whose degrees were awarded by a degree mill. Good staff work would have revealed the backgrounds of the nominees before the appointments were made.

Smith's victory margins in the 1968 primary and general elections were comfortable, if not overwhelming, but he was regarded as somewhat unproven electorally, since many observers felt that his primary victory was more an indication of the weakness of his liberal opponent, Don Yarborough, than of his strength. Additionally, Ben Barnes, at that time widely regarded as a handsome, articulate young politician with a bright future, was overwhelmingly elected lieutenant governor and inherited much of Connally's organizational and economic support.

Smith's performance as governor reflected both the weakness of his political position and his ambivalence toward the role of the governor. He presented a legislative program that was surprising in its ideological moderation, given his reputation as a staunch conservative. The program emphasized improvement in the state's vocational-technical education program, development of new medical schools in Houston and Lubbock, and enactment of a state minimum wage. He pledged support for constitutional amendments to increase the compensation of legislators and lower the voting age to 18. His budget proposals consisted essentially of Legislative Budget Board recommendations plus increases for selected programs, but he did recommend sources for the additional revenue needed to finance his spending recommendations.

Smith pursued his recommendations with mixed diligence. A few were actively and successfully supported (e.g., new medical schools and occupational education), but most seemed to receive little attention from either Smith or the legislature. His tax recommendations were disregarded. When it appeared that agreement on taxes would be difficult, the legislative leadership decided to appropriate funds for the first year only of the biennium, for which funds were adequate, and delay action until a special session on second-year appropriations and taxation a year later. Smith did not indicate objections to this procedure, but when the appropriations bill reached his desk, he vetoed it and announced that he would recall the legislature to consider a biennial appropriation act.

A similar disinclination to press his view occurred in 1971, when he allowed approval of a tax bill that contained an unacceptable increase in the gasoline tax and then announced that he would veto the bill if the gasoline provisions were not removed. Both incidents apparently resulted from the governor's hesitancy to "dictate" to the legislature. The same motivation may have influenced his position in 1969, when he indicated, during legislative consideration of removing the exemption of food from the sales tax as part of an omnibus tax bill, that he would accept whichever bill the legislature approved.

Smith's second term as governor was marred by allegations that he was involved in the Sharpstown Bank scandal. The allegations were revealed in 1971 near the beginning of the term, and he became a political lame duck. An indication of his difficulties was his inability to secure senatorial confirmation for appointments to the Insurance Commission, whose rate-setting policies were under criticism. His relations with the legislature were complicated by Barnes's active but eventually unsuccessful pursuit of the governorship.

Smith left office in 1973 with only a limited record of accomplishment. He did not propose as much legislation as did his predecessors in the contemporary era, and he did not have as aggressive a concept of the governorship. Nevertheless, he was not willing to adopt a completely passive approach; he eventually intervened on crucial matters, even though his poor timing served to reduce the impact of his efforts.

Dolph Briscoe: Unaggressive Personality Dolph Briscoe became governor in 1973 with a background very different from that of his politically experienced predecessors. Briscoe had served in the legislature in the 1950s and in 1968 had unsuccessfully sought the Democratic nomination for governor; he also had engaged in some activities of concern to his business interests, including support for a state-sponsored screwworm eradication program. Otherwise, he was not especially active politically. During the period in which he was out of public office, he had accumulated great personal wealth (he was rumored to be the state's largest individual landowner), and to a considerable degree he personally financed his unsuccessful 1968 and successful 1972 campaigns. Perhaps as a consequence of this method of campaign finance, he entered office with few programmatic commitments. Among those he did have were opposition to increased taxation and support for strengthening the criminal laws and law enforcement, and those themes remained the cornerstone of his policy proposals.

Briscoe seemed almost tentative in taking control of the governorship. After the general election in November, he returned to his South Texas ranch, but the usual announcements of staff appointments were slow in coming. When he took office, his staff was only partially complete; several members of Smith's staff were invited to remain on a temporary basis, and some eventually remained permanently. The new appointees tended to be former campaign workers who had little experience in state government.

Briscoe's legislative program and budget recommendations were revealed slowly and were not very extensive. He did recommend a temporary two-year plan for improving the system for financing the public schools, but it was not released until after the education committee of the House had favorably reported a different plan. He successfully resisted a tax increase, but his spending proposals were delayed until after both the House and Senate had completed hearings on the general appropriations bill.

The featured aspects of Briscoe's legislative program dealt with law enforcement, including restoration of the death penalty for certain crimes, denial of bail to habitual criminals, toughening of drug laws, legalized wiretapping, and expanded use of oral confessions. A drug reform law, which received considerable attention because of its reduction of marijuana possession penalties, was enacted. Four years later, a constitutional amendment authorizing denial of bail to habitual criminals was adopted, but the desired wiretapping and oral confession legislation was not enacted until after he left office.

Although there were occasional exceptions, strong, aggressive leadership did not characterize the Briscoe governorship. He played a negligible role in the constitutional convention of 1974, and in 1975 and 1977 he did not vigorously pursue extensive legislative programs. He did present numerous suggestions in his "State of the State" addresses but tended to leave them with the legislature and not to work vigorously for their enactment; much of the legislation similar to his recommendations that was enacted appears to owe its passage to factors other than the governor's support.

Public school and highway finance are examples of policy areas where Briscoe's influence was more apparent than real. In 1975 he recommended a new system for distributing state aid to local schools, and the legislature eventually enacted a temporary plan that increased the amount of state aid. In 1977 a similar situation occurred, except that a permanent plan eventually was enacted. Highway interests had worked vigorously throughout 1976 to secure additional funding for highway construction, and Briscoe recommended a plan to the 1977 legislative session for providing additional funds. The legislature eventually approved additional funds, but the amount was considerably less than that recommended by Briscoe, and the method of providing it was different.

Overall, Briscoe's relationship with the leaders of the legislature was friendly. During his first term, relations with Speaker Price Daniel, Jr., whom many thought an ally of Attorney General John Hill, a prospective opponent for the governorship, were cool; but Daniel was succeeded by Bill Clayton, a conservative West Texan much closer to Briscoe. Lieutenant Governor Bill Hobby was also considered a possible gubernatorial opponent, but he eventually made it clear that his plans did not include a challenge to Briscoe, and relations between the two were cordial.

Briscoe's good relations with the two presiding officers were not converted into great influence with the legislature. His popular support appeared broad but not intensive, and such support did not lead legislators to fear popular retribution if they opposed him. At the same time, he did not make active, effective use of personal contact to persuade legislators to support him and his programs.

Dolph Briscoe did not dominate the Texas political scene as have some governors. His major accomplishment—which was not sufficient to win renomination in 1978—in both his and the voters' perceptions was the absence of revenue-raising legislation. Otherwise, his legislative accomplishments were sparse. However, he did not appear philosophically to accept a passive or deferential role for the chief executive. He undertook such aggressive actions as threatening to veto revenue-raising legislation and indicating in a special message delivered during the final minutes of the 1973 session that he would refuse to call a special session to deal with public school finance if the legislature failed to approve a bill during the regular session. Such assertiveness was not characteristic of Briscoe. Bo Byers, an experienced and able journalistic observer of Texas government, concluded that Briscoe preferred to propose plans and then allow the legislature to settle issues without much pressure from the chief executive's office. He reported that lawmakers and lobbyists gave low ratings to Briscoe's staff, whom they found not very knowledgeable about the legislative process, and concluded that the staff's "lack of push" was a result of Briscoe's approach to the governorship.[37]

Another conclusion might be that, given the occasional outbursts of aggressiveness, Briscoe's nonaggressive attitude was derived more from an unassertive personality than from a philosophical approach to the role of governor. Byers noted that Briscoe had an image of aloofness, rarely holding press conferences for the capital press corps, seldom socializing in Austin, and frequently departing Austin for relaxation at his Uvalde ranch, and concluded that he cared little for the day-to-day drudgery of governing. Regardless of whether his lack of assertiveness was philosophical or psychological, Byers's summation of Briscoe's governorship seems accurate: Briscoe was honest, well meaning, and cautious but neither an imaginative nor a strong leader.[38]

THE GOVERNORSHIP IN RETROSPECT

As we have seen, the normal condition of the Texas governorship is not that of a powerful chief executive. Although an able and politically strong individual may use the informal bases of influence inherent in the governorship, the office is legally weak, and the structure of Texas politics is such that the governor does not ordinarily possess political resources and influence adequate to overcome that weakness and provide effective leadership in the formulation and execution of policy for state government. Such has not always been the case, for in the

nineteenth and early twentieth centuries the governors were the political leaders
of the state, and effective governors, of whom Jim Hogg was the most notable,
succeeded in establishing extensive and controversial programs.

The one-party system with nomination by primary elections destroyed
coherent political parties, the most effective base available to governors for mobilizing support. Since use of primaries became well established, governors have
provided strong leadership in the initiation and adoption of public policy only
under unusual conditions. Jim Ferguson secured the adoption of an impressive
program during his first term in office, and Jimmy Allred used the conditions
accompanying the Great Depression to bring a mild version of the New Deal to
Texas. In the aftermath of the Depression and World War II, Beauford Jester led
a modernization effort that enjoyed broad support. Otherwise, the record of
leadership in state government during the one-party era was one of legislative
domination and drift.

The record of leadership of governors in the contemporary era is not much
better than that of their predecessors of the one-party era. Allan Shivers and John
Connally were undoubtedly the strongest governors of the post–World War II
period, if strength is measured by the force of their personalities, legislators'
respect, and accomplishing what they desired. Both had aggressive concepts of
the governorship and a vision for the state requiring change in state government.
Shivers wanted to modernize state services while encouraging economic development, and he made extensive recommendations and achieved enactment of many
of them by the legislature. He probably was Texas's most successful governor in
the modern era.

Shivers's efforts resulted in the modernization of the facilities and treatment
methods at the state's mental health and mental retardation facilities, but otherwise his accomplishments as governor in improving state services were not great
(as lieutenant governor he was instrumental in the legislature's approval of
Jester's program for modernizing education and highways). He helped create a
political climate favorable to economic development through his proposals for
regulating labor-management relations and his taxing and spending policies, but
the system of taxation did not provide the revenue for substantial improvement
in services. After an initial burst of improvements in mental hospitals and schools
for the retarded, those institutions exhibited little progress for a decade. The
absence of greater programmatic accomplishments during Shivers's governorship
was, more than anything else, the result of his conservatism, for he focused on
improving services, not innovative problem solving. Many of his programs, rather
than aiming at improvement, were designed to maintain existing conditions, as
was notably the case in race relations, where he supported school segregation and
favored the use of the doctrine of interposition of state sovereignty against actions
by the federal courts, and in labor law, where he supported many antiunion
measures designed to maintain the low level of unionization of the state's work
force.

The impact of Texas's other "strong" postwar governor, John Connally, is
similar to that of Shivers. Like Shivers, Connally had a vision requiring governmental change. He wanted to encourage economic development through the

creation of an educational system that would produce the scientists and engineers to attract high-technology industry. Most of his accomplishments, however, were managerial and organizational, not programmatic, and their long-term success is questionable. The limited nature of his success is attributed by some critics to his tendency to neglect his programs after an initial success. A more fundamental cause may be that his approach was organizational and managerial because he was not disposed to challenge basic programs and power relationships. If the new organizations were to have a lasting impact, they needed his continuing interest and support; the problems faced by the old organizations were more than just managerial, reflecting a balance of influence among competing groups. An example is Connally's first triumph, the Parks and Wildlife Department.

When the Parks and Wildlife Department was created in 1963, the state's parks, administered by a parks board, were underfinanced and poorly located; whereas the Game, Fish, and Oyster Commission had ample funds from dedicated sources but was a poorly run agency whose leadership was buffeted by pressures from competing sports, landowning, and commercial interests and often overrode the advice on technical matters of its staff. The creation of a new agency did not change the basic problem. In a compromise accepted by Connally to make the legislation more acceptable to hunters and fishers, game and fish funds cannot be used for parks. Conflicts continued among the competing sports, landowning, and commercial interests. Park funds are still dispersed among many locations, which have been determined more by historical and political factors than by the needs of the state's population.

A fundamental cause of Connally's failure to leave a more substantial record of accomplishment is the same as Shivers's—his essentially conservative philosophy led him not to challenge existing conditions, not to chart new programs and press for their adoption. A major exception would appear to be the creation of the comprehensive community mental health and mental retardation program, but the impetus for this program actually came from the national government, which, in response to new attitudes of programmatic specialists favoring noninstitutional care, had established a grants-in-aid program for community mental health and mental retardation centers.

Among the other governors of the contemporary era, Dolph Briscoe and Preston Smith shared both a lack of vision of accomplishment and a comprehensive conception of the role of the governor; their accomplishments and their impact on Texas government were comparatively minor. Price Daniel, Bill Clements, and Mark White held aggressive concepts of the governorship but cannot be considered strong, successful governors who contributed greatly to shaping Texas government. Daniel had an aggressive concept of the office without a decisive personality to match the concept, and his legislative program seems more a piecemeal response to conditions than a coherent program. Clements had the personality to match his aggressive conception of the office, but his vision of a smaller, more responsive, and better managed government was utopian. He did not leave a great imprint on Texas government. Mark White, who never revealed an overall vision of what he wanted to accomplish, sometimes adopted a confrontational style but was unwilling or unable to make the hard choices needed to bring the revenue system and the level of state services into balance.

The failure of constitutional reform in the 1970s destroyed, for the foreseeable future, the possibility of legally strengthening the governorship, but just as political developments weakened the governorship, political change is beginning to strengthen it. The one-party system with nomination by the Democratic primary, which weakened the governorship, no longer exists. As competition between parties increases, partisan loyalty has become a useful tool in securing support, but it remains secondary in the overall legislative context and is likely to remain so until the legislature organizes itself along partisan lines. Organization of the legislature by party caucuses faces a formidable obstacle, however, for it could weaken the power of the presiding officers. Nevertheless, a governor whose party organized even one house undoubtedly would find that his or her influence with that body would be considerably enhanced.

NOTES

1. Leslie Lipson, *The American Governor from Figurehead to Leader* (Chicago: University of Chicago Press, 1939).
2. *Fiscal Size Up Texas State Services 1984–1985 Biennium* (Austin: Legislative Budget Board, 1984), p. 160.
3. *Texas Observer,* October 4, 1968, p. 5.
4. Fred Gantt, Jr., *The Chief Executive in Texas* (Austin: University of Texas Press, 1964), p. 327.
5. For a general account of Texas history that provides a description of the overall political context in which the development of the governorship occurred, see Rupert Norval Richardson, Ernest Wallace, and Adrian N. Anderson, *Texas: The Lone Star State* (Englewood Cliffs, N.J.: Prentice-Hall, 1981). An older work that focuses more on the role of the governors is Ralph W. Steen, *History of Texas* (Austin: Steck, 1939).
6. Llerena Friend, *Sam Houston* (Austin: University of Texas Press, 1954), p. 111.
7. For an account of Texas politics from the end of Reconstruction through the beginning of the twentieth century, see Alwyn Barr, *Reconstruction to Reform* (Austin: University of Texas Press, 1968).
8. The following account of Hogg's governorship is based on Robert Cotner, *James Stephen Hogg* (Austin: University of Texas Press, 1959), chaps. IX, XIV.
9. Ibid. pp. 233–238.
10. Ibid., p. 233.
11. Ibid., p. 313.
12. Barr, *Reconstruction to Reform,* pp. 206–207, 248–251.
13. Ibid.
14. Steen, *History of Texas,* pp. 388–389.
15. Ibid., pp. 395–396.
16. Arthur M. Schlesinger, Jr., *The Politics of Upheaval* (Boston: Houghton Mifflin, 1960).
17. Richard Morehead, *50 Years in Texas Politics* (Burnet, Tex.: Eakin Press, 1982), p. 350. For a more devastating critique of O'Daniel's governorship, see Robert A. Caro, *The Path to Power* (New York: Vintage Books, 1983), pp. 694–703.
18. Caro, *Path to Power,* pp. 734–740.
19. Morehead, *50 Years in Texas Politics,* p. 358.
20. Sam Kinch and Stuart Long, *The Pied Piper of Texas Politics* (Austin: Shoal Creek, 1973), p. 49.
21. Joseph Schlesinger, "The Politics of the Executive," in *Politics in the American States,*

2d ed., ed. Herbert Jacobs and Kenneth Vines (Boston: Little, Brown, 1971), and ibid., 4th ed., 1983.

22. The following account of Shivers's governorship is based primarily on Kinch and Long, *Pied Piper of Texas Politics.*

23. Ibid., p. 44.

24. The following account of Connally's governorship is based on Ann Fears Crawford and Jack Keever, *John Connally* (Austin: Jenkins, 1973), and Paul Burka, "The Truth about John Connally," *Texas Monthly,* VII (November 1979): 156ff.

25. Crawford and Keever, *John Connally,* pp. 148–149.

26. Clifton McCleskey, "Some Changes for the Better," *Texas Observer,* 27 (December 1974): 58–59.

27. Crawford and Keever, *John Connally,* p. 39.

28. Paul Burka, "King of the Mountain," *Texas Monthly,* IX (January 1981): 94–95.

29. *Austin American Statesman,* August 29, 1987, pp. A1, B1.

30. *Austin American Statesman,* December 23, 1990, pp. A1, A13.

31. Ibid.

32. The following account of Daniel's governorship is based primarily on newspaper accounts of the period. Particularly valuable was the file of clippings on Daniel in the Legislative Reference Library. All references are from that file.

33. *Dallas Morning News,* November 17, 1957.

34. *Austin American Statesman,* March 15, 1959.

35. *Dallas Morning News,* January 10, 1960.

36. *Houston Chronicle,* July 8, 1984, sec. 1, p. 32.

37. *Houston Chronicle,* April 10, 1977, sec. 1, p. 10. For a more critical view, see Griffin Smith, Jr., "Why Does Dolph Briscoe Want To Be Governor?" *Texas Monthly,* IV (February 1976):80ff.

38. McCleskey, "Some Changes," p. 58.

chapter 7

The Administrative System

Texas state agencies occupy a number of new buildings in the capitol area in Austin.

Although the press, the public, and social scientists often concentrate their attention on electoral politics, the chief executive, the legislature, and—somewhat less often—the superior appellate courts, the day-to-day work of government is performed in administrative agencies. Chief executives, legislatures, and courts may make decisions, but the task of carrying out those decisions is performed by the administrative agencies. They enforce laws, provide services, and regulate various activities; it is with the administrative units that most citizens have almost their entire experience of direct personal contact with government.

An infinite variety of arrangements exists for structuring the overall organization of the administrative units of government. Analysts have long identified two types of structures, however, and most administrative systems resemble one or the other. Students of administration have generally favored the *integrationist* model: This model calls for an administrative structure that is headed by a chief executive and has all the activities of the government grouped into a small number of departments, each headed by a single person who is appointed and removable by the chief executive. The *weak-executive* model provides for a chief executive who has limited influence over the administrative units; agency heads are not subject to appointment or removal by the executive, and authority is not centralized in the chief executive.

The weak-executive model existed without challenge in most state governments well into the twentieth century. The governor more often than not was designated chief executive but had little control over the administrative agencies, which were headed by elected officials or boards and commissions whose members served overlapping terms. Those agencies often acted independently of and even contrary to the wishes of the governor, whose influence on agency decisions was exercised, if at all, through informal political means. Professional students of administration and citizen reform groups look with disfavor on the weak-executive model, and a long-standing reform movement has attempted to force revision of the administrative structures of state governments.

The integrationist model aims at strengthening the governor's influence over the state's administrative agencies by formal authority over their decisions. Proponents argue that such action would reduce the proliferation of independent agencies, eliminate the duplication of work that accompanies such proliferation, and overcome the diffusion of authority and responsibility inherent in the weak-executive model.

The reform movement in the past half-century has scored impressive, if partial, victories in a number of states. When major changes are made by conventions or legislatures, they tend toward the integrationist model. Nevertheless, neat administrative hierarchies that make the governor responsible for the management of the executive branch do not exist in most states. The usual pattern is for a large number of administrative units, some of which enjoy independence from the governor, to exist. The failure of even the states so inclined to develop integrated systems is attributable to the complexity of governmental programs, which develop through a general accretion of new functions. The tendency when a new problem arises is to adopt the most readily available administrative solution: creation of a new agency. Thus, even states committed to the integrationist model have difficulty meeting their commitment. For example, New York, a reformed state, has constitutionally limited the number of its departments to 21, but it uses one of them as a catchall for unrelated functions.[1]

The structure of the executive branch of government in Texas is a classic example of the weak-executive model. Three factors combine to make Texas an exaggerated case of the fragmentation of executive power.

First, there is a tremendous number of separate administrative entities. An exact count of the separate units is difficult, if not impossible, to obtain; it is difficult even to define what constitutes a separate administrative unit. There are departments, agencies, officials, boards, commissions, advisory boards, and advisory commissions. If one limits the count to agencies or officials having operating or ministerial responsibilities who are not subordinated to a higher authority other than the governor or the legislature, the number of agencies is about 160. Table 7.1 presents an approximate tabulation of the administrative agencies, grouped by predominant function, as of the beginning of 1987. Such a tabulation

Table 7.1   ADMINISTRATIVE AGENCIES IN THE TEXAS STATE GOVERNMENT
             BY FUNCTION AND TYPE OF CONTROL, 1990

Type of Agency	Total	Appointed by Governor	Ex Officio	Elective	Appointed by Others	Mixed
General government	23	8	6	4	0	5
Public safety and correction	12	6	2	0	0	4
Health and hospitals	10	7	2	0	0	1
Education	21	16	4	1	0	0
Welfare and employee benefits	14	10	0	0	1	3
Economic regulatory and promotional	57	46	1	2	1	7
Conservation, recreation, and culture	19	17	1	1	0	0
Transportation	2	2	0	0	0	0
Total	158	112	16	8	2	20

Source: Originally based on Guide to Texas State Agencies, 4th ed. (Austin: Lyndon B. Johnson School of Public Affairs, University of Texas, 1978). Updated by the authors from a variety of sources.

presents an image of dispersion that is somewhat misleading, for many of the agencies perform activities of little consequence. For example, the 25 agencies in the "general government" category include not only the departments headed by the attorney general and comptroller but also the Aircraft Pooling Board, which has ministerial responsibility for the performance of very routine functions. Among the agencies classified as "economic regulatory and promotional" are over 30 licensing-examining boards; like numerous others, the Funeral Service Commission and the Polygraph Examiners Board are important to limited segments of the population but do not loom very large in the overall operation of state government. Also included in the tabulation as state agencies are the Texas members of interstate compacts; in several instances (e.g., compacts on juveniles, mental health, and parole), state officials who perform related duties have been designated compact representatives from Texas.

The second factor contributing to the fragmentation of executive power is the existence of nine elective officers and boards having administrative responsibility. The Constitution of 1876 provided for the popular election of not only the governor but also the lieutenant governor, comptroller of public accounts, treasurer, attorney general, and commissioner of the General Land Office. In 1891 an amendment provided for the election of the three members of the Railroad Commission. In this century the legislature has provided for the election of the commissioner of agriculture (1907) and the members of the State Board of Education (1949). Additionally, the legislature in 1939 provided for the selection of five members of the Soil Conservation Board by conventions held in each of the five districts created by the Soil Conservation Act. In most states the creation of new elective state offices ended in the past century, but Texas has continued the practice into the twentieth century.

The third and most important factor contributing to the fragmentation of executive authority is the means of control the legislature has devised for the agencies not headed by elective officials (see Table 7.1). Many of these are headed by boards at least some of whose members serve ex officio because they occupy other positions. A couple have heads appointed by someone other than the governor. Of the remaining agencies, most have heads appointed by the governor, but several are headed by boards and commissions appointed in a mixed manner (in most instances, the governor appoints part of the membership, and the remainder are appointed by other officials or serve ex officio).

Of the agencies whose heads are appointed by the governor, almost all are headed by boards and commissions whose members serve overlapping terms. In the entire executive branch, only about a dozen agencies are headed by single officials, and that figure includes the elective officials (but excludes the representatives on interstate compacts). Most of the members of the boards serve on a part-time basis, and agency activities are directed by a chief administrative officer.

The governor thus appoints over 100 boards to head administrative agencies. Included in this number are most of the largest and more significant state agencies. But the governor's ability to influence the boards is limited by the existence of overlapping terms for board members, restrictions on freedom to select appointees, and limitations on removal authority.

Several factors have contributed to the fragmentation of executive power. Jacksonian democracy, with its emphasis on popular election, and the goal of depoliticizing administration, which led to the boards with members serving overlapping terms, are influences of a national scope that affected Texas. Three additional factors of a peculiarly Texan nature have also been at work.

First, the Reconstruction experience left many Texans with a distrust of governmental power, especially of concentrated executive power. Second, the Texas legislature is a traditionally independent body whose members have distrusted executive leadership. Legislative politics has operated in a manner that produces two strong leaders, the lieutenant governor and the speaker, who are competitors with the governor for power and influence. Finally, the politics of the administrative process is such that the fragmentation of executive power works to the advantage of various groups concerned with administrative policy making, and they have exerted their influence to prevent reforms aimed at developing an integrated executive structure.

MAJOR ADMINISTRATIVE AGENCIES

A description of the activities and responsibilities of all of the administrative agencies of the Texas state government would be difficult and dull, for many of them perform minor or perfunctory tasks. Others, however, are of broad and general interest; still others, while little known, perform important functions in state government or carry on activities of importance to limited segments of the population. The following sections, using the classification of governmental activities presented in Table 7.1, describe some of the more important state agencies and their responsibilities.[2]

General Government

Of the 158 agencies tabulated in Table 7.1, 23 are classified as "general government." Their responsibilities are of a varied nature, involving the management of the government or responsibilities for services to other governmental agencies. A majority—including the Surplus Property Agency, Board for Lease of University Lands, Surplus Property Agency, and Commission on the Arts—are of little consequence. Among the more significant agencies are those responsible for fiscal, legal, and administrative services.

The Comptroller of Public Accounts and the Treasurer   These two agency heads are responsible for the operation of the state's fiscal services. The comptroller's responsibilities fall into three areas: (1) central accounting, under which that department maintains the accounts for all appropriations made to state agencies and audits and approves, in advance of payment, all expenditures to be made from state funds; (2) tax administration and enforcement, under which most, but not all, of the state's tax laws are administered; and (3) revenue estimating, involving the estimation—for the legislature and the governor—of the amount of money that will be available for expenditure for each fiscal year and certification that the amounts approved in appropriations bills will in fact be available.

The comptroller of public accounts is an elected official, but turnover in the office has been small. In the 60 years preceding the beginning of John Sharp's term in 1991, only three persons held the office: George Sheppard for 18 years, Robert S. Calvert for 26 years, and Bob Bullock for 16 years. Sheppard and Calvert were seldom involved in broader political issues, but Bullock was an active participant in state politics who was interested in the governorship but eventually settled for the lieutenant governorship. His successor, John Sharp, is a politician of broad political interests who appears unlikely to be a career comptroller in the Sheppard/Calvert tradition.

The treasurer heads a department with responsibility for receiving state funds, acting as their custodian, and paying obligations upon authorization by the comptroller. The department has custody of securities owned by several state investment funds, as well as those required by law to be deposited by various businesses. Essentially, the treasurer is the state's banker, but as such most of the office's activities are routine, even clerical. The political significance of this office is enhanced, however, by the treasurer's membership on the State Banking Board and the State Depository Board (the banking commissioner is also a member of the two boards, and the governor appoints a third member of each). The banking board must approve charters for new state banks, a potentially lucrative form of patronage. The depository board selects the banks in which funds held by the treasury are deposited, and such deposits may be a form of patronage. The treasurer's influence on the depository board is enhanced because the treasurer's department also administers matters relating to the depositories. This position is thus of greater significance than the otherwise routine functions might indicate. Like the comptroller, the treasurer is an elective official, but the office became a career position for Jesse James, who held it from 1941 until his death in 1977.

Kay Bailey Hutchinson in 1991 became the third person elected to the office since James's death and the first Republican in contemporary times to hold the office. She perhaps benefited from Democratic opponent Nikki Van Hightower's strong identification with militant feminism and name similarity to controversial Agriculture Commissioner Jim Hightower, who was defeated for reelection in the same election. Hutchinson is a politician with varied interests who appears more likely to follow the path of her immediate predecessor, Governor Ann Richards, than the career orientation of James.

The Attorney General   As the state's lawyer, the attorney general heads an office responsible for two primary functions: representing the state in civil litigation and giving advice in the form of opinions to public officials. In civil litigation, the attorney general serves as the lawyer for state agencies and acts independently in direct legal representation of the state. Much of the work is routine, but occasionally cases are of great importance and are highly publicized. John Hill's successful effort to establish Texas as the official residence of deceased billionaire Howard Hughes and thereby gain for the state the inheritance tax on his estate, Mark White's defense of the state prison system, and Jim Mattox's defense of at-large systems for electing district and appeals court judges all resulted in considerable public attention for recent attorneys general.

The furnishing of legal advice in the form of opinions perhaps is at least as important a function of the attorney general as the representation of the state and its agencies. Only authorized public officials (a sizable group, including the governor, heads of state agencies, chairpersons of legislative committees, and numerous local officials) may request opinions, which may not be on matters of strictly private concern. These opinions are of great significance: Many of the issues that are the subjects of opinions are never litigated, and although the opinions are not binding on state courts, they are regarded as persuasive and are rarely overruled.

Attorneys general occasionally face conflict between their responsibilities to advise and defend their clients and their personal policy inclinations, and this conflict may be enhanced by their ambition for higher office. Of the post–World War II attorneys general, only two have not sought the governorship, and both were tainted, probably unfairly, by major governmental scandals. Their record of success is not great, however; only Price Daniel and Mark White have been successful, and Daniel served a term in the United States Senate between his service as attorney general and governor.

The State Purchasing and General Services Commission   This agency provides a broad range of administrative services to state government, the most important of which is central purchasing. Other services include management of the state building construction and leasing program; security for state buildings; traffic control in the capitol complex; centralized telephone, mail, and messenger services in the capitol complex; and computer services for small state agencies. The commission is also responsible for administering the state's building construction programs (although there are important exceptions to its jurisdiction). The commission is composed of three members, appointed by the governor with the consent of the Senate; an executive director acts as chief administrative officer.

Public Safety and Corrections

Of the 12 agencies in this category, the most significant are the Department of Public Safety, the Department of Criminal Justice, the Youth Commission, and the Adjutant General's Department.

The Department of Public Safety (DPS)   This department has responsibilities in three areas: traffic law enforcement, criminal law enforcement, and management of emergencies. Its primary responsibility in traffic law enforcement is the policing by the highway patrol of traffic on public highways, with primary emphasis on unincorporated areas. Among its other traffic enforcement responsibilities are the administration of the driver's license and motor vehicle inspection laws.

Although law enforcement is essentially a local function, the DPS has responsibility in several areas. The department maintains an extensive set of police records and operates a statewide police-communications system and laboratories that are available to local law enforcement officials. The Texas Rangers are the most famous division of the DPS responsible for field services in the law enforcement area. Their field of operations is broad: protection of life and property, suppression of riots and insurrections, apprehension of fugitives, and investigation of major crimes. Although their mandate is broad, their activities are more limited, since there are only 110 rangers. They provide assistance to local law enforcement agencies and coordinate activities that cross jurisdictional lines. The DPS also maintains enforcement units concerned with criminal intelligence and organized crime, vehicle theft, and narcotics.

The department has responsibility for emergency management of natural and other disasters, civil unrest, and hostile military and paramilitary actions. Most of its efforts are devoted to coordinating the efforts of other agencies and local authorities. Civil unrest and hostile military actions have not been a problem in recent history, but the special hurricane preparedness program for the Gulf Coast is activated periodically, and recurring emergency situations requiring responses include hazardous material spills, missing airplanes, and problems resulting from severe weather. The DPS is headed by a director who operates under a three-member commission appointed by the governor with the consent of the Senate.

The Department of Criminal Justice   As has been the case throughout the twentieth century, the prison system is controversial. In earlier decades the system occasionally operated at a profit that was produced by leasing prison labor to private entrepreneurs and by selling prison-produced goods, mostly agricultural, for a profit. The system was never as successful with industrial activities, although for the first two decades of the century a railroad and an iron-manufac-

THE GIRLS IN THE BAND

Attorney General Jim Mattox, a combative liberal Democrat, was the most controversial recent attorney general. In the continuing debate over whether attorneys general should be lawyers doing the bidding of their client—the state and its agencies—or advocates of the public interest, Mattox usually chose to be "the people's lawyer." His legal strategy and actions were controversial im several areas, but perhaps the action that aroused the greatest controversy was his settlement of a suit against Texas A&M University in 1984.

In its days as the Agricultural and Mechanical College of Texas, Texas A&M was an all-male institution that required all students to be members of the reserve officers training corps. As the school evolved into a major multipurpose university, female students were admitted and ROTC was made voluntary, but the Corps of Cadets continued to play a major role in university activities. Cheerleaders at athletic activities are corps members, and the band that performs at halftime of football games and similar activities is a special unit of the corps. Females were eventually admitted to the corps, but they continued to be excluded from its special units, including the band. A female student brought suit charging that such exclusion constituted illegal sex discrimination, and the university responded that requirements of national security allowed military units to adopt special rules regarding the sex of their members. After the suit dragged on for five years, Mattox agreed to a settlement that required the university actively to encourage females to join the band and other all-male corps organizations.

The settlement aroused great criticism from supporters of the univer-

turing plant were operated in the hope of huge profits, but both were very unprofitable. State laws prohibiting the leasing of convicts and federal laws prohibiting the sale in interstate commerce of prisoner-produced goods ended the pursuit of profit but not the pursuit of self-sufficiency, a goal long sought after but never achieved.

Treatment of prisoners has been a problem throughout the twentieth century. Allegations of mistreatment, legislative investigations of the allegations, and reforms designed to correct abuses have occurred approximately once each decade. The most important and successful reform program was begun in 1947. Texas prisons in the 1940s have been described as "the most miserable in the country. . . . The guards were nasty, the buildings were awful, the work was killing, and the convicts were badly fed, sick, terrified, and mean."[3] By the 1970s, however, the prison system was widely considered the best state system in the country. Extensive rehabilitation, educational, and vocational programs were offered, with emphasis on the production of agricultural and industrial products that were consumable within the system or by other state agencies.

sity, who contended that the attorney general should not settle suits over the objections of the party being sued. Mattox responded that defense of the suit could cost up to $300,000 and that it was ridiculous to think that women in the band would endanger the national-security interests of the nation.

In the 1985 session of the legislature the Republican contingent in the House of Representatives introduced and secured committee approval of legislation popularly called "Bum Bright's revenge," in honor of a wealthy Dallas businessman who owned the Dallas Cowboys football team and who was serving as chairman of the university's governing board at the time of the settlement. It prohibited the attorney general from settling lawsuits without the consent of the state agency involved when such settlement would result in a provision of the state constitution, state law, or agency rule being declared unconstitutional. In floor debate the bill's supporters charged that laws were being changed at the whim of the attorney general and that he was becoming a second governor and vetoing bills. Opponents responded that the bill would take power from an elected official and give it to appointed bureaucrats. A preliminary vote approved the bill by a vote of 74 to 65, with all 52 Republicans voting for it, but Mattox undertook an active lobbying campaign, arguing that it was just a Republican publicity stunt. He also declared that he would rule it unconstitutional because the Texas Constitution made the attorney general responsible for representing the state. His critics responded that he could only issue an opinion, for only courts can rule a law unconstitutional. A second vote resulted in a tie, which effectively killed the bill.

The physical plants, constructed by an in-house program utilizing inmate labor, were modern and clean, and the food, largely produced within the system, was wholesome and plentiful. Although the ratio of guards to inmates was much lower than recommended by correctional specialists, the prisons were comparatively safe, with much lower assault and homicide rates than prisons in comparable states. The cost per day per inmate was the lowest in the country.[4]

Although generally considered a success, the Texas prison system was not without its critics. The system was highly authoritarian, and there were allegations that prisoners were brutalized by guards who dispensed summary physical punishment. The low guard-to-inmate ratio allegedly was maintained by giving inmates authority over other inmates; prison officials contended that "building tenders" had only janitorial duties. In 1972 a group of inmates filed suit in federal district court alleging that the treatment of inmates by the Department of Corrections was unconstitutional. At about the same time, a dramatic increase in the number of inmates began that resulted in a doubling of the population of 16,000 to approximately 32,000 by 1982.

The complex suit, in which the U.S. Justice Department intervened on behalf of the inmates, was not decided until 1981. The court found the prisons overcrowded, understaffed, and dangerous, with inadequate medical care and guard violence against inmates. The pattern of treatment was found to violate the prohibitions in the U.S. Constitution against cruel and unusual punishment and denial of due process of law.[5] The order rendered by the court addressed many areas of operations of the prisons, with major emphasis on overcrowding, under-staffing, and medical care. The system was ordered to stop giving inmates author-ity over other inmates, a practice it denied but eventually, in a consent decree, agreed to stop. The immediate effects of the court ruling included an expanded construction program to reduce overcrowding, a reduction in the guard-to-in-mate ratio, and construction of a hospital facility at the University of Texas Medical Branch at Galveston.

Prison officials pointed to another consequence of the court ruling. Inmate disturbances and violent acts against other inmates increased; in the decade preceding the ruling, prison authorities reported 23 homicides, but in 1981 the number already approached 50 percent of that figure.[6] In succeeding years vio-lence continued at high levels as prison gangs battled among themselves and intimidated other inmates, sanitation became a problem, and productivity in vocational programs declined. Construction of new prisons was accelerated and legislation was enacted providing for the early release of prisoners, but the sys-tem's population continued to increase. For short periods the system has refused to accept additional prisoners, and many inmates have remained in county jails for extended periods after their sentences have begun.

The construction program increased the number of prison units to 31 with a capacity of over 45,000 in 1989, and another 12 units were either in the planning or construction process. The construction program is costly, and court-mandated changes in services and procedures added additional costs. In an attempt to slow the increase in spending, laws were enacted providing for probation for more offenders and earlier releases on parole for others. Many of those released eventu-ally returned to prison, and the eventual response of the legislature was a reorga-nization that created a Department of Criminal Justice that performed the func-tions previously assigned to three state agencies—the Department of Corrections, the Board of Pardons and Paroles, and the Adult Probation Commission. The new department, headed by a director responsible to a nine-member board ap-pointed by the governor with Senate concurrence, thus was a response to dissatis-faction with the criminal justice system and specifically to a perceived lack of coordination in the system. It remains to be determined whether the new organi-zation can manage its responsibilities more effectively than did its predecessors.

The Youth Commission   The Youth Commission administers the juvenile cor-rections system of the state. Youths committed to the commission fall into two basic categories: (1) those who have committed offenses against persons or prop-erty and (2) those who have been involved in truancy, runaway, and other status offenses and have violated a court order. Most juveniles committed to the com-mission are first placed in a statewide reception center at Brownwood, where their cases are evaluated and placements determined. All violent offenders are placed in one of four high-security facilities where they must stay at least 12 months; the others may be placed in one of the other training schools, in halfway houses operated by the commission, or in privately operated community child-care facilities. In 1989 over 1200 of the 1900 juveniles in the custody of the commission were in the training schools. Juvenile judges ordinarily do not give determinate sentences, and committed youths remain under under the commission's authority until age 18. Jurisdiction may be extended to age 21 for youths who meet certain criteria. In reaction to allegations that juveniles who committed serious crimes escaped justice when the commission's jurisdiction expired, a determinate sentencing law was enacted that allows juvenile sentences of up to 30 years for enumerated serious offenses. The sentence is initially served in a Youth Commission facility, but when the youth reaches age 18, jurisdiction is transferred to the Department of Criminal Justice. The commission operates a parole system, and a child whose parole is revoked may be returned to a training school or placed in another program. In 1989 over 1800 youths were on parole.

The Youth Commission is composed of six members appointed by the governor with the consent of the Senate; day-to-day operations are the responsibility of an executive director. The commission shares responsibility with the Department of Human Resources for dependent and neglected children. For decades the commission operated state homes for such children, but use of foster homes and other community programs reduced the number of referrals, and the homes have been discontinued.

The Adjutant General's Department   The adjutant general is appointed by the governor with Senate concurrence, and the department is responsible for the operation of the National Guard. Since a large part of the mission of the guard is a national responsibility, financing of the units is national, and many of the training requirements are established by the national government. The state, nevertheless, is responsible for command, administration, recruitment, and training. During peacetime, the guard may be called upon in emergencies to assist in the maintenance of order. There are almost 180 army and air force units of the Texas National Guard, with an authorized strength of over 26,000.

The adjutant general is also responsible for the operation of the Texas State Guard, the successor to similar units dating back to World War II, when much of the Texas National Guard was activated. The mission of the State Guard, which is little known and even less used, is to handle emergencies that would otherwise be the responsibility of the National Guard when the National Guard is called into federal service.

Health and Hospitals

The Department of Health   Several state agencies carry on programs in the health field, but the most important is the Department of Health, which is responsible for the planning and development of health policy, for maintaining a comprehensive state health plan, and for aiding areawide health-planning groups. Direct public health services for the most part are provided by health units responsible to local governments, but the department operates regional offices that provide services in counties without organized services, as well as hospitals in San Antonio and Harlingen that are historical accidents. As part of its system of eleemosynary institutions, Texas once operated a series of tuberculosis hospitals that for the most part performed chest surgery. As reorganizations occurred that dispersed eleemosynary institutions among agencies along functional or programmatic lines, the hospitals were eventually placed in the Department of Health, which is responsible for control of tuberculosis. As the number of tuberculosis patients declined, the statutory treatment authority was broadened first to include all chest-related diseases and then all other diseases for which the department operates programs. In 1989 the San Antonio hospital was given primary responsibility for tuberculosis services, and the Harlingen hospital was converted into a general medical facility for the Rio Grande Valley.

The health services programs of the department fall into three broad categories: prevention of contagious disease, personal health services, and environmental and consumer health protection. Although in recent years emphasis has shifted away from controlling epidemics to the delivery of personal health services and environmental control, the disease prevention category is probably the service most familiar to the general public. Several million antigens are administered annually, primarily to preschool and school-age children, for the prevention of communicable diseases such as mumps and polio. Major programs are administered to control venereal disease, tuberculosis, and rabies, and in recent years an acquired immune deficiency syndrome (AIDS) program was added.

Services directed toward preventing and remediating health conditions have received increased emphasis over the past decade, and the number of conditions for which financial assistance is available has been expanded. Some 30 services are offered, with the largest programs providing maternal and child health care and assistance, aid to chronically ill and disabled children, and kidney care.

The Department of Mental Health and Mental Retardation (MHMR) The MHMR board, composed of nine members appointed by the governor with the consent of the Senate, appoints a commissioner responsible for operation of the department. The department constitutes a system of residential and community services that includes 8 mental hospitals, 13 schools for the retarded, a center for emotionally disturbed youths, a recreational rehabilitation center, a program of grants for 32 community mental health and mental retardation centers, and 5 prototype centers called "centers for human development," which essentially are day-care facilities for the mentally ill and retarded.

Texas's mental health and mental retardation programs have a controversial history. Prior to 1949, mental hospitals and schools for the retarded were operated by the Board of Control, the predecessor agency of the State Purchasing and General Services Commission, and services and physical plant were of poor quality. A reform effort created a Board for State Hospitals and Special Schools and funds were provided to improve the facilities and provide care under the supervision of professionals. The state program, however, consisted exclusively of institutional care, and the programs existing in local communities for treating persons prior to or after discharge from institutions were not coordinated with the treatment programs at the institutions.

In 1965 another reform movement replaced the Hospital Board with the Department of Mental Health and Mental Retardation, which was given responsibility for the mental hospitals and schools for the retarded as well as some mental health programs formerly administered by the Health Department. Community mental health and mental retardation centers were also authorized, with funding from national, state, and local sources and some supervision by the department. The reorganization supposedly signaled a change in philosophy that emphasized continuity of treatment in the patient's home community.

Despite the creation of the community centers, the bulk of the MHMR budget is devoted to the institutions; only slightly over 20 percent of the department's general revenue appropriation is devoted to the centers. The population of the mental hospitals has declined as improved treatment techniques, most notably in drug therapy, and the availability of community-centered programs have resulted in shorter periods of institutionalization. The hospitals have become primarily centers for short-term, intensive treatment. As community programs have become available, a similar but less extreme development has occurred at the schools for the retarded, where the population is now smaller than a decade ago but composed of more severely retarded persons.

Departmental and appropriating authorities have been criticized for their priorities among the programs conducted by MHMR. The critics, who desire greater emphasis on community programs, suspect that the tendency of entrenched bureaucrats to support their programs and of legislators to support construction projects that are physical proof of their endeavors on behalf of their districts accounts for the underemphasis on community services. Defenders of the department point out that the costs of intensive treatment of the severely ill and retarded who need institutionalization are very high, and that treatment programs at the Texas institutions have much lower per-patient costs and higher staff-patient ratios than are considered desirable by mental health and mental retardation specialists.

The administration of MHMR has been characterized by conflict. The first major conflict was between those primarily concerned with mental retardation and supporters of mental health programs. In a victory for medical doctors and their association over the Texas Association for Retarded Citizens, primarily made up of parents of students at the schools for the retarded, the 1965 authorizing legislation in effect ensured that a mental health professional would always head the agency by requiring that the commissioner be a medical doctor when most retardation specialists were psychologists. This conflict occasionally reappears, but two others are more prominent. Regional rivalries among institutions have intensified as resident populations have declined and mention of closing institutions appeared. Of even greater importance has been the competition between institutions and community centers for funds. One result of the many conflicts has been high turnover rates among the top administrators and instability and discontinuity in program administration.

Reprinted by permission.

In the late 1970s, class-action lawsuits were instigated by relatives of clients of the department which alleged that minimum services required to provide due process of law as required by the state and national constitutions were not being provided by MHMR. In 1981 and 1983 the department agreed to settlements in federal court which, within fiscal constraints imposed by legislative appropriations, would provide improved care and redistribute funds to follow clients as they progressed from institutions to less restrictive settings. Institutional populations have been reduced and more funds per patient provided for those who remain, but community facilities have been overburdened. As the 1990s began, the department remained under the supervision of a federal judge.

Education

The Central Education Agency In 1949 the Texas legislature enacted the Gilmer-Aikin law establishing a foundation school program. The program was the culmination of a long but heretofore piecemeal involvement by state government in public education. Land had been set aside for support of schools during independence, and the Constitution of 1876 committed a portion of state revenue and of the public domain to support schools. In 1884 legislation was enacted providing for increased support of the public schools, and an elective position of superintendent of public instruction was created. A per capita apportionment of state aid was provided for all school districts, and eventually a special program of aid to rural schools was created.

In the nineteenth century local support of schools was slight; in 1899 less than a fourth of the expenditures were raised by local taxation. The twentieth century witnessed a greater willingness to provide local support, and by 1940 half of public school expenditures was raised by local taxation. A compulsory attendance law was enacted in 1915, and in 1918 the constitution was amended and legislation eventually enacted providing free textbooks for use in public schools. In 1929 an appointive state board of education was created, but it was always overshadowed in influence by the elective superintendent.[7]

The Gilmer-Aikin law constituted an effort to guarantee to every student the opportunity to obtain a minimally adequate level of education. The legislation abolished the elective superintendency and appointed board and created in their place the Texas Education Agency, composed of an elective State Board of Education, with a member from each of the state's congressional districts, a commissioner appointed by the board, and a State Department of Education, which under the supervision of the commissioner administered the system of state aid, services, and controls that constituted the foundation school program. The program was considered quite progressive for its time.[8]

For the first two decades of its existence, the Texas Education Agency was relatively uncontroversial, but in the past two decades its programs have been highly controversial, with most but not all of the controversy involving the method of distributing state aid, a problem discussed in greater detail in Chapter 9. Other controversies involved educational and managerial issues, including the degree of state control, the specificity of state regulations, and even the eligibility of students for extracurricular activities. In the 1980s the board was reduced in size and was temporarily made appointive, with the governor and the legislature involved in the appointment of the commissioner. Currently the board consists of 15 members elected from single-member districts; the board nominates the commissioner, who then is appointed by the governor with Senate concurrence.

Higher Education   The state's institutions of higher education are governed by a variety of governing boards, usually called *boards of regents,* appointed by the governor with the consent of the Senate. Several of the state's universities (there are 35 general academic campuses) have boards that are responsible for the operation of individual schools, but in other instances boards are responsible for the operation of multicampus systems. The Board of Regents of the University of Texas is responsible for the operation of its several general academic branches, medical and dental schools, and special institutions. The Board of Directors of Texas A&M University oversees the operations of the main university and several general academic institutions, three maritime-related units in Galveston, and a variety of agricultural and engineering agencies. Other multicampus systems are the University of Houston, East Texas State University, Lamar University, and the Texas State University System, which includes four of the small to medium-size state universities.

The Coordinating Board, composed of 18 members appointed by the governor with Senate concurrence, is responsible for coordinating higher education policy. The board, with a staff headed by a commissioner of higher education, also administers the state grants to community colleges, a program of tuition equalization grants for students attending private colleges and universities, and various federal grants-in-aid programs. Another component of the state's higher education system is the Texas State Technical Institute, a 4-campus system with over 7500 students, governed by a 9-member board appointed by the governor with the concurrence of the Senate. Courses of study are offered in specialized vocational-technical areas.

Welfare and Employee Benefits

The state operates a number of social service programs that are administered by special agencies (included are commissions for the blind, deaf, veterans, and the aging) and several retirement programs. But the most important programs in this classification are conducted by the Department of Human Resources, Employment Commission, and Rehabilitation Commission.

The Department of Human Services (DHS)   This department, which through much of its history was named the Department of Public Welfare, is headed by a 6-member board appointed by the governor with Senate concurrence. Once primarily concerned with providing financial assistance to the needy aged, blind, disabled, and families with dependent children, plus medical assistance (Medicaid) to the recipients of those same programs, DHS now is responsible for a variety of additional programs but is no longer responsible for aid to the needy aged, blind, and disabled. Most of its services are encouraged, if not required, by the national government and at least partially funded through federal grants. Several programs provide services that are not income-related—protective services for children and elderly and disabled persons, licensure of child-care facilities, and disaster assistance—but most provide services to persons near or below federal poverty guidelines.

A broad range of services are offered for low-income persons, but they can be classified into 4 groups: (1) income assistance, including aid to families with dependent children; (2) health care, including Medicaid; (3) family self-support services, including support for child care and job training; and (4) nursing home and community care services for the aged and disabled, including payment to nursing homes and home-delivered meals. The DHS caseload fluctuates in response to changing economic conditions and revision of federal law, and anticipating such changes is difficult. The consequence is recurring crises and public and legislative criticism, most of which involve the financing rather than the performance of services.

The Texas Employment Commission (TEC)   The TEC is responsible for two major programs—employment insurance and employment services. The employment insurance program collects an unemployment tax from covered employees and pays benefits to the justifiably unemployed. The entire program operates under considerable control by the U.S. Bureau of Employment Security, although the state has some control over standards of eligibility for benefits. The employment services program is conducted through a system of 180 free public employment offices. In addition to the two major programs, the TEC administers the state's minimum wage, child labor, and payday laws and conducts programs funded through federal grants directed toward the training and job placement of the hardcore unemployed. The three commissioners, who occupy full-time positions, are appointed by the governor with the consent of the Senate.

The Texas Rehabilitation Commission The commission, composed of six members appointed by the governor with the consent of the Senate, is responsible, through its executive director, for the administration of two programs: (1) the disability determination program, funded entirely through federal grants, which determines eligibility of the disabled for social security and supplementary security income payments, and (2) the vocational rehabilitation program, which provides a broad range of services to persons determined to be legally disabled except the visually impaired, who are served by the Commission for the Blind. Most of the rehabilitation programs' funds are provided under federal grants, but the state provides some matching funds. The commission operates an extended rehabilitation program, which provides work and residential living for persons whose handicaps are too severe for them to benefit from regular rehabilitation services. This program is funded entirely by the state and is considered cost-effective because most participants would otherwise be institutionalized.

Economic Regulatory and Promotional

Although more state agencies are classified as "economic regulatory and promotional" than are included in any other category, this group does not contain a large number of the more significant state agencies. Perhaps this is because the state's economic regulatory and promotional activities have only a marginal influence on the economy. The most significant economic policies are made by the national government, while state regulation tends to be of particular activities or industries. The state regulates a number of professions and occupations: Over thirty of the agencies classified as economic regulatory and promotional are licensing and/or examining boards, ranging from the Board of Architectural Examiners to the Board of Veterinary Medical Examiners. The state also regulates a somewhat smaller number of industries, among the more important being the liquor industry, regulated by the Alcoholic Beverage Commission; state-chartered banks, by the Banking Department of the Finance Commission; and insurance, by the Board of Insurance. The regulation of industries tends to be for the purpose of preventing abuses (or, in fact, to promote the well-being of those being regulated), and the overall economic impact is relatively small. Exceptions are the Railroad Commission and the Public Utility Commission.

The Railroad Commission The Railroad Commission was once the exception to the contention that state economic regulation has only a marginal economic impact. The commission was established to regulate railroads, and eventually its authority was expanded to include trucks and buses in intrastate service. The most important regulation of transportation is at the national level, however, and only the authority to regulate intrastate trucking remains of any significance.

The Railroad Commission has been assigned a variety of duties, including regulating the surface mining of coal, uranium, and iron ore for safety and conservation, the liquid petroleum gas industry in matters of safety, and, on appeal from the decisions of municipalities, the rates charged by natural gas utilities. Its most important duty, however, involves the regulation of the exploration, production, and transportation of oil and natural gas. The commission's concerns began with safety and conservation, but excess productive capacity in the 1930s led to the regulation of the volume produced in order to influence prices. Since Texas was by far the largest producer of petroleum among the 50 states, Railroad Commission decisions had a significant impact on the price of petroleum. Changes in the 1970s in the domestic petroleum industry eliminated economical excess productive capacity, and the commission's decisions now restrict production only for conservation reasons. The three commissioners, who are elected officials, have been closely allied with the petroleum and trucking industries.

The Public Utility Commission (PUC)   The Public Utility Commission is composed of three full-time commissioners appointed by the governor with the consent of the Senate. The commission has original jurisdiction over telephone and telecommunications companies throughout the state and over electric utilities operating in unincorporated areas. Municipalities have original jurisdiction over all electric utilities operating within their limits, and the commission has appellate jurisdiction over nongovernmental electric utilities operating in cities. Gas utilities are regulated by cities and the Railroad Commission and water utilities by the Water Commission, which also regulates water rights and hazardous waste and solid waste disposal.

When PUC was created in 1975, Texas was one of the last states to create a commission to regulate utilities. Consumer groups supported and utilities opposed creation of the PUC, and the commission has been a continuing source of controversy between the two. The basic problem of utility regulation is to strike a balance between consumers' interest in lower rates and maintaining the financial integrity of the utilities in order to provide a rate of return sufficient to induce investment. In its first years the PUC attempted to strike such a balance when it established the precedent for determining the base upon which rates should be set.[9] The legislation creating the commission specified that it follow an "adjusted value of capital" base that was a compromise between original cost (favored by consumer groups) and replacement cost (favored by utilities). The commission essentially defined adjusted value of capital as original cost but set rates at a level adequate to attract investment. Utilities wanted construction work in progress included in the base, but consumer groups were opposed to this; a compromise was developed that allows a percentage of work in progress to be included.

Consumers welcomed the first major decision of the commission, which granted Southwestern Bell only one-fifth of its requested rate increase, but after that decision, attitudes changed. Governors Dolph Briscoe and Bill Clements appointed to the commission business-oriented conservatives who believed that economic growth required prosperous utilities able to finance expanded services, and by 1979 the electric utilities were unsuccessfully supporting legislation to give the commission original jurisdiction over electric rates in cities. The PUC became an issue in the 1982 gubernatorial election between Mark White and Clements, with White criticizing the commission and promising to appoint consumer-oriented commissioners. After White's election he was able to appoint all three members of the commission when the two holdover members resigned to protest his criticism, and increases in the cost of electricity moderated; the reason probably had more to do with stable fuel prices than the policies of White's appointees.

For a time, controversy over the commission receded, but during Clements's second term, the PUC again became a subject of public debate. Changes in 1986 in federal tax laws had reduced the tax burdens of utilities, and consumer groups contended that rates should be adjusted downward. The commission staff worked out a settlement with Southwestern Bell that provided each customer with a one-time credit, and in turn Bell promised an extensive modernization program. The settlement was approved by the commission without going through the full hearing process. Bitter animosity developed between the White appointee still on the commission and the two Clements appointees, who approved the settlement. The White appointee called for legislation to prohibit waiving the hearing process when negotiated settlements were not approved by all interested parties. One of the parties that did not approve the Southwestern Bell settlement was the Office of Public Utility Counsel, which was created in 1983 to represent the allegedly underrepresented interests of residential and small commercial customers.

The Board of Insurance   Regulation of the insurance industry originally was intended to ensure that companies met minimum capital requirements and thus were financially sound. The responsibility of the Board of Insurance now encompasses a comprehensive set of regulations designed to ensure the financial soundness of the industry while protecting the interest of consumers in the state (and it is important to note that insurance is the only highly regulated industry in the financial sector of the economy that the national government leaves almost entirely to state regulation).

The Board of Insurance conducts financial examinations of insurance companies and approves rates in most property/casualty lines of insurance. Companies in financial difficulty may be placed under a special form of supervision called conservatorship, which attempts rehabilitation, or in liquidation, which operates under court order to dissolve insolvent companies. The three full-time board members, appointed by the governor with Senate concurrence, have initial jurisdiction over policy, rules, and rates and hear appeals of administrative rulings of the commissioner of insurance, who is appointed by the board and serves at its pleasure but who otherwise is statutorily responsible for the operation of the agency.

The Board of Insurance tends to operate without much public scrutiny except in times of scandal (as in the 1950s, when nonregulation resulted in the failure of a number of undercapitalized companies) and in periods of sharp rate increases. The insurance industry tends to be politically active, and the companies and the network of local agents have exercised considerable influence on the appointment of board members.

In recent years, rate increases and a few highly publicized company failures have generated additional interest in the Board of Insurance. In 1987 consumer criticism led to the creation of a division of consumer protection, which is headed by a public counsel appointed by the governor and is charged wth representation of consumers before the board. In 1991, after making the board an issue in her gubernatorial campaign, Governor Ann Richards, as a first step in reorienting the board toward greater openness and more effective regulation, successfully demanded the resignations of the two board members appointed by her predecessor, Bill Clements.

Conservation, Recreation, and Culture

Included among the agencies in this category are several river compact commissioners who represent Texas on interstate compacts designed to conserve (or exploit) interstate rivers and a mixed group of other minor agencies. The most important agency in this classification, however, is the Parks and Wildlife Department. This department is headed by a nine-member commission, appointed by the governor with Senate concurrence, which, in turn, names an executive director responsible for directing agency activities. The department has two major responsibilities: game and fish management and park management. In the game and fish area, it conducts management and research programs, enforces state laws regulating hunting and fishing, and sells sand, shells, and gravel from public waters and streams.

The department is responsible for the operation of the state park system of about 130 recreational, scenic, and historical parks. Admission is charged at some of the more popular and heavily used parks, with proceeds used for the acquisition and development of new parks. The state park system, which was almost undeveloped into the 1960s, has made considerable progress since the present department was created in 1963.

Transportation

The only transportation agency of any consequence in Texas is the Department of Highways and Public Transportation, which is headed by a three-member commission appointed by the governor with the concurrence of the Senate. An engineer-director administers the department, which is responsible for both the construction and maintenance of highways. The department performs most of its own maintenance operations, which include picking up litter, beautifying rights-of-way, and repairing damages. Construction is performed by private contractor selected through competitive bidding, although plans are drawn by the department's engineers. More employees participate in maintenance than construction, but construction accounts for three-fourths of the department's budget. Generally, the leadership of the department works closely with the Good Roads and Transportation Association, an organization dominated by highway contractors but including other groups committed to "good" roads. Even the critics of the department's policies, who charge that it is too oriented to the automobile, concede the excellence of the Texas highway system.

The Highway Department administers a public transportation fund that helps finance local public transportation capital improvement projects; matching local and federal funds provide the remainder of the financing. The public transportation fund amounts to less than 1 percent of the department's budget.

THE PERSONNEL SYSTEM

The personnel system of the Texas state government is decentralized, with the operating agencies largely responsible for personnel management. Decentralization is practiced to such a degree that a study conducted by the Texas Research League concluded that in a very real sense there are no state employees, only employees of particular agencies.[10] Much of the following account of the personnel system is dependent on this study.

The legislature does establish some basic policies, either through statutes or rider provisions of the appropriations act. Certain conditions of employment have been established, including a 40-hour work week. There are prohibitions on conflict of interest, publicizing individuals, attempting to influence the outcome of an election or the passage or defeat of legislation, and specified forms of nepotism. Discrimination on the basis of race, religion, color, sex, national origin, and age (for those between 21 and 65, with exceptions for such positions as law enforcement officers) is prohibited. Veterans or their widows and orphans are entitled to a preference in employment over other applicants not having better qualifications. The state laws governing conditions of employment, however, are not part of an integrated general framework of personnel policies; they are a hodgepodge of provisions enacted over time to deal with particular problems.

The policies established by the legislature governing employee benefits are more comprehensive and consistent than those affecting conditions of employment and employment practices. State employees are provided 13 paid holidays, vacation and sick leave, and retirement, social security, and group insurance. Separate policies on holidays, group insurance, and retirement apply to the units of the higher education system.

Prior to 1961, wage and salary administration was not uniform, and rates of pay and qualifications for similar employment often varied from agency to agency. In that year the legislature approved a position classification plan designed to establish classes of work for most positions and to assign each job class to a pay grade within a salary-classification schedule. Agency administrators are responsible for determining that employees are properly classified, and the state auditor has authority to determine that the classifications are correct. The positions comprising the salary plan are listed in the general appropriations act, and the legislature occasionally reclassifies positions or reallocates them to other salary groups. The legislature can also exempt positions by specifying the salary in a line-item appropriation, and most sensitive policy positions and many professional positions are exempt. Units of the state system of higher education are not covered by the plan. Limited responsibility for administration of the position-classification system is vested in a classification officer appointed by the state auditor. This officer maintains a current listing of all classified positions; provides descriptions for new positions; aids state agencies in the application of the plan; and conducts studies for and makes recommendations to the budget offices, governor, and legislature on the operation of the plan and on salary rates in other governmental units and industry.

Each biennial general appropriations act sets out a salary schedule applicable to positions included in the classification plan, which covers about 80 percent of non–higher-education employees. The salary schedule establishes salary groups to which all positions are assigned, and within each group a series of steps provides for different salary levels. At present there are 20 groups and 8 steps within each group. Generally, there is a differential between groups of 6.8 percent and a difference of 3.4 percent between steps within groups. The legislature has regularly increased the salaries of state employees by revising the schedule upward, usually by multiples of 3.4 percent, but the fiscal crises of the 1980s has resulted in smaller increases in what was fortunately a period of low inflation.

Most state employees are on the lower steps of their group because the legislature has not provided funds for awarding a large number of step (or merit) increases; high turnover rates also contribute to the concentration of employees on the lower steps.

The adequacy of the salary schedule is a matter of dispute. The Texas Public Employees Association, the dominant state employee association, which is actively antiunion and is committed to furthering the interests of state employees through traditional lobbying tactics, regards it as inadequate. There are other indications that state salaries are competitive. Salaries paid by state government in Texas compare favorably with salaries paid in neighboring states; they are also apparently competitive in the Texas labor market, with the exception of high labor-cost areas such as Dallas and Houston.

Within the context of the policies established by the legislature, the major responsibility for personnel management resides with the state's operating agencies, where there is great variation in personnel practices. Some agencies have developed sophisticated personnel management staffs with responsibility for recruiting and testing prospective employees, developing and coordinating agency training programs, and counseling employees on personnel matters. Others, including a few of the large agencies but predominantly those with a small number of employees, leave all personnel activities to supervisory officials. A majority of state agencies, including those that employ an overwhelming percentage of employees, do use such procedures as qualifying tests, orientation programs, probationary periods for new employees, and exit interviews at the time of separation; but many, including a few large agencies, do not.

Since there is not a central contact point, such as a state personnel office or civil service commission for prospective state employees, the agencies resort to a variety of sources for finding applicants. Many use the Employment Commission, but others use private employment agencies and college placement centers. Still others depend on walk-ins or employee referrals.

To discourage discrimination on ethnic and sexual grounds, all agencies must submit affirmative action plans to an Equal Employment Opportunity Office in the Texas Employment Commission, and all openings for jobs with state agencies in Travis County (Austin) must be listed with the Employment Commission.

Policies also vary in other areas of personnel management. Most major state agencies have formalized procedures for handling employee complaints, but some smaller agencies do not. Many small agencies do not have formal systems of performance evaluation, but the large agencies that employ most state employees do. An exception to the decentralization of personnel administration were the agencies participating in the Merit System Council, which was created in 1940 in response to federal laws that conditioned the receipt of grants-in-aid upon the administering agency's participation in a merit system of personnel administration. In a reflection of the unpopularity of anything resembling a formal civil service system, the council was allowed to die in 1985, and the agencies that formerly were members now perform their personnel functions independently.

Three problems are identifiable within the personnel system of Texas state government. First, there is no system to protect most state employees from political pressures and removal without cause for "spoils" purposes or to protect the public from use of state employees by politicians to enhance their chances for reelection. Such a system is provided in the national government and in many states through civil service systems, usually administered by an independent commission. But there is little interest in or support for a civil service system for state employees in Texas. The Texas Public Employees Association concentrates primarily on employee benefits and has not supported extension of the merit system to all state agencies.

In its report on personnel management in state government, the Texas Research League concluded that a merit system was unnecessary because the use of the independent board system to head most state agencies provided insulation from political pressure for state employees. Furthermore, the league concluded that the flexibility the Texas system now provides should not be exchanged for a more authoritarian system that might produce a cadre of personnel unresponsive to public needs, not accountable for job performance, and consequently inefficient and indifferent.[11]

Although the insulation from political pressure afforded by the independent board system can be overstated, most state agencies do not have high turnover rates of rank-and-file employees attributable to changes in political control. There are occasional examples of the spoils system at work, and employees of agencies headed by elected officials often are expected to contribute to or participate in their campaigns. But for the most part Texas state government has escaped the more flagrant spoils-system abuses.

The second problem with the personnel system involves the administration of the salary system. A sound salary system recognizes meritorious performance by awarding salary increases, with increases not limited to promotions to more responsible positions but awarded for performance on the same job. The Texas system recognizes this principle by providing for a series of eight steps; within each salary group an employee can be rewarded with step increases. The legislature has provided very little money for merit increases, often simply allowing funds appropriated for other purposes but not spent to be used for merit increases. Agency heads try to have the positions of employees whom they desire to reward for meritorious performance reclassified to higher salary groups; this provides higher salaries but defeats the principle of equal pay for equal work upon which the classification plan was based.

The failure to provide adequate merit salary increases is a result of the process by which the salary program is established. Since riders to the general appropriations act establish the salary schedule and provide for the administration of the system, the salary program is subjected to fiscal rather than administrative review. This violates a principle of public personnel administration that while salary levels (the amount of salary increases) necessarily depend on the overall fiscal situation, the elements of salary administration (who gets raises) should not be so related. The legislature tends to favor awarding across-the-board increases since such increases are more likely to be attributed by the employees to the beneficence of the legislators. The Texas Public Employees Association is less than enthusiastic in its support of merit salary increases, preferring that what funds are available be used for increases for all employees.

The third problem with the state personnel system is the absence of a focal point in administration. There is no center of responsibility concerned with where the state is going in terms of personnel: with the number of employees needed in future years, where they will come from, and what skills they will need. There does not appear to be any serious movement to develop a mechanism for developing and coordinating state personnel policy.

THE POLITICS OF THE ADMINISTRATIVE PROCESS

A long-held ideal in the United States was that politics and administration should be separated. Politics was identified with the process of determining which goals were to be pursued by governmental policies and the content of those policies; administration was thought of as the process of carrying out those policies. Ideally, goals and policies should be established by those who are politically responsible (the chief executive and the legislative body), and administration should be by those who are technically competent (officials in the administrative agencies). Students of public administration now recognize, however, that in most situations this ideal is not attainable. The application of policy almost inevitably involves making policy choices, for policy is almost never enacted in a form that anticipates all policy questions. In many instances policy is left deliberately vague, and on other occasions legislatures delegate policy-making responsibility to administrative agencies. Further, administrative officials regularly participate in the formulation of policy; they have knowledge that other participants feel should be used, and they are individuals with their own views and preferences.

Administration actually is a process suffused with politics, and participants in the administrative process often are engaged in making policy choices, promoting group interests, struggling for power and influence, and maneuvering for partisan advantage. Political scientists once advanced a formalistic perspective that viewed administration as dominated in policy matters by the top-level, politically appointed administrators. But they have come to view administration as a process in which agencies interact with their entire environment, including not only the chief executive, the legislature, and the courts but also the general public, party and factional groups, other administrative agencies, and clientele. Agencies are faced with situations in which the policy choices they make are to the greater advantage (or lesser disadvantage) of certain elements of their environment than to others.

Administrative Politics in Texas

Agencies respond differently to various groups in the community. In Texas, administrative agencies exist in a political environment that encourages their response to follow well-established patterns. The administrative process operates within a governmental structure and political context that fragments authority and is conducive to the dominance of policy making by the organized clienteles of agencies. More often than not the most influential elements of agency clienteles are conservative business groups. The governor is in a relatively weak position; although the office is the most important in the state, and a strong and popular occupant conceivably could dominate the policy process, decisive gubernatorial influence is more the exception than the rule.

The legislature is a strong contender with the governor for influence in the administrative process, but it suffers from the weaknesses of fragmentation and division that are common to legislative bodies in providing policy leadership. While the presiding officers are influential, neither the speaker nor the lieutenant governor is selected through a process that encourages the development of extensive legislative programs. Effective initiative in policy development lies elsewhere than with the legislature and its leaders; for the most part, administrative agencies and organized interest groups provide such leadership.

Throughout the United States the interests of the administrative agencies and representatives of pressure groups tend to converge, and administrative agencies develop close relationships with the representatives of organized groups interested in their activities. This tendency is abetted in Texas by the governmental structure and the pattern of politics.

The governmental structure encourages close relationships between administrative agencies and clientele groups by placing the agencies in positions that insulate them from the general political process. The agencies headed by elective officials tend to be unnoticed by the public unless a scandal occurs or those segments of the public with which the agency has day-to-day contact voice criticisms. Incumbents are ordinarily reelected and in effect have career positions unless they attract a great deal of unfavorable publicity; only personal scandal and clientele dissatisfaction threaten their security. If the organized groups that constitute an agency's clientele are content, they provide campaign support for the incumbent, and opposing candidates find it difficult to develop an effective base of support for their campaigns.

In the past 40 years only six elected agency heads have been defeated for reelection (two others who were appointed to office were defeated in their first attempt at election). The first five of the six were involved in special circumstances—identification with scandals, choking a member of the news media, use of a derogatory racial epithet, and supporting Republicans for office in the period of total Democratic domination, and all occurred in the Democratic primary (prior to 1990, Democrats had not lost an election for a position in the executive branch other than governor). A basic rule of Texas politics was that "lesser" state officials could, barring special ineptitude and/or most unusual conditions, maintain their positions as long as they were responsive to their clienteles (for example, the state treasurer to banking, the commissioner of agriculture to farm groups, and the railroad commissioners to the petroleum and trucking industries).

The development of straight-ticket voting for Republicans eventually posed a threat to Democratic elected agency heads, and in 1990 Republicans finally won two such positions. Agriculture Commissioner Jim Hightower, a self-styled populist, had offended large commercial agricultural interests in several areas, the most notable of which involved pesticide application regulations, and the Farm Bureau developed a vigorous campaign to prevent his reelection. For tactical reasons the major challenge was by a Republican in the general election, but six otherwise unknown farmers (the "Texas six-pack") filed against Hightower in the Democratic primary and continually attacked the operation of his agency in an effort to weaken his position in the general election. Rick Perry, a Democratic legislator, switched parties to run as a Republican and defeated Hightower in the general election. In the same year Republican Kay Hutchinson was elected state treasurer. Democrats are likely to undertake vigorous campaigns to retake the two offices, and general partisan considerations rather than clientele service may play a significant role in future campaigns for positions as head of state agencies. Jim Hightower's defeat, however, came about because of his alienation from the most powerful group in his clientele and does not disprove the proposition that elective agency heads in effect have career positions if they serve their clienteles and avoid scandal.

Economic groups whose well-being is affected by administrative agencies encourage their members to contribute to and participate in gubernatorial elections; such contributions undoubtedly help explain the large expenditure on elections to an office that otherwise is not extremely influential. Among the influential clienteles and the agencies of particular interest are highway contractors and the Highway Department; medical doctors and the Board of Medical Examiners and, to a lesser degree, the Department of Health; outdoor sports enthusiasts and local tourist interests and the Parks and Wildlife Department; the chemical and other heavy industries and the Air Control Board; the beer, wine, and liquor industry and the Alcoholic Beverage Commission; banks, thrift institutions, and small loan companies and the Finance Commission; organized labor, industrial companies, and plaintiff's attorneys and the Workers' Compensation Commission; insurance companies and insurance agents and the Board of Insurance; and telephone and electric companies and large commercial users of their products and the Public Utility Commission.

Contributions and other forms of electoral support may not ensure favorable appointments, but they do tend to aid access, or the ability to be heard, in the maneuvering that often occurs over appointments. Interest-group members also contribute to and participate in elections for positions in the Texas Senate, where the two-thirds requirement for approval of nominations affords an influential clientele a reasonable opportunity to block the appointment of a nominee it views with disfavor.

The consequence of both the elective and appointive methods of selecting the policy-making leadership of Texas administrative agencies is that it is very friendly to those being served and regulated. This is especially the case where the clienteles are business and occupational groups that command enough resources to organize and pursue their interests. The Department of Health is very responsive to the policy preferences of the medical profession, the Insurance Board has close relations with the insurance industry, and the Highway Department is very responsive to the wishes of highway contractors and the trucking industry.

Occasionally conflicts occur between segments of an agency's clientele. For example, there is a long-standing conflict between "chain" optometry companies and independent optometrists, with the independent optometrists supporting the adoption of rules by the Optometry Board that make the operation of chains difficult. When such conflict occurs, either a winner or a truce based on compromise may emerge (optometrists in effect are allowed to work for chains, but there must be separate entrances to their workplace and the chain's retail outlet). Occasionally, the conflicts within an agency's clientele reflect more general factional conflict: for example, a conflict between labor and management over policies of the Employment Commission or the Workers' Compensation Commission, or between liberal environmentalists and industrial groups over policies controlling water and air pollution. In such instances, the business and industrial groups tend to prevail over labor and liberal interests. This is a reflection of their overall political success, which translates into favorable legislation and appointments to key administrative positions.

There is a tendency in the United States for policy to be made within specialized subsystems of the overall political system composed of the administrative agency, organized clientele, and interested portions of the legislative body. The process often operates in an insulated context in which such matters as party platforms or the program of the chief executive seldom impinge. In Texas that tendency has been aggravated by the absence of meaningful party programs and a strong chief executive; the political strength of business interests; and the weakness of organized labor and consumer, environmental, and minority groups. The consequence is that the organized segments of the agencies' clienteles dominate policy making, although that dominance may have lessened somewhat in recent years as two-party politics impinged on a broader range of issues and overall political considerations became more important during the governorships of Bill Clements, Mark White, and Ann Richards.

Bill Clements entered his first term of office after having largely financed his campaign from personal funds, and his upset victory was unanticipated by the leaders of most of the trade associations and other interest groups. He organized a talent search for appointees under the direction of South Texas rancher/businessman Tobin Armstrong that reached beyond the usual group of political activists and campaign contributors. Although the appointees were for the most part business-oriented conservatives, they tended to be freer of identification with interest groups than past appointees had been.

Mark White largely returned to the traditional method of making appointments. One survey found that 61 of his 90 appointments to major boards and commissions were campaign contributors.[12] His appointments aroused some liberal criticism, although they probably did recognize somewhat the increased strength of ethnic minorities, labor, and liberal groups in the Democratic party. Ann Richards's initial appointments also followed the traditional pattern of appointing contributors to office, but the liberal base of her support, including financial support, may have lessened the influence of business and commercial clientele groups over the agencies in which they hold special interests.

The Sunset Review Process

Conditions in Texas are not unlike those that exist in many other states; and in Texas, as in other states, efforts have been undertaken to reform the executive branch by adopting an integrated administrative structure with the governor at its head. The most comprehensive proposal was developed in the early 1930s by a consulting firm, Griffenhagen and Associates, for a Joint Legislative Committee on Organization and Economy.[13] The Griffenhagen plan, which was quite thorough and moderately expensive, proposed consolidating all existing agencies into 19 departments, each headed by a single person responsible to the governor; departments with important policy-making, rule-making, investigatory, or fact-finding functions were to have advisory boards. Nothing came of the report. Since that time, occasional governors, social scientists, and the League of Women Voters have periodically voiced support for change, but comprehensive reform has not been attempted. Reorganizations have occurred in a number of areas; agencies have been abolished, combined, and created, and activities have been transferred from agency to agency. Nothing, however, has been accomplished in the way of drastically reducing the number of departments, or of giving the governor power to appoint, remove, and direct single heads of such departments. These are the actions that would be necessary to create an integrated executive structure.

In 1977 Texas adopted a *sunset review law* that embodies a different approach to administrative reform. Similar laws, based on the concept that governmental agencies and programs should have an established life span, have been enacted in numerous states. The Texas sunset law scheduled state agencies (and advisory committees), with the exception of agencies of higher education, for review at biennial intervals from 1979 to 1989, after which the process was repeated. Agencies are automatically terminated unless the legislature extends their terms. Renewals are for a period of 12 years.

A Sunset Advisory Commission, composed of four senators and a public member appointed by the lieutenant governor and four representatives and a public member appointed by the speaker, is responsible for reviewing the agencies

and submitting recommendations to the legislature. The sunset review law specifies 13 criteria to be used by the commission (and allows others to be added) in
performing its evaluations, including such matters as the efficiency with which
the agency performs its work, the extent to which the agency has identified and
achieved its objectives, the extent to which the jurisdiction and activities overlap
with those of other agencies, and the promptness and efficiency of the agency in
answering complaints. Agencies that are terminated are given a year to conclude
their business, at which point their property and records are transferred to the
State Purchasing and General Services Administration; unspent funds revert to
the general revenue fund; and indebtedness is transferred to an appropriate state
agency designated by the governor.

The Sunset Advisory Commission operates on a biennial cycle that begins
when the agencies scheduled for review, typically 25 to 30 entities, submit self-
evaluation reports. The commission's staff then prepares a performance evaluation report on each agency, the commission develops its recommendation, and
the legislature then determines the fate of the agency. The first Sunset Advisory
Commission established two precedents that have been subsequently retained.
First, it was decided that a majority of the appointees of each appointing authority
had to approve a recommendation for it to be submitted to the legislature. Second,
the commission developed 11 principles for application to agencies under review.
Among the most important of the "across-the-board" principles were requirements that agency expenditures be subject to the appropriation process (many
simply spent the money derived from fees they charged); that public members
(i.e., persons not engaged in the regulated activity) be included on all boards; and
that specific provisions be included in law that related to conflict of interest.

The Texas sunset review process generally receives commendations from
observers, even including consumer advocate Ralph Nader.[14] In a survey for the
public interest group Common Cause, Nader reported that Texas was among the
states benefiting most from the sunset process. The staff reports have been thorough, the commission has taken its work seriously, and members have been
sponsors of legislation it approved. There have been few instances in which the
commission has been unable to agree on a recommendation, and in those instances disagreements on the commission usually have become the basis for
competing bills considered by the legislature. The legislature has given the c
mission's work serious consideration, and the "across-the-board" prin
which generally are conceded to be the most important contributi One
commission, have usually been followed. The least successful princi
requiring inclusion in the appropriation process.   public
                                                                  lify the
Most of the successes of the sunset process have been in agencies
accountability and responsiveness, but some changes have 7 through
administrative structure. The accomplishments in cons   6 had their
and eliminating others are quite real. In the full 12-yea new agencies
1989, the commission reviewed 167 entities: 30 b uding the Pink
functions transferred to other agencies, 129 were ard, and others
were created. Several of the agencies abolished
Bollworm Commission and the Stonewall J

were almost inactive. For example, the Board of Tuberculosis Nurse Examiners was created to license specialized tuberculosis nurses, but since the last school graduating tuberculosis nurses was closed in 1961, the board was restricted to granting annual license renewals.

The sunset process is oriented to agency-by-agency review, and the Sunset Advisory Commission has not attempted ambitious consolidations, such as consolidation of all examining-licensing authority into a single occupational licensing agency. The commission, although noting that cosmetologists and barbers perform similar services (and in fact have jurisdictional conflicts that present problems for practitioners), did not recommend combining the two agencies. It has also been hesitant to recommend discontinuing activities; the sunset review staff reported that the Burial Association Rate Board had taken 17 years to promulgate adequate rates, that the board had not met in 14 years, and that burial association memberships had declined greatly. But the commission nevertheless successfully recommended that the board's functions be transferred to the Board of Insurance.

Forces still at work in directions contrary to the sunset process complicate the drive toward simplification and reduction in the number of agencies. The Sunset Advisory Commission successfully recommended that the Board of Landscape Architects and Board of Architectural Examiners be merged, but the merger left the status of landscape irrigators unclear. The irrigators' trade association, which the commission staff reported had succeeded in having the Board of Landscape Architects design licensing standards that reflected their wishes, succeeded in having a new Board of Irrigators created. In 1979, during the first sunset cycle, the legislature was busy creating six new agencies and advisory committees, a practice that has continued in each cycle. The commission has even contributed to the increase in the number of agencies with its successful recommendation that the Department of Water Resources, created in 1977 by combining three agencies, be divided into two agencies.

The record of success of the sunset process is not unblemished, and expectations of change in the basic policies of administrative agencies, especially as they interact with the organized segments of their clienteles, should not be great. When the Sunset Advisory Commission has recommended changes opposed by trade associations and other organized groups, more often than not the groups have ⟨been⟩ successful. Such groups as morticians, barbers, and cosmetologists have ⟨succee⟩ded in thwarting key recommendations, even though they do not compare ⟨in⟩ ⟨influ⟩ence with truckers, lawyers, and medical doctors, all of whom have ⟨success⟩ully fought off what they regarded as attacks on their interests during the ⟨sunset proce⟩ss.

⟨The re⟩view's successes have overwhelmingly been in areas where agen-⟨cies were⟩ weak or indifferent, or the ⟨agency b⟩oards accepted the changes. The review and reauthorization of the ⟨Board of Pharmacy⟩ is often cited as a major success of the sunset process. The ⟨board, which approv⟩als and licenses pharmacists and administers the law governing ⟨the sale of⟩ drugs and medicines, prepared a detailed, thoughtful ⟨report that eventu⟩ally resulted in the addition of public members to the board and a revised pharmacy law that authorized pharmacists to substitute generic drugs for more epensive brand-name products. Pharmacists and consumer groups had long advocated such authority, which was opposed by the Texas Medical Association as infringing on the prerogatives of medical doctors. Pharmacists were, however, able to maintain the status of the board outside the appropriations process, which is regarded, at least by legislators, as an important tool for securing responsiveness to the public.

The controversy over generic drugs during reauthorization of the Board of Pharmacy is illustrative of a regular development in thc sunset process: Sunset review often becomes involved in policy and political matters that have little to do with the existence of an agency. Thus the reauthorization of the agency headed by the commissioner of agriculture became enmeshed in the personality, policies, and political future of the incumbent commissioner, Jim Hightower, with Hightower's critics threatening to defeat legislation aimed at continuing the existence of the agency.

The disposition in 1979 of the Sunset Advisory Commission's recommendations on the State Bar may be illustrative of what happens to its recommendations when powerful political interests are offended. The bar, to which all practicing lawyers must belong, exists in a confusing legal condition. For some purposes it is a licensing-examining board, but in other respects it is a trade-association type of corporation. It chooses its own officers, levies fees, and spends its own money. The commission recommendations would have clarified its legal status by making it a state agency, whose board of directors would be appointcd by the presiding judges of the two superior appellatc courts and whose revenue would be deposited in the state treasury and available only after appropriation. The bar opposed the recommendations, especially the provision that subjected the bar to the appropriations process. Eventually six nonlawyers were added to the board of directors, and the Supreme Court was given some supervisory powers over the budget, but all other reforms were defeated. A legislative supporter of the Sunset Advisory Commission's recommendations referred to the changes actually made as tokenism and cosmetic, but some improvement.[15]

Power and Responsibility

The Texas administrative structure is characterized by fragmentation of authority and influence, and the politics of the administrative process contributes to the fragmentation. Although the governor's influence in the administrative process is relatively weak, the office has the appearance of power. The Texas Constitution seems to give broad responsibility for overseeing state administration to the governor, and the public often holds the governor responsible for almost everything that happens in the executive branch of government—if not in all of state government. But the governor's legal powers and political position do not grant the authority adequate to meet the broad responsibility; in reality, the position is one of responsibility without formal power.

Why has Texas persisted in the use of the weak-executive system when "good government" groups and social scientists have so widely favored the inte grated executive model? The answer lies in the nature of the reorganization task and the balance of power among the political forces favoring and opposing reorganization. The legal and constitutional tasks confronting reorganizers are quite formidable. In addition to a monumental amount of statutory revision, the constitution would have to be revised to give the governor power to appoint, direct, and remove lesser administrative officials and to eliminate numerous references to elective officials and independent boards and commissions.

The balance of power now existing between the proponents and opponents of administrative reorganization constitutes an even more formidable obstacle than does the technical problem of statutory and constitutional revision. Other than participants in and supporters of the reform movement, who tend to lack political influence and skill, about the only support for reorganization comes from occasional governors. Groups that enjoy more favorable access to the governor than to the legislature or administrative agencies might also be expected to support the creation of an integrated executive structure, but any such group is difficult to identify. Groups in the liberal/labor coalition who have not enjoyed favorable access to the legislature more often than not have not been favorites of the governor and have not favored strengthening the governorship.

The opposition to administrative reorganization comes from three sources: (1) the administrative agencies, which prefer autonomy from interference by the chief executive, who they fear might make use of agency positions for patronage or might disrupt existing practices and policies with which they have become comfortable; (2) the organized interest groups that enjoy favorable access and fear any disruption of the existing distribution of influence, especially a governor who appeals or responds to the unorganized and potentially conflicting interests of the general electorate; and (3) the legislators, who are distrustful of anything they perceive as threatening the strength of the legislature vis-à-vis the governor and thus oppose all changes that would restrict their ability to deal directly with agency administrators. The sunset review process is a legislative process; it was established by the legislature, the commission is dominated by legislators, and the process has not shown any inclination to strengthen the governor.

Changes in governmental machinery of the magnitude necessary to establish an integrated executive branch are difficult to achieve under any circumstances, for those resisting change in effect have the force of inertia as an ally. Given the political strength of the opponents of reorganization, attempts at administrative restructuring have been easily defeated. The abortive effort in 1974 to rewrite the constitution illustrates the weakness of the proponents of reorganization. At the same time the constitutional convention bestowed limited removal power on the governor, limited the life of state agencies to ten years unless they are renewed through legislative action, required the governor to submit periodic reorganization plans for legislative consideration, increased the number of officials whose election was mandated in the constitution, guaranteed the continued existence of most agencies established in the Constitution of 1876, and defeated ts to restrict to a stated figure the number of administrative agencies that e created by the legislature. Almost certainly the provisions would have d the existing weak-executive system.

NOTES

1. Joseph Schlesinger, "The Politics of the Executive," in *Politics in the American States,* 2d ed., ed. Herbert Jacobs and Kenneth Vines (Boston: Little, Brown, 1971), pp. 210–211.
2. For information on a particular agency, the best source is its annual report. A good summary source is the most recent version of the biennially published *Fiscal Size Up Texas State Services* (Austin: Legislative Budget Board).
3. *Guide To Texas State Agencies,* 5th ed. (Austin: University of Texas, Lyndon B. Johnson School of Public Affairs, 1978) p. 120.
4. Lawrence Wright, "Reporter," *Texas Monthly* VII (March 1981): 92.
5. *Ruiz* v. *Estelle,* 506 F. Supp. 1265 (S.D. tx., 1980).
6. *Dallas Morning News,* November 28, 1981, pp. A1, 8.
7. Ralph Steen, *Twentieth Century Texas* (Austin: Steck, 1942), pp. 139–141.
8. Stuart MacCorkle and Dick Smith, *Texas Government,* 3d ed. (New York: McGraw-Hill, 1956), p. 197.
9. The following account of the early activities of the Public Utility Commission is based on James Anderson, "The Public Utility Commission of Texas," *Public Affairs Comment* 36 (February 1980).
10. *Quality Texas Government* (Austin: Office of the Governor, Division of Planning Coordination, 1972), p. 21.
11. *Ibid.,* p. 6.
12. *Dallas Times Herald,* October 6, 1985, p. 1.
13. *The Government of Texas* (Austin: A. C. Baldwin, 1932–1933).
14. *Fort Worth Star Telegram,* March 16, 1982, p. 1.
15. *Houston Chronicle,* January 5, 1979, p. 1.

chapter 8

The Judicial System

Many citizens become involved with the courts as jurors, witnesses, litigants, and defendants.

The English philosopher John Locke, writing three centuries ago, concluded that people are forced into political society because they perceive the need for a common superior to judge disputes between themselves and their fellows.[1] Present-day government has created an elaborate set of structures and practices for judging the many conflicts that cannot be resolved privately among the members of a community. The nature of this judgmental process has been disputed. One tradition emphasizes the impartiality of the judges themselves, who are pictured as dispassionate appliers of general rules to particular cases. The judge does not create law but simply draws out the details implicit in the constitutional or legislative edicts in question.

A tradition of legal realism has challenged this Olympian view of law and judgeship with considerable success in recent years. This realistic view holds that becoming a judge does not suddenly cleanse one of all prejudices or immunize against social pressures. A judge's actions, like those of other human beings, will depend on personality, background, attitudes and beliefs, likes and dislikes. A judge is not merely an automaton consistently applying rules in particular cases. Rather, a judge creates law while dispensing it because cases must be decided when laws or precedents are unclear, contradictory, or ambiguous. The realists have further attacked the contention that the judicial process is equally open to all, and they have called attention to the varying patterns of compliance that characterize the enforcement of court decisions.

The legal realists affirm that the judicial system is very much concerned with politics, or with what David Easton calls the "authoritative allocation of values and resources for a society."[2] These allocations are in the form of policy outputs and are authoritative in the sense that they are made by government and are backed by the coercive power of the state. Judges, like legislators and executive officials, make decisions that benefit some citizens at the expense of others.

The great majority of the legal business of Americans begins and ends in state courts, such as those in Texas. These courts decide most civil disputes between individuals or companies as well as the great bulk of cases where persons are charged with violations of criminal law. Every year hundreds of thousands of Texans have business in these courts. On the civil side, the matters considered can vary from uncontested divorce proceedings to a $10 billion jury verdict for Pennzoil in a bitter business dispute with Texaco. Criminal court decisions, on the other hand, have placed over 40,000 people in overcrowded state prisons.

In addition to judging civil disputes between persons or companies and determining the guilt or innocence of persons charged with criminal acts, courts in the United States also exercise the power of judicial review. This means that judges have the power to both interpret what the law or Constitution means in specific cases, and to declare null and void any law or other official action that they view as conflicting with the Constitution. The U.S. Supreme Court has exercised this power on numerous occasions with profound consequences in areas such as abortion policy (for example, in *Roe* v. *Wade,* a 1973 case, the court invalidated the Texas abortion statute and legalized abortions in all states). State courts were generally more cautious, but some states such as New Jersey and California have developed a tradition of aggressive state judicial review. Texas courts, led by the state supreme court, have clearly been moving toward a more assertive posture.

The most prominent example of the growing political power of Texas courts occurred in January 1991 when the Texas Supreme Court ruled, for the second time, that the state's system of financing public schools failed the constitutional requirement that an "efficient" educational system be established. The Supreme Court then instructed the Texas Legislature either to correct the disparities in funding between the 1047 school districts in Texas or have the court step in and impose a solution. Since funding public schools is the greatest fiscal responsibility of state and local governments in Texas (total costs are about $15 billion a year), this decision has enormous political implications.

We thus see that the courts are a very important part of the political process in Texas. But the court system is also fundamentally different from other segments of the Texas political system. The judicial system operates in a highly formalized, structured manner. Decision-making roles are more clearly spelled

out than in other policy-making areas. While personal values, biases, and prejudices undoubtedly affect judicial decisions, Texas political leaders rarely, if ever,
try to dictate court rulings, and direct partisan involvement in the judicial process
is usually minimal.

These general considerations aside, the following sections discuss the
staffing and structure of the court system and the nature of the judicial process
in Texas. Additionally, attention is directed to several problems associated with
the state judicial system and some of the reforms that have been suggested to meet
these difficulties.

STAFFING THE JUDICIAL SYSTEM

The Texas Bar

The Texas Bar Association includes all persons admitted to practice law in the
state—now about 60,000 lawyers. The composition of the bar is important, not
just because it includes the attorneys representing contesting parties in courts or
other legal matters, but also because the judiciary is recruited from within its
ranks. In contrast to the practice in most European countries, the office of judge
in the United States is not treated as a distinct profession separate from that of
lawyer. Most lawyers are eligible for service on the bench at any time.

Texas lawyers have traditionally been Anglo men, often from high-status
and high-income families. This pattern has changed somewhat in recent years,
as many more women have graduated from law schools in the state and several
thousand black and Hispanic attorneys have entered practice in Texas. Nonetheless, members of the legal profession still constitute a rather uniform socioeconomic group: They are often from middle- or upper-income families, frequently
have relatives who have been lawyers, are mostly educated at a handful of law
schools, and are still predominantly Anglo males.

Not too much should be made of the homogeneity of Texas lawyers as a
class, because there are important differences within the profession. For example,
the income, status, and legal interests of a corporate lawyer in a big Houston firm
are very different from those of a trial lawyer in Corpus Christi or a prosecuting
attorney in Big Springs. Such intraprofessional differences among lawyers are of
considerable significance, as we will note in later sections of this chapter.

The number of lawyers has been increasing rapidly in Texas. In 1950 there
was 1 lawyer for every 953 persons in the state, and in 1960 the ratio was 1 per
every 924 persons. However, by 1982 this ratio dropped to 1 lawyer for every 420
persons, and in 1991 the ratio is 1 to 300. More lawyers are practicing in Texas
than the United Kingdom; more practice in Houston alone than in all of Japan.

Judicial Selection

The Texas Constitution, faithful to the principles of Jacksonian democracy,
provides for the popular election of judges. Trial judges are elected for four-year
terms, appellate judges for six-year tenures. The majority of judges, however, first

reach the bench by appointment. T. C. Sinclair and Bancroft Henderson found that of the state judges serving during the 1940–1962 period, 66 percent first came to their office by appointment.[3] The governor fills vacancies in district and appellate judgeships. County commissioners courts, the nonjudicial governing body of county government, make appointments when vacancies occur at lower levels, except for the municipal courts, where appointment practices vary. An appointee's term expires at the next general election. Traditionally one had little trouble holding the position. Incumbent judges, whether appointed or elected, were seldom challenged and almost never defeated.

The Texas Constitution requires that district and appellate judges be citizens of the United States and Texas who have practiced law, or have been lawyers and judges of courts of record, within the state for at least four and ten years, respectively. Legal training and experience are usually not required for posts below the district judge level. In general, those making appointments have a free hand in filling vacancies. Governors may seek advice and counsel on judicial appointments from a wide range of friends, political allies, and representatives of the bar, but they retain the decisional power. The Texas Senate, though possessing the power to block gubernatorial appointments, rarely disapproves a nominee. In a state not noted for its competitive politics or strong party organizations, the governor can resist almost any political pressure in selecting a choice. Of course, one is likely to seek someone who will not discredit the administration and can be reelected. So while governors select individuals on the basis of friendship and partisan support, they usually insist that nominees be competent and qualified. Generalization about the 254 commissioners courts' appointive patterns is difficult, but friendship and political support appear to be crucial, with competency stressed less.

As noted, most judges came to the bench via appointment and could expect to be reelected without much difficulty. That pattern is changing, however, as more candidates contest judicial races and incumbent judges are increasingly defeated. In 1980, for example, a respected recent appointee to the Texas Supreme Court, Will Garwood, was defeated by C. L. Ray. And in 1982 Judge Carl Dally of the Court of Criminal Appeals finished fourth in the May Democratic primary. Not only are statewide judicial contests more frequent and hard fought, but many more district and county judges must defend themselves at the polls. Such is especially the case in large urban counties. In Harris County there were just 2 general contests for local judicial office in 1978, but there were 17 contested races in 1980, 32 contests in 1982, and 37 in 1986. The reason more judicial contests are occurring is simple: Incumbent judges can now be defeated. With Texas judges elected on the partisan ballot along with governors and presidents, the shifting tides of party fortune have imperiled judicial officials. This is especially the case in large urban counties like Dallas, Harris, and Tarrant, where most voters cannot keep track of individual judicial candidates and often end up voting a "straight ticket" for all the nominees of one party or the other. This straight-ticket voting has meant that in a "good" Democratic year like 1982, when White was defeating Clements, many qualified Republican judges were defeated around the state. Conversely, nearly all challenged Democratic judges in urban counties were defeated in the Reagan-led Republican landslide of 1984. Voters seem to be more inclined to split their tickets in recent judicial elections, and very few incumbent Democratic or Republican judges were defeated in the 1990 elections.

In addition to increased partisan conflict, judicial selection is featuring a more explicit involvement by organized subgroups of lawyers. In the past, the Texas bar would poll its members by mail, and the candidate who led usually won contested races. The general bar effort has been supplanted by much more vigorous advocacy on behalf of candidates by specialized lawyer groups. The Texas Trial Lawyers group, whose members often represent people suing large corporations and insurance companies, has been especially active in recruiting and supporting judicial candidates. Their success in this regard has led defense counsels, who represent the established interests, to get involved in judicial races. This means that contests like the 1990 Phillips-Mauzy race for chief justice of the Supreme Court are not just partisan elections between a Republican (Tom Phillips) and a Democrat (Oscar Mauzy) but are also battles between plaintiff lawyers (backers of Mauzy) and defense lawyers (supporters of Phillips).

The increased partisan and interest-group conflicts over judicial elections have led to cries for reforming the selection process. The prospects for change are discussed in a later section.

The state operates a judicial retirement system, and district and appellate judges must retire at age 75; they qualify for increased pensions if they leave office upon or before reaching the age of 70. In an effort to provide a mechanism for removing the unethical or incompetent, a 1965 constitutional amendment provided for the establishment of a Commission of Judicial Conduct. The commission is composed of two appeals court justices and two district court justices appointed by the Supreme Court, two lawyers appointed by the directors of the state bar, and three nonlawyers appointed by the governor. The commission can issue private reprimands, public censures, or even recommendations for removal of judicial officials ranging from judges of the highest appellate courts to local courts of limited jurisdiction. Recommendations for removal are submitted to the Texas Supreme Court for action. The impact of the commission is difficult to assess, since the most serious cases are apparently disposed of by resignation before commission action is completed.

Juries

The jury system provides a means for involving the ordinary citizen in the judicial process. Two types of juries are used in Texas: *grand juries,* which indict persons alleged to have committed crimes if the evidence warrants; and *petit* or *trial juries,* which decide cases. The grand jury is composed of 12 persons, 9 of whom must concur in an indictment. District judges have considerable control over the composition of grand juries, since they appoint the commissioners who select a group of 20 county residents, from whom the judge selects 12 for jury service. Critics of the process have complained that grand juries are usually made up of individuals from the more affluent segments of society. That this occurs is probably due as much to the fact that most salaried employees cannot afford the time for service during the typical three-month grand-jury term as to the biases of the judges. Grand juries are usually dependent on the office of the district attorney for legal advice, and indictments often represent the sentiments of that office as much as those of the grand jury.

Texas makes extensive use of juries for deciding cases. All serious crimes must be tried by a jury, and jury trial is available on request for all other cases, civil and criminal. Trial jurors are randomly selected from among those eligible for service, that is, registered voters who reside in the county. Over the years statutes allowing numerous categories of persons to claim exemption from jury service were enacted, presumably because of the overriding importance of their activities to the community. In actuality, it was because group spokespersons had enough legislative influence to have their group added to the exemption list. Most of the exemptions have been repealed, with mothers of small children and students constituting important exceptions.

Judges may excuse people from service, and many are excused for business and occupational reasons. Others are excused from particular trials because the opposing attorneys and the judge believe they are disqualified for some reason: for example, a prospective juror might have preexisting opinions or biases. Additionally, each attorney is allowed a limited number of peremptory challenges to disqualify potential jurors. This form of negative selection undoubtedly prevents juries from accurately representing a cross-section of the population. Not enough is known about the process to indicate which social groups are underrepresented or overrepresented, although the poor and ethnic minorities constitute a smaller portion of jury membership than they do of the general population.

Conclusion

Quite clearly the judicial system is staffed by a relatively select segment of the population. The legal profession itself is of course unique, in that lawyers have undergone special training and possess skills not common to the populace as a whole. But beyond this, the bar and the state judiciary are socioeconomically and politically atypical. The question can legitimately be raised as to what difference all this makes. Can lawyers and judges and grand juries objectively apply the law, irrespective of their partisan, sexual, ethnic, or social characteristics? National studies support the view that, at least in certain types of cases, judicial background correlates with judicial decisional patterns.[4]

Unfortunately, the relationships between judicial characteristics and judicial decision making in Texas have not been tested. Although personal background may not lead to conscious prejudice on the part of judges, it may well provide a general social and political orientation or evaluative framework that is reflected in judicial rulings. If this is the case, the narrow base from which Texas judges are recruited may be of substantial import to the operation of the state's judicial system.

Whatever the uncertainties are in this regard, there is no doubt that courts and judges have become much more embroiled in political controversy. Much of this reflects, as noted earlier, the intrusion of party and interest-group politics into

the judicial arena. But the politicization of the judiciary also reflects a growing
public concern about the issues addressed by this part of the political process:
more specifically, about crime and punishment.

THE STRUCTURE OF THE COURT SYSTEM

The Texas court system is complicated, diffused, and at times confusing, with
series of layers and special courts within layers (see Table 8.1). The Texas Constitution provides for a supreme court, a court of criminal appeals, courts of appeals,
district courts, county courts, and justice of the peace courts. In addition, the
legislature has created a number of other courts. Courts may be classified into
three types: local trial courts of limited jurisdiction, trial courts of general juris-

Table 8.1 **TEXAS JUDICIAL STRUCTURE**[a]

Type of Court	Name of Court	Jurisdiction Criminal: original
Trial court of limited jurisdiction	Justice of the Peace	Misdemeanors with no confinement and fines not exceeding $200
	County Court	Class A and B misdemeanors (fines of $2000 or less and/or one year or less of confinement in the county jail)
Trial court of general jurisdiction	District Court	All felonies
Appellate courts	Court of Appeals	None
	Court of Criminal Appeals	None
	Supreme Court	None

[a]Corporation (municipal) courts and probate proceedings not included.

diction, and appellate courts.[5] Generally, trial courts are responsible for making the basic decisions in cases, and appellate courts review their findings. Emphasis in review is placed on legal questions, and on factual questions appellate courts defer to the findings of trial courts. In Texas, however, there is considerable overlapping between layers, with courts sharing jurisdictions and exercising original jurisdiction over some cases and appellate jurisdiction over others.

Trial Courts of Limited Jurisdiction

Probably the greatest variety in the names, kinds, and jurisdictions of Texas courts occurs among the trial courts of limited jurisdiction, most of which are structurally part of county or municipal governments. The constitution estab-

Jurisdiction		
Civil: original	Criminal: appellate	Civil: appellate
Cases where amount does not exceed $2500; decisions are final for amounts of $20 or less	None	None
Concurrent with JP courts, $200–$2500; concurrent with district courts,[b] cases $500–$5000; $20–$100 are final	All cases from JP court (trial *de novo*)	All cases from JP court (trial *de novo*)
All cases over $1000; concurrent with county courts, $500–$5000; specified cases	None	Mental competency cases from county court; decisions are final
None	All cases involving confinement and/or fines exceeding $100 from county and district courts	All cases over $100 from county and district courts; decisions in divorce litigation are final
None	From trial courts: all cases in which the death penalty has been assessed. From courts of appeals: discretionary review on petition by parties or on its own motion	None
Writs against judicial, state government, and political party officials	None	From trial courts: validity of state statutes or administrative actions. From courts of appeals: dissents, conflicts, invalidity of statute revenue of the state, Railroad Commission cases

[b]Some county courts have higher concurrent jurisdictions granted by legislative acts.

lished two such courts (justice of the peace and county courts), with limitations based on the importance of the cases they handle, and the legislature has established several courts to handle cases based on specialized subject matter.

The court at the bottom of the judicial hierarchy is the justice of the peace, or JP, court. The Texas Constitution provides that each commissioners court shall divide its county into not less than four or more than eight justice precincts, with a court in each. In precincts where there is a city of 8000 or more inhabitants, the constitution provides for two JP courts. JPs are elected by the voters of the precinct for four-year terms; the only requirement is that the holder must be a qualified voter of the state.

JP courts have jurisdiction over criminal cases involving misdemeanors (minor criminal offenses) not punishable by confinement and/or fines of over $200 and in civil cases where the amount involved is less than $2500. The JP courts handle a tremendous variety of minor cases, most notably traffic and hunting and fishing violations and small claims. A person charged with a misdemeanor may request a jury trial, and either party in a civil case may request a jury trial, although the requesting party must pay a small jury fee. Juries in JP courts are composed of six persons; there is a right of appeal to county court, where the cases are tried anew *(de novo)* in all criminal cases and in civil cases involving more than $20.

The JP performs several other roles. If the county does not have a coroner (most rural counties have not created this position), the Justice of the Peace acts in that capacity. The JP also serves as magistrate at arraignment proceedings, making a preliminary determination of whether an accused person should be discharged, have bond fixed, or be remanded to jail. Additionally, the JP has authority to issue warrants for the apprehension of persons charged with crimes. As a magistrate, the JP may perform weddings; since tradition demands remuneration and fees are not provided by law, the practice of tipping makes the position quite profitable in many urban areas.

In each incorporated municipality, there is a municipal court, commonly known as traffic court. Municipal courts have jurisdiction over all criminal cases arising under municipal ordinances, and they have concurrent jurisdiction with JP courts over criminal cases falling under JP jurisdiction. They have no civil jurisdiction. In the larger cities the municipal court judge is a full-time official, but in smaller cities and towns the mayor, city clerk, or other municipal official serves as judge. Appeals from municipal court go to the county court.

In each county there is a county court presided over by the county judge, who is elected by the voters of the county for a four-year term and who must be "well versed in the law." County courts have original jurisdiction over all misdemeanors not under the jurisdiction of the JP courts (those punishable by confinement or fines of over $200) and concurrent jurisdiction with JP courts in cases involving from $200 to $2500. In civil cases involving from $500 to $5000, county courts have concurrent jurisdiction with state district courts. They also have jurisdiction over the commitment of mentally ill persons to mental hospitals. The county courts serve as appellate courts for appeals from decisions of the JP courts; in civil cases involving less than $100 and in criminal cases not involving imprisonment or fines over $100, their decisions are final. Appeals from the county courts in mental competency cases are directed to state district courts; otherwise, appeals are directed to the courts of appeals.

In the larger urban areas the judicial functions of county judges conflict with their other duties as officials of county government by making demands on their time, and the docket may include more cases than even a full-time judge could handle. In a number of such counties, the legislature has established courts called *county courts at law,* presided over by elected judges, who assume many of the judicial responsibilities of the county judge. In some cases these courts are specialized, with county civil and criminal courts at law.

Over the years a variety of special courts were created in the urban counties to handle specialized problems at the trial court level. Students of judicial administration prefer courts of general jurisdiction, and the legislature has moved in that direction in recent sessions by creating only district courts and converting existing special courts to district courts. The 1977 legislature, for example, converted 31 courts of domestic relations and juvenile courts into state district courts. Appeals from remaining special courts generally go to the courts of appeals.

Trial Courts of General Jurisdiction

The chief trial courts are the district courts, which handle both civil and criminal matters. The state is divided into judicial districts; a district judge, elected by the voters of the district for a four-year term, presides over each district court. In rural areas, districts often include several counties, and in the larger urban counties there are several judicial districts, each encompassing the entire county. Some of the latter are statutorily established to handle criminal or civil cases only. District judges must be residents of the district for 2 years immediately preceding their election, must be at least 25 years old, and must have 4 years of experience as a lawyer or judge. In 1991 there were 377 district courts, and new courts are added nearly every legislative session.

District courts have original jurisdiction over all criminal cases involving felonies (offenses punishable by lengthy confinement) and civil cases involving over $1000; as noted, they share jurisdiction with county courts for amounts of $500 to $5000. Additionally, they have original jurisdiction over misdemeanors involving official misconduct, suits for damages and slander, controversies over land titles, contested elections, and suits in behalf of the state to recover penalties, forfeitures, and escheats. Any party to a suit may require that trial be before a 12-person jury, but in civil cases the request must be made by one party to the suit, who is required to pay a small jury fee.

Appellate Courts

The procedures used by appellate courts differ considerably from those of trial courts. In trial courts plaintiffs present evidence designed to prove their cases; if they succeed in presenting enough evidence to demonstrate a legitimate case, the defendant must then present evidence in rebuttal. Witnesses are examined and cross-examined, and attorneys summarize the case; the jury then decides. During this process lawyers may object to the introduction of evidence, challenge the interpretation of the law by the judge, and undertake other legal maneuvers designed to call attention to errors by the judge. If they lose the case, they can appeal to a higher court to reverse the decision because of an error.

Appellate courts ordinarily do not retry cases (an exception in Texas is appeal from JP courts, when a complete new trial is held). Instead, they review the record of the original trial to determine if errors that justify the reversal of the decision were committed by the trial court. Ordinarily appellate courts accept the findings of fact of trial courts and concern themselves with questions of law, although they may insist that the record reveal substantial evidence to support the findings of fact of the trial court. In reviewing the record of the trial court, appellate judges may consider the written record of the trial, the allegations of error contained in the appeal, and the briefs on the law and the oral arguments presented by opposing attorneys. If the court discovers a reversible error, it may send the case back for retrial, dismissal, or other appropriate action; if not, the original decision must be executed.

An unusual feature of the Texas court system is that at the highest level it divides into two branches, one for civil matters (the Supreme Court) and one for criminal cases (the Court of Criminal Appeals). The Constitution of 1876 created a Court of Appeals with jurisdiction over both criminal and civil appeals originating below the district court level. This court's decisions were final. Appeal of civil cases originating in the district courts was to a Supreme Court. In 1891 the judicial article was rewritten with the civil jurisdiction of the Court of Appeals being removed and the name changed to the Court of Criminal Appeals. Intermediate Courts of Civil Appeals were created to hear the civil cases formerly heard by the Court of Appeals and to hear appeals of civil cases from district courts. Journalist Paul Burka attributes the creation of the special criminal appeals court to the draconian nature of frontier justice in Texas. More precisely, the constitution's framers believed that speed in hearing criminal appeals was essential and that a Supreme Court hearing both criminal and civil cases could not keep ahead of the hangman.[6]

Regardless of motivation, the Court of Criminal Appeals has survived, but as the state grew and crime increased, its workload became enormous. The original court had only three members, but the number has been increased to nine judges who are authorized to consider cases in three-member panels. The judges, one of whom is designated presiding judge, are elected for six-year overlapping terms. Enlargement has not solved the overload problem. By 1984 the Court of Criminal Appeals disposed of 3534 cases (a monstrous number when one considers that opinions have to be written in all cases) and had 1423 pending. By comparison, the Texas Supreme Court disposed of 1626 cases the same year and had just 427 pending.[7]

In partial response to this overload, a constitutional amendment was adopted in 1980, giving the courts of civil appeal jurisdiction in criminal cases. These courts were enlarged and renamed *courts of appeals.* The amendment provided that these courts were to have appellate jurisdiction in all criminal cases tried in the county and district courts, except those involving the death penalty, which were to be appealed directly to the Court of Criminal Appeals. Decisions of courts of appeals as to facts in criminal cases are final, and review on matters of law is at the discretion of the Court of Criminal Appeals, which can conduct review with or without a petition from either party in a case. As a consequence of the 1980 amendment, the Court of Criminal Appeals is limited to reviewing death penalty cases and issues involving case law.

Texas is now divided into 13 intermediate courts of appeals areas, with one court in each save the Houston metropolitan area, which has two courts. These are presided over by a chief justice, and they range in size from 3 to 12 judges. The appeals courts are allowed to consider cases in three-member panels, but permanent specialized civil and criminal panels are forbidden. Judges are elected for 6-year overlapping terms by the voters of the districts and must be citizens of the United States and residents of Texas, at least 35 years of age, and practicing lawyers or judges of courts of record for at least 10 years. (These are the same qualifications as are required by the constitution for the Texas Supreme Court and the Court of Criminal Appeals.)

The civil jurisdiction of the courts of appeals extends to cases from district courts, county courts, and the various special courts, excepting those cases decided by county courts involving $100 or less. Court of appeals decisions are final in divorce matters, cases of slander, and contested elections other than for state office or when the validity of a statute is questioned. Otherwise, cases may be appealed to the Texas Supreme Court, but only on questions of law, not the facts of a case.

The highest civil court in the state is the Supreme Court, which is composed of nine members, one of whom is designated chief justice. Members are elected for six years and serve overlapping terms.

As Thornton Sinclair notes, the Supreme Court is easily the most important and prestigious court in the state:

> The Texas Supreme Court stands at the head of the civil judicial system of the State. Since civil law is so overwhelmingly important to lawyers, and the court of criminal appeals is pushed into the background, the Texas Supreme Court emerges in bar circles as the unrivaled head of the Texas judicial system. In this capacity, the court performs in fact or in theory many functions. First of all, it is the last resort in the State for deciding civil cases, and thus for developing the case law in this area. The court makes the rules of civil procedure, which bind civil courts and the lawyers who work in them. It is the supreme court which prescribes and administers the rules and examinations for admission to the bar, and in so doing, states the minimum requirements for legal education. . . . The court draws up rules of ethics which serve as the basis for disciplining and expelling bar members. The supreme court is the instrument for removal of judges (including judges of the theoretically coordinate court of criminal appeals). Insofar as there is any centralized administration of courts in Texas (and there is very little), the supreme court or the chief justice is in charge.[8]

Framers of the amendment to the Constitution of 1876 creating the framework within which the Texas Supreme Court still operates hoped that the existence of a two-layer appellate system for civil cases would allow the courts of civil appeals to handle the correction of errors by trial courts. The Supreme Court could then devote its attention to achieving unity of decision making among the courts of civil appeals and to developing case law by handling only the difficult legal problems facing the state courts.[9] Three developments have frustrated these intentions.

First, there is a small but potentially important group of cases in which the Supreme Court has original jurisdiction. The statutes provide that the court or any justice thereof may issue various writs against district and appellate court judges, officers of state government, and political party officials. Party officials were included so that persons ruled off the ballot might obtain quick relief.

Second, the legislature has provided that appeals may be taken directly from trial courts to the Supreme Court from any order granting or denying an injunction on the ground of the constitutionality or unconstitutionality of any state statute, or on the ground of the validity or invalidity of any administrative order issued by any state board or commission under any state statute. This in effect provides for the direct appeal from trial courts of cases in which state administration might be frustrated over a long period of time by fully deliberative judicial processes.

Third, and most important, the legislature has expanded the scope of Supreme Court review of court of civil appeals decisions beyond earlier intentions. Six categories of cases may be appealed to the Texas Supreme Court: (1) cases in which judges of a court of civil appeals disagreed, (2) cases in which two or more courts of civil appeals disagreed, (3) cases in which a statute was held void, (4) cases involving the revenue of the state, (5) cases in which the Railroad Commission is a party, and (6) cases in which it appears that an error of substantive law that affects the judgment in the case has been committed by a court of civil appeals. The first three categories are essential to the purpose of securing a court whose objectives are unity of decision making and development of difficult case law through the handling of cases presenting difficult legal problems. The last three categories add to the caseload of the Supreme Court, even though the cases may not be of great public importance; this is especially true of the *substantive error* category, which obligates the court to review a case if the judgment of the civil appeals court appears erroneous and which, in effect, merely gives litigants a second chance in the appellate process.

THE JUDICIARY AND THE POLICY-MAKING PROCESS

The courts intervene in the policy-making process through the settlement of disputes. Controversies in the courts may concern almost any form of political activity, and judicial participation may occur at almost any point in the policy-making process; however, policy-making in the courts differs from that in other governmental institutions because special legal factors influence the judicial process, and legal concepts limit the scope of court decisions. Courts may only decide cases and controversies. They cannot levy taxes or appropriate funds, although decisions on particular cases may influence the distribution of power or wealth in the community. This is especially the case when courts possess the authority to rule on the consistency of statutes with the constitution as in the case of Texas's school finance law.

The highest appellate courts have by far the greatest political significance; through a process of elimination they get the most controversial cases with the most at stake, since these are the cases most likely to be appealed to the end of the judicial process. The courts of last resort are the ultimate decision makers in the judicial process and, occasionally, in the political process. As Kenneth Vines emphasizes, in stressing the importance of appellate courts the policy-making functions of trial courts should not be neglected. Their interpretation of statutes and application of law necessarily involve them in the making of important policy decisions. They make the initial decisions and may shape the manner in which the case is approached by appellate courts. Furthermore, for most litigants the trial courts are also the courts of last resort, for only a small portion of cases are appealed. Nevertheless, most of the highly controversial cases of major political significance are appealed to higher courts.[10]

The Texas Supreme Court

The political role of Texas courts has not been thoroughly examined by social scientists, but a good deal of attention has been focused on the Texas Supreme Court. Thorton Sinclair's exploration of the Supreme Court in the 1960s found a court that was hard-working and legally competent but limited in its ability to select important cases and only mildly innovative as a policy-making body. All the justices from 1949 onward were identified with the conservative faction of the Democratic party, but Sinclair's analyses of Supreme Court cases with liberal/conservative implications found that a slight majority of decisions favored the liberal position.[11]

Supreme Court judges and journalistic observers generally agreed with Sinclair's observations and noted there were no established blocs on the court adhering to philosophical positions. Rather, they suggested that members "bounced back and forth."[12] The decision-making processes of the Texas Supreme Court are designed to discourage the development of cliques or blocs. In contrast with the United States Supreme Court, where the chief justice or senior associate justice makes opinion-writing assignments, in Texas these tasks are rotated. The process begins with the receipt of an appeal, usually called an *application for writ of error,* with each judge receiving one-ninth of the appeals. The judge reviewing the case circulates a memorandum summarizing the facts and issues, along with a recommendation as to whether the writ application should be granted. At weekly conferences, the justices decide which cases involve errors that affected the outcome of the cases. If three judges agree to grant a writ of error (fewer than 20 percent are granted), oral arguments are set. Just before the justices go into the courtroom to hear arguments on the day of the week set aside for that purpose, each of the three judges in rotation for assignment selects one of the three slips, placed face down on a table, representing one of the three cases to be heard that day. After the judges have heard the lawyers' arguments and read their briefs, the judge who drew the slip writes and presents an opinion on the case to the weekly conference of judges.

Although the traditions of the Supreme Court generally encourage harmony, the conferences are exceptions. Decisions are closely scrutinized both grammatically and legally and are often substantially revised. If the designated judge's written opinion inspires a dissent, the dissenter prepares an opinion for a later conference; this opinion becomes the opinion of the court if a majority approves it.

The Supreme Court continued on the course described by Sinclair into the 1970s. Members continued to be drawn from the conservative faction of the Democratic party, but their election campaigns received little attention, and incumbent judges rarely faced serious challengers. The most influential group in the selection of the judges, whether they were first appointed by the governor or elected, consisted of members of large urban law firms, often called corporation lawyers, who often represented large industrial and manufacturing concerns, financial institutions, and insurance companies. The court's most important cases involved interpreting statutory and common law and attracted little attention. The court's reputation was for legally sound, noninnovative decisions that emphasized the importance of *stare decisis,* the doctrine that precedents established in earlier cases should be accepted as authoritative in similar later cases. The Supreme Court had the power of judicial review of legislative action, but its conservative makeup and traditional legal philosophy combined to prevent the court from issuing many new constitutional interpretations.

The uncontroversial nature of the Texas Supreme Court suddenly changed in the early 1980s, although the roots of the change occurred earlier. In 1949 a group of plaintiff attorneys specializing in tort cases (i.e., cases involving wrongful acts, other than breach of contract or trust, that result in injury to another and for which the injured party is entitled to compensation) organized the Texas Trial Lawyers Association. Plaintiff attorneys ordinarily are paid only if they win their cases, usually receiving a predetermined percentage of any settlement. Though as a group they tended to be politically liberal and active, for many years they did not focus particularly on appellate judicial offices.

In the 1970s two developments refocused the political interest of plaintiff attorneys. The exodus of conservatives to the Republican party weakened the conservative wing of the Democratic party, and the Sharpstown Bank scandal resulted in the election of a legislature and an attorney general oriented to consumer protection. Attorney General John Hill (1973–1979), a former president of the Texas Trial Lawyers Association, encouraged the enactment of a strong deceptive trade practices and consumer protection act and other laws protecting debtors, tenants, and people buying from door-to-door salespersons. The electoral and statutory changes offered both the opportunity and incentive for changing the Texas Supreme Court, and the plaintiff attorneys eventually responded.

The political action committee of the trial lawyers' group adopted a strategy of making monetary contributions only in contests for the state legislature, while encouraging individual members to contribute in judicial contests, especially for

Reprinted by permission.

the Supreme Court. Between 1978 and 1982 six new members were elected to the nine-member court with the strong support of plaintiff attorneys.

The 1983 term of the Texas Supreme Court saw the fruits of these changes with a sharp reversal in the treatment of torts. In perhaps the most publicized case, the court held an employer liable for the negligence of a drunken employee who caused a fatal automobile accident after being sent home from work. The Supreme Court held that when an employer exercises control over an employee, the employer has an affirmative duty to prevent the employee from causing harm to others *(Otis Engineering v. Clark).* Other decisions expanded the opportunities for plaintiffs to recover damages. In *Sanchez* v. *Schindler* the court overturned a nineteenth-century precedent that the parents of a child who was wrongfully killed could not recover money for mental anguish associated with the death but could only be awarded money representing the income the child might have provided to the home before reaching maturity. Judge Franklin Spears, writing for a 6–3 majority, ruled that the traditional interpretation was grounded in an antiquated concept of the child as an economic asset, and that if the rule were literally followed, the average child would have a negative worth; strict adherence to it could lead to the negligent person being rewarded for saving the parents the cost and expense of rearing a child.

In addition to a number of decisions that expanded the opportunities for plaintiffs to recover damages (27 according to one tally from 1981–1986),[13] in 1985 the Supreme Court allowed prejudgment interest in personal and wrongful death cases *(Cavnar* v. *Quality Control Parking).* Prior to this decision, Texas precedent allowed interest to accumulate only after a court awarded damages, but the Supreme Court reversed that position and ordered that interest be calculated from a date six months after the event occurred, thereby allegedly removing the incentive for defendants to prolong settlements. The only dissenters in this decision argued that interest should be paid from the occurrence of the event.

Decisions such as those affecting the wrongful death of a child and prejudgment interest have had significant economic consequences and contributed to a rapid increase in liability insurance rates that was already under way around the country. Strong pressures from business and defense lawyers' groups have focused on the need for tort reform at the legislative level, and the Texas Supreme Court has come under attack from a number of quarters.

Prominent critics of the court's new orientation include former Chief Justices Robert Calvert and Joe Greenhill. Calvert saw the mid-1980s court moving away from its tradition of applying the law in the same manner in every case to all litigants without regard to personal notions of justice. Instead, judges were more likely to construe the law to reach what they considered a fair result. Judges are acting like legislators, according to Calvert, which reflects the fact that most Supreme Court judges are now elected rather than appointed and have typically held other public offices before coming to the bench.[14]

The electoral success of plaintiff-backed judges stimulated a counterattack. Since 1980 a corporate lawyers' organization, the Texas Association of Defense Attorneys, has become more active in supporting candidates for the Supreme Court. They had little success in 1982 or 1984 but successfully backed one candidate in 1986. In 1988 when, owing to midterm retirements, six seats were up, the defense bar supported three winners, including newly appointed Chief Justice Tom Phillips. In 1990, Phillips was reelected to a full term, along with another defense-oriented candidate. The 1990 election left a court closely divided on party lines (five Democrats and four Republicans), as well as between defense- and plaintiff-supported members.

Antiplaintiff forces have also sought change in the legislative arena. In 1986 several groups formed the Texas Civil Justice Coalition to support reforms in tort and liability laws. Included were the Texas Medical Association, the Texas Bankers Association, and major corporations like Exxon, Dow Chemical, and Union Carbide. The coalition emphasizes its business and professional members, not defense attorneys and insurance companies. Major legislative goals include limiting damages for pain and suffering and punitive damages, and revising the "joint and several liability" rule to limit a defendant's liability to the portion of responsibility borne for damages rather than the entire amount of damages. They also support limitations on contingency fees paid to attorneys and favor reversing the prejudgment interest decision handed down by the Supreme Court in 1985.

This group was a key supporter of a new workers' compensation law passed by the legislature in 1990 over bitter opposition from trial lawyers and labor unions. However, they have had little success in changing the general tort and liability rules adopted by the Supreme Court in the mid-1980s. And with Governor Ann Richards in office through 1994, the prospects for legislative reversal of proplaintiff rules appear dim (Richards's largest campaign contributions came from plaintiff attorneys).

The Court of Criminal Appeals

The reputation of Texas's other superior appellate court, the Court of Criminal Appeals, is quite different from that of the Supreme Court. For most of its history the Court of Criminal Appeals has suffered from an image of being more concerned with legal technicalities than with substantive issues. In 1910 the American Institute of Criminal Law charged the court was "one of the foremost worshippers among the American appellate courts of the technicality."[15] Between 1900 and 1927 the court reversed 42 percent of the cases it reviewed. In one case it reversed the conviction of a man charged with receiving stolen property from persons unknown because in the course of the original trial the prosecutor discovered who it was who had transmitted the stolen goods.[16]

The record of the Court of Criminal Appeals in reversing convictions began to change in the late 1940s, after two famous cases subjected it to intense criticism. Both cases involved faulty indictments. In one murder case a conviction was reversed because the indictment did not specify that the substance in a bathtub used to drown the victim was water; in the other, the charge did not state that the weapon used to stomp the victim to death was the defendant's feet. By the 1960s the court had swung in the opposite direction, reversing just 3 percent of the cases it heard in 1966. Defense lawyers now viewed the court as strongly proprosecution. Criticisms of the quality of its work continued. Robert Dawson of the University of Texas Law School charged that the court's opinions were entirely lacking in reasoning and that it was beyond doubt the worst court of last resort in the United States.[17] Contributing factors to the court's problems were its small size (three judges) and very heavy workload.

In 1967 the court was enlarged to five members (it has since increased to nine), and its makeup changed owing to retirements and defeat of an incumbent. The reconstituted court began to give more extensive consideration to cases and to issue more defensible opinions. Defense attorneys and the District and County Attorneys Association became more active in efforts to influence elections and appointments—usually in support of different candidates. Divisions on the court along philosophical lines became more pronounced, and reversal rates again increased.

As before, the court had a sharp eye for technical processes, especially in the nature and wording of indictments. Although critics insist that indictments must contain only the information needed to give the defendant notice of the charges, the court insists that indictments are the foundation of the case and requires that they be precisely worded and that they completely inform the defendant of the charges. Critics argue that this leads the Court of Criminal Appeals to apply highly formalistic rules of law that have no real connection to individual rights. Cases cited in support of this argument included a reversal in which the indictment had charged theft from Montgomery Ward and Company, Incorporated, while the state's witness had referred only to Montgomery Ward.

Another reversal faulted a capital murder indictment because the victim in a related rape was not named, even though the defense attorney had been allowed to see the entire file on the case.[18]

Members of the Court of Criminal Appeals, including some with "law-and-order" reputations, defend the court against charges of overemphasis on formalities and technicalities. Former Judge Carl Dally, for example, has expressed concern about the tendency for the media to report that the court has freed a criminal on a technicality when that technicality is based on constitutional rights. Dally argues that the court "is here to protect the freedoms of the innocent, the guilty, and even those guilty of heinous crimes," and that in drawing up indictments as well as in other areas, the district attorney must get everything right.[19] Essentially, this is a libertarian argument that the state, with all its power and resources, must follow strict procedural requirements when it attempts to restrain the liberty of an individual.

Others are not convinced; they include journalist Paul Burka, who called for the abolition of the court in a 1982 *Texas Monthly* article. Critics like Burka see the fundamental problem of the Court of Criminal Appeals as overspecialization.

> The nine judges on the Court of Criminal Appeals know the criminal law inside out. That have spent a lifetime in it, as prosecutors, defense attorneys, trial lawyers, or all of these; if anything, they are too familiar with it. The judges accept the technicalities unquestioningly. . . . Their background as specialists has a lot to do with the court's technical and hairsplitting approach to the law. They are like the medieval monks who debated how many angels could dance on the head of a pin; their cloistered lives lead them to explore questions that are meaningless. . . .
>
> The sad truth is that Texas criminal law is never going to reflect common sense so long as it remains the exclusive domain of specialists.[20]

A decade has passed since Burka's assault, and the Court of Criminal Appeals remains controversial. A "law-and-order" group endorsed a slate of nominees for the five seats that were up in the 1990 general election, arguing that a majority of the court was too concerned about criminal rights as opposed to victim rights. Despite growing public concern about reversals of convictions and early release of prisoners (resulting from *federal,* not state court orders), the conservative slate fared poorly at the polls. That being the case, little change in criminal appellate processes seems likely.

JUDICIAL PROBLEMS

Structure and Administration

Students of judicial administration believe that justice is best served by a unified and simplified court system, a belief that has led to considerable criticism of the Texas system. At the top of the Texas system are two branches of appellate courts, a division found in only one other state. There is even more duplication at the trial-court level, where district courts, justice of the peace courts, and municipal courts all operate.

Other problems arise from the nature of judicial districts in Texas. State district and civil appeals courts vary greatly in the populations and caseloads they serve. Courts in metropolitan centers like Dallas and Houston frequently have caseloads that are many times larger than those of their rural counterparts. The Supreme Court can shift cases and judges about at the appeals level, and metropolitan areas can hire underemployed district judges from outside the area to assist with their dockets. The state is divided into nine administrative judicial districts, with each district presided over by one of the district judges designated by the governor with the concurrence of the Senate. The presiding judge may assign judges in the district to hold court in any county in the district in order to dispose of accumulated business or to replace a regular judge who is absent, disabled, or disqualified.

The Texas Judicial Council makes recommendations to the legislature, courts, and individual judges for changes in the structure and operation of the courts. An Office of Court Administration, which provides staff for the council but operates under the direction of the Supreme Court, works with the presiding judges of the administrative judicial districts and courts of appeals and compiles statistics on the court system. The efforts of these agencies have not solved the problems resulting from unequal judicial districts because the aid received by overburdened urban courts has not been extensive.

The absence of equitable districts has contributed to a most serious problem in the Texas judicial system—the delay in bringing cases to trial. Concern about slow criminal procedures led the legislature to adopt "speedy trial" provisions wherein a defendant may request and receive an early trial date, and the state must bring persons accused of violent crimes to trial within a 90-day period from when they are arraigned in court. On the civil side, however, no such relief is available. In urban counties like Harris and Dallas, tens of thousands of civil district cases await resolution at any time, and it takes from one to five years for a case to come to trial.

Selection of Judges

There has been continuing debate in the United States regarding the desirability of electing judges. The formal Texas system of election, which usually results in appointment, has drawn fire from both sides. Critics contend that the appointment system makes politicians into judges and the election requirement makes judges into politicians. They maintain that governors and commissioners courts use their virtually unrestrained appointive powers to elevate friends, cronies, and political supporters to the bench and that considerations of competency and ability are only secondary. At the same time, objection is raised to the necessity for judges to stand for election or reelection every four or six years. Electioneering takes judges from their benches for considerable periods and raises the possibility that in their search for popular support they may incur political obligations that will affect their independence and impartiality. Additionally, there is likely to be

THE RISE AND FALL OF A JUDGE

The most meteoric career in the Texas judiciary was experienced by former Supreme Court Judge Don Yarbrough. Prior to his successful race for a position on the court, he was little noticed. After law school he worked for two state water agencies and the Campus Crusade for Christ, and then established a law practice in Houston and became involved in several business and banking enterprises. In 1974 he made an almost unnoticed race for state treasurer.

In 1976 Chief Justice Charles Barron of the San Antonio Court of Civil Appeals won the support of leaders of the bar association and apparently had an easy race for an "open" seat on the Texas Supreme Court, for Yarbrough, his only opponent, apparently was not a serious contender. During the campaign Barron emphasized his judicial background, won the bar association poll, and outspent his opponent; Yarbrough's only visible support derived from his evangelical religious activity. Yarbrough received 831,621 votes and Barrow 537,394; political analysts attributed the victory to the resemblance of Yarbrough's name to that of Don Yarborough, a popular liberal Democratic candidate for governor in the 1960s.

The state's lawyers were surprised, but surprise shortly became shock. Yarbrough held a press conference and indicated that God put him in the race and won him the nomination. He added that his decisions would be interpreted in harmony with God's word. Shortly thereafter, the media discovered several civil suits that were pending against Yarbrough, as well as complaints to the bar association dating back to August 1975. In June

little relation between a candidate's vote-getting abilities and qualifications for judicial service.

Concern about the selection of judges took on a new urgency in the 1980s because, as noted earlier, more and more judges faced electoral challenges and more incumbents were defeated. The increasing number of judicial candidates means that voters, especially in big urban counties, must contend with very long election ballots. With voters having so many judicial candidates to choose among, voting tends to be either random in these cases (voting for people because one likes their names) or along straight party lines. In either case there are considerable risks. People who have nice-sounding or somewhat familiar names often turn out to have no qualifications whatsoever to serve as judges (see the accompanying box on former Texas Supreme Court Justice Don Yarbrough). And political parties, which nominate judicial candidates in open primaries where almost any lawyer can file for judge, have no control over the people who get on the general election ballot under the party label.

A number of legal scholars and practitioners have urged the adoption of a modified system of appointment-election, sometimes called the *Missouri Plan,* for a jury found him guilty of civil fraud, and throughout the summer of 1976 additional suits and bar grievances were filed.

Efforts were begun to prevent Yarbrough's election. He did not have a Republican opponent, and the most likely write-in candidate, former dean of the Texas law school Page Keeton, decided a campaign was impractical. Two would-be candidates undertook write-in campaigns, but Yarbrough won overwhelmingly.

Yarbrough's troubles mounted as indictments for forging an automobile title and perjury in testimony before a grand jury were added to the charges against him. At the conclusion of a special summer session in 1977, the legislature began proceedings to address him out of office, but he announced his resignation from the court.

Shortly after his resignation, an associate of Yarbrough informed the Harris County District Attorney's office that, while a sitting member of the Texas Supreme Court, Justice Yarbrough had plotted the murder of another man involved in one of Yarbrough's many legal controversies. A legal taping of a conversation between the informer and Mr. Yarbrough confirmed the former justice's involvement in the planned "hit."

Yarbrough was eventually tried and convicted of perjury and sentenced to prison. However, while out of jail on bond, he fled to Grenada, a Caribbean country that does not have an extradition treaty with the United States. In 1983, however, Yarbrough was arrested outside Grenada and returned to Texas. He was immediately placed in state prison.

use in Texas. Under this plan the governor would fill vacancies on the bench from a list submitted by a nonpartisan nominating commission. After the newly appointed judge had served a specified period, his or her name would be placed on the ballot for voters of the area to determine whether the judge should be retained on the bench. Such referenda would be held periodically so the electoral nexus would not be broken.

Various bar association groups, spurred by the leadership of former Texas Supreme Court Chief Justice Robert Calvert, have strongly urged the adoption of the Missouri Plan, or something akin to it. Surveys of judges and lawyers have also shown support for such a selection system. During his three years on the Supreme Court, Chief Justice John Hill emerged as the foremost advocate of an appointive/retention election system, strongly urging legislative action in this area. Hill continued pressing the issue after leaving the court in January 1988.

The Texas Legislature has not acted on reforming judicial selection, and future prospects seem dim. The basic reason is that the general public likes the idea of electing judges, whatever the practical problems associated with such elections. Another reason why change is unlikely is that the present system works reasonably well in the small and medium-size counties of the state. Such counties have relatively few judges; so if a judicial candidate is a crook or fool, that will likely become known to enough voters to defeat the individual. Unqualified candidates have a much better chance of slipping into office in urban counties like Harris, where over 50 local judicial positions may be on the ballot in a given year. A final reason for keeping the present system is that reform advocates cannot agree on what to replace it with. Some favor nonpartisan elections, others want to eliminate straight-ticket voting in judicial races, while others want the afore-mentioned Missouri Plan with the governor making appointments and retention elections after judges have served a term in office.

Does the Voting Rights Act Apply to Judicial Elections?

In addition to the continuing debate over electing versus appointing judges, a serious new challenge to Texas's court system has emerged. More than 90 per-cent of the judges in Texas are Anglos, while about 40 percent of the state's population is Hispanic or black. That fact led the League of United Latin American Citizens to file a 1989 lawsuit in federal court arguing that Texas's system of electing judges in large urban counties discriminates against minori-ties in violation of the U.S. Voting Rights Act. The NAACP also joined the suit. Minority plaintiffs specifically challenged the use of at-large elections for district judges in big urban counties like Bexar, Harris, Dallas, Tarrant, El Paso, and Travis. They contended that such at-large elections deprived minor-ity voters of the opportunity to elect candidates of their choice, in violation of Section Two of the Voting Rights Act.

The case was tried in Midland before Judge Lucius Bunton in the late summer of 1989. After a three-week trial, Judge Bunton found for the plaintiffs in *Lulac* v. *Mattox* and ordered that a new election system be used for the 1990 elections. The judge's order shook the courthouses in every big city of Texas as judges and lawyers contemplated a massive, hasty restructuring of judicial elec-tions that would almost certainly retire many veteran members of the judiciary. The near-panic subsided, however, when the U.S. Fifth Circuit Court stayed Judge Bunton's order and left the old rules in place for 1990.

Some months later the Fifth Circuit overruled Judge Bunton, holding that Section Two of the Voting Rights Act did not apply to judicial elections because judges were not "representatives" like legislators, county commissioners, or city council members. However, this ruling conflicted with another federal appellate court decision, so the final result awaited a U.S. Supreme Court decision. In June 1991 the U.S. Supreme Court overruled the Fifth Circuit Court, holding that judicial elections were covered by the Voting Rights Act.[21] The implications of the Supreme Court's decision are unclear because it said only that suits challeng-ing judicial elections could be brought. What sort of relief plaintiffs are entitled to if they bring and prevail in suits challenging judicial elections will have to be determined in future cases. In the interim, Governor Richards will be under increased pressure to appoint more Hispanics and blacks to available court vacan-cies.

The Poor and the Law

The concept of equal treatment before the law is a principle widely acclaimed and deeply cherished as an integral part of our political system. But is this principle realized in fact? Evidence points to the contrary. The legal system in the United States, including Texas, is highly complex, and legal practitioners have knowledge, skills, and techniques relevant to this system not possessed by the general public. Their specialized knowledge is available to the public, but usually on a laissez-faire fee basis. This fee system tends to restrict legal advice and assistance to those who can afford it. From the outset, then, Texans of low income are at a disadvantage in their dealings with the law.

There is irony in this, for the poor are often the economic group most in need of legal services. To begin with, the poor, because of patterns of education and socialization associated with poverty, are generally unfamiliar with the law and their rights under it. Two observers conclude, "Urban poor, in particular, often are abused by the legal process because they are ignorant of even the most elementary of its principles. They frequently submit to illegal acts and baseless legal claims."[22]

Though ignorant of the law, the poor cannot escape involvement with it. Most individuals charged with criminal offenses are from low-income groups. Additionally, the national and state governments have created new classes of entitlements—social security, job benefits, retirement benefits, and welfare—that are available to the poor. They have a right to these programs, but fulfillment of their right often depends on legal efforts on their behalf. The poor also have ordinary legal needs with respect to housing, wages, civil rights, consumer transactions, and domestic relations; these legal needs are perhaps more pressing than those of other segments of society because of the economic marginality of the poor. However, few lawyers are interested in the problems of the poor because little money can be made in handling their cases.

An increased awareness of the needs of the poor in legal matters has developed in recent years. The federal courts, recognizing this need in a series of decisions, have prodded the states toward ensuring greater legal equality in criminal cases. Texas adopted a revised code of criminal procedure in 1965 that provides procedural guarantees for persons suspected of criminal offenses. Police are required to inform individuals they arrest of their basic legal rights, and the state must see that legal counsel is provided in cases in which individuals cannot themselves afford it. In many areas of the state, the organized bar has assisted in providing competent counsel for indigents.

Although progress has been made in reducing the impact of poverty in Texas's system of criminal justice, similar steps in civil law have lagged behind. The poor have no problems finding lawyers in personal injury cases *if defendants with resources can be identified* because attorneys will represent such clients on a contingency basis (if they win, they get a percentage—usually a third or so—of what is recovered; if they lose, there is no fee charged). However, such cases represent only a small portion of the legal needs of working-class and poor Texans. Broader services for the poor in civil matters have traditionally been provided by legal aid offices financed partly by federal funds. Such funding came under sharp attack during the Reagan administration (1981–1989), and these meager assistance programs have been cut back. The state, facing enormous fiscal problems in the 1990s, is not likely to assume additional burdens in this area.

Prospects for Reform

The possibilities for extensive judicial reform in Texas are reduced by the basic inertia of the governmental system. As with most reform efforts, the public is not very interested in the issue, and their lack of interest is shared by many political leaders. Past attempts at substantive reform of the judicial system have produced little in the way of results.

In the early 1970s a Task Force for Court Improvement recommended a thoroughgoing set of reforms that would have reshaped the court system and simplified it and would have combined the Court of Criminal Appeals with the Supreme Court. Adoption of the Missouri Plan for judicial selection was urged, and the method of selecting district attorneys, county attorneys, and sheriffs— all currently elective officials—would have been left to the legislature. Supporters of these reforms were able to get a modified version of their plan into the new constitution that was put before the voters in 1975. However, voters overwhelmingly rejected the judicial changes along with the other constitutional changes.

Since then supporters of judicial reform have concentrated on narrow and specific objectives. They have scored some limited structural successes, such as getting the Court of Criminal Appeals enlarged and giving the new courts of appeals criminal as well as civil jurisdiction. More basic problems, such as judicial selection, have not been addressed and will likely not be addressed unless federal courts order changes. Substantive issues, such as the aforementioned legal problems of the poor, remain on the back burner in the state government kitchen.

NOTES

1. John Locke, "An Essay Concerning the True Origin, Extent and End of Civil Government," in *Social Contract* (New York: Oxford University Press, 1962), pp. 51–52.
2. David Easton, *The Political System* (New York: Knopf, 1953).
3. T. C. Sinclair and Bancroft Henderson, *The Selection of Judges in Texas* (Houston: Public Affairs Research Center, University of Houston, 1965), p. 21.
4. See John R. Schmidhauser, "The Justices of the Supreme Court: A Collective Portrait," *Midwest Journal of Political Science* 3 (February 1959): 2–37, 40–49; Stuart S. Nagel, "Testing Relations between Judicial Characteristics and Judicial Decision-Making," *Western Political Quarterly* 15 (September 1962): 425–437; and S. Sidney Ulmer, "The Political Party Variable in the Michigan Supreme Court," *Journal of Public Law* 11 (Fall 1962): 352–362.
5. Herbert Jacobs and Kenneth Vines, "State Courts and Public Policy," in *Politics in the American States,* 3d ed., ed. Herbert Jacobs and Kenneth Vines (Boston: Little, Brown, 1971), pp. 246–247.
6. Paul Burka, "Trial by Technicality," *Texas Monthly,* April 1982, p. 210.

7. *Fiscal Size Up Texas State Services 1986–1987 Biennium* (Austin: Legislative Budget Board, 1986), p. 160.

8. Sinclair and Henderson, *Selection of Judges,* p. 41.

9. Ibid., p. 42.

10. Kenneth Vines, "Courts as Political and Governmental Agencies," in Jacobs and Vines, *Politics in the American States,* pp. 241–243.

11. Sinclair and Henderson, *Selection of Judges,* p. 59.

12. *Austin American Statesman,* April 13, 1980, sec. C, p. 1.

13. *San Antonio Express,* April 13, 1986, p. 1.

14. *Austin American Statesman,* December 29, 1985, sec. C, p. 6.

15. Burka, "Trial," p. 131.

16. Ibid., p. 210.

17. Ibid.

18. Ibid., p. 212.

19. *Houston Chronicle,* January 4, 1978, p. 14A.

20. Burka, "Trial," pp. 215, 241.

21. *New York Times,* June 21, 1991, p. 1.

22. Norman L. Miller and James C. Daggatt, "The Urban Law Program of the University of Detroit School of Law," *California Law Review* 54 (May 1960): 1009.

chapter 9

Local Government

A county courthouse serves citizens on a local level, including visiting schoolchildren.

Although in geographical terms local governments are closest to the people (or the "grass roots"), they are frequently less salient and "visible" than the state and national governments. Popular attention is attracted by the important events and large controversies that occur at the state capital and in Washington. Issues involving such matters as foreign policy, income tax reform, or energy shortages are more likely to stir the citizen's interest than the construction of a new sewage disposal plant or the budget for the sheriff's office. Moreover, the happenings at the state capital and in Washington are likely to be better reported by the news media, and the distance at which they transpire probably serves to enhance their glamour.

Yet, local governments have a direct, immediate, and large impact on the day-to-day lives of most citizens—their convenience, comfort, safety, and happiness. It is local governments that bear primary responsibility for operating public schools; supplying water, garbage collection, and sewerage services; providing police and fire protection; keeping public records; maintaining parks and recrea-

Reprinted by permission.

tion facilities; administering many public health and welfare programs; controlling traffic and maintaining streets; and regulating land use by planning, zoning, and other means. Many of these activities are taken for granted, especially by the urban dweller, notwithstanding their vital nature and their substantial cost. (See Table 9.1.)

Paradoxically, while the average citizen may be little informed on local government matters (and little interested, as indicated by the low turnout in local elections), the value of local government, often referred to as local *self-*government, is a traditional theme in American politics. The supporters of local government argue that it is "closer to the people" than the national and state governments and is therefore more representative and responsible in operation. Related to this is the contention that local control and decentralization are

Table 9.1 DIRECT EXPENDITURES BY GOVERNMENTS IN
TEXAS, 1986–1987 (IN THOUSANDS OF DOLLARS)

State government		15,491,827
Local governments		31,787,879
Counties	4,176,316	
Cities	11,229,193	
Special districts	3,964,161	
School districts	12,418,209	

Source: U.S. Department of Commerce, Bureau of Census, *Government Finances in 1986–1987* (Washington, D.C.: Government Printing Office, 1988), p. 90.

desirable goals in themselves. Politicians have much to say concerning the virtues of grass-roots democracy and the need to return government closer to the hands of the people. This was one of the professed objectives of the Nixon administration's "New Federalism." Another argument on behalf of local government is that it provides an opportunity for many citizens to participate and obtain experience in governmental affairs at a readily accessible level. Certainly the existence of a variety of local governments increases greatly the opportunities for holding elective offices. In Texas there are over 24,000 elected local government officials. Many thousands more served on appointed boards, commissions, and committees. Still another argument is that local government permits experimentation and flexibility in the development and implementation of public programs. Local governments can take into more particular account the varying needs and circumstances of their constituents.

The existing pattern of local government is not without its critics, however. A common contention is that there are too many local governments and that they are characterized by overlapping activities and inefficiency, with substantial inequalities existing in the number and quality of services provided by various units. Moreover, the critics assert, local officials are often shortsighted and parochial. Further, the existence of the long ballot and many elected officials is said to confuse the voter and hamper rather than promote popular control of local government. Finally, doubt is expressed over whether decentralization is a desirable goal, at least when it leads to an excessive fragmentation of power among too many local governments.

In this chapter we will not attempt to resolve the controversy over local government. The reader should, however, remember the various arguments and form some tentative conclusions concerning their relative merits, keeping in mind also that an argument is not necessarily a description of reality.

Whatever their motivations, there is no denying the fact that Americans have created a multitude of local governments and that they take a variety of forms. In 1987, the U.S. Bureau of the Census reported the existence of 83,166 local governments in the United States (in addition to the national and state governments). This figure included 3,042 counties, 19,205 municipalities (cities, towns, and villages), 16,691 townships, 14,741 school districts, and 29,487 special districts. Texas, with its total of 4,413, ranked third among the states in number of local governments. The leader was Illinois, with 6,627 units; Hawaii, with 19 units, had the fewest. The average number of units per state was 1,663.

At this point we need to raise the question of what a local government is. What characteristics must a governmental entity possess to be considered a unit of local government and not simply an agency of another government? A widely accepted definition is that used by the U.S. Bureau of the Census in its surveys: "A government is an organized entity which, in addition to having governmental character, has sufficient discretion in the management of its own affairs to distinguish it as separate from the administrative structure of any other governmental unit." Analysis of this definition yields three criteria for a "government." First, an *organized entity* is one that has specified powers and is organized to carry them out, having its own officers, administrative structure, and so on. Second, *govern-*

Is local government equipped to meet today's problems?

mental character means that the entity performs activities that are regarded as governmental in nature, may possess the power to levy taxes, and is characterized (at least formally) by public accountability, as by the election of its officials or public reporting of its activities. Third, the entity must have substantial financial and administrative autonomy, as when it can impose taxes or adopt a budget without the approval of other local governments and when it is not really controlled by another government. In Texas, for instance, mosquito-control districts are governed by the county commissioners court and do not possess the autonomy needed to classify them as units of local government. Rather, they are administrative appendages of county governments. Under the definition, a wide and disparate variety of governmental units are classified as local governments, ranging from New York City with its several million inhabitants to a Texas water district with its half-dozen constituents.

Numerical changes and trends in local governments in Texas in recent decades are illustrated by Table 9.2. Texas has no townships, a form of rural local government especially prevalent in the Northeast and Midwest. The number of Texas counties has remained constant at 254 since 1924, when the last county was organized. Three trends are especially noticeable: (1) The number of municipal

Table 9.2 LOCAL GOVERNMENTS IN TEXAS, 1952–1987

	1952	1957	1962	1967	1972	1977	1982	1987
Counties	254	254	254	254	254	254	254	254
Municipalities	738	793	866	884	981	1066	1121	1156
Special districts	550	645	733	1001	1215	1425	1681	1891
School districts	2479	1794	1474	1308	1174	1138	1124	1111
Total	4021	3484	3327	3447	3624	3883	4180	4413

Source: U.S. Department of Commerce, Bureau of the Census, *Census of Governments* for 1952, 1957, 1962, 1967, 1977, 1982, and 1987.

or city governments has been constantly growing, which reflects the increasing urbanization of the state's population. Most of these new city governments are located adjacent to existing urban areas. (2) School districts have been decreasing in number, as districts with small enrollments are consolidated to provide more adequate educational programs and as *dormant districts* (those that have not operated a school for two consecutive years) are merged with adjoining districts in compliance with the Gilmer-Aiken Law (Texas) of 1949. (3) Special districts have greatly increased in number because of various factors, which are discussed later in this chapter.

Local governments are dispersed throughout the state, although the number differs very much from one county to another. Four thinly populated rural counties (Borden, Glasscock, Kennedy, and King) have only two local governments each, whereas three highly populated counties (Harris, Dallas, and Tarrant) had 349, 66, and 69, respectively, in 1982. Generally, local governments are especially numerous in the urban and metropolitan areas.

The various types of local government, some of their political aspects, and the problems of metropolitan areas will be treated in this chapter. The different categories of local government will be taken up separately for ease of discussion. However, this should not be taken to mean that they exist and act independently of one another. The various local governments in an area often serve the same public, and they frequently cooperate in their operations. For example, they often raise revenue from the same source (e.g., taxes on property) and collect it for one another. Even when they do not cooperate, they will be affected by what others do, whether it involves law enforcement, road and street maintenance, the annexation of territory, or the operations of territory. There is no way, for example, that the many local governments in the Dallas-Fort Worth area can simply ignore each other, whatever their inclinations. Also, open conflict between local governments is not a rare occurrence, as in "annexation wars" or disputes over the location of garbage disposal facilities.

COUNTY GOVERNMENT

Among the American states only Alaska, Connecticut, and Rhode Island do not have county governments. Traditionally, and particularly in the South and West, the county has been the principal unit of local government. This is still the case in rural areas. The 1980 population census revealed that approximately 175 Texas counties have populations of less than 20,000 each and thus can be fairly classified as rural counties.

County-State Relationships

According to legal doctrine, the county is established by and exists for the convenience of the state government to enforce and administer state laws and programs. Unless the state constitution provides otherwise, the state government formally has complete legal control over the structure, legal authority, and very existence of the county government. The county can undertake only those programs and activities that are authorized by the state constitution and legislation. This is a fairly accurate statement of one facet of the state-county relationship today in Texas. On the other hand, in practice there is very little supervision by state officials of the everyday operations of county governments. Once a given activity is authorized or delegated to the counties or their officials, they are left largely on their own. For example, the county sheriff enforces state criminal laws, but there is little if any state control over how this is done or over the prosecution of offenders by the district attorney. Moreover, since county officials are elected locally and hence are accountable to a local constituency, localism influences their actions. As has been observed:

> Although counties are created to carry out a common policy of the state and not mainly to advance the interests of a particular locality, the fact that a county is a local area, and that county officials are elected by a local rather than a state-wide electorate, brings about an anomalous situation in which county officials tend, in most instances, to apply state laws and regulations in the light of local conditions rather than with reference to conditions in the state as a whole.[1]

Thus, some counties collect personal taxes on automobiles, while many others do not; all are supposed to on the basis of existing law.

Direct confrontations between the state government and county or other local governments are rare. Bargaining, cooperation, and accommodation rather than coercion are more likely to characterize state-local relationships. State legislators are usually quick to accede to the requests of local officials for special legislation. Also, associations of local officials often have sufficient political power to secure desired legislation and to ward off or modify what is unwanted. Opposition to the Texas Tort Claims Act, which curtailed somewhat the immunity of local governments from damage suits, came from such organizations as the Texas Municipal League, the City Attorneys Association, and the County Judges and Commissioners Association. Although they failed to prevent its adoption, they did succeed in restricting its scope.[2] (The doctrine of immunity of governments from suit is archaic, stemming from the old notion that "the king can do no wrong.")

Since the early twentieth century, proponents of reform in county government have advocated home rule for counties, under which counties could do whatever they wanted in organizational and policy matters so long as they did not contravene the state constitution and laws. Home rule for cities has been long established and accepted.

Home rule would provide counties with greater flexibility and operating discretion and permit them to deal with problems more expeditiously and effectively. The experience with city home rule seems, on the whole, to have been quite satisfactory. Nonetheless, there continues to be strong opposition to county home rule, and the balance of political power appears to rest with the opposition. Many county officials, especially elected ones, have strongly resisted home rule. Thus one county attorney indicated a belief that home rule could lead to "managerial-type government" in which a county manager might appoint various officials now elected. Such opposition is based partly on the belief that such officials should properly be elected. (On the other hand, a frequent criticism of county government is that too many officials are elected.) There is also in this opposition, though usually denied, a strong element of job protectionism. Some see home rule as a step toward "metro government," in which the governmental units in a metropolitan area are consolidated into a single unit. This they find highly disturbing.[3] Some basic opposition to change as such also blends in. Also, it should be noted that county government is not very visible or salient to much of the population, nor has it attracted the attention of reformers, as has city government. While county home rule may seem like a good idea to many people, there has not been strong pressure in its support. In contrast, the intensity of the opposition enhances its power.

As the situation now stands, counties must ask the state legislature for permission to do many things that home-rule cities do as a matter of course, such as adjusting speed limits on county roads, concluding contracts with other governments, and removing fire hazards on private property. Some authorizations are general in nature, such as a law that permits all counties to adopt rabies control measures. More commonly, however, the laws granting regulatory power to counties deal with specific local circumstances. Thus in 1975 the legislature enacted laws authorizing (1) certain West Texas counties to regulate lighting installations near the McDonald Observatory and (2) counties of over 235,000 population to regulate parking in lots adjacent to a county courthouse. Such laws illustrate the dependence of county governments on legislation to enable them to deal with problems in their local communities.

Moreover, counties generally lack *legislative,* or rule-making, authority, whereas home-rule cities have broad legislative power. For example, compare the positions of city and county health officers. Both are expected to follow the rules and regulations of the State Board of Health. However, the city can also adopt ordinances relating to health and sanitation and have these enforced by the health officer, whereas the county has no such authority.[4] The lack of rule-making power handicaps counties as units of general local government. In recent years, proposals in the state legislature to grant general rule-making authority to counties were defeated, largely because of the opposition of organized real estate groups. They have feared that counties would use such authority to regulate land use and development adversely to their interests, as by regulating the construction of housing in flood plain areas or the adoption of building codes.

County Governmental Organization

The structure of county government is set forth in much detail in the state constitution and laws. Although all counties have certain officials and bodies, there are variations among counties in their structure of offices, depending on the size of their populations; in special laws pertaining to them; and in accepting local practices, such as simply not filling some positions, whether elective or appointive. Predictably, the more populous counties have considerably larger, more elaborate administrative systems than do rural counties. We will not attempt to describe the structure of county government in detail. Some categorizations are possible.

1. Each county has a governing body called the county commissioners court, whose members are elected for four-year terms.

2. Each county has a number of other officials, elected for four-year terms in partisan elections. They may include the following: sheriff, treasurer, county clerk, county attorney, tax assessor-collector, district clerk, county surveyor, county superintendent of schools, one or more justices of the peace, one or more constables, county board of school trustees, and inspector of hides and animals. (This last position is still open to counties on an optional basis. A person who was elected to this position in Harris County in 1976 apparently had no duties.) The familiar generalization that the structure of all county governments is essentially the same lacks complete accuracy, as there are many variations from one county to another.

According to law, in counties with fewer than 10,000 residents, the sheriff also serves as tax assessor-collector. However, some counties with populations below that figure still fill the office separately. Some have recently dropped below the 10,000 figure; most, however, have either never had 10,000 residents or have long been below that figure.

The jurisdiction of the county attorney is given to the district attorney in some small counties (as is also the case in populous Bexar County), while others simply leave the office vacant. The office of county surveyor is filled mostly in the larger, urban counties, where the occupant may develop close ties with real estate developers and promoters.

All counties elect at least one justice of the peace, with the number varying from 1 each in several counties to 16 in Harris County. The number of constables varies from none in many counties to 8 (the maximum possible) in a handful of counties. Although by law each county is to elect at least 4 justices and 4 constables, many do not. Some counties do not hold elections for some positions, while in others low or nonexistent salaries discourage the appearance of candidates.

3. There are a number of appointed officials and boards or commissions. Each county is required to have a health officer (a "competent, licensed physician") who is appointed by the commissioners court. In counties with over 35,000 population or $15 million in property tax evaluations, there is an auditor, who exercises oversight of county financial practices. In counties with over 225,000 people, this individual becomes the chief budget officer. The auditor is appointed by the district judge or judges having jurisdiction in the county. Most counties participate in the agricultural extension and home demonstration programs and have appointed county agents in charge. Some counties, especially larger ones, have a variety of appointed officials or boards to head programs authorized but not required by law. Examples include the medical examiner, county librarian or library board, fire marshal, probation officer, and juvenile board.

4. Each county may have a number of administrative departments, such as

the health department, welfare department, county library, or county clerk's office, presided over by an elected or appointed official. These administrative departments, especially those headed by elected officials, operate with substantial independence because of the belief on the part of other officials that "you can't tell an elected official what to do" and the absence of any coordinating power.

The county commissioners court is the principal governing body in the county (it is not a judicial body despite the word *court* in its title). It consists of four commissioners, one elected from each of the four commissioner's precincts into which the county is divided, and the county judge, who is elected from the county at large. The county judge serves as presiding officer of the commissioners court and has a vote but no veto power over decisions.

The boundaries of the precincts from which the commissioners are elected are established by the commissioners court itself. In many counties these precincts were highly unequal in population size, either as a consequence of deliberate action or as a result of population changes without realignment of precincts. A study published in 1965 found that approximately 60 counties had not redrawn their commissioner's precincts since 1900.[5] As with legislative malapportionment at the state level, urban areas within counties received the short end of this situation.

Legal action challenging the constitutionality of inequality in commissioner's precincts was started in Midland County, where one precinct containing the city of Midland had 97 percent of the county's population, and the other three precincts had the remainder. In 1968, in *Avery* v. *Midland County,* the U.S. Supreme Court held that commissioner's precincts had to be set up on the basis of the one person-one vote criterion used in legislative reapportionment cases and had to be of substantially equal population size.[6] Many counties subsequently took action in accordance with this decision. In recent years Chicano groups have been exerting pressure for reapportionment to give them a better opportunity to elect county commissioners.

County reapportionment may result in the commissioners court's giving more attention to the municipal areas within a county, especially when there is a single large city containing most of the population. The Supreme Court indicated in the Avery case that it believed this was necessary. Concerning the condition that had existed in Midland County, the Court remarked: "Indeed, it may not be mere coincidence that a body apportioned with three of its four members chosen by residents of the rural area surrounding the city devoted most of its attention to the problems of that area, while paying for its expenditures with a tax imposed equally on city residents and those who live outside the city."[7] Moreover, the realignment of commissioner's precincts may improve the opportunities of Republicans and ethnic minorities to gain direct representation on commissioners courts.[8]

A principal basis for the importance of the commissioners court in county government is its control of county finances. Although the kinds of taxes that can be collected and the maximum rates that can be levied are specified in the state constitution and laws, the commissioners determine which taxes will be used and to what extent to raise revenue for the county. The county's annual budget is prepared by the county judge (or the county auditor in large counties) and adopted by the commissioners court, which usually displays much interest in budgetary details and can raise or lower budget requests from various officials and departments. The entire county budgetary process attracts little public attention, and little effort is made to inform or involve the public. In all, the commissioners court has much discretion in budgeting, and it can use its power to attempt to influence or control county officials and agencies over whom it has no formal authority. Also, the commissioners themselves directly handle the expenditure of a large portion of appropriated funds, particularly for roads and parks.

The commissioners court also decides whether the county will undertake programs or activities that are authorized but not made mandatory by legislation. In some cases these authorizations apply to one or a few counties (e.g., authority to prevent littering on public beaches); in other cases they are open to all counties. Thus, whether a given county has such programs as food stamp distribution, county parks, pollution control, or county hospitals depends on action by the commissioners court. The trend in recent years has been continual expansion of such authorizations, which has served to increase the discretionary power of the commissioners court. The officials who direct the administration of such programs are usually appointed by the court unless the programs come under the jurisdiction of regular county officials. The court also fills vacancies when they develop in many elective county and precinct offices; their appointees hold office until the next general election.

In most counties each of the four commissioners is in charge of the county road and bridge program in the precinct, with the available money usually being allocated equally among the precincts. Each commissioner has road crews, equipment, and sheds; contracts for the purchase of construction materials; and authority to determine what will be done and where. So important is road construction and maintenance that in many counties the commissioners are called "road commissioners." One-third of total county expenditures go for roads, with some rural counties spending as much as half their funds for this purpose. In planning the road program, each commissioner usually acts unilaterally, making little if any effort to coordinate activities with those of the other commissioners. In 1947 the legislature enacted the Optional Road Law, which permits the voters in a county to adopt a unified road system that would be under the supervision of a professional county highway engineer. Basic road policy would still be made by the commissioners court. Although a unified road system probably would eliminate waste and duplication, among other things, only around 20 counties (including Bexar, Brazoria, Galveston, and Potter) currently operate on this basis. Most commissioners prefer the existing individualized arrangement because of the power it gives them, while most voters are too satisfied, uninformed, or uninterested to demand change.

The county judge has a variety of legislative, administrative, and judicial duties. As presiding officer of the commissioners court, the county judge participates in the exercise of its power and in most cases prepares the county budget. Along with the sheriff and county clerk, the county judge is a member of the County Election Board and has numerous duties relating to the administration of elections. In some counties, this individual may also serve in such capacities as ex officio county school superintendent or as a member of the Juvenile Board (which is concerned with the treatment of juvenile lawbreakers). And, as the title indicates, this person presides over the county court, which is part of the state judicial system and should not be confused with the county commissioners court.

There is no formally designated chief executive in a county, although in some counties the county judge may appear to act in this fashion. If so, it will be primarily because of personality, leadership abilities, political standing, or tenure in office rather than official authority. This lack of a chief executive, frequently cited by reformers as a major defect in county government, often leads to fragmentation and particularism in the operation of county government. Other factors also contribute. Commissioners tend to resist "outside" control or interference in their precincts. A controversy in Tarrant County over the county's role in maintaining dumpgrounds caused a reporter to state that "each commissioner feels that his precinct is his sole domain, that the other three commissioners should keep their hands and, in this case, their noses out of his affairs."[9] As county services expand in urban areas, there is a tendency to assign primary responsibility for certain departments (e.g., welfare) or certain programs (e.g., parking facilities) to each of the commissioners. The election of a number of administrative officials also serves to hinder the development of common policies and coordinated action in the implementation of policy. Just as there is a reluctance to tell elected officials what to do, so too are they reluctant to take outside direction. A proposal to set up a central computer system in Harris County was opposed by the elected county clerk because, he said, "no one is going to tell me how to run my office."[10] Executive leadership, which is a preferred value in the literature of public administration, is a scarce item in Texas county government.

It is not possible to present a neat, comprehensive review of the functions counties are authorized to perform or the functions they actually do undertake. A multitude of general and special laws and constitutional provisions variously authorize, prescribe, or limit what some or all counties can or must do. Generally, though, county functions fall into two groupings. First there are duties they are required to perform as administrative arms of the state government. Included are such functions as administering and collecting some taxes; enforcing criminal laws; servicing the state courts by, for example, providing clerks and prosecuting attorneys; keeping records of births, deaths, deeds, and other matters; registering voters and administering elections; and enforcing health laws. Second, there are functions they perform as units of general local government, especially for people outside of municipalities. Examples are road construction and maintenance; provision of parks and recreation facilities; operation of county hospitals, libraries, and airports; administration of local welfare services; and control of environmental pollution. Generally, urban counties operate a more extensive variety of programs than do rural areas.

MUNICIPAL GOVERNMENT

Over 80 percent of Texans now live in urban areas, and as a consequence municipal government has become the most significant form of general government.

(Table 9.3 conveys a sense of the growth rate of Texas cities.) Municipal, or city, governments perform a variety of protective and welfare activities (e.g., police and fire protection, public housing and health programs) and provide many services (e.g., water and sewerage systems, parks and recreation programs) that are of great importance for the safety, convenience, and well-being of city dwellers. The tendency is for the demand for municipal services to increase as urban population continues to grow. Necessity more than ideology shapes the response to such demands.

Legally, cities are regarded as "municipal corporations" that have received operating charters from the state government. A city charter, which is akin to a constitution, sets forth a city's boundaries, governmental structure, legal authority, sources of revenue, and methods for selection of officials. It is intended to grant the power of local self-government to a community at its own request. The legal authority of city governments is not unlimited, however, because they have only that authority permissible under the state constitution and laws. Cities must also conform to the relevant provisions of the U.S. Constitution and laws (which restrain but do not empower cities), such as those pertaining to civil rights and minimum wages; cities are also subject to some supervision by state administrative agencies. City governments, in short, operate within the context of an extensive network of legal guidelines.

American courts traditionally follow the practice of narrowly interpreting the powers granted to cities by their charters and state laws. This standard of interpretation is known as *Dillon's Rule*, after its nineteenth-century formulator, Judge John F. Dillon.

It is a general and undisputed proposition of law that a municipal corporation possesses and can exercise the following powers and no others: First, those granted in express words; second, those necessarily or fairly implied in or incident to the powers expressly granted; third, those essential to the declared objects and purposes of the corporation not simply convenient, but indispensable. Any fair, reasonable substantial doubt concerning the existence of power is resolved by the courts against the corporation and the power is denied [11]

Table 9.3 THE TEN MOST POPULOUS CITIES IN TEXAS

City	1990	1950	% Change
Houston	1,630,553	1,595,124	2.2
Dallas	1,006,877	904,077	11.4
San Antonio	935,933	785,877	19.1
El Paso	515,342	425,259	21.7
Austin	465,622	345,493	34.8
Fort Worth	447,619	385,164	16.2
Arlington	261,721	160,113	63.5
Corpus Christi	257,453	231,999	11.0
Lubbock	186,206	173,979	7.0
Garland	180,650	138,857	30.1

Source: U.S. Department of Commerce, Bureau of the Census, *Census of Population,* *1990.*

Although in recent years it appears that the courts have been more lenient in their interpretation of municipal powers, considerations of legal power are still quite important in the operation of city governments. The city attorney is often a pivotal figure in the decision-making process, and judicial review of municipal activity is rather extensive.

The goal of municipal reformers and others seeking greater self-government for cities has long been to free cities of excessive dependence on the legislature for legal authority, with the attendant possibility of legislative "interferences" in city affairs. Until the middle of the nineteenth century, Texas cities were governed only under special charters issued directly on an individual basis by the legislature. In 1858 the legislature enacted a general law under which cities could be incorporated by meeting stated requirements, but little is known of experience with this legislation. A major change in the state-city relationship came with the Constitution of 1876. It provided that cities and towns with populations of 10,000 or less (the figure was reduced to 5000 or less by a 1909 amendment) could be incorporated only under general laws, whereas only cities over 10,000 (later 5000) could have charters issued and amended by special acts of the legislature. The movement toward more local self-government culminated in the adoption of a constitutional amendment in 1912 permitting home rule for cities with more than 5000 residents.

Under the home-rule amendment, eligible cities are able to draft their own charters and put them into effect with the approval of a majority vote in a referendum. *Home rule,* which is intended to allow cities to set up their governmental structure and undertake programs with a minimum of state control, permits a city to do anything not prohibited by the state constitution and laws. In other words, a city operating under a home-rule charter is not limited to doing only what is clearly authorized by existing law. The practical effect of this is substantially to overturn Dillon's Rule as a guiding principle for home-rule cities, but not for general-law cities. Home-rule cities are still subject to legislative policies, such as those defining the work week of firefighters, authorizing cities to levy sales taxes with voter approval, and reducing the immunity of cities from tort liability. Home rule does relieve cities of the necessity of seeking legislative authorization every time they want to engage in a new activity.

For charter purposes, Texas cities can presently be classified as general-law and home-rule cities. Cities with fewer than 5000 inhabitants are governed in accordance with general state statutes. There are several hundred small municipalities in this category. Those over the 5000 mark have a choice between general-law and home-rule status; almost all (279 in 1989) have opted for home rule. Home-rule cities have more discretion in the adoption of governmental structure, as well as broader powers of taxation and annexation. Beyond these matters, there do not appear to be great differences in the operating authority legally available to each category. Also, it should be noted that particular home-rule cities may be affected in what they can do by special, or *bracket,* legislation passed by the state legislature. This results when local problems or conflicts—as over police pensions—are carried to the legislature for resolution.

Forms of Municipal Government

Municipal governments in the United States, including Texas, display considerable variation in their organization and policies as a consequence of their adaptations to local interests and conditions. It is possible, however, to group them under three general forms on the basis of their structural characteristics: the mayor-council, council-manager, and commission forms.[12] Most general-law (small) cities use the mayor-council form, while the council-manager form is most popular among the larger home-rule cities. (Like home rule, the council-manager form is associated with the municipal reform movement.) Some, mostly general-law, cities still cling to the commission form.

The *mayor-council* form is both the traditional and the most common form of city government in use. Indeed, in the nineteenth century it was the only form of municipal government. It features an elected mayor and an elected council chosen at large or by wards or by some combination of the two. In the *strong-mayor* variations, the mayor is vested with strong administrative and legislative authority, including the appointment (subject to council approval) and removal of most department heads, the preparation of a budget for the council's consideration, and (usually) veto power over council actions. The council acts primarily as a legislative body. The strong-mayor form thus concentrates much power in the mayor, who is thus both an administrator and a political leader. Some express a preference for this type on the ground that it concentrates responsibility and provides for, or at least facilitates, strong executive leadership in city government. These are seen as requisites for effective municipal government. (See Figure 9.1.)

A second variation, the *weak-mayor–council* type, has a mayor with minimal administrative authority and usually no veto power over actions of the council. Most city departments are headed by persons who either are elected or are appointed by other officials, such as a majority of the council. This results in a fragmentation and dispersion of power, which in turn diffuses responsibility.

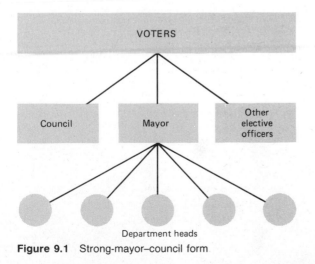

Figure 9.1 Strong-mayor–council form

The voters may find the whole system rather confusing. Dissatisfaction with the lack of clear leadership and direction in its operation has caused most municipalities of substantial size to abandon this form of government. (See Figure 9.2.)

The *commission* form of city government developed early in the twentieth century, with Galveston being its accepted place of origin. Dissatisfaction with the existing city government was compounded by the task of rebuilding the city following the disastrous hurricane of 1900. Moreover, needed state financial assistance was apparently conditioned on reform of the city's government. Consequently, a charter was obtained from the legislature providing for a five-member commission to govern the city. All legislative and executive functions were combined in the commission. Collectively, under the "Galveston Plan," the commission adopted ordinances or policies. Individually, each commissioner administered a specific department. Thus, the original Galveston charter provided for a mayor-president and commissioners of finance and revenue, waterworks and sewerage, streets and public property, and fire and police.[13]

The commission form gained rapid popularity among municipal reform groups, and by 1920 some 500 cities across the nation were using it. The development and rapid diffusion of the commission form suggests two conclusions: Innovations in governmental structure are sometimes as much a product of chance as of deliberate design, and the adoption of governmental structures and practices is sometimes a form of emulative behavior. Interest in and use of the commission form soon waned, however.

As exemplified in the Galveston Plan, the commission form is no longer used by Texas cities. (Galveston abandoned the commission form in 1960.) Two major causes for its disappearance were administrative problems, created by electing commissioners who doubled as department heads, and a growing preference for the council-manager form, which promised more effective executive leadership. Although a number of Texas cities are still listed as using the commission form, what they actually have is usually closely akin to the council-manager

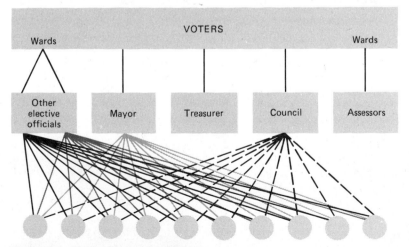

Figure 9.2 Weak-mayor–council form

form. A city commission composed of a mayor and two commissioners makes policy decisions and selects a manager to administer day-to-day city operations. Members of the commission have no individual authority over city departments. Municipal government organized along the lines of the Galveston Plan can still be found in a few cities in the nation, such as Cedar Rapids, Iowa.

The *council-manager* is the most recent major innovation in municipal government forms and has enjoyed much popularity in recent decades. This form has a small, part-time council, usually elected at large in nonpartisan elections, which possesses all legislative power. The mayor, who is either elected by the voters or chosen by the council from among its members, presides over council meetings and serves as the political and honorific head of the city government. Control of the city administrative system, however, is vested in a professionally trained city manager, who is appointed by the council and is accountable to it. The city manager has the power to appoint and remove department heads, prepare the city budget, and implement policies made by the council. Municipal reformers and many others have found this form attractive because of such attributed virtues as strong administrative leadership by a professional manager, the separation of policy-making and administrative activities, efficient operation, and nonpartisanship. Among large Texas cities, Dallas, Fort Worth, San Antonio, Corpus Christi, and Austin use it; Houston and El Paso use the strong-mayor–council form. (See Figure 9.3.)

In actuality, the council-manager form often does not provide a separation of administration from politics and policy making. Although managers usually avoid partisan politics, they often become deeply involved in the politics of policy making, both making (especially if they seek to be innovative) and being expected

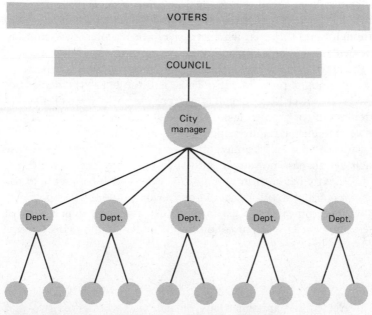

Figure 9.3 Council-manager form

to make policy recommendations. Certainly it is accurate to regard as political in nature such actions as recommendations for tax increases or bond issues, the refusal to recommend a salary increase for public employees, or the proposal of a new housing or street improvement program. Not only do managers make such recommendations, but they also usually seek to develop support for them within permissible limits. Some managers work primarily through official channels, while others look for support in the general community. On matters that are strongly controversial, such as electoral law changes and the handling of minority grievances, however, managers are less active in policy formulation.

General-law cities may choose any of these forms of government, although what the statutes designate as the "commission" form appears more like the mayor-council form. In comparison, home-rule cities are free to adopt a charter providing whichever organizational structure for their governments they desire. However, once a charter is adopted, the form of government so provided cannot be changed by charter revision or amendment at less than two-year intervals. Voter approval is required for all changes in home-rule charters, and sometimes sharp political conflicts may arise over proposed changes. But apathy often prevails. A charter revision election in Dallas in 1973 attracted fewer than 5 percent of the registered voters, while in El Paso in 1977 fewer than 13 percent turned out for a charter revision election in which single-member districts were adopted for the city council.

No particular form of city government will automatically provide "good" government, notwithstanding the large amounts of time and argument devoted to the question of which is the best form of city government. While formal governmental structure may indeed affect the character or style of government in a community, it is by no means necessarily *the* crucial variable, as some apparently assume. Formal authorizations are certainly one basis for the possession and exercise of power. However, whether a mayor is "strong" or "weak" in fact, for instance, will depend not simply upon the formal powers of the office but also upon how the mayor uses those powers, the amount of political support in the community, the kinds of prevailing problems, and the like. Whether or not the mayor has the veto power is significant, and from the perspective of mayoral power it is better to have it than to lack it, but it should not be assumed that without this power the mayor is automatically less able to block council action than is a mayor with such power. The mayor may be able to persuade or otherwise cause the council not to pass unwanted ordinances, while a mayor with veto power may be sufficiently hemmed in by political pressures to be unable to use that power. In short, formal structure should be viewed as the starting point for the analysis of the governmental process in cities. An understanding of formal structure is a necessary but insufficient condition for understanding how government operates.

Electoral Activity in Texas Cities

Prior to 1958, all elected and appointed city officials in Texas served two-year terms. In 1958, a constitutional amendment provided that, with the approval of their voters, cities could specify either two-, three-, or four-year terms for their officials. If a city were to select four-year terms for its council members, election would have to be by majority rather than plurality vote (where whoever gets the most votes wins, whether the amount is half of the total number or not), thereby sometimes necessitating runoff elections. Some home-rule cities do utilize plurality elections.

In an effort to insulate municipal politics from state and national politics, city elections are usually held in "off-years" (i.e., odd-numbered years), when state and national elections are not held. They are also usually nonpartisan, with no political party designations for candidates appearing on the ballot. Reformers have contended that nonpartisanship would help take "politics" out of city government, raise the quality of candidates seeking public office, focus campaigns on local rather than national and state issues, and contribute to efficiency in municipal government. It is not really possible to determine conclusively the effect of nonpartisanship on city politics. It probably has lessened the impact of political parties on local politics and, at the same time, caused greater emphasis on personal popularity and relationships in local elections and less stress on policy issues and differences.

Local political organizations have arisen in some cities and have shown considerable continuity. Such organizations may screen and "nominate" slates of candidates, finance and manage their campaigns, and influence those elected once they are in office. Examples are the Communities Organized for Public Service (COPS) in San Antonio, the Citizen's Committee for Good Government in Wichita Falls, and the Amarillo Citizens Association. The Good Government League and the Citizen's Charter Association, which long dominated politics in San Antonio and Dallas, respectively, have faded from power in recent years. The Good Government League, which was a conservative, business-oriented group, was displaced by COPS, which draws its strength from liberal and Mexican-American elements in San Antonio. This marks a distinct change in the nature of politics in San Antonio.[14] In Dallas, no group has yet developed to replace the Citizen's Charter Association. In Crystal City, La Raza Unida dominated city politics for several years in the 1970s before losing power because of internal factional conflicts.

Notwithstanding political organizations of this sort, it is more common for local candidates either to run as individuals, as in Austin or Houston, or to join together and run as an informal slate, as in El Paso.

Nonpartisan politics of this sort, unstructured by political parties, works to increase the influence that pressure groups, downtown associations, or the press can have on elections. Without party labels to aid them in identifying and sorting out candidates, voters must rely on other means such as newspaper or pressure-group endorsements or personal contacts. Those seeking office, especially in larger cities, have to develop campaign organizations and secure financial support on their own without the aid of a party organization. (Contractors and others hoping to do business with the city are often a fertile source of campaign contributions.) Personal relationships appear to be especially important in smaller cities and towns.

Several election systems are used by cities for selecting council members.[15] One is the *at-large system,* whereby the voters in the entire city select all the members of the council; each voter is entitled to cast votes for as many candidates as there are positions to be filled. In the absence of slates, each candidate in effect runs against all other candidates. Another is the *ward* (or *district*) *system,* whereby council candidates must reside in the ward or district they seek to represent and are elected by the voters of that ward alone. A third is the *place system.* This provides for the election of all council members on a citywide basis; but each candidate runs for a particular seat, or place, on the council—as place one, place two, and so on. Candidates file for a particular place and run only against the other candidates seeking that place. Finally, cities can use some combination of these three systems. For example, in Houston eight members of the council must live in and are elected by particular districts of the city, while five others run for places and are elected by the voters in the entire city. Many cities, such as Abilene, Beaumont, and Texarkana, use the combination of residence in wards and election by the entire city. In home-rule cities, the place system or some variation thereof is the most frequently used electoral device. (General-law cities do not have legal authority to use the place system.) Only a few home-rule cities, such as San Antonio, use the ward system, which was the traditional form of municipal election and is often associated with such bad things as machine politics and boss rule.

What difference does it make whether one or another of these systems is used? What are the consequences? Those who prefer at-large elections (including the place system) contend that such elections cause council members to consider the needs of the city as a whole, whereas under the ward system, council members are said to do "nothing but run local errands" in the interests of their constituents and to be amenable to logrolling.[16] Whether this is really the case is open to question and empirical analysis. Under the place and at-large systems, it is quite possible for most council members to come from one area of the city and to identify the interests of their area and friends with those of the whole city. Certainly one can find many examples in Texas where some sections of a city receive more or better services than other sections. At-large elections, with or without the place system, were adopted in some cities to prevent racial minorities from electing council members, as they well might under a ward or district system.[17] Whatever their actual effects, election systems are not regarded by many as neutral in impact, and those in dominance will usually select a system that seems best geared to serve their interests.

In the 1970s considerable pressure developed in support of election of city council members from single-member wards or districts. Cities such as San Antonio, El Paso, Waco, Paris, Houston, and Dallas converted at least partially to single-member districts. They were encouraged or required to do so by legal action based on the Voting Rights Act of 1975.[18] Citywide elections were legally attacked for diluting the vote (i.e., reducing the electoral opportunities of minority groups). In 1977, in the first election in San Antonio held under the single-member district scheme, those winning election to the city council were five Anglos (including the mayor), five Mexican-Americans, and one black. Until then, the Council had been dominated by Anglos. Also in 1977, single-member districts contributed to the election of a Mexican-American to the Waco City Council, the first in its history.

Voter participation is usually quite low in city elections; probably less than 25 percent of the potential electorate turns out for most elections. In Austin during the 1954–1964 period, according to one study, the turnout in city elections ranged from around 20 percent to about 6 percent.[19] A hotly contested mayoral election in Houston in 1973 brought out 40 percent of the registered voters. In the 1980s mayoral elections in nine large Texas cities had turnouts of from 9 to 35 percent of the registered voters.[20] The usual low turnout in city elections is the result of such factors as the low salience of local politics for many voters, holding city elections in "off-years" when state and national elections do not help attract voters to the polls, nonpartisanship, and the frequency of local elections.[21] Most Texas city elections are nonpartisan, and available evidence indicates that turnout is typically lower in nonpartisan than in partisan elections. In the latter, the parties help to generate interest, define issues, and get voters to go to the polls.[22] Low voting turnout likely has a conservative impact on city government because it means low participation by lower socioeconomic groups. Officials are thus most likely to be concerned with the attitudes and interests of the middle-class voters who go to the polls and tend to be more conservative.

Another facet of municipal politics, and of local politics generally, is the widespread use of the voter referendum, which provides for direct popular participation in the decision-making process. Cities and other local governments usually must secure the approval of the voters to issue bonds and, occasionally, to change tax rates. We have already noted that city charter revisions require voter approval. Other matters may be submitted to the voters in order to get a "sense of the community," as on a proposed zoning ordinance or housing code. In 1967 the legislature authorized cities to levy a 1 percent sales tax after approval in a local referendum. Winning approval in most instances, the local sales tax was instituted in 923 cities as of January 1980. Another notable illustration of the referendum involves "liquor by the drink." As a result of a 1970 constitutional amendment and subsequent legislation, when approved in local option elections in "wet" precincts of counties, liquor may be sold by the drink. By the mid-1980s, the sale of mixed drinks had been approved in all or parts of 85 counties.

The percentage of voters who participate in referenda is usually low, and the amount of information available to them on the issue at hand is likely to be minimal. (Voters in liquor-by-the-drink referenda are unlikely to feel the need for much information, being either "for or agin' it." It tends to be an emotional issue to which voters often have a "gut reaction.") It has also been said that "Widening the scope of the decision-making arena inevitably means the inclusion of a high percentage of people to whom the proposal will mean little or nothing."[23] As a form of "participatory democracy," the referendum has not proved to be a particularly encouraging experience. As much as anything, continued use of the referendum in many instances reflects the notion that local officials cannot be fully trusted, especially on financial matters. In some other instances, such as liquor by the drink, it becomes a way for elected officials to avoid having to make decisions alone on controversial matters.

SPECIAL DISTRICTS

Special districts, although little known and even less loved, except perhaps by real estate developers, are the fastest growing form of local government in Texas. The 1987 *Census of Governments* reported the existence of 1891 special districts in the state. Included in this total were water control, improvement, and supply districts; housing authorities; conservation and reclamation districts; soil and water conservation districts; hospital districts; levee improvement districts; drainage districts; navigation districts; rural fire prevention districts; airport authorities; noxious weed control districts; and miscellaneous districts. Although school districts are also a form of special district, because of their number and importance they are treated separately in this chapter.

The number of special districts grows apace, especially in the state's urban areas. While some become inactive or are abolished (as when water or municipal utility districts are absorbed by city annexation), more are created each year. In the 1960s and early 1970s, large numbers were created by special laws enacted by the legislature. (One Houston legislator alone was credited with "batting in" over 50 water districts in 1970.) Now, as a consequence of reform legislation enacted in 1973, most special districts are created by the Texas Water Commission. Few inhabitants of Texas do not come under the jurisdiction of and help support at least one special district, whether they are cognizant of it or not.

In contrast to county and municipal governments, which possess general governmental powers, special districts are usually created to provide one or a few services for the inhabitants of a defined area. Few are authorized to regulate or control the behavior of people. The diverse characteristics of special districts are well pointed up in the following statement.

> Special districts are the most varied of all governmental units. . . . Thus some districts may tax, but others may not. Some may incur debt, but others may not. Many are governed by elected officials, many by appointed officials. A number possess police powers, but some do not. Most districts are intrastate, but a few are interstate. Many are more or less affiliates of another government, but a large number are virtually autonomous. A handful are highly responsive to public opinion, yet most operate in the shadows. Many are staffed by unpaid, part-time amateurs, many by highly paid professionals. A majority are informal, personal, and intimate; a minority are formal, impersonal, and autocratic. Some are "grass-roots" in the extreme, others are multi-purpose million-dollar operations. Most are well-established governments; however, a considerable number are sheer speculations.[24]

The Creation of Special Districts

As with other units of local government, special districts trace their legal origins to general or specific state laws and constitutional provisions. A number of hospital districts have been authorized by constitutional amendments. In most instances the general laws permitting the establishment of special districts require that they be approved by a majority vote (of those actually voting) of the district's resident property owners. This is usually done in perfunctory fashion, and often only a few dozen voters or fewer cast votes. A notable exception was the controversy in Harris County over the establishment of a hospital district. It was twice rejected by the voters before winning approval in 1965, following an extensive campaign for it by city and county officials and community leaders.

A number of factors have contributed to the establishment and proliferation of special districts. First, regular local governments may have defects or inadequacies that special districts are intended to overcome. In some instances, it appears easier to set up a new governmental unit to handle an activity than to try to alter existing units. The area boundaries of existing governments are inflexible, and their geographical jurisdiction may be larger or smaller than necessary to carry on a desired activity. For example, the residents of a river-basin area may want a flood-control program, but the area that should be covered may exceed the jurisdiction of existing local governments. Financial restrictions on city and county governments, as on tax rates and debt limits, may be avoided by resorting to special districts for particular programs, such as hospital districts or airport authorities. Or the officials of a general local government may simply want to shift a costly activity elsewhere. Administrative deficiencies, especially in county governments, may also encourage resorting to special districts.

A second general cause cited for the creation of special districts is political expediency. Special districts usually can be set up with comparative ease to handle new activities. Reorganizing or altering an existing government may bring much opposition from local officials and interests who perceive a threat to their positions and relationships. Special districts do not appear to disrupt the status quo and offer quick solutions to given problems.

Third, special districts may be viewed as a means for taking an activity "out of politics." By virtue of the special-district device, the activity is taken away from the politicians who dominate the city hall and county courthouse and is put into the hands, perhaps, of nonsalaried, public-spirited businesspersons or local people who will operate it in an efficient manner. The desire to take activities out of politics is a tradition of long standing in the United States. Whether it really can be done and whether it should be done are quite different matters.

Fourth, considerations of personal gain may motivate those seeking to have special districts established. Water districts in particular can be easily created; they have in the past been subject to little or no supervision and operate in semisecret style. Special districts may be established to create business opportunities, turn a quick profit, or provide jobs for friends and relatives. In urban areas, most notably the Houston metropolitan area, they have been used for promotional purposes by real estate developers. Districts have been established and millions of dollars in bond issues voted by a half-dozen or fewer voters to provide water supplies and sewer systems to new developments. These would have to be paid for by the developer in the absence of the special (water) district. When the territory covered by such promotional districts is annexed by the nearby city, as often happens, the city assumes liability for payment of the bond issues.

Governmental Structure and Administration

In their formal organization, special districts encompass a plethora of forms.[25] Approximately three-fourths of them are governed by boards of elected officials, usually commissioners or directors, with 5 members being common. (The appointed boards of river authorities may have as many as 24 members.) The rest are controlled by appointed officials. In most instances the governing officials are selected for two-year terms, although some may serve longer. Generally, they are part-time officials and receive only expenses or a small per diem allowance.

All soil conservation districts and many of the water districts have elected officials. For water districts with appointed officials, the appointing is usually done by the Texas Water Commission or other creating agencies. Directors of river authorities are usually appointed by the governor. The governing bodies of housing authorities are customarily appointed by the mayors of the cities in which they are located, whereas city councils do the appointing to urban renewal authorities. The county commissioners normally make selections for hospital, noxious weed, and rural fire-prevention districts. For some special districts, the selection process can become quite involved. For example, control of the Reagan County Water Supply District is lodged in a five-member board of directors appointed by a three-member citizen's committee. One member of this citizen's committee is chosen by the Reagan County commissioners, one member by the Big Lake city council, and the third member by the first two. What becomes of democratic accountability or popular control in a situation such as this?

The primary sources of revenue for special districts are property taxes and user charges for their services. All except soil conservation districts have authority to issue revenue bonds to finance their activities, using their reserve sources as backing, but in some cases this requires voter approval.

While a few special districts are large operations employing hundreds of people, many of them have no full-time staff whatsoever. Woodworth G. Thrombley concludes that, with the exceptions of housing and urban renewal authorities, hospital districts, and a few water districts, the administrative operations of special districts are "decidedly amateur" in style:

> Few of these districts make use of the tools of professional management. Such things as merit and budget systems, machine operations, double-entry accounting, and competitive purchasing are unknown to these little governments. Most of them do little or nothing in the way of reporting their activities. And many do not even maintain offices. (Their addresses may be the offices of a local attorney or the county clerk.) District employees are almost always employed on a part-time basis, and often such functions as property assessment and tax collection, annual audits, legal actions, and the conduct of elections are "farmed out" to other local governments. A number of districts, namely soil conservation districts, have no paid employees.[26]

Special districts, in short, usually do not fit the image that most of us have of a "government."

Criticism and Reform

Many persons have been critical of the extensive use of special districts, alleging that they are undemocratic because they are obscure in operation and resistant to effective popular control; that by their vast number they fragment, confuse, and complicate the local government scene; and that their small scale of activities often renders them uneconomical in operation. Clearly, the proliferation of special districts does contribute to the decentralization of governmental authority. In some counties, for example, the control and development of water resources are dispersed among a considerable number of special districts and other governmental units. This dispersion of authority makes comprehensive and integrated handling of local problems difficult and hampers popular control of government at the grass-roots level. Operating costs are often higher. For instance, the operating costs of sewage treatment plants operated by two small special districts in Dallas County are more than twice those of a nearby, larger City-of-Dallas plant. Interest rates on special-district bonds tend to run high because of their poor credit ratings.[27]

In 1973 complaints about the operation of water districts, coupled with a reformist atmosphere in Austin, led to legislative adoption of a package of 13 statutes intended to reform their operation. Under them, districts are required to maintain offices in their districts and keep their records open to the public. Annual audits by certified public accountants must be filed with the Texas Water Commission, which was given increased power of supervision. Petitions to create districts must be sent to cities within whose extraterritorial jurisdiction they lie. Relatives and employees of developers cannot serve as directors, tax assessors, or collectors in districts in which the developers own property. Those who buy property within a water district must be informed of its existence. Whether this legislation will prevent the abuses often associated with the use of water districts depends upon the vigor with which it is administered, especially by the Texas Water Commission. One change that is apparent is that most special districts are no longer established by special acts passed by the legislature. Also, the pace at which special districts are created has slowed down since the early 1970s; they do, however, continue to proliferate.

SCHOOL DISTRICTS

In 1987 there were 1111 independent school districts in Texas. (The legislature in 1979 converted some 100 common school districts into independent districts.) Operating both elementary and secondary schools, these independent school districts enroll approximately 3 million students. Of these, about 70 percent are enrolled in the elementary grades. The school districts vary greatly in terms of such characteristics as the number of students enrolled, the racial and ethnic composition of their student bodies, the nature and quality of their educational programs, the value of taxable property within their jurisdictions, and their property tax rates. In addition to educational programs, the schools provide students with counseling, health and nutrition services, transportation, and extracurricular activities.

The independent school district is a regular unit of local government, having its own governing body (the board of trustees), defined territorial jurisdiction, and the power to levy taxes. In most districts the school board is comprised of seven part-time, unsalaried members who are elected for three-year terms by the district voters in nonpartisan, at-large elections, with the candidates receiving the largest number of votes being elected. Because of special laws that apply to some districts, there are various exceptions to these generalizations. In some districts, terms are longer, the place system is used, a majority of the votes cast are needed to win election, and so on. The school board acts as the legislative body of the district, making decisions on tax rates and bond issues, adopting the budget, approving the appointment of teachers and other personnel, making disciplinary rules, and formulating other school policies. The board also selects the superintendent of schools, who is the chief administrative officer of the district and is in charge of the day-to-day operation of the school system.

Although conventional wisdom holds that education should be kept out of politics or vice versa, in practice the operation of local school systems is often highly political in the sense that this means conflict and struggle over policy. School-board elections are often hotly contested; liberal and conservative groups put up slates of candidates in some districts, while urban-rural cleavages appear in others. Conflicts in districts may develop over the location of new school buildings, the level of tax rates, the performance of the superintendent, the nature of the instructional program (with many assertions concerning "frills," the three *R*s, and the like), the desegregation of schools, disciplinary and dress codes, and drug abuse.

Reprinted by permission.

Public school desegregation became an important, volatile, and acrimonious issue in the mid-1950s. Major progress in desegregation followed the enactment of the national Civil Rights Act of 1964, and by the early 1970s most public schools had been officially desegregated. De facto segregation based on residential patterns was more resistant to change, however. Potent symbols and issues in the desegregation struggle include "freedom of choice," "neighborhood schools," "busing," "magnet schools," and "affirmative action." One also hears of "second generation discrimination," which refers to unequal treatment of black and white students within formally unitary schools.

In 1980 bilingual education, which had been a matter of controversy for some time, flared into a major political issue. A federal district judge held that the state's bilingual education program, which provided two-language instruction for public school students in kindergarten through the first grade, discriminated against minorities whose native language was not English. He ordered the state to implement a bilingual program for kindergarten through the twelfth grade. While his decision was being appealed to a higher federal court, the legislature in 1981 enacted a law providing for bilingual education through the sixth grade, with individual school districts being given an option to provide it through the eighth grade with state aid. Bilingual education continues to be a potent political issue.

The independent school districts receive their operating funds from a combination of national, state, and local sources. (Construction of school facilities is customarily financed by the proceeds of local bond issues.) For the 1988 school year, 44.3 percent of total funds ($6.23 billion) came from local sources, 40.8 percent ($5.74 billion) from the state, and 7.6 percent ($1.07 billion) from the national government. (The remaining 7 percent came from bond revenues and other sources.) The trend in recent years has been toward increasing the state and national contributions. Local districts depend heavily upon property (ad valorem) taxes for their own revenues and usually encounter strong resistance to increases in property-tax rates, which in some cases require voter approval. It is often easier to look elsewhere for needed funds, which, whether intentional or not, becomes a way of shifting the financial burden of local schools beyond the district.

The system of public school financing in the state historically has been characterized by great inequalities among school districts, as measured by spending per student, because the districts vary greatly in their capacity to raise local funds. Some districts contain much more taxable property per student than do others; consequently, rich districts can raise more money with lower tax rates than poor districts can with higher tax rates. And they do. As a consequence, even though legislative efforts have been made to provide more state funding for property-poor districts, substantial inequalities in funding among districts continue in the public school system. For two decades, public officials and others in the state have wrestled with the task of reducing inequality in public school finance. We will consider a few major events in this struggle.

In December 1971 a three-judge federal district court held that the use of property taxes to provide local school funds caused such disparities in levels of support among Texas school districts, because of disparities in the value of property on which taxes were levied, as to violate the Fourteenth Amendment's guarantee of equal protection of the laws.[28] As the court explained: "The current system of financing public education in Texas discriminates on the basis of wealth by permitting citizens of affluent districts to provide a higher quality of education for their children while paying lower taxes . . ."[29] The Edgewood school district in San Antonio, where the case originated, then had $5,900 of taxable property per student; the nearby wealthy Alamo Heights district had $49,000 in taxable property per student. The Edgewood district, composed mostly of Mexican-Americans, taxed its residents at a higher rate but raised only $26 per student compared to the $333 raised per student for Alamo Heights. When added to the minimum foundation program funds each district received from the state, these locally generated funds produced substantial differences in the total funds spent in each district. The district court gave the state two years to develop an alternative financing system.

The state appealed the case to the U.S. Supreme Court. While the appeal was pending, something of a crisis atmosphere existed. Many groups, official and private, studied the problem of school finance and made recommendations for change.[30] School finance was a major issue on the state legislative agenda in 1973. Then, in March 1973, the Supreme Court overturned the district court's decision by a five-to-four vote.[31] Speaking for the majority, Justice Lewis F. Powell, Jr., held that the right to an education was not of such fundamental character as to justify a finding of unconstitutional discrimination because of differences in educational expenditures among districts. Nor was there sufficient evidence of discrimination against a "suspect" class (such as racial group) as to warrant such a decision. On the other hand, Justice Powell did not endorse the status quo, going on to state:

> The need is apparent for reform in tax systems which may well have relied too long and too heavily on the local property tax. And certainly innovative new thinking as to public education, its methods and funding, is necessary to assure both a higher level of quality and greater uniformity of opportunity. These matters merit the continued attention of scholars who already have contributed much by their challenges. But the ultimate solution must come from the lawmakers and from the democratic pressures of those who elect them.[32]

The Supreme Court's ruling took some of the pressure for change away from the legislature. In 1975 and 1977 the legislature made more funds available for the equalization of spending in the school districts. This legislation, however, made no basic or major changes in school expenditure patterns. In 1984, in response to recommendations from the Select Committee on Public Education, chaired by Dallas billionaire H. Ross Perot, the legislature passed the Education Reform Act. This statute reorganized the State Board of Education, made many changes in the operation of schools, and changed the pattern of state funding so as to lessen spending disparities among school districts.

In 1984 the constitutionality of public education funding was challenged under the Texas Constitution in the state courts. The Edgewood school district and a number of others argued that the school finance system violated the Texas

Reprinted by permission.

Constitution because it did not provide equal educational opportunity. This contention was upheld by an Austin district judge in 1987. This decision was reversed a year later by the court of appeals in Austin, whose decision in turn was overruled in October 1989 by the Texas Supreme Court.

In the case of *Edgewood* v. *Kirby,* the nine members of the Texas Supreme Court unanimously held that the public school financing system violated Article 7, Section 1 of the Texas Constitution, which states: "A general diffusion of knowledge being essential to the preservation of the liberties and rights of the people, it shall be the duty of the Legislature of the State to establish and make suitable provision for the support and maintenance of an efficient system of free public schools." The court gave the legislature until May 1, 1990, to enact a constitutional finance plan for the schools that would ensure that districts had "substantially equal access to similar revenues per pupil at similar levels of tax efforts."

Meeting in the spring of 1990, the legislature needed four special sessions to hammer out a new state educational funding system that was acceptable to the governor. State funding for the public schools was increased, and formulas were adopted that directed more state funds to poorer districts. Considerable funding disparities remained among the districts, however. Within weeks, the legislature's handiwork was challenged by attorneys for several dozen property-poor districts and was held unconstitutional by the district judge with jurisdiction in the case. That decision was unanimously upheld by the Texas Supreme Court in early

1991. This meant that once again the legislature had to confront the issue of public school finance.

During its regular session in 1991 the legislature worked out a new school finance bill that was quickly approved by Governor Richards. This legislation increased state funding for public schools by an estimated $1.7 billion for the 1991–1993 biennium. School districts were required to levy a minimum required property-tax rate. Higher rates could be levied for "unequalized enrichment" of operations and facilities. Also, 188 county or multi-county education districts were created. Within them, some property-tax revenues would be shifted from wealthier to poorer school districts. In all, it was estimated that this plan would greatly reduce but not eliminate disparities in per pupil school funding.

The new legislation immediately was challenged in the courts. Some wealthy school districts alleged that it unconstitutionally established a state property tax and transferred local tax monies from one district to another. A number of poorer districts contested the law on the ground that it did not provide adequate funding for the construction of school facilities. The law remained in effect pending decisions on those challenges. There the matter stood in the fall of 1991.

Mention should be made here of the state's free textbook program, which was authorized by a constitutional amendment adopted in 1918. A 15-member textbook committee is appointed annually by the State Board of Education to evaluate textbooks and develop a list of recommended titles for use in the public schools. The committee holds public hearings at which persons may appear and express support or opposition for particular textbooks. Representatives of fundamentalist groups can usually be counted on to appear and oppose the approval of biology textbooks that present evolution as "a fact, rather than a theory." Or it may be advocated that "creation theory" be given equal treatment with evolutionary theory. Whether history books give proper treatment to American heroes and heroines is another common concern. Women's rights groups have protested the stereotyped treatment of women in various textbooks. Another critic protested a sixth-grade health book because it told students that "a pesticide should not be used when a flyswatter will do"; this was a "hysterical reaction" caused by the "pollution bugaboo."[33] Use of the *American Heritage Dictionary* was rejected in 1981 because it contained "offensive words." Books that make it onto the approved list are provided free to districts, who must select basic texts from that list. Supplementary texts do not have to come from the approved list, but a district must then pay for them itself, which obviously is an incentive for further use of approved books. The Texas system of textbook selection is the most centralized and restrictive in the nation.[34]

METROPOLITAN AREAS

There are now 28 metropolitan statistical areas (MSAs) in Texas (see Table 9.4). The U.S. Bureau of the Census defines an *MSA* as an area that includes a central city of at least 50,000 people and its adjacent urban areas. So defined, metropolitan areas contain over three-fourths of the state's population. The Houston, Dallas, Fort Worth, and San Antonio metropolitan areas include about half the

Table 9.4 METROPOLITAN STATISTICAL AREAS IN TEXAS, 1980–1990.

Name	Population	
	1980	1990
Abilene	110,932	119,655
Amarillo	173,699	187,547
Austin	536,688	781,572
Beaumont-Port Arthur	375,497	361,226
Brazoria	169,587	191,707
Brownsville-Harlingen	209,727	260,120
Bryan-College Station	93,588	121,862
Corpus Christi	326,228	349,894
Dallas	1,957,378	2,553,362
El Paso	479,899	591,610
Ft. Worth-Arlington	973,138	1,332,053
Galveston-Texas City	195,940	217,399
Houston	2,735,766	3,301,937
Killeen-Temple	214,656	255,301
Laredo	99,258	133,239
Longview-Marshall	151,752	162,431
Lubbock	211,651	222,636
McAllen-Edinberg-Mission	283,229	383,545
Midland	82,636	106,611
Odessa	115,374	118,934
San Angelo	84,784	98,458
San Antonio	1,071,954	1,302,099
Sherman-Denison	89,796	95,021
Texarkana	75,301	81,665
Tyler	128,366	151,309
Victoria	68,807	74,361
Waco	170,755	189,123
Wichita Falls	121,082	122,378

Source: U. S. Department of Commerce, Bureau of the Census, *Census of Polulation,* 1990.

state's population. This represents a marked contrast with 1900, when Texas was a predominantly rural state with only one city (San Antonio) of more than 50,000 residents. Today the typical Texan is an urban dweller (albeit, perhaps, with a pickup truck), and in the future even more Texans will be urban dwellers, as the movement away from small towns and rural areas into the cities continues.

Metropolitan Problems

A great many of the domestic problems confronting all Americans are essentially metropolitan problems. Typically, when a person thinks of urban or metropolitan problems, such things as police and fire protection, water supply, garbage and sewage disposal, traffic congestion, parks and playgrounds, and land-use planning come to mind. And, indeed, these often are problems with which urban dwellers become well acquainted when the water pressure decreases or disappears in the summer, when they sit in a car on a clogged freeway, or when they search for open recreational space only to find people and clutter. These traditional urban problems have been compounded by the rapid metropolitanization of the population.

Many other problems that have a place on the public agenda and are often regarded as national problems because of their scope and the attention they attract from national policymakers are also essentially metropolitan problems. Poverty and welfare, racial conflict and civil rights, environmental pollution, mass transportation, slum housing and center-city decay, crime and juvenile delinquency, even unemployment: These are problems of the city and not of the countryside. "Crime in the streets" is of little immediate concern to Dime Box, while air pollution is not much of an issue in Marathon. How these problems are dealt with has much importance for the safety, comfort, and quality of life in the metropolitan areas. Increasingly, policymakers are expected to come to grips with these problems and provide "solutions" for them, preferably at low financial cost.

A number of factors that handicap and complicate the efforts of metropolitan-area governments in dealing with their problems are frequently cited. These include the lack of financial resources; restrictive provisions in state constitutions and laws; public and official indifference; diversity and conflict among social, ethnic, and economic groups; the fragmentation of governmental authority; and lack of knowledge concerning the causes of some problems. The fragmentation of governmental authority has especially attracted attention, perhaps because Americans seem intrigued with the effort to solve public problems by tinkering with governmental structure. The failure to treat adequately such problems as slum housing, however, is undoubtedly often more due to lack of will and concentrated effort than governmental structure.

Still, there is no denying the fact that, in Texas, metropolitan areas contain local governments in abundance. The 1982 Census of Government reported that the state's four most populous MSAs contained a total of 1171 units of local government: Houston had 622; Dallas-Fort Worth, 392; San Antonio, 77; and Austin, 80. If many metropolitan problems require policy unity and areawide action for effective treatment at the local level, then this proliferation of governments and fragmentation of authority must have a negative impact. Reorganization and reduction in the number of local governments is often recommended.

One should, however, make the distinction that Edward Banfield and Morton Grodzins do between problems that "exist in metropolitan areas" and problems that "exist by virtue of the inadequacies of governmental structures in metropolitan areas."[35] Thus, such problems as a lack of parks and recreational areas, inadequate garbage collection, discrimination in public employment and services, unpaved and rutted streets, billboard blight, and abusive behavior by the police can probably be handled without any reorganization of local government. Ask yourself why such problems persist. If you answer "who cares?" you have come up with part of the answer. If your response attributes them to a "sick society" or the local "establishment," or something else equally unimaginative and unhelpful, try again, and strive to be more precise. Are there easy solutions?

Other problems, such as air and water pollution, mass transportation, urban sprawl, and inadequate water supply are not respecters of governmental boundaries, and areawide handling appears to be required. But a government with jurisdiction over a metropolitan area will not automatically generate workable or adequate solutions for such problems if it lacks political leadership, financial resources, or public support. Moreover, there is likely to be conflict as to what should be done among those favoring action. There is, after all, more than one way to provide for clean air or mass transportation facilities. With these considerations in mind, we can briefly survey some of the policies that have been proposed or tried for ameliorating, if not solving, metropolitan problems.

Possible Solutions

Annexation   *Annexation* involves the absorption and incorporation of new territory into existing cities as a means of preventing urban sprawl and the development of many small, independent municipalities ringing the central city and choking off its growth and jurisdiction. Generally, Texas cities have stronger powers of annexation than do cities in most other states. Under the Municipal Annexation Act (1963), cities may annex up to 10 percent of their land area each year; unused allocations are usable in the future up to a limit of 30 percent in any one year. Annexation is accomplished unilaterally by the use of city-ordinance power and does not require the approval of residents of the area being annexed. In states where their approval is required, it often results in rejection of the proposed annexation. The Texas annexation law also gives cities extraterritorial jurisdiction ranging from 0.5 to 5 miles (for cities of over 100,000) beyond their corporate limits, depending on their size. Although a city cannot levy taxes within its extraterritorial area, it can exercise control over the development of subdivisions in it, and the residents therein are restricted in their ability to incorporate as separate cities or towns. Once an area is annexed, it must be provided with city services within three years or it can be disannexed by court order upon petition by residents and property owners. In actuality, this is unlikely to occur.

One observable consequence of the use of Texas annexation laws is that they have helped prevent central cities in the state's metropolitan areas from being surrounded and hemmed in by suburban cities to the extent that they are in most states. Most of the population in MSAs in Texas is located in the central city. Whether this has resulted in the more effective handling of urban needs and problems is not self-evident.

Special Districts   The special district having authority to undertake some activity on an areawide basis is another approach to metropolitan problems. Perhaps the best-known illustrations are the Port of New York Authority and the Bay Area Rapid Transit Authority in the San Francisco area. Although the special district is widely utilized in Texas, only limited effort has been made to adapt it to metropolitan problems. Some countywide hospital districts have been created in populous counties. The Gulf Coast Waste Disposal Authority was established in 1969 to abate pollution in three heavily industrialized Gulf Coast counties (Harris, Galveston, and Brazoria), and an airport authority controls the new Dallas-Fort Worth Regional Airport. Also, in recent years mass transit authorities have been established in the Houston, Dallas, San Antonio, and Austin areas.

Special districts can provide services or facilities that exceed the authority or capabilities of existing city and county governments. Some believe, however, that extensive use of special districts could further divide authority and compound the problem of governmental coordination in metropolitan areas.

Governmental Consolidation   Some students of urban government have been much interested in various forms of governmental consolidation in metropolitan areas. They point to the federated government adopted by Toronto (Canada) and its suburbs, the Nashville-Davidson County (Tennessee) consolidation, and the metro government of Dade County-Miami (Florida) as examples of the possibilities. Texans, however, have manifested little interest or enthusiasm for such innovations, which are difficult to effect under existing laws. Some consolidations, mostly of smaller cities, have occurred, such as that of Freeport and Velasco in the Gulf Coast area. Although there has been considerable interest in and support for consolidation of the El Paso city and county governments, this has not yet happened.[36]

More significant, perhaps, has been the movement toward greater use of county governments, with their broader jurisdiction, for handling programs and services in large urban areas.[37] Thus, Ector County (Odessa) almost completely supports the public parks system; Tom Green (San Angelo) and Ector counties support all library facilities; Jefferson County (Beaumont) operates a commercial airport; Tarrant County (Fort Worth) handles all purchasing for state highway rights-of-way; and Harris County has its domed stadium. Since most of the population of most Texas MSAs resides within a single county, the county is a logical unit for providing areawide services. Legal authority for such developments is provided by a 1970 constitutional amendment that authorizes consolidation of governmental functions within counties and by the Interlocal Cooperation Act of 1971, which granted local governments broad authority to contract with one another for the provision of services.

Councils of Government (COGs)   *COG*s are "multi-jurisdictional organizations of local governments created in an effort to provide forums for the consideration of common urban and regional problems."[38] Beginning with the North Central Texas Council of Governments in 1966, 24 of these organizations have been created in Texas. Of them, 20 include within their areas the state's 26 MSAs. COGs are voluntary organizations and are controlled by councils composed largely or entirely of representatives of member local governments. They are supported by financial contributions from their member governments and by state and federal grants; each has a permanent staff and an executive director.

COGs perform two basic functions for their member governments. One is regional planning on such matters as transportation, land use, water and sewerage facilities, and health services. There are many federal grant-in-aid programs for which evaluation and comment by a regional planning body is required, although favorable comment by that body is not always required before a grant application is approved. However, the sanction of negative review and the possible withholding of federal funds do encourage local governments to negotiate changes in their proposals so as to bring them into closer accord with regional plans. Second,

COGs also provide a variety of services for their members, including technical assistance in seeking federal grants-in-aid, the development of information systems, the operation of a police academy (in the Dallas-Fort Worth area), and help in developing modern personnel systems. Many of the councils run in-service training programs and engage in research and planning activities for their member governments.[39]

Member governments of each COG remain independent and have full control over their own policies and finances. There is no effective way by which a COG can compel them to do something they consider adverse to their interests. The COGs must depend for their effectiveness on the value of their services and recommendations and their skill in persuasion. They can move no faster in bringing about governmental and policy changes to provide regional coordination than their member governments are willing to move. In actuality, they have had to be fairly deferential to the central cities in their areas as part of the cost of organizational survival.

Revenue Sharing   Two familiar complaints from urban representatives have been that (1) cities have inadequate financial resources to meet their many needs and problems, and (2) federal grant-in-aid programs (over 500 existed in the 1970s), while providing needed funds, are often too narrow, restrictive, and complicated and are focused on national objectives. Many have said that *general revenue sharing,* under which the national government would make funds available on an unrestricted basis to state and local governments, is needed. State and local officials have often argued that they are in the best position to develop solutions to local problems, including metropolitan problems.

In October 1972, Congress, with the urging of the Nixon administration, adopted the State and Local Assistance Act, which authorized the provision of $30.2 billion to state and general local governments over a five-year period; within broad limits, the money could be used as they saw fit. In late 1972 the first checks, totaling $5.7 billion, were mailed to some 38,000 general-purpose governmental units. The state of Texas received $81.5 million, and its city and county governments received $163 million. They received slightly larger amounts in subsequent years. Practically all Texas cities and towns, whether Houston or Cotulla, Dallas or Impact, received funds based on such criteria as their population and tax effort. In 1976, under strong pressure from state and local officials, Congress extended the revenue-sharing program for another four years, and it was extended again in 1981. However, the program was ended in 1986 because of the fiscal pressures on the national government. During the period of its existence a total of $86 billion was distributed to state and local governments.

Studies of the revenue-sharing program indicate that cities and other local governments generally used most of the funds received for existing programs rather than new or innovative programs.[40] Some governments did use their funds to reduce local taxes, as critics of the program contended would happen. A study of the use of revenue-sharing funds by the 15 most-populated Texas counties found that about two-thirds of their funds were used for five general areas of activity: courthouse and jail construction and repairs, roads and bridges, voting machines, data processing, and law enforcement.[41] Local governments found revenue sharing to be a desirable source of funds; those who used the money to finance operating expenses rather than capital improvements (e.g., streets and buildings) became especially dependent upon it. For example, in 1986 revenue-sharing funds constituted 19 percent of total revenues for Starr County (a smaller county located along the Rio Grande).

Categorical grant-in-aid programs that support specified activities, however, have been a greater source of federal revenue for cities, and particularly for larger cities. Revenue sharing obviously did not have the impact on urban problems that some of its more enthusiastic advocates contended it would. Money is a necessary but not sufficient condition for the solution of urban problems.

Concluding Comment The various solutions for urban problems discussed here perhaps can ease or mitigate some of these problems. They are not panaceas. Much depends, ultimately, on politics—on the will and desire of citizens and their public officials to come to grips with their problems, devise alternatives for redressing them, compromise their differences and adopt policies, and follow through with necessary implementing actions. There is no easy or scientific formula for good, effective government.

NOTES

1. A.J. Thomas, Jr., and Ann Van Wynen Thomas, *Vernon's Annotated Constitution of the State of Texas,* vol. 2 (Kansas City, Mo.: Vernon Law Book Company, 1955), p. 630.
2. C. Ed Davis, "Waiver of an Ancient Doctrine: The Texas Tort Claims Act," *Public Affairs Comment* 15 (September 1969): 1–4.
3. *Houston Chronicle,* February 3, 1974, sec. 1, p. 1.
4. Robert E. Norwood, *Texas County Government: Let the People Choose* (Austin: Texas Research League, 1970), pp. 21–22.
5. Charldean Newell, *County Representation and Legislative Apportionment* (Austin: University of Texas, Institute of Public Affairs, 1965), pp. 13–14.
6. *Avery* v. *Midland County,* 88 S. Ct. 1114 (1968).
7. Ibid.
8. Minor B. Crager, "County Reapportionment in Texas," *Proceedings of the Eleventh County Auditors' Institute* (Austin: University of Texas, Institute of Public Affairs, 1969), p. 10. See also Minor B. Crager, "County Reapportionment in Texas," *Public Affairs Comment* 17 (March 1971): 1–4.
9. *Fort Worth Star-Telegram,* August 22, 1969. Quoted in Norwood, *Texas County,* p. 64.
10. *Houston Chronicle,* September 22, 1968. Quoted in Norwood, *Texas County,* p. 67.
11. Quoted in Duane Lockard, *The Politics of State and Local Government,* 2nd ed. (New York: Macmillan, 1969), p. 129.
12. This discussion draws on *Forms of City Government,* 7th ed. (Austin: University of Texas, Institute of Public Affairs, 1966); and Gary Halter, *The Council-Manager Form of Government: A Citizen's Guide* (Austin: Texas City Management Association, 1983).

13. Bradley Robert Rice, *Progressive Cities: The Commission Government Movement in America, 1901–1920* (Austin: University of Texas Press, 1977).

14. See David R. Johnson, John A. Booth, and Richard J. Harris, eds., *The Politics of San Antonio* (Lincoln: University of Nebraska Press, 1983).

15. Roy E. Young, *The Place System in Texas Elections* (Austin: University of Texas, Institute of Public Affairs, 1965); and Philip Barnes, "Alternative Methods of Electing City Councils in Texas Home-Rule Cities," *Public Affairs Comment* 16 (May 1970): 1–4.

16. Young, *Place System,* p. 13.

17. Ibid., p. 21.

18. On San Antonio, see Charles L. Cottrell and R. Michael Stevens, "The 1975 Voting Rights Act and San Antonio, Texas: Toward a Federal Guarantee of a Republican Form of Government," *Publius* (Winter 1978): 79–88.

19. Harry Holloway and David Olsen, "Electoral Participation by White and Negro Voters in a Southern City," *Midwest Journal of Political Science* 10 (February 1966): 108–109.

20. Kenneth R. Mladenka and Kim Quaile Hill, *Texas Government: Politics and Economics* (Monterey, Calif.: Brooks/Cole, 1986), p. 232.

21. See, generally, Delbert A. Taebel, "The Municipal Reform Movement, Elections and Constitutional Revision," *Municipal Matrix* 5 (December 1973) (Denton: North Texas State University, Center for Community Services), pp. 1–4.

22. Thomas R. Dye, *Politics in States and Communities* (Englewood Cliffs, N.J.: Prentice-Hall, 1969), pp. 224–226.

23. Lockard, *Politics,* p. 251.

24. Woodworth G. Thrombley, *Special Districts and Authorities in Texas* (Austin: University of Texas, Institute of Public Affairs, 1959), p. 6. The discussion of special districts relies heavily on this study, which remains a leading work on its topic. Also of much value has been David W. Tees, "A Fresh Look at Special Districts in Texas," *Governmental Authority and Organization in Metropolitan Areas* (Arlington: University of Texas at Arlington, Institute of Urban Studies, 1971).

25. See Tees, "Fresh Look," p. 47, for a tabular summary.

26. Thrombley, *Special Districts,* p. 11.

27. See, generally, Virginia Marion Perrenod, *Special Districts, Special Purposes* (College Station: Texas A&M University Press, 1984).

28. *Rodriguez* v. *San Antonio Independent School District,* 37 OF. Supp. 280 (WD Tex 1971). A similar California case was *Serrano* v. *Priest,* 5 Cal. 3rd 584 (1971).

29. Ibid., p. 291.

30. See the discussion in *Texas Observer,* December 15, 1971, pp. 1–6.

31. *San Antonio School District* v. *Rodriguez,* 36 L Ed 2d 16 (1973).

32. Ibid., pp. 57–58.

33. *Houston Post,* September 22, 1973, sec. A, p. 9; also *Houston Chronicle,* September 16, 1973, sec. 1, p. 24.

34. House Study Group, *The Texas Textbook Controversy.* Special Legislative Report No. 101 (Austin: May 9, 1984).

35. Edward Banfield and Morton Grodzins, *Government and Housing in Metropolitan Areas* (New York: McGraw-Hill, 1958), p. 32.

36. See *Unite El Paso* (Austin: Texas Research League, 1970).

37. Norwood, *Texas County Government,* chap. 3; and James W. McGrew, "The Texas Urban County in 1968; Problems and Issues," *Public Affairs Comment* 14 (March 1968): 1–4.

38. Philip W. Barnes, "Councils of Government in Texas: Changing Federal-Local Relations," *Public Affairs Comment* 14 (July 1968): 1.
39. See, for example, Richard P. Nathan, Allen D. Manuel, and Susannah E. Calkins, *Monitoring Revenue Sharing* (Washington: Brookings Institution, 1975); and Richard Nathan et al., *Revenue Sharing: The Second Round* (Washington: Brookings Institution, 1977).
40. For a summary of council of government activities, see *Regional Councils in Texas* (Austin: Texas Advisory Commission on Intergovernmental Relations, 1984).
41. Richard L. Raycraft, *Metropolitics and County Government in Texas* (Ph.D. dissertation, University of Houston, 1976), chap. 5.

chapter 10

Government and Money

Highway construction provides a visible example of "tax dollars at work."

The preceding chapters have been concerned with the structure of Texas government and the process by which demands are expressed and decisions made in the state political system. This chapter focuses on the substance of governmental activity—on outcomes of the political process. The analysis of policy outcomes may be approached by describing and analyzing policy in various substantive areas. An alternative approach is to ask where the government gets its money and what it spends the money on. That is the approach used in this chapter; concern is for the sources of state revenue, the process by which the state government decides to spend this money, and the general pattern of state expenditures.

Admittedly, analysis of government and money does not provide a description of all governmental policy, but much policy does involve either securing or spending money. Certainly, decisions on taxes and expenditures constitute some of the most basic and important political decisions that governments make. Their outcome plays an important part in the determination of who will be benefited by government activity and who will pay the financial costs of government.

Consequently, taxation-expenditure decisions often produce conflict and controversy. Such conflict provides a convenient area in which to examine the influence on policy outcomes of the factors analyzed in previous chapters. Of special interest will be the influence of party and factional divisions and relations between, and relative strength of, the governor and the legislature.

GETTING THE MONEY

Taxes and expenditures are often viewed as two sides of the same coin, but such a view is somewhat misleading. Taxes finance governmental programs, but they also allocate the material costs or burdens of government among its citizens. The politics of taxation often appears fairly distinct from the politics of expenditure, and politicians find that their constituents respond more favorably to increased spending than to increased taxes. Economists may argue that decisions on taxation and expenditure should be part of a total process in which the marginal utility of additional expenditure for one objective should be weighed against the utility derivable from its expenditure for another objective and/or against the utility derivable from leaving funds in the private sector of the economy. But such calculations are for all practical purposes impossible.

Nevertheless, taxation and expenditure decisions of necessity are interrelated in the American states; because they lack the flexibility the national government derives from the operation of a central treasury, the states must closely relate receipts and disbursements. The order of decisions varies. When policymakers are primarily interested in programs, expenditure decisions are made first; but, on other occasions, the level of revenue to be raised is first determined (often the product of either the existing system or the existing system with specified alterations), and then the amount is divided among governmental activities.

In Texas the procedure used throughout the 1950s and 1960s was for the Legislative Budget Board to develop an estimate while preparing its budget of the cost of continuing existing programs at roughly the current level of operation, and then to compare that figure with the revenue that would be provided by existing law. Estimates were then made of the costs of the program changes for which the greatest need or support existed, and the various participants began to plan taxation policies. The governor then presented a budget with spending and taxation proposals, and that tax plan became a first approximation of an expenditure ceiling. Through a complex process of opinion formation and negotiation among legislative leaders and the governor, an appropriation bill was prepared that often required adjustments in that ceiling. After final spending totals were determined, legislation to raise the necessary revenue was enacted; from the end of World War II through 1971 every legislature enacted revenue-raising legislation.

After 1971 the process of making taxation expenditure decisions changed. Successive governors insisted that the state operate within the income produced by the existing revenue system, and attention focused on allocation among competing programs. Governors were successful in establishing such a ceiling not only because the real, uninflated rate of increase in state expenditure slowed slightly but also because of tremendous increases in revenue from oil and gas severance taxes and large increases from the sales tax.

In the 1980s a third pattern emerged. The Legislative Budget Board developed a budget reflecting the priorities of its members, but the revenue that would be produced by the existing system was inadequate to finance that budget. Measures to increase revenue were enacted, and a spending ceiling was thereby established. Items in the budget were then reduced or eliminated until revenues and expenditures were in balance.

In 1991 the Budget Board returned to the original pattern of basing expenditures on available revenue, but it also prepared a "current services" spending plan that was about 10 percent higher and that supported services at existing levels, including increases for population growth and inflation.

Legal, Ideological, and Economic Considerations

The U.S. Constitution does very little to limit the power of the states to tax. They may not tax imports or exports without the consent of Congress; they may not use the taxing power to deny persons equal protection and due process of law or levy taxes that burden interstate commerce, a provision that frustrated some attempts by the legislature to levy natural-gas-gathering taxes.

Typically, state constitutions contain a variety of limitations on the legislature's taxing power. Limits are placed on some taxes; others, such as income taxes, may be entirely prohibited; and exemptions of various sorts are granted. Texas is less restrictive than most states, with few significant limitations included in the constitution. Among those that do exist are the requirement that taxation be equal and uniform, and the exemption from all taxation of farm products in the hands of the producer and family supplies for home and farm use, except by vote of two-thirds of the membership of both houses of the legislature. A new limitation was added in 1978, limiting the rate of growth of appropriations from state tax revenues not dedicated by the constitution to the rate of growth of the state's economy. The ceiling provides considerable room for maneuver and may be suspended by majority vote of the membership of each house of the legislature. It has not been an operable factor in decisions on expenditure levels since its adoption. Taxation of incomes is explicitly authorized, although some authorities contend that it cannot be graduated because of the "equal and uniform" requirement.

Thus, tax issues in Texas are essentially political issues to be resolved in the legislature through the political process rather than by recourse to the courts and the constitution. There are a variety of factors that may affect the outcome of tax controversies.

Revenues and expenditures of a state are determined not only by legislation establishing revenue sources and rates and expenditure objectives, but also by economic forces that determine the amount of revenue a source produces and the costs of goods and services purchased by the state. The state, in effect, purchases a "market basket" of goods and services and finances it from taxes on a separate "market basket" in the economy. Changes in one market basket may or may not be paralleled by changes in the other. Major innovations in a state's tax system are usually stimulated by some type of crisis involving either changes in economic conditions or strong pressures for increased expenditure. The failure of the tax system in use in Texas in the 1950s to produce revenue that would allow expenditures to increase as rapidly as population growth and inflation led to the Texas legislature's enactment in 1961 of the first broad-based tax in the state's history—the general sales tax.

The timing of decisions on major taxes also appears to influence tax choices.[1] The states having major income taxes adopted them in the early 1930s or before. Since World War II, the sales tax has usually been resorted to when additional taxes are needed. The high level of national income taxes and the general level of affluence seem to have lessened the appeal of progressive state taxation on incomes.

Notions as to the proper theory of taxation also affect tax decisions. The theory of *progressive taxation* holds that taxation should be based on the principle of "ability to pay" and favors higher rates of taxation as a person's income increases. Those who accept this theory show a preference for graduated income taxes. Another theory holds that those who benefit from governmental programs should pay for them. This theory is manifested in the earmarking of motor-fuel taxes for highway construction and maintenance. Another notion is that all citizens should make some contribution to the support of their government, a notion that is satisfied by the sales tax.

Beliefs are motives for action, but people are influenced in tax decisions by more than notions of what is correct or proper; they are influenced by considerations of material advantage. Very few people enjoy paying taxes, and most (no matter what their income bracket) show a marked preference to let someone else do it. Consequently, the balance of political forces (which often reflects the strength of economic interests in a state) helps determine who pays.

Taxes that are selective in their impact are often easier to enact than those of general effect. The selective tax is less visible and, as fewer are affected, the opposition may be weaker; selective taxes are often levied on persons or groups whose ability to resist is particularly weak. Some selective taxes, such as those on hotel and motel rooms, are directed against tourists; others are placed on items regarded as "evil," such as liquor and cigarettes. The demand for these last items is rather inelastic, and consequently higher taxes yield higher revenues rather than discouraging their use. The knowledge that taxes on liquor and cigarettes produce substantial revenue has resulted in the imposition of high tax rates on these items in most states, including Texas.

Interstate competition also affects taxation. That one state has a particular tax will often serve as an argument for its adoption in neighboring states. Conversely—and despite a substantial volume of evidence indicating that such factors as availability of natural resources, skilled labor, and transportation facilities are decisive—the argument is still made that higher taxes will keep out new industry or drive away existing businesses. Occasionally, reductions are justified in order to allow competition with similar industries in other states, as in 1963 when the state tax on sulfur was reduced to enable Texas sulfur to compete better with sulfur from Louisiana and Mexico. One liberal senator was quoted as saying that the Texas sulfur companies "had a legitimate, reasonable argument."[2]

The Current Revenue System

The present Texas revenue system represents the culmination of a century of development and comprises a variety of taxes, fees, interest and sales receipts, and miscellaneous items, plus a substantial amount of federal grant-in-aid money.[3] Tax decisions tend to be cumulative, and, once adopted, a tax that is a good source of revenue is not likely to be abandoned (although modification or tinkering with it is quite possible). As state spending has increased and existing taxes have proven inadequate, new taxes have been added or existing taxes increased in piecemeal fashion, and nontax revenues have been sought.

Rather than discuss in detail the many tax and revenue sources, their rates, exemptions, yield, and impact, the following discussion simply outlines the patterns of revenue. Major categories are noted, along with some illustrations of each. Table 10.1 illustrates the yield of various taxes since 1960, and Figure 10.1 indicates the relative importance of various sources of revenue in fiscal 1990.

Article VIII of the Constitution of 1876 authorized income, property, occupation, and poll taxes in Section 1, and then, in Section 17, provided that the specifications of the objects and subjects of taxation should not deprive the legislature of the power to require either subjects or objects to be taxed. The legislature historically chose not to use the general clause and instead relied on the delineated taxes in order to remove any doubt as to their legality. That policy was abandoned in the 1950s, but before that time many taxes were labeled occupation taxes that actually were other types of taxes; that is, when the oil severance tax was levied in 1905, it was defined as a tax on the occupation of producing oil. In the discussion that follows, economic reality, not technical legal form, is followed in classifying taxes.

General Sales Tax   After an intense political struggle whose outcome determined the direction of tax policy into the present period, the legislature adopted a 2 percent general sales tax in 1961. Subsequent legislatures enacted increases, with the most recent in 1991 resulting in a 6.25 percent state tax. Since many cities levy a 1 percent tax, which the state collects and then rebates to the cities, most Texans now pay a 6.75 percent sales tax; many others pay an additional cent which can be levied by transit districts in several large metropolitan areas. The sales tax is levied on most sales of personal property and merchandise and is collected by the seller from the purchaser.

As originally enacted, the general sales tax applied to tangible personal property, but in a reflection of political and ideological considerations, several items were exempted from its coverage. A still-maintained exemption for food and prescription medicine made the tax acceptable to some liberal legislators and, some economists argue, makes it regressive only when moderately high income levels are reached. Agricultural machinery and equipment were not taxed but nonagricultural machinery was; in 1961 courts had not intervened in apportion-

Table 10.1 DEVELOPMENT OF TEXAS TAX REVENUE (MILLIONS OF DOLLARS)

Tax	1960 Amount	1960 Percent	1970 Amount	1970 Percent	1980 Amount	1980 Percent	1990 Amount	1990 Percent
Sales								
General	—	—	559	28	2521	38	7589	53
Motor fuel	185	24	312	16	481	7	1515	11
Motor vehicles	27	3	97	5	438	7	1092	7
Tobacco	86	11	187	10	322	5	432	3
Alcoholic beverages	35	5	58	3	200	3	335	2
Subtotal	(333)	(43)	(1204)	(62)	(3962)	(60)	(10,963)	(76)
Severance								
Oil	123	16	172	9	786	12	516	4
Natural gas	52	7	96	5	734	11	568	4
Other	8	1	4	—	5	—	4	—
Subtotal	(183)	(24)	(272)	(14)	(1525)	(23)	(1088)	(8)
Business								
Corporation franchise	60	8	110	6	341	5	587	4
Insurance companies	31	4	55	3	176	3	526	4
Other	19	3	41	2	187	3	223	2
Subtotal	(110)	(15)	(206)	(11)	(704)	(11)	(1336)	(10)
Miscellaneous								
Motor vehicle registration	76	10	148	8	278	4	644	5
Property	38	5	64	3	47	1	—	1
Inheritance	13	2	23	1	76	1	131	1
Other	17	2	12	1	30	—	115	—
Subtotal	(144)	(19)	(247)	(13)	(431)	(6)	(890)	(7)
Total	770		1929		6622		14,277	

Source: Annual Reports of the Comptroller of Public Accounts.

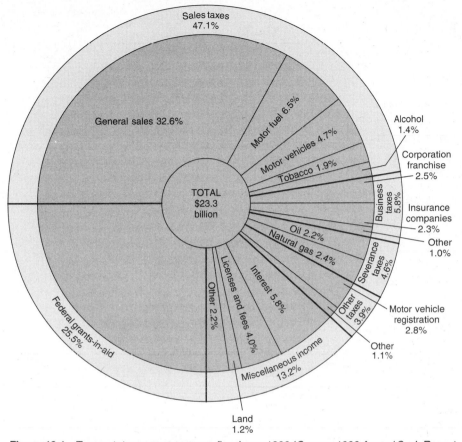

Figure 10.1 Texas state revenue sources, fiscal year 1990 (*Source: 1990 Annual Cash Report*, Volume I [Austin: Comptroller of Public Accounts, 1990], p. 7.)

ment matters, and rural interests were overrepresented in the legislature. Services were not covered by the tax; they were thought to be difficult to collect and were not as important as in the contemporary economy. Desire for additional revenue resulted in the addition of some services in 1987 (credit reporting, debt collection, property services such as landscaping and janitorial services, insurance services such as appraisals, and security services by private agencies, among others), but the services provided by the politically powerful professions of law, accounting, and medicine were not included. In the same year legislation was enacted that provided for a phasing-out from coverage of nonagricultural machinery and equipment. The argument of business interests that the tax on machinery discouraged investment that would produce additional jobs proved effective during the recession then underway.

Selective Sales Taxes   These are taxes, sometimes called excise taxes, that are levied on particular goods and services. As with general sales taxes, it is assumed that they fall on the consumer, although the tax is often paid by a wholesaler and included in the retail price. Major selective sales taxes in Texas are levied on gasoline and diesel fuel (when used for highway travel); cigarettes, cigars, and chewing tobacco; alcoholic beverages; and sale and rental motor vehicles. To illustrate further, the levies on alcoholic beverages are $2.40 a gallon for distilled spirits, $6 a barrel for beer, and 20.4 to 51.6 cents a gallon for wine.

Severance Taxes   Taxes are levied on oil, natural gas, and sulfur when they are extracted from the ground. Originally developed because of the difficulty of determining the value of natural resources for property taxation, taxes are imposed on the market price at the time of production. The oil and gas taxes are assessed at the rate of 4.6 percent and 7.5 percent, respectively.

Major Business Taxes   Significant among these are the corporation franchise tax, paid by corporations for the privilege of doing business in the state and based on their net worth; various gross receipts and production taxes charged against public utilities and other businesses as a percentage of their receipts; and a tax on gross premiums of insurance companies, graduated according to the percentage of their assets invested in the state.

Motor Vehicle Registration Fees   All motor vehicles must have licenses to operate on the public highways. Although technically a fee, this source of revenue is treated here as a tax; it is a significant source of revenue earmarked for the highway patrol and the construction and maintenance of highways, and, given the state of public transportation in Texas, many Texans do not have a choice in its payment. The amount of the fee is based on the vehicle's weight and age and is collected by the counties.

Miscellaneous Taxes   In addition to the major revenue sources, Texas levies several other taxes. The property tax, once the mainstay of the revenue system, was for a long time inconsequential and was abolished by constitutional amendment in 1982. The inheritance tax, while not repealed, has been substantially revised to reduce the revenue it produces by limiting the state tax to the federal credit (the amount by which the federal inheritance tax is reduced by payment of a state tax). The hotel/motel tax is similar to a sales tax in that it taxes a percentage of the consideration paid by the occupant. It is an attempt to reach tourists and other travelers, many of whom are from out of state; since it is so targeted it is not treated as a sales tax. The inheritance and hotel/motel taxes each produced about 1 percent of state tax revenues in 1990. Others, including the cement, bingo, and amusement machine taxes, produce even less, and several minor occupation taxes do little more than cover administrative costs. Some taxes, notably the controlled substance tax on dealers in illegal drugs, are levied more to discourage activities deemed undesirable and to aid law enforcement than to produce revenue.

Nontax Revenue   In 1990 almost 19 percent of the state's income came from nontax sources. Significant sources of nontax revenue include college tuition and fees; game, fish, and other licenses and fees; pay patient collections; interest income; and land income. Interest and land income produce considerable revenue because of the existence of two great landed trusts, the Permanent School Fund and the Permanent University Fund. The most important source of nontax revenue, however, is federal grants-in-aid. The portion of state revenue derived from federal aid has varied somewhat over the years as federal and state policies have changed (an increase in the federal gasoline tax increases aid to highways, the enactment and subsequent repeal of an unearmarked revenue-sharing program raised and then lowered the percentage, and increases in state spending brought on by increased tax revenue lowers the federal portion) but has remained between 25 and 30 percent over the last three decades. Although the revenue derived from federal grants is significant, Texas has not always pursued federal aid fully and enthusiastically. The conservatism of state policymakers in the 1950s and 1960s meant that many of the welfare and social services funded by federal grants were not viewed favorably, especially if they required the expenditure of matching funds. Although the ideological objections, which never reached such programs as grants for highway construction, have declined in recent years, the comptroller of public accounts reported that in 1990 state and local governments failed to receive $2 billion in federal aid because of state-level actions and that $1.7 billion of that would not require the expenditure of additional state funds.[4]

Taxation and Politics

The Texas tax system relies on sales, severance, and a collection of business taxes for most of its revenue. The relative contribution of each is a result of a combination of political decisions and economic trends. Political decisions occur with the enactment of new taxes and increases or decreases in others, but economic trends may affect the contribution of a particular tax without any changes occurring in the tax laws. Of course, political decisions and economic trends interact, as they did in Texas to eliminate state use of the property tax. Economic trends led to sharp increases in the value of residential and agricultural property, but locally elected assessors tended to undervalue that property in comparison with business property. Business interests in turn felt that they were paying too much of the burden and supported the efforts of local officials to make the property tax the province of local government; and, after decades of reducing dependency on the tax, it was finally eliminated in 1982. In a sense, political decisions are always present, at least implicitly, when economic trends either increase or decrease the revenue produced by a tax; legislation could be enacted to counter the trend, but most politicians do not perceive or act upon that alternative. They tend to be thankful for extra revenue when economic trends produce additional revenue (this was certainly the case in Texas from 1973 onward, when severance taxes yielded massive increases in revenue without any changes in the tax); to sympathize with the plight of taxees when economic trends result in a decrease in the revenue produced by a tax; not to increase the tax rates to prevent revenue loss (this was the case with the oil and natural gas severance taxes between the late 1950s and 1974, when revenue produced by those taxes grew more slowly than the overall tax revenue system as well as state expenditures, and again in the 1980s, when revenue actually declined); or even to reduce taxes (as in the case of the sulfur industry in 1963).

A comparison of Table 10.2, which lists the major revenue legislation enacted from 1959 onward, with Table 10.1 indicates that in the 1960s, political action was the predominant force in shaping changes in the relative contribution of the different types of taxes. The share of sales taxes increased from 43 percent to 62 percent, and the share of business and severance taxes declined; this clearly reflects legislative action, as the legislature first enacted a 2 percent general sales tax and then expanded its coverage and increased the rate (and the comparable rate of the motor vehicle tax) throughout the decade. The only changes in business taxes were two small increases in the corporation franchise tax effective in the 1967–1968 and 1969–1970 bienniums, and severance taxes were unchanged except for a decrease for competitive reasons in the sulfur tax in 1964–1965.

Between 1970 and 1980, economic forces were the major contributors to changes in relative shares of the tax system. Only in the first two bienniums of the decade was revenue-raising legislation enacted, and that legislation focused heavily on sales taxes. The share of tax revenue contributed by sales taxes declined, however, from 62 percent to 59 percent, while the share of severance taxes increased from 14 percent to 23 percent. The only statutory change in a severance

Table 10.2   MAJOR REVENUE-RAISING LEGISLATION, 1960–1989

Fiscal Biennium	Legislation
1960–1961	Increased selective sales taxes on cigarettes, liquor, wine, motor vehicles, automobiles, radios, television sets, and phonographs; increased corporation franchise tax; enacted new selective sales taxes on radio, television, and phonograph components, jewelry and furs costing over $25, hotel and motel rooms, boats and outboard motors, air conditioners, and tobacco (except snuff)
1962–1963	Enacted general sales tax
1964–1965	Removed exemption from general sales tax of outer clothing costing less than $10 and "to go" restaurant food
1966–1967	Cigarette tax increased
1968–1969	General sales, motor vehicle, and corporation franchise taxes increased
1970–1971	General sales, cigarette, natural gas, and corporation franchise taxes increased; liquor and beer brought under general sales tax; drinks served in private clubs taxed
1972–1973	Sales tax increased; 10 percent gross receipts tax on mixed drinks enacted
1984–1985	Accelerated payment schedule adopted for several taxes; numerous fees increased; increased all sales taxes; increased corporation franchise, insurance, amusement machine, hotel/motel, and motor vehicle registration taxes
1986–1987	Increased general sales and motor fuels taxes
1988–1989	Increased general sales, motor vehicles, and hotel/motel taxes

Reprinted by permission.

tax was a small increase in the natural gas tax, but it became effective in 1970 and therefore was in effect through the entire 1970–1980 period. The business share did not change appreciably, increasing from 11 percent to 12 percent, but the miscellaneous category declined drastically from 13 percent to 6 percent. That decline is attributable to the rates for registering motor vehicles not being increased in an inflationary period and moves toward eliminating the state property tax.

The major economic development affecting the tax system between 1970 and 1980 was a sharp increase in oil and natural gas prices and consequent sharp increases in revenue derived from severance taxes. The increase in severance tax collections was so great that the growth in sales tax collections produced by general prosperity still resulted in a decline in the sales tax portion of tax revenue.

A combination of economic trends and political action shaped the changes in the sources of tax revenue between 1980 and 1990, with the economic trends making political action necessary. The decade began with a serious national economic recession that initially did not have a major impact in Texas. In 1982 and 1983, however, two blows struck the Texas economy. First, the Mexican peso was devalued, and communities along the Texas border with Mexico experienced an economic depression as retail sales to Mexican nationals declined. Second, and of greater long-term consequence, the price of petroleum dropped sharply, and petroleum prices eventually adversely affected the price of natural gas. The increase in oil and gas prices in the 1970s masked a major development in the industry. While prosperity prevailed, production was actually declining. The combination of a national recession, peso devaluation, and declining oil and gas prices and production resulted in a severe economic recession. Real estate values declined, and many of the state's financial institutions eventually failed.

The economic developments had serious consequences for state revenue. From the end of World War II through fiscal 1973, significant revenue-raising legislation had been enacted for every biennium, but from 1974 through 1983 the existing system had produced revenue that the policymakers deemed adequate. The remainder of the 1980s, however, resembled the earlier decades, with major revenue legislation enacted for each biennium. In contrast with the 1970s, when revenue legislation was largely avoided and revenue increased from $1.6 to $6.6 billion, the increase from $6.6 billion to $14.2 billion in the 1980s was largely attributable to legislative action. One estimate places the increase that would have occurred with legislation at only $2.4 billion.[5] Every tax specifically listed in Table 10.1 was increased at least once.

Although a variety of taxes were increased, the emphasis was on the sales taxes. There were four increases in the general sales tax, three increases in the taxes on alcohol and/or tobacco, and two increases in the tax on motor vehicles. There were increases in business taxes; the tax on insurance companies was increased once and the corporation franchise tax twice, although the second franchise tax increase was temporary and was allowed to lapse. Two other legislative actions indicate the degree to which consumer sales taxes were emphasized in the 1980s. The first was the exemption from the sales tax of nonagricultural machinery and equipment described previously. The second was the inclusion in the sales tax base of basic telephone service and intrastate long-distance service when the sales tax base was expanded in 1987; a tax on telephone companies was repealed in the same legislation.

The result of both economic trends and political decisions in the 1980s was to increase the dependence of the revenue system on sales taxes. The portion of tax revenue derived from sales taxes increased from 60 percent to 76 percent, with the percentage derived from the general sales tax alone increasing from 38 percent to 53 percent. The percent of tax revenue derived from severance taxes declined from 23 percent to 8 percent, with actual dollar amounts declining substantially even though rates were unchanged. Economic trends reduced the contribution of severance taxes, and, since the other sources of revenue did not experience comparably dismal circumstances, the severance tax contribution to total tax revenue would have decreased and that of other taxes increased without political action. Political decisions, however, sharpened the increase in the portion derived from sales taxes.

An analysis of changes in the relative contributions of different types of taxes directs attention to the economic factors that affect revenue receipts and the relative political strength of competing political forces, but such an analysis should not obscure the overall nature of the tax system. The enactment of the general sales tax established the basic structure of the tax system:.Texas relies primarily on sales taxes, with a secondary and declining emphasis on severance taxes and a significant contribution from an assortment of business taxes. Sales

taxes fall directly on the consumer; and, although the impact varies and is difficult to determine, many business taxes are undoubtedly passed along to the consumer in the form of higher prices. The impact of severance taxes is even more difficult to determine (though it is especially attractive to many Texans because a major portion is passed on to out-of-state consumers). Nevertheless, the Texas tax structure probably is substantially regressive, in that its burden tends to rest more heavily on low-income groups, for the proportion of income paid in sales and property taxes (upon which local governments remain very dependent) declines as income rises.

The desirability of regressive or progressive systems of taxation depends on the values of the person passing judgment. The type of tax system in use, however, reflects the balance of political forces in the state and the relative influence of economic groups with those forces. Upper-income and business groups have enjoyed favorable conditions of access to the conservative faction of the Texas Democratic party, whose members have controlled the important policy positions in both the executive and legislative branches of state government.

Business-oriented conservatives thus have been the dominant influence in shaping the system of taxation. Conservative Democrats have shown a marked preference for sales taxes, and Texas conservatism has generally been associated in public finance with opposition to progressive taxation of income, frugality in governmental expenditures, and encouragement of business and industrial development through a tax structure attractive to business and industry.

Taxes do not touch all economic activity with an equal impact; a tax may be used punitively, but significant revenue can be derived from a tax without greatly harming the activity being taxed. The revenue that Texas secures from the oil and gas industry is not an indication of political weakness, and, in fact, that industry is quite influential. The severance taxes are sufficiently moderate that oil and natural gas producers in Texas do not suffer in competition with producers either in neighboring states or internationally. Agricultural interests have historically been quite influential in Texas, as indicated by the major role played by agriculture in the abandonment of the state property tax and the maintenance of the exemption from the general sales tax of farm machinery.

Although some areas of economic activity receive more favorable treatment than others, the Texas tax system reflects the influence of agricultural, commercial, and industrial interests to the detriment of the influence of organized labor and liberals, who have generally lost the battles over tax policy. Liberal Democrats have favored taxation of natural resources, business taxes, and a corporate income tax while offering little public support for a personal income tax, although the absence of such support may be more a reflection of political reality than personal preference. The only real examples of liberal influence were the inclusion of increases in the corporation franchise and natural gas severance taxes in omnibus tax legislation in the late 1960s and early 1970s at the insistence of a strong liberal contingent in the Texas Senate, and the increases in the corporate franchise and insurance company taxes for the 1984–1985 biennium. The latter increases were a reflection of the development of two-party competition. The Democratic legislative leadership, fearing that Republicans would not vote for tax increases of any kind, supported increasing business taxes in order to obtain liberal votes for the tax bill.

The fiscal preferences of Texas Republicans tend to be antitax and antispending and have emphasized reductions in expenditures rather than tax increases. Republican legislators for the most part voted against the tax increases in the 1980s. Indications are, however, that if forced to choose, Texas Republicans favor sales over income and business taxes. Republican Governor Bill Clements, for example, indicated that he considered the general sales tax the best and fairest tax in use in Texas and grudgingly accepted an omnibus tax bill for each biennium during his second term that emphasized sales taxes.

Regardless of philosophical and partisan considerations, the enactment of revenue-raising legislation is a politically difficult process. Beneficiaries of expenditures often do not identify their benefits with revenue legislation, and very few interests favor being taxed. Time, energy, and political capital such as appointments to office, obligations for past favors, promises of future benefits, and personal friendships are depleted in the enactment of revenue legislation. Political leaders favor a revenue system in which changes in revenue are correlated with changes in demand for expenditure. Close correlation seldomly exists, and at times the correlation is inverse; for example, the demand for social services increases during recessions when revenue growth from sales and income taxes slows or even declines. A revenue system that produces a growth in receipts that parallels somewhat population increases and inflation is achievable, however, but the Texas system falls well short of such growth. Almost 40 percent of Texas revenue is derived from nontax sources and is thus not closely related to population growth and inflation. Of the major taxes, income derived from severance taxes is unaffected by population and inflation, and the gasoline, alcoholic beverage, and tobacco taxes are based on volume and thus are not responsive to inflation but do tend to increase with population. Factors other than population, such as fuel efficiency of automobiles, and drinking and smoking patterns, however, may temper the relationship to population growth. The general sales, motor vehicle, corporation franchise, insurance, and utilities taxes grow with the economy, and together they provide slightly over 40 percent of state revenue.

At the beginning of the 1990s the governor and legislature are confronted with the need to enact revenue-raising legislation in order to finance existing levels of service. A similar situation existed prior to the enactment of the general sales tax in 1961, but the addition of that tax to the revenue system made few major tax battles necessary in the 1960s and 1970s. The first significant discussion of an income tax in contemporary Texas politics began in 1991 when both the outgoing and incoming lieutenant governors indicated their support for such a tax. As with the sales tax, receipts from a tax on income are directly affected by inflation and population.

THE BUDGET MACHINERY

There are several ways in which budgets may be described. First, a budget can be viewed as a financial document, a statement of estimated revenues and pro-

Reprinted by permission.

posed expenditures to guide financial activities for the period covered. Second, budgets are also policy statements indicating priorities among policy areas, levels of activity within policy areas, and overall spending. In this sense budgets are "political" matters, in that they entail choices among competing and conflicting interests, and there is never enough money to satisfy everyone. Third, a budget can be a means of administrative management, an instrument for directing the administrative system. In Texas, however, the budget has little of this last characteristic because of the absence of a comprehensive budget execution system.

A familiar way of classifying budgets is on the basis of who has major responsibility for their preparation. Such a classification yields three types: the *executive budget,* prepared by the chief executive; the *legislative budget,* prepared by an instrumentality of the legislature; and the *commission budget,* formulated by a board composed jointly of legislative and executive officials. Among students of public administration there is a marked preference for the executive budget, and indeed it is the most common type in American governmental systems. Its advocates contend that it permits the chief executive to lay a comprehensive, systematic program before the legislature; facilitates evaluation of both total spending and spending for particular programs in relation to one another; serves as a tool of executive management; helps increase citizen understanding of governmental activity; and contributes to strong and responsible executive leadership in government. Since one of the general consequences of the executive budget is to strengthen the chief executive, opponents of the extension of executive power occasionally oppose the pure executive budget; they argue that many of the alleged benefits are derivable from any comprehensive budget.

A budget of any type represents a change from nineteenth- and early twentieth-century practice, when there was typically neither a central budget agency nor a comprehensive budget, and each administrative agency drew up its own budget and sent it directly to the legislature. The budget machinery of each state developed somewhat differently, since constitutional provisions and political traditions differed in each state. In Texas this development led to an unusual system in which there are two separate budget agencies, each of which develops and submits a budget for legislative consideration.

Constitutional Framework for Budget Procedures

Three provisions of the Texas Constitution establish the framework within which budget procedures developed. First, Article VIII, Section 6 provides that money shall not be withdrawn from the treasury except in pursuance of specific appropriations and that appropriations shall not be made for a period longer than two years. Since regular sessions of the legislature are held at two-year intervals, the state's budget is normally adopted for a two-year period, or *biennium.* Each biennium is composed of two fiscal years, with each fiscal year running from September 1 of one calendar year through August 31 of the next and taking its name from the calendar year in which it ends. Most authorities recommend annual budgets on the ground that they permit more careful and precise planning. But a minority contends that the process of preparing and adopting a budget is so complex and lengthy that a 12-month fiscal period is too short. Experience on the national level offers some support for the minority position: Budget requests and recommendations for a forthcoming year must be prepared before the appropriations for the current year are known, and appropriations bills for a fiscal year often are not enacted until after the fiscal year begins.

Article IV, Section 9 requires the governor to present estimates of the amount of money required to be raised by taxation for all purposes at the commencement of each regular session of the legislature. This gives the governor a constitutional role in the process of financial planning. The governor's role is further specified in the budgetary process by the grant in Article IV, Section 14, of power to veto appropriations, including the veto of specific items of appropriations in general appropriations acts. This veto can be overridden by a two-thirds vote in each house of the legislature.

Article III, Section 49a provides that the comptroller of public accounts will submit to the governor and legislature an itemized estimate, based on the laws in effect, of the revenue that will be available for expenditure during the forthcoming biennium. Appropriations in excess of the anticipated revenue may not be made, and bills containing an appropriation cannot be considered as passed and sent to the governor until the comptroller certifies that the amount appropriated from a fund is within the amount estimated to be available. When the comptroller finds that an appropriation exceeds the estimated revenue, the bill containing the appropriation is returned to the legislature, where steps must be taken to bring it within the estimate. A four-fifths vote in each house can override the finding, but that has never occurred.

The constitutional provision for estimating revenue, which became effective in 1947, grew out of dissatisfaction with continuing deficits in the treasury in the 1930s and 1940s and was designed to eliminate deficit spending. Texas is the only state that gives responsibility for making revenue estimates to an elected state official other than the governor, and its requirements for overriding the official estimate are among the most stringent of the states. Students of public administration generally favor placing ultimate responsibility for the estimate in the hands of the person responsible for recommending expenditure and revenue measures, but the Texas system is another example of the distrust of a strong chief executive. Proponents of the Texas system argue, however, that by removing the revenue-estimating function from the budget-writing process, a check is created that eliminates the temptation to be overly optimistic in achieving a balance between revenue and expenditure.

The independent revenue estimate by the comptroller thus was meant to be a conservative check to prevent spending more than was in the treasury, and in most years it has worked that way. The average forecast for the key general revenue fund for the first 20 years was one-third lower than actual collections.[6] In 5 of those years, however, collections were less than estimates; 4 of those were in the 1958–1961 period, when receipts from the severance tax on oil were badly overestimated. A Middle Eastern oil crisis resulted in increased demand for Texas oil, but after the crisis subsided there was a sharp increase in Middle Eastern oil production, and Texas production declined faster than the comptroller estimated.[7] In that period the comptroller essentially used extrapolative or mechanical methods that projected past performance into the future. In the late 1960s the techniques became more sophisticated, but throughout the inflationary 1970s revenue was consistently underestimated.

In the late 1970s the comptroller began the development of more sophisticated methods of estimating revenue, and the accuracy of the estimates increased. Two economic models, one of the state's economy and another of the revenue system, were developed. The economic model, based on multiequations that simulate relationships between national economic factors such as gross national product, inflation, and energy prices and Texas economic performance in such areas as income, employment, and retail sales, predicts how the Texas economy will perform. The model of the revenue system is then used to predict income from the major revenue sources. The first estimate using the models, made in 1980 and used in 1981 in determining appropriations for the 1982–1983 biennium, was only 3.1 percent below actual collections.

The econometric models, of course, are only as good as the economic assumptions upon which they are based, and through most of the 1980s the assumptions produced reasonably accurate estimates. In 1986, however, problems developed. The estimate of January 1985, which estimated revenue for the remainder of fiscal 1985 and the 1986–1987 biennium, had assumed a steady decline in per-barrel oil prices from the $29 average in the summer of 1984: $28 in January 1985, $27 at the end of fiscal 1985 in August, an average of $25 in fiscal 1986, and an average of $24 in fiscal 1987.[8] The assumptions were conservative through November 1985, when a decline began that halved the $28 price in four months. Comptroller Bob Bullock announced that the general revenue fund was expected to have a large deficit for the biennium; and, after calling on state agencies to reduce expenditures, Governor Mark White called a special session, which increased the general sales and gasoline taxes but which still left the state with a $1 billion deficit at the end of the biennium in August 1987.

The "pay-as-you-go" provision of the Texas Constitution thus is not a guarantee against deficits because actual receipts may be less than estimated. The complex fund structure also allows deficits to exist in some funds while there are surpluses in others. In earlier periods of Texas history deficits regularly occurred in the general revenue fund, and banks discounted state warrants, which the treasury issues instead of checks and which are commitments to pay at a future time rather than actual negotiable instruments. In the post–World War II period the treasurer has persuaded banks to honor warrants on the general revenue fund at face value even if they could not be redeemed immediately in return for receiving non-interest-bearing deposits of money from funds with surpluses. Since 1979 the treasurer has been authorized to transfer cash from other funds to prevent deficit balances caused by cash flow problems during a year, and cash management notes can now be used to even the flow of cash.

AGENCIES AND FUND STRUCTURE

Texas has developed budget machinery and procedures within the framework of these constitutional provisions. Prior to 1949, Texas did not have an effective system of budgeting, and financial procedures were criticized for being haphazard, fragmented, and arbitrary. The legislature in that year created a Legislative Budget Board and required all state agencies to submit their appropriations requests to it. The board consists of four members from each house, plus the lieutenant governor and speaker of the house, who in effect appoint the other members. The chairs of the appropriations and revenue and taxation committees of the House and the finance and state affairs committees of the Senate must be included. Consequently, the Legislative Budget Board includes some of the most influential members of the legislature. The creation of a budget agency responsible to the legislative leadership was indicative of the legislature's desire for independence from and suspicion of gubernatorial power; the legislature had not been willing to grant the governor authority and adequate staff aid for preparing a state budget. The first budget board began the development of a professional staff, and later boards continued the emphasis on strong staffing; the combination of competent professional staff and the makeup of the board has meant that its recommendations carry much weight.

The creation of the Legislative Budget Board meant that Texas had two state budget agencies, for the Board of Control was also responsible for preparation of a budget. The Board of Control's budget division had never been adequately staffed, and its budget was not held in very high esteem by the legislature. In 1951, following the recommendation of both the Legislative Budget Board and Governor Allan Shivers, the legislature transferred responsibility for preparation of an executive budget to the governor. Preparation of the executive budget is handled by the Office of Budget and Planning in the governor's office.

The budget prepared by the Legislative Budget Board in 1951 included all funds in the state treasury for the first time. The state's fund structure made this difficult, however, for like many states Texas follows a policy of dedicating or earmarking revenue to specific purposes. The comptroller of public accounts classifies the approximately 450 funds, which technically are accounting entities used to divide up the state's money for specific purposes, into nine categories: general state operating and disbursing funds, constitutional funds expendable for specific purposes, federal funds, trust or pledged funds, constitutional nonexpendable funds, tax clearance funds, petty cash funds, trust funds, and suspense funds. Most of the categories are technical and of little interest to anyone other than administrators and accountants. Some of the funds are revenue funds that temporarily hold money that is allocated to expenditure funds, but others are both revenue and expenditure funds.

The funds of general interest are the general state operating and disbursing funds and the constitutional funds. There are six nonexpendable constitutional funds, but only two are of general significance—the permanent school fund and the permanent university fund. These are endowments based on landed trusts whose earnings become the available school and university funds, which are constitutional expendable funds earmarked for the public schools and the University of Texas and Texas A&M University systems. Of the 37 general operating and disbursing funds, the most important is the general revenue fund, with the remainder consisting of funds that receive revenue earmarked for a particular purpose. The fees collected by most licensing and examining boards, for example, are deposited in special funds, and money from these funds is appropriated to pay the operating costs of the boards. Several such boards collect the money and spend it without depositing it in the treasury and having it appropriated to them; such receipts and expenditures are not included in the figures in this chapter based on reports of the comptroller of public accounts. The 47 constitutional expendable funds are similar to the general operating and disbursing funds but are earmarked by the constitution rather than statute, and include such major funds as the highway fund as well as such minor funds as the Confederate pension fund.

A statutorily earmarked fund can be used for other purposes only if special legislation is enacted authorizing its use, and that occurs infrequently; not even the legislature can authorize the use of constitutionally dedicated funds. The practice of earmarking revenue has some undesirable consequences; for example, limitations on the flexibility of budgetmakers to allocate funds where needs are greatest and the tendency of those with dedicated funds to be better financed than those competing for general revenue. The beneficiaries of dedicated funds, however, strongly and usually successfully resist efforts to end earmarking.

Figure 10.2 presents a simplified version of an estimate by the Legislative Budget Board at the beginning of the 1990–1991 biennium of the operation of major interrelated funds that together account for $28 billion of the $37 billion state budget. The general revenue fund receives most of the major state taxes, including the general and motor fuels sales taxes, the severance taxes, the corporation franchise tax, and various occupation and selective sales taxes. Money is then allocated to other funds on a priority basis established by statute. In addition to the allocations specifically shown in Figure 10.2, the other priority allocations category includes important allocations to the state parks fund; fish, game, and water safety fund; and retirement funds. The residual $15.4 billion in the general revenue fund supports higher education, mental health and mental retardation

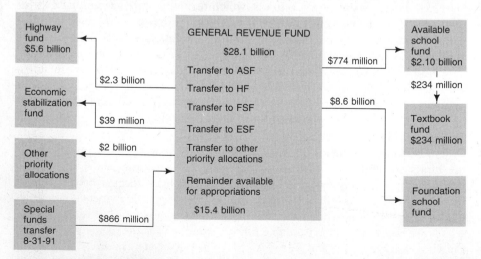

Figure 10.2 Flow of funds that affect the general revenue fund, 1990–1991 biennium (*Source: Fiscal Size Up Texas State Services* (Austin: Legislative Budget Board, 1990), p. 2–16.

programs, youth correctional programs and the prison system, and many regulatory and service programs.

One-fourth of the revenue from the tax on motor fuels is constitutionally dedicated to the public schools. That money is allocated to the available school fund, which also receives the income of the permanent school fund. After allocations to the textbook fund to finance purchase of textbooks for public school pupils, the remainder of the money in the available school fund is distributed to local school districts on the basis of the number of pupils in average daily attendance.

The foundation school fund is essentially a distribution device by which the school districts receive the difference between the state's share of the foundation school program and the amount received from the available school fund. Most of the money for the fund is allocated from the general revenue fund and includes the constitutionally dedicated portion of all receipts defined as occupation taxes.

The highway fund receives the bulk of its revenue from federal funds, motor vehicle registration fees, and transfer from the general revenue fund of the three-fourths of the motor fuel sales tax constitutionally dedicated to highways. It also receives an allocation earmarked for use on farm-to-market roads. The money from the highway fund can be spent only on construction and maintenance of highways and the administration and enforcement of traffic laws.

The newest of the major state funds is the economic stabilization fund, popularly known as the "rainy day fund." In the 1970s revenue collections often exceeded estimates, and when there was a surplus at the end of a biennium the comptroller included the surplus in the amount available for expenditure in the succeeding biennium. The economic and fiscal difficulties of the 1980s led to charges of profligate spending. In 1987 the legislature proposed and the voters approved a constitutional amendment that restricted the surplus that could be spent in a succeeding biennium and established a fund that would be available in the event of future revenue decreases.

The economic stabilization fund receives one-half of any general revenue surplus and 75 percent of the amount by which oil and natural gas tax collections exceed 1987 receipts. The amount of revenue in the stabilization fund may not exceed 10 percent of total general fund receipts and may be appropriated by a three-fifths vote of each house of the legislature for a biennium in which the comptroller forecasts a decline in revenue. A three-fifths vote is also needed to approve the use of the fund to remedy deficits that develop after the approval of the appropriations act. Otherwise, appropriations from the stabilization require a two-thirds vote. The stabilization fund appears unlikely to receive money from oil and natural gas tax receipts, but substantial money may become available from general revenue surpluses. The initial experience with the fund indicates, however, that its requirements can be readily circumvented.

THE BUDGETARY PROCESS

The budgetary process can best be understood as a continuous pattern of activity with several distinguishable but not entirely separate stages. The various people

THE BOOKKEEPING BILL

The complex fund structure and the requirement that the comptroller certify that the amount appropriated from each fund be available for expenditure occasionally require special measures to bring all funds into balance. Such measures usually involve comparatively small amounts of money, but in 1989 the balancing of receipts and expenditures from the general revenue fund for the 1990–1991 biennium involved significant amounts. Governor Bill Clements had adamantly opposed the enactment of revenue-raising measures, but the $28.1 billion appropriated from the general revenue fund was over $1 billion more than the estimate of available revenue. The problem was resolved by the enactment of legislation containing several measures that either increased the amount of money available for appropriation or shifted expenditures out of the 1990–1991 biennium. This legislation became known as the Bookkeeping Bill.

The Bookkeeping Bill contained several provisions, but four were most important. Two provisions prevented money from being transferred to the recently approved rainy day fund: a prepayment of $150 million was made at the end of fiscal 1989 to the foundation school program, and the remaining general revenue balance of $167 million was appropriated to an emergency appropriation fund on the last day of fiscal 1989 and then returned to the general revenue fund the following day. A third provision delayed the transfer of the state's contribution to the teacher retirement trust fund for the final three months of fiscal 1991 until after the end of the fiscal year, thus moving the expenditure of $190 million into fiscal 1992. The most important provision made an additional $866 million available to the general revenue fund during the 1990–1991 biennium by transferring balances from other funds to general revenue on the final day of the biennium and then transferring them back the next day.

The Bookkeeping Bill made available almost $1.4 billion for appropriation from the general revenue fund in the 1990–1991 biennium, but in doing so it frustrated the intention of the creation of the rainy day fund and reduced the revenue available for expenditure in the 1992–1993 biennium. Another bookkeeping bill can be enacted to make money from the 1994–1995 biennium available to 1992–1993, and the process could continue indefinitely. It could also be construed as a form of deficit financing in which each biennium borrows from its successor.

and agencies concerned with raising and spending money can be located in this process and their roles indicated, thereby providing information on both their particular activities and their relationships to the total process. In the budgetary process decision makers tend to develop particular perceptions and expectations; these are often associated with institutional patriotism. In the discussion that follows, the policy inclinations of various participants are described; references to spending levels generally are to spending for discretionary general purposes, that is, general revenue and related funds.

The budgetary process consists of four basic stages: (1) preparation of the budget, (2) authorization of the budget, (3) execution of the budget, and (4) the audit of expenditures. With such considerations in mind, we describe the budgetary process for the biennium beginning September 1, 1991, and ending August 31, 1993.

Preparation of the Budget

June–December 1989   Both the executive and legislative budget staffs begin initial planning. General policy problems are considered, and the two staffs, working independently, engage in research on various finance-related problems of state government.

January–September 1990   The next phase involves the preparation and analysis of agency requests for funds. Early in the year, budget instructions developed jointly by the two budget offices are sent to the agencies. The instructions are largely technical, but in 1973 an important innovation was instituted when the instructions required that requests be zero-based. *Zero-based budgeting* supposedly requires that the entire request be justified, not just changes from the current budget, as allegedly occurs under conventional budgeting. A notable feature of zero-based budgeting in Texas has been that it uses a programmatic format and requires alternative spending levels, including, but not limited to, amounts that vary from current levels by specified percentages. Agency officials then begin to work up their requests, often consulting with officials of the two central budget offices along the way. The agencies, not unexpectedly, are advocates of increased spending. Their concern is that their programs operate at an optimum level; they are not concerned with the overall size of the budget or the necessity for new revenue sources. The highest level of requests often represent increases of two-thirds or more, and requested increases of over 100 percent are not unknown.

After the agency requests are prepared, they are submitted to the two budget offices, where the examiners begin the analyses of the proposals. In the summer, hearings are conducted jointly by the governor's budget staff and the legislative budget staff; agency officials appear to explain their budget requests. Once these hearings are concluded, joint activity by the two budget agencies is ended, and they go to work independently to develop budget recommendations for the governor and the Legislative Budget Board.

September–December 1990   The next phase in the budget cycle involves the actual preparation of the overall budgets. Each staff continues its analysis of the requests and eventually prepares recommendations for those who are responsible for preparation of the budget.

Traditionally, budget offices tend to regard the operating agencies as spenders who are more interested in programmatic excellence than economy and efficiency and who have only a narrow, agency-oriented perspective; they also perceive that they have a responsibility to protect the taxpayers from such attitudes by functioning as guardians of the treasury. The legislative budget staff consequently recommends large reductions in agency requests. The board tends to make marginal rather than major changes in the staff recommendations; it works through a consensual process that secures agreement, and votes are almost never taken. The budget developed by the board sharply reduces the requests of the agencies. The process of preparing the board's budget is completed by late December, and the budget is presented to the governor and the legislature for their consideration in early January.

Meanwhile, the governor's staff has been working on the executive budget. Acting on the basis of general guidelines as to what the governor wants to emphasize in the budget, the executive budget staff works in a fashion similar to its legislative counterpart. The staff recommendations are usually presented to the governor in a summary fashion for review; the governor usually does not conduct an item-by-item, detailed review of the budget (as does the Legislative Budget Board). The governor's budget also recommends large reductions in the budget requests.

Throughout the 1950s and 1960s, during the terms of governors Allan Shivers, Price Daniel, and John Connally, the governor's budget usually was larger than the Legislative Budget Board's and more likely to contain recommendations for new or significantly expanded programs. It was also more likely to exceed existing revenue. The governor thus acted more as advocate or innovator. This situation changed during the governorship of Preston Smith, who in attitudes toward spending and taxation was more conservative than the budget board and generally recommended lower spending totals. Programmatic innovations also came to be less often initiated in his office and more likely to be recommended by the agencies, the Legislative Budget Board, or individual legislators. Governors Dolph Briscoe, Bill Clements, and Mark White recommended smaller budgets than the Legislative Budget Board, and programmatic innovations that increased spending were less likely to receive support in their budgets than in the legislative budget.

Although changes in gubernatorial attitudes played an important role in the reversal of attitudes toward spending by the governors and the Legislative Budget Board, an equally important change occurred in the policy of the board. Changes in the position of staff director and membership of the board resulted in a less conservative, more aggressive board.

During the 1950s and early 1960s, under the leadership of Lieutenant Governor Ben Ramsey and a conservative group of senators he repeatedly appointed to the board, the Legislative Budget Board followed a policy of developing a base upon which the legislature could develop its own spending plan, popularly called the "bare bones" budget. Personnel changes on the board and staff resulted in the abandonment of the bare bones approach in the late 1960s. The board, under the leadership of Lieutenant Governor Ben Barnes (1969–1973) and his successor, Bill Hobby, who has served from 1973 to 1991, gradually began developing a plan in line with what the board members wanted the legislature eventually to enact. Barnes and Hobby have tended to look with more favor on spending for state services than the occupant of the governor's office. A contributing factor to their greater inclination toward spending may be that, unlike governors, lieutenant governors are neither required nor expected to recommend revenue sources.

The executive budget is presented to the legislators in December; early in the regular session in January, the governor presents an overall financial plan (including, if necessary, proposals for raising additional revenue) in an address to the legislature. Newly elected governors do not present their budgets until after their inauguration, but the outgoing governor still is responsible for presenting a budget in December. Thus, when there is a gubernatorial transition, the legislature has not two but three budgets presented to it. The recommendations of the outgoing governor are ignored.

Both the governor and the Legislative Budget Board recommend considerably smaller expenditures than the total amounts requested by the spending agencies. There is a definite incentive for both to reduce the spending requests; reductions in requests lessen the amount of revenue that must be raised, and raising revenue is always a painful process. According to the Texas Constitution, the governor must recommend where revenue should be obtained to meet expenditure requirements. The budget board is not required by law to recommend sources of revenue, but the board members are likely to be leaders of the legislature, which would be required to increase taxes. Although the two budgets recommend spending less than requested, they always allow for increases over current spending levels.

Budget Authorization

Budgets are proposed plans of expenditure; the spending still must be authorized, and that is the task of the legislature. When the legislature meets in January, a bill enacting the recommendations of the budget board is introduced in each house and referred to committee.

January–March 1991 The appropriations process in the committees of the two houses is similar, but differs in one important respect. In the Senate, the bill is referred directly to the Finance Committee, and consideration is limited to that committee. In the House, the various substantive committees (e.g., Health and Welfare, Agriculture) consider the portion of the bill for which they have legislative responsibility and recommend amounts for those agencies. The recommended amounts may be reduced or increased by the Appropriations Committee, but increases require a two-thirds vote.

In effect, the substantive committees establish a ceiling that will be lifted only under extraordinary circumstances. The substantive committees take a special interest in "their" agencies, and, consequently, their recommendations are higher than the amount eventually approved by the Appropriations Committee, which must fit all the pieces into an overall budget. The key point of decision is in the Appropriations Committee.

The House and Senate committees hold separate hearings, most of which are rather perfunctory. In their appearances before the committees and elsewhere, agencies are expected to be advocates of their original budget requests; this is unlike the situation at the national level, where agencies are expected to support the president's budget. If an agency is seeking to increase an item recommended by the board, it may utilize a higher recommendation in the governor's budget to support its position. But otherwise the agencies tend to explain why they need the amount requested, or at least more than was recommended by the board.

When the hearings are completed, the committees decide what to recommend for each agency on a program-by-program basis. Various influences are focused on the committees in the course of their deliberations. Agency officials lobby for their requests, pressure-group representatives attempt to influence decisions on selected items, and the governor seeks approval for favored proposals. Although attention is focused on committee members, especially the chair, interested parties may also seek to work through the lieutenant governor and the speaker, to whom the committee members are usually quite responsive.

Reprinted by permission.

The committees work from the budget and appropriations bill prepared by the budget board. Ordinarily, the board's recommendations are accepted as a base, and changes involve additions. The bills are then reported to the two houses for floor consideration, which is usually rather perfunctory and seldom results in substantial changes.

At no stage in the authorization process is there a thorough, general debate. Agreement with the pattern of expenditure; limitations of time and knowledge; lack of alternatives, given the statutory commitment of so much money and the political commitment of even more; and fear of antagonizing those in control of the bill and consequent loss of items important in one's district all contribute to the sparseness of debate. In recent years the House has devoted a significant amount of time to the bill, and changes have been made of important marginal consequence. A Senate tradition of pride in not amending the bill has developed, wherein senators argue that the floor is not the place to write legislation as complex as the general appropriations act.

April–May 1991   Because the bills passed by the two houses differ, the stage is set for the conference committee, since institutional patriotism is sufficiently strong to ensure that neither house will accept the other's bill. Historically, the conference committee, composed of five members of the appropriating committees of each house, actually wrote the appropriations bill. It was not limited to resolving the differences between the two bills, but could and did add entirely new items and struck out items already agreed to by both houses.

Since 1973, the appropriations act has been prepared by conferees restricted to adjusting differences between the two bills; nevertheless, they make numerous changes that are not strictly adjustments of differences. Statutory and other changes that occur between the preparation of the bill by each house and its final approval by the conferees make a strict adherence to the limitation difficult, if not impossible. If for no other reason, the rapid changes having ramifications for appropriations that occur in basic statutes during a session that legislates in 140 days for a two-year period require some flexibility. Many of the conferees' changes involve technical corrections not apparent until after the passage of the bills by the two houses, provide additional money, or can otherwise be attributed to legislative action. Still other changes, however, involve new policies. The salaries of officials may be increased to put them on a level with similar positions in other state agencies, and some changes are attributed simply to the availability of updated information. Under the joint rules adopted by the legislature, the changes that do not adjust differences in the two bills must be authorized by concurrent resolution.

The actions of the two houses differ, although not in the pattern at the national level, where the Senate is said to be the "upper" body because it usually increases the appropriations recommended by the House. The pattern in Texas tends to be ideological rather than institutional, with the body that is less conservative in its ideological makeup likely to approve higher spending. When agreement is finally reached, the staff drafts a final appropriations bill. This is reported to the two houses, where it must be accepted in whole or rejected in whole; if rejected, a new conference committee would be appointed. The conference committee bill is invariably approved, usually with only perfunctory debate.

Since the founding of the dual-budget system in 1953, four periods are discernible in the attitudes of the two houses toward the budget. Prior to 1963 the House was the less conservative of the two bodies, and it approved higher spending levels (exceptions were the legislative sessions of 1953 and 1957, when both houses had strong conservative majorities). From 1963 through 1971, the Senate contained a larger portion of moderate and liberal members and approved higher amounts (an exception was 1967, when the presiding officer of the Senate, Preston Smith, who was more conservative than his House counterpart, Ben Barnes, used his authority over appointments to place staunch conservatives in control of the appropriating process in the Senate). Throughout most of the 1970s, the differences in spending totals were less significant, as both houses tailored spending to available revenue. In the 1980s, the Senate, generally less conservative than the House and strongly influenced by Lieutenant Governor Bill Hobby, has been more oriented to maintenance of state services in a period of financial difficulty than has the House and has approved higher spending totals.

That pattern seems likely to remain through the early 1990s as the Senate remains the less conservative of the two bodies and its presiding officer, Bob Bullock, is more supportive of state programs than his House counterpart, Gib Lewis.

June–July 1991   Upon completion of action by the legislature, the appropriations bill goes to the comptroller for certification that the amounts appropriated will be available and then to the governor for approval. The governor can veto the entire bill, as Governor Preston Smith did in 1969 to a one-year bill, or specific line items while allowing the remainder to become law. The latter procedure is the standard pattern of gubernatorial action, with particular items regarded as wasteful, unnecessary, or of benefit to political opponents being eliminated. Since the bill ordinarily comes to the governor near the end of the legislative session, the vetoes in effect are absolute. The item veto gives the governor greater control over appropriations than does the general veto, which gives only a choice between all or nothing—with neither being a desired alternative in many cases.

The Final Product

In addition to appropriations, the bill contains policy directives, or *riders,* which the legislature includes as a means of exerting control over the agencies. The appropriations act for 1992–1993 included provisions for administration of the salary schedule, the schedule of architectural fees, a prohibition on the use of appropriated funds for the payment of salaries of employees who imbibe alcoholic beverages while on duty, and a prohibition on the practice of discrimination based on race, creed, sex, or national origin.

Riders are legitimate if they assert controls over the spending of state funds, but they are invalid if they attempt to make basic changes in state policy. Governors, however, may find them objectionable and on occasion have announced that they were vetoing riders. Many of the provisions are also legally questionable, and the attorney general not infrequently rules them invalid. Article III, Section 35 of the constitution prohibits bills from containing more than one subject, so an appropriations bill can contain only appropriations and valid limitations on their expenditure. The distinction between a valid limitation and the enactment of policy is not always clear, but the attorney general tends to be rather restrictive in interpretation, which usually is definitive. It is important to word the riders properly if there is to be hope for their legality. Thus, the rider that provides that none of the monies appropriated be used to pay the salary of any employee who uses alcoholic beverages while on active duty would, if properly challenged, be more likely to be upheld than the more generally worded prohibition against discrimination. The latter restriction provides that appropriated funds may not be spent by agencies practicing discrimination; as such, it is not directly tied to the expenditure of funds but instead prohibits funds from being spent by agencies pursuing designated policies. Of course, such riders may be of greater importance as statements of legislative intent than as legal restrictions.

The process of budgeting is incremental. Spending agencies begin with their current appropriations as a base (this is the case under the misnamed zero-based budgeting system, which in reality is a program budget presenting alternative spending levels developed, on specific instructions, in increments from a base defined as a percentage of current spending); the budget offices develop their recommendations (which tend to be based more on current spending than on agency requests); the legislature works from and adds to the budget prepared by the Legislative Budget Board; and the governor exercises an item veto, which may be important either to specific services and projects or to the governor's bargaining power but does not greatly affect overall spending. In the end the appropriations provide much less than was requested but allow for growth in expenditures.

The legislature has a more significant role in budgeting in Texas than in most states, where use of a single executive budget gives the initiative to the governor. The governor's influence depends on informal powers and political relationships rather than on formal budget powers. Governors who enjoy a favorable political situation and aggressively support innovative recommendations occasionally have a major impact; otherwise, the gubernatorial impact is largely to set a ceiling on expenditures through taxation policies and to lobby for select items. The governor's influence over priorities within the ceiling has declined as governors Preston Smith, Dolph Briscoe, and Bill Clements have not developed programmatic innovations. Mark White supported programs of state aid to public schools and indigent health care that had major budgetary implications, but decisions on these programs largely occurred outside the budgetary process.

Execution of the Budget

Once the appropriations bill becomes law, the agencies revise their spending plans for the forthcoming fiscal year to bring them into accord with the amounts appropriated. With the beginning of the first year of the biennium (in our example, September 1, 1991), the third phase of the budgetary process, the spending of the money, is ready to begin. Many states have formal machinery, usually under the control of the governor, that provides for centralized planning and control over execution of the budget. Financial authorities are generally agreed that a system of budget execution is desirable. Among the particular controls that such authorities believe should be given the governor are the powers to require the submission of work programs for approval, to establish allotments (controls over the rate and volume of spending), to approve transfers between categories of expenditures or even appropriations items, and to reduce appropriations.

In Texas there is little formal system of budget execution; at the onset of the fiscal year, the agencies are largely free to begin spending the funds provided—within the limitations set out in the appropriations act. The legislature has used riders to establish gubernatorial controls, similar to those used by states having executive budget execution systems, requiring approval of the governor prior to expenditure of specified items of appropriation. Rulings by the attorney general, however, held such requirements unconstitutional on the grounds that they violated the separation of powers clause of the constitution by delegating legislative authority to determine appropriations.

Recent governors have favored a budget execution system, but rulings by the attorney general interpreting the separation of powers clause of the Texas constitution prohibited requirement of executive approval of appropriations. A constitutional amendment was approved in 1985 during the administration of Mark White that provided that the legislature could require the prior approval or the emergency transfer of any funds appropriated, but by the time the legislature met, Bill Clements had become governor. The Democrats in the legislature were reluctant to adopt authorizing legislation but eventually did so as an incentive for Clements to approve revenue-raising legislation. The language in Article XVI, Section 8, conceivably is broad enough to allow full-fledged budget execution involving executive approval of operating budgets and periodic allocation of appropriations, but the system adopted is of limited scope and divides authority between the governor and the Legislative Budget Board, who must concur in any action. The focus is on handling emergencies, not coordination in the management of state government. During the first biennium in which the new authority was available, the governor, who must initiate proposals, made 13 proposals involving $9.2 million, of which proposals affecting $8.9 million became effective. The impact of the budget execution system thus initially was not great.

The Audit of Expenditures

It is generally agreed that sound financial administration requires an independent audit after the expenditure of funds by the operating agencies. This task is handled in Texas by the state auditor, who is appointed—with Senate approval— for a two-year term by the Legislative Audit Committee. The committee is composed of the lieutenant governor, speaker, and the chairs of the Appropriations and Revenue and Taxation committees of the House and the Finance and State Affairs committees of the Senate. The auditor, who must have had at least five years of experience as a certified public accountant prior to appointment, is directed to audit the financial records of all state agencies at least once every two years. This is to ensure that the agencies use proper accounting procedures and to determine whether there is illegality or irregularity in expenditures. Reports embodying the state auditor's findings and recommendations are sent to the governor and legislature. In short, the auditor is supposed to keep the agencies "honest," and the thought is that this can best be done by someone who is not a member of the executive branch.

THE PATTERN OF EXPENDITURES

The general trend in government expenditures—national, state, and local—in the United States in the twentieth century has been ever upward. While attention is often called to the great increase in national government spending, state and local spending has also increased tremendously.

A few figures will illustrate the point. In 1902 all governments in the United States collectively spent $1.7 billion.[9] Texas state government now spends several times that by itself in a year. The 1902 total figure was allocated among the three levels of government as follows: national government, $572 million; state governments, $188 million; local governments, $959 million. Thus, over two-thirds of total government spending was done by state and local governments.

By contrast, in 1988 total actual spending by all governments amounted to $1,776 billion: $1,012 billion by the national government, $542 billion by state governments, and $495 billion by local governments. Spending by the national government constituted about 57 percent of government spending. But, if spending on defense and international relations is eliminated by subtracting $330 billion, only $782 billion remains for national spending on domestic activities,[10] and state and local governments still spend more for domestic programs than does the national government. Intergovernmental transfers are considered expenditures by the originating government; a substantial portion of the national expenditures are actually grants to state and local governments, and the ultimate expenditure of those funds is by those governments. If spending is a measure of governmental power, not all power has "gone to Washington."

Nevertheless, there has been a huge increase in governmental spending, and much of the growth has been on the part of the national government. Several factors have contributed to the growth of government. A common complaint attributes growth to power-hungry, inefficient bureaucrats and politicians, an ideologically satisfying explanation that may apply to particular situations but that lacks real explanatory power. Inflation undoubtedly accounts for part of the growth in dollar figures, but the governmental portion of gross national product has increased in this century. Much of the increase in national spending stems from the breakdown of isolationism, the increasing involvement of the United States in international affairs, and the commitment to maintaining a permanent defense establishment able to exert worldwide military power.

In the domestic arena, a number of broad, long-term socioeconomic and political developments have given rise to needs and demands for increased spend-

ing. Population growth has necessitated increased spending for traditional programs to provide services or protection for larger numbers of people. As the
population has increased, it has also become more urbanized and industrialized;
urban populations have more need for governmentally provided services, such as
police and fire protection, sewerage and water systems, and parks and recreational
facilities. Along with population growth, urbanization, and industrialization have
come rising standards of living, which result in greater demands for services and
still higher costs.

The result is an urban-industrial society in which independence and self-
sufficiency have been replaced by interdependence as part of the human condition.
As the economic hazards of life—old age, sickness, accident, unemployment—
increase, government is called on to provide security, and consequently welfare
programs originate and proliferate. The guarantee of human welfare becomes an
accepted, if not applauded, responsibility of government.

The dominance of officeholders identified with the conservative faction of
the Democratic party has not prevented Texas state government from participating in the nationwide growth of governmental expenditures (Table 10.3). In three
of the decades of this century, expenditures tripled, and only in the depression
decade of the 1930s did they fail to double. Much of the growth is attributable
to increases in population and inflation. If per capita expenditures of constant
dollars are considered, the growth was much more moderate—except in the first
two decades of the century, when increases in the small dollar amounts represent
very large percentage increases. Nevertheless, per capita spending in constant
dollars increased from $3 in 1900 to $378 in 1988.

Texas state government spends in support of a variety of activities, and the
amount of expenditure is not necessarily a reflection of the importance of an
activity. With the caveat that service-providing activities generally are more
expensive than regulatory activities, it should be noted that almost two-thirds of

Table 10.3   STATE EXPENDITURES IN TEXAS,
             ACTUAL AND PER CAPITA

Year	Actual Expenditures (in Millions)	Per Capita Expenditures (1967 Dollars)
1900	$ 4.8	$3
1910	10.9	6
1920	33.5	35
1930	103.1	48
1940	165.7	64
1950	527.3	84
1960	1184.4	130
1970	2954.7	239
1980	10211.9	293
1988	19329.1	378

Sources: Population and expenditure data are from the Texas Almanac, 1990–1991
(Dallas: A. H. Belo, 1984). Data on the value of the dollar are based on the producer's price
index in the Statistical Abstract of the United States, 1988 (Washington, D.C.: Government
Printing Office, 1988); and Historical Statistics of the United States, 1789–1945 (Washington, D.C.: Government Printing Office, 1949), pp. 233–234.

state spending goes to support three services: education, highways, and welfare (Table 10.4). The figures actually understate spending on these services because of the accounting and classification system used by the comptroller of public accounts. The "all other" classification includes the remaining conventional functional classifications (general government, regulation of business and industry, health and sanitation, law enforcement, development and conservation of natural resources, and parks), as well as a miscellaneous group not based on the activities of government (debt payment, grants to political subdivisions and others, and state contributions to employee retirement and social security). The latter group could more properly be allocated to the functional classifications that generated the expenditures. Over a third of the "all other" expenditures are for nonfunctional purposes.

An analysis of the changes by decade in the portion of state spending devoted to each classification in Table 10.4 indicates that a combination of social, economic, and political developments produce gradual but major shifts in emphasis. The "all other" classification almost tripled between 1960 and 1990, but little can be learned from that classification since much of the expenditure actually is for other functions in Table 10.4. The increase probably does represent a greater willingness to spend on general or overhead activities, including the legislature; the judiciary; and the general-purpose agencies of the executive branch such as the offices of the governor, attorney general, and comptroller of public accounts.

An additional factor was growth in spending on employee benefits, which resulted when the state began making contributions in 1971 toward the insurance premiums of employees.

The portion of spending devoted to mental health and corrections did not change from 1960 to 1980 but increased between 1980 and 1990. The increase from 5 to 7 percent is entirely attributable to spending on corrections, which increased from 1.5 to 3.6 percent between 1980 and 1990 under the impetus of an increased prison population and a federal court order to improve services. Otherwise, the significant variations in state spending occurred in the three major revenue-consuming classifications—education, highways, and welfare.

Between 1960 and 1990 the percentage of state spending devoted to the public schools decreased from 32 to 31 percent and the percentage devoted to higher education increased from 7 to 14 percent. The increase in the higher education share is a consequence of demographic changes (the post–World War II "baby boom" and great in-migration to Texas) and changes in social attitudes resulting in a greater portion of college-age persons actually enrolling in post–high school programs. Note the increase in the higher education portion from 7 to 12 percent in the 1960–1970 decade, when the postwar babies reached college age.

Political developments played the major role in the fluctuations in the portion of state expenditure devoted to public education. The 1960s were a period in Texas politics in which the emphasis was on higher education, and other than changes in the salary schedule of public school teachers, the system of state support did not undergo significant change, and the portion of state spending devoted to the public schools changed little. By the end of the decade, however,

Table 10.4 STATE EXPENDITURES IN TEXAS, BY PURPOSE (MILLIONS OF DOLLARS)

Purpose	1960		1970		1980		1990	
	Amount	Percent	Amount	Percent	Amount	Percent	Amount	Percent
Public education[a]	375	32	961	33	3735	37	7107	31
Higher education	83	7	344	12	1315	13	2950	13
Highways	387	33	633	21	1581	15	2580	19
Mental health and correctional	62	5	141	5	514	5	1672	7
Welfare	188	16	554	19	1601	16	4266	19
All other	89	7	322	11	1475	14	4219	19
Total	1184		2953		10,221		22,794	

Source: Annual Reports of the Comptroller of Public Accounts.
[a]Includes all teacher retirement.

state policymakers began to feel significant pressures for additional state aid. As school enrollment increased and more sophisticated programs resulted in increased costs, the property tax, the primary source of local revenue for schools, became burdensome. The consequence was support from agricultural interests and the home-owning middle class for a series of legislation throughout the 1970s that increased the state's portion of the foundation school program from 82 percent in 1974 to 88 percent prior to a major revision that became effective in fiscal 1985. Between 1970 and 1980 the portion of state spending devoted to the public schools increased from 33 to 37 percent.

The increasing portion of spending on public education in the 1970s was achieved without the enactment of revenue-raising legislation, but changes in the 1980s required such measures or reductions in the level of support for other services. Nevertheless, there was strong pressure in the 1980s for improvement in the performance of the public schools. The result was the enactment of major legislation effective in fiscal 1985 and some additional changes in the remainder of the 1980s, which were financed primarily by increasing the local share of the program. In fiscal 1985 the state's share was reduced to 70 percent and in the following biennium to 67 percent. Not all spending on public schools is part of the foundation school program, but if overall spending is considered, the same pattern emerges; the state's contribution to total spending (federal, state, and local) declined from 48 percent in 1985, the first year of the decline of the state's portion, to 44 percent in 1989.[11] The result of the transfer of the financial burden from state to local sources is that the portion of state spending devoted to public education declined from 37 percent in 1980 to 31 percent in 1990. The additional state expenditures arising from the court-mandated reforms enacted in 1990 do not become effective until fiscal 1991 and may increase the public education portion slightly.

The portion of state spending devoted to highways experienced a consistent decline between 1960 and 1990. Between 1960 and 1980 the gasoline tax was unchanged at five cents and construction costs for the interstate system, which began in the 1950s, decreased as work on the system was largely completed. The energy crisis of the 1970s resulted in more fuel-efficient cars and lower gasoline consumption, and the rate of growth of revenue earmarked for highways was less than the rate of inflation. In 1977 legislation was enacted diverting unearmarked general revenue to the highway fund, but even that did not reverse the trend. The decline in the highway portion of state spending continued between 1980 and 1990. During the decade the gasoline tax was increased from 5 to 15 percent, but the diversion of unearmarked general revenue was ended, and spending on highways increased at a lower rate than overall state spending. The 33 percent share in 1960 had fallen to 11 percent in 1990.

In the period following World War II, spending on welfare peaked at a fourth of the total, with most of the money going to the politically attractive program of aid to the needy aged. As an increasing portion of the elderly became eligible for social security, that program declined in cost. However, the politically unattractive program of Aid to Families with Dependent Children (AFDC) was growing. By 1960 only 16 percent of state spending was on welfare, but the portion increased to 19 percent in 1970. The increase was attributable to the federally mandated Medicaid program. Not only was medical assistance costly, but its existence caused the costs of the categorical assistance programs to increase as a larger percentage of persons eligible to receive assistance from those programs applied for it. In the 1970s the welfare share declined, primarily because the national government assumed responsibility for the adult assistance programs. In 1980 welfare accounted for only 16 percent of state spending. During the next decade, however, eligibility for the AFDC and Medicaid programs was expanded, and the economic recession in Texas contributed to an increased caseload in most programs. The welfare portion of state expenditures returned to 19 percent.

TEXAS AMONG THE STATES

Comparative studies indicate that the levels of taxation and expenditure are determined more by a state's level of economic development (as measured by industrialization, urbanization, and income and educational levels) than by such political variables as party competition, voter participation, liberal-conservative political divisions, or legislative malapportionment. (Other analyses indicate that the political variables do have a more important influence than economic variables on the allocation of burdens and benefits across income lines.)[12] While there is substantial variation among the states, the wealthier, more economically developed states tend to spend more, the poorer states to spend less. Nevertheless, particular states do, at least temporarily, move ahead or behind the norm for their level of development, and there seemingly are some deviant cases.

When compared with other states, Texas emerges as a low-taxation and low-expenditure state. (The comparisons that follow are of combined state-local figures because differences in the distribution of responsibilities between state and local governments among states distort comparisons that include only state government expenditures.)

In 1988 Texas ranked thirty-fifth among the 50 states in per capita state-local expenditures, spending $2913, compared with an average national average of $3365. Per capita revenue was $3081 and the national average $3598, ranking Texas thirty-eighth. Another measure of state fiscal policy involves the percentage of personal income extracted by state and local taxes. This measures effort. The average amount of revenue per thousand dollars of personal income for the 50 states was $162. In comparison, Texas extracted only $157, ranking it thirty-first among the 50 states.[13]

The level of expenditure, revenue, and effort may represent a lag between economic development and urbanization, which occurred later in Texas than in the industrialized Northeast and Midwest, and the translation of those developments into political outputs. Over the past three decades the Texas rankings in expenditure, revenue, and effort have risen from among the lowest to somewhat below average. Additionally, it should be noted that many variables affect such comparisons, and at times they can be misleading. For example, the cost of living varies considerably from state to state, and states with lower costs of living may provide similar services at less cost than high-cost states. Nevertheless, Texas is undoubtedly a low-revenue, low-expenditure, low-effort state with a relatively low level of public service; that reflects the dominance of conservative antigovernment sentiment.

NOTES

1. Clara Penniman, "The Politics of Taxation," in *Politics in the American States,* 3d ed., ed. Herbert Jacobs and Kenneth Vines (Boston: Little, Brown, 1976), p. 433.
2. *Texas Observer,* May 2, 1963, pp. 10–11.
3. A historical view is presented in Read Granberry and John T. Potter, "Some Texas Tax Trails," *Texas Quarterly* 7 (Winter 1964): 125–142.
4. *Dollars We Deserve, Part V* (Austin: Comptroller of Public Accounts).
5. *Fiscal Size Up Texas State Services 1990–1991 Biennium* (Austin: Legislative Budget Board, 1990), pp. 2–10.
6. *Fiscal Notes* 85 (January 1985):3.
7. *Revenue Estimating for Texas State Government* (Austin: Texas Research League, 1968), pp. 9–26.
8. *Summary of the Biennial Revenue Estimate, 1986–1987* (Austin: Comptroller of Public Accounts, 1985), pp. 3–4.
9. *Historical Statistics of the United States, 1798–1957* (Washington, D.C.: Government Printing Office, 1960), pp. 69–77.
10. *Governmental Finances in 1987–1988* (Washington, D.C.: Government Printing Office, 1990), p. 2.
11. *Fiscal Size Up 1990–1991,* p. 4–10.
12. Thomas R. Dye, *Politics, Economics, and the Public* (Chicago: Rand McNally, 1966), chaps. 4–6; Bernard Booms and James Halderson, "The Politics of Redistribution: A Reformulation," *American Political Science Review* 67 (September 1973): 924–933.
13. Revenue, expenditure and effort data are from *Governmental Finances in 1987–1988,* pp. 101–107.

PHOTO CREDITS

Index

Abortion, 60, 92, 93, 94, 227
Act-Up Against AIDS, 94
Adjutant general, 203
Administrative system. *See* Agencies, administrative
Affirmative action, 215
Agencies, administrative, 193–224. *See also* Executive branch
  and budget procedures, 306–311, 312
  and clientele groups, 217, 218, 219
  election of heads, 217–219
  gubernatorial appointments to, 146, 147–148, 166, 196, 219–220
  in legislative process, 124–125
  of local government, 259–260
  major, 196–213
  numbers and types of, 194–195
  personnel system of, 213–216
  reorganization of, 224
  and sunset review process, 220–223
Agriculture interest groups, 81, 218, 302
Aid to Families with Dependent Children (AFDC), 6, 323, 324
Aikin, A. M., Jr., 108
Air Control Board, 218
Aircraft Pooling Board, 195
Alcoholic Beverage Commission, 218

Alcoholic beverages
  and liquor-by-the drink referenda, 271
  and Prohibition, 158, 159, 160, 163
  taxes on, 292, 294, 296, 298, 300, 303
Allred, Jimmy, 150, 162–163, 189
Amarillo Citizens Association, 269
Amendments. *See* Constitution, Texas, amendments to; *specific amendment to U.S. Constitution*
American Farm Bureau, 81
American GI Forum, 82
American Independent party, 70
American Medical Association, 92
Americans for Democratic Action, 179–180
Anderson, John, 70
Anglos
  in legal profession, 228, 248
  party affiliation of, 64, 66
  political power of, 45–46
  population decline of, 27
  socioeconomic status of, 28
  voter participation of, 32
Annexation
  of metropolitan areas, 283
  of Texas, 151, 152
Antilynching law, 165
Appellate courts, 232, 233, 234–238

327

Constitution, Texas (*Continued*)
175, 185, 187, 230, 236–237,
268–269, 271, 280, 318
articles of, 12
Bill of Rights, 12
and budget procedures, 304–305, 306,
313, 318
and election practices, 14, 30, 34–35,
39, 101, 195
evaluation of, 14–17
framing of, 7–8
and governmental organization,
12–13, 15, 16, 99, 100, 108, 133
and gubernatorial powers, 121, 122,
142–144, 145, 148
and judicial system, 12–13, 228, 229,
230, 232, 233–234, 236–237
length of, 11–12, 14
and local government, 13–14, 16,
264, 268–269
prior versions of, 7, 151, 153
and public policy issues, 14
revision of, 17–20, 224
and taxation, 293
Constitution, U.S., 12, 13, 202
amendments to. *See specific
amendment*
and executive power, 141
and federal system, 2–5
methods of development, 8
and taxing power, 291
Constitutional conventions
calling, 17, 18–19
of 1845, 151
of 1866, 153
of 1875, 7–8, 153
of 1974, 19–20, 224
Constitutional revision commission, 17,
19
Control Board, 164, 307
Controlled substance tax, 296
Convention system, 156, 157
Cope, Glen Hahn, 16
Cornyn, John, 50
Corporation franchise tax, 294, 296,
298, 300, 302
Corruption, government, 18, 40–41,
121, 160, 172, 186, 218
Council-manager form of municipal
government, 266–268
Councils of Government (COGs),
284–285
County attorney, 259
County auditor, 259, 261
County board of school trustees, 259
County clerk, 41, 259

County commissioners' courts, 40, 53,
234, 255, 259, 260–261, 262, 274
County conventions, 51
County courts, 232, 234–235, 262
County courts at law, 235
County election board, 41, 261
County executive committee, 52
County government, 255, 256–262, 284
County inspector of hides and animals,
259
County judge, 41, 234, 235, 260,
261–262
County surveyor, 259
County tax assessor, 41
County treasurer, 259
Court of Criminal Appeals, 13, 229,
232, 237, 250
reversals of, 243–244
workload of, 236
Courts, federal, 206. *See also* Supreme
Court, U.S.
on prison conditions, 201–202
on reapportionment/redistricting, 36,
37, 101, 103, 104, 105, 126
on school funding, 277–278
Courts, Texas 227–250. *See also* Judges;
Lawyers; *specific court*
constitutional provisions for, 12–13,
228, 229, 230, 232, 233–234,
236–237
equal treatment principle in, 249–250
judicial review in, 227
and jury system, 230–231, 234
and legislative process, 125–126
political role of, 227, 231–232,
238–244
problems of, 244–248
on redistricting, 36
reform of, 250
on school funding, 278–279
and separation of power, 13
structure of, 232–238, 244–245
Courts of appeals, 232, 235, 236–237
Courts of Civil Appeals, 236, 237–238
Cox, Jack, 171, 181
Criminal Justice, Department of,
199–200
Criss, Lloyd, 91
Criswell, Reverend, 84–85
Culbertson, Charles, 156

Daiell, Jeff, 70
Dallas, Texas
and redistricting, 102–103, 105
voting rights in, 43
Dally, Carl, 229, 244